Human Behavior
in the Social Environment

A Social Systems Approach
Fifth Edition

D1057181

Ralph E. Anderson (1928–1997)
The essence of Ralph by Gary R. Lowe

Human Behavior in the Social Environment

A Social Systems Approach

Fifth Edition

**Ralph E. Anderson and Irl Carter
with Gary R. Lowe**

transaction

ALDINE TRANSACTION
A Division of Transaction Publishers
New Brunswick (U.S.A.) and London (U.K.)

Reprinted 2007
Copyright @ 1999 by Diane B. Anderson and Irl Carter.

This book is printed on acid-free paper that meets the American National Standard for Permanence of Paper for Printed Library Materials.

Library of Congress Catalog Number: 98-45357
ISBN: 978-0-202-36116-1
Printed in the United States of America

Library of Congress Cataloging-in-Publication Data

Anderson, Ralph E.
  Human behavior in the social environment: a social systems approach /
Ralph E. Anderson and Irl Carter with Gary Lowe.—5th ed.
        p. cm.—(Modern applications of social work)
  Includes bibliographical references and index.
  ISBN 0-202-36115-2 (cloth: alk. paper).—ISBN 0-202-36116-0 (paper: alk.
  paper)
    1. Social systems. 2. Social institutions. 3. Human behavior.
  I. Carter, Irl. II. Lowe, Gary R, 1943-. III. Title. IV. Series.

HM51.A54   1999
306-dc21   98-45357
                                                                     CIP

3/19/07

Table of Contents

Acknowledgments   xi

Introduction to the Fifth Edition   xiii

Introduction (1999)   xvii

1   Social Systems Theory

Introduction:
Providing Meaning to Theory   1
I. Essence and Ancestry:
   The Atomistic/Holistic Continuum   4
II. Energy/Information:
   The Necessary Element   9
III. The Four Basic Energy Functions   11
IV. Organization:
   The Sufficient Element   14
V. Causation, Feedback Loops, and Chaos Theory   16
   Conclusion   19
   Suggested Readings   20
   Literary Sources   21
   Films and Videos   21

2   Aspects of Social Systems

Introduction:
Energy—Evolutionary, Structural, and Behavioral   23

I. Evolution of Social Systems:
    The Interplay of Change and Maintenance   24
II. Structural Characteristics   28
III. Behavioral Aspects of Social Systems   35
     Conclusion   39
     Suggested Readings   39
     Literary Sources   40
     Films and Videos   41

3   Culture and Society

Introduction   43
I. Species and Culture:
    Unique Aspects of the Human Species   48
II. Analytic Dimensions of Culture:
     Qualities of a Society   55
     Conclusion   66
     Suggested Readings   67
     Literary Sources   68
     Films and Videos   68

4   Communities

Introduction   73
I. Community as System   74
II. Definition of Community   76
III. The Community in Critical Condition   94
     Conclusion   96
     Suggested Readings   97
     Literary Sources   98
     Films and Videos   98

5   Organizations

Introduction   101
I. Theories of Organization   103
II. The Open Systems Perspective:
     The Systems Model   113
     Conclusion   133
     Suggested Readings   133
     Literary Sources   135
     Films and Videos   135

6   Groups

Introduction		137
I.	Types of Groups	139
II.	Dimensions of Groups	144
III.	Aspects of Group as System	146
	Conclusion	162
	Suggested Readings	162
	Literary Sources	164
	Films and Videos	164

7   Families

Introduction		165
I.	Approaches to Family Analysis	166
II.	A Social Systems View of Families	182
	Summary	192
	Suggested Readings	193
	Literary Sources	194
	Films and Videos	195

8   The Person

I.	Theoretical Approaches	197
II.	The Critical Phases of the Life Cycle	226
	Conclusion	257
	Suggested Readings	257
	Literary Sources	259
	Films and Videos	260

Epilogue

I.	Holonistic Thought	264
II.	Implied Values and Ethical Positions	267
	Bibliography	271
	Literary Sources	285
	Glossary	287
	Name Index	297
	Subject Index	301

Acknowledgments

We wish to acknowledge the inclusion of Dr. Gary R. Lowe, Dean of the School of Social Work at East Carolina University, in the authorship of this edition. Gary is our longtime colleague (at the University of Iowa), collaborator and friend. We invited him to join us in this edition, a fortunate decision, and are grateful for his contribution, both in content and in support over many years. He would like to thank Taia Younis and Sammy Dorsey for their editorial assistance in the initial and final preparation.

This edition greatly benefits from the continuing editorial and administrative support of fine people at Aldine de Gruyter: Dr. Richard Koffler, Executive Editor; Arlene Perazzini, Managing Editor; and Mike Sola, who did a superb job of copy editing. We continue to be proud of a quarter-century with a publishing company of such quality.

Finally, and most of all, we wish to acknowledge two persons who have not previously been recognized, but who have served as consultants, sounding boards, constructive critics, and contributors for the past quarter-century: Diane B. Anderson and Sharon K. Carter.

Introduction to the
Fifth Edition

> What I propose . . . is very simple; it is noth-
> ing more than to think what we are doing.
> —Hannah Arendt, *The Human Condition*

The publication of this edition marks the twenty-fifth year since the first edition of this book appeared. A quarter-century ago, systems theory was a relatively obscure set of suppositions and observations, and *social* systems had little recognition or status; in fact, it was largely regarded as one more attempt to "scientize" ideas about human behavior, a fad with a short career. Early in the preparation for this edition, we raised the question whether we could now legitimately call social systems a *theory* rather than an approach. We believe the threshold for status as a full-fledged theory (or body of theories) has been reached, and we will call it an "approach" less frequently. Occasionally, we will continue to call social systems a *model*; this is consistent with its "new" status. Systems theory is an acknowledged source of some of the most exciting ideas in science, including the social sciences and the field of human behavior. We will, however, retain some modesty about the status of social systems *theory*, and skepticism regarding some applications of it to human behavior. It will, of course, be interesting to check on the status of social systems ideas in another twenty-five years. We will be glad to let you know; or *you tell us*.

Three new themes emerged as we rewrote this book: *self-development*, *caring*, and *postmodernism*. The first, self-development, has become a central theme in systems theory, notably in the work of Ilya Prigogine in

Belgium and Humberto Maturana in Chile. This concept integrated naturally with the other two themes.

The second theme, *caring*, emerged as we explored recent writings about women's development and came to see social relationships, caring in particular, as a fundamental aspect of culture that was omitted from most writing on culture, including previous editions of this book. We are indebted to these writers and theorists, in particular those cited in the section on women's development; we strongly agree with those feminist writers who assert that caring must be a *cultural* characteristic, and that men must be supported in developing and expressing this characteristic.

We discovered that the third theme, *postmodernism*, already characterized the earlier editions of this book without being explicit: we were "postmodern" twenty-five years ago! (Does that make us *pre*postmodern, or *post*postmodern?) Our readers then (most of them coerced into reading a required text) would recognize the similarities to postmodernism as described below. The clearest, and perhaps briefest explication of postmodernism that we've seen is by W. Richard Scott:

> Postmodernism is a recent intellectual movement and still a work in progress. During the past decade, a steady stream of loosely related ideas and critiques, primarily generated by European social and cultural theorists, has begun to challenge many of the central assumptions underlying contemporary social science. . . . This work shares much in common with other natural open system perspectives. . . . [I]t emphasizes the central role of power in shaping social institutions. . . . [I]t stresses the overriding importance of cultural beliefs and symbolic processes. (W. R. Scott, 1998:313–314)

In the postmodernist view, our social world is constructed socially, and "what we 'see' and believe depends on the social situation and our location in it" (ibid.:314). That is, all knowledge is *contextual*. Social science is the reporting of experience from multiple perspectives. Further, our interpretations of the world are not simply reports of events external to us, but also of *ourselves* (this adds another layer of interpretation to Arendt's comment, quoted above: "to think what *we* are *doing*"). Therefore, it is impossible to separate knowledge from power. *Who* is interpreting events, from what *perspective*, and with what *credence, authority, and power*? are questions that are as important as the "facts" being presented. Thus the emphasis on "deconstruction," to show the bases being used for such interpretations and claims to truth.

"The task of the analyst is to understand 'what is "going on" in a situation,' recognizing that there is no one correct version, including that developed by the analyst. Truth is recognized to have many aspects and to speak with many voices" (ibid.:315). A postmodernist view emphasizes *diversity*. "If uniformity exists, it is because diversity has been suppressed; if consistency dominates, it has been arbitrarily imposed" (ibid.). We interpret postmodernism as a "view from below." Its view derives from those less powerful, as opposed to the rationalist (modernist) view "from above," by those who want or need "order" and "control." The former is an "outsider's" view, the latter an "insider's" view.

We point out the kinship of this book to postmodernism, in part, to defend it against the charge that, like macrofunctionalists or macrosystem determinists, social systems theory protects the status quo—that it favors the existing social structure and distribution of power. Not in this book—we refer anyone who holds that opinion to our first and later editions. We said then what we say now: Change is a constant, and there are no reserved seats in this arena. In fact, there are no seats; we are all participants. At least, that's *our* theory.

Introduction*

> When we mean to build,
> We first survey the plot, then draw the
> model.
> —William Shakespeare, *Henry IV*, Part 2

This book is an attempt to map the territory of human behavior. It is intended to introduce students in the human services to ideas and theories that are fundamental to understanding human behavior. Students in social work, nursing, education, home economics, child development, and other disciplines that provide human services require an acquaintance with a vast body of knowledge about the behavior of humans. Today it is impossible to present enough information in one book to accomplish this.

In our teaching and in our students' learning, we found that we came nearest to accomplishing this task by writing this book and using it as a global map of human behavior. It designates the major levels of knowledge of human behavior and enables students to recognize the human systems that most concern them. It is designed to organize human behavior content into an understandable whole.

Along with most of our students, we have found this book useful as a large-scale map in a "survey" of human behavior. We know from our experience that its utility in any particular sector of human behavior may be limited; therefore, we provide "small-scale maps" in the suggested readings at the end of each chapter. These sources provide more detailed explorations of particular human systems. This book, however, serves to place knowledge of human behavior within a broad context to remind us

* Revised 1999

that one's theory and one's practice are "a piece of the continent, and a part of the main," as the poet John Donne put it.

The manner in which this book and the more specialized resources fit together varies with the terrain. For example, a great many books and articles deal with *organizations* as systems, and it is fairly clear how the large- and small-scale maps of organizational behavior can be integrated. However, the integration of the two scales is less clear as they converge in the behavior of *a person*, where the relation of the part and the whole is always at issue. One recurrent question, for example, is whether a person should be regarded as the basic unit, a system capable of being subdivided, or only as a subsystem of some larger system such as society. Our intent is to demonstrate that these are all legitimate perspectives, to be used selectively in accord with the criteria explicated in this book.

Our objectives in this book are to explain how our map is designed and to establish its utility. We have sought an "umbrella" theory under which various theoretical perspectives would fit, or—to shift the metaphor—a "skeleton" framework upon which various theories can be affixed and fleshed out toward a comprehensive theory of human behavior. In our experience, no single theoretical perspective can encompass all aspects of human behavior.

Courses in human behavior have had various organizing themes, including:

1. *Normal vs. abnormal behavior.* This perspective provides knowledge of individual and family dynamics, which is invaluable in understanding and dealing with behavior of individual persons, but is of doubtful validity when applied to groups, institutions, communities, and societies.

2. *Developmental patterns of the person.* This perspective includes groups, communities, and society, but only from the standpoint of their effects on the development of the person. Inherent in this approach is a view of the person as an "adjuster" or "adapter." Human behavior is seen as adjustment to social stresses. Intervention possibilities are dichotomized, *either* working toward helping the person to adjust to the social situation *or* attempting to change the social situation so that it would be supportive to the person.

3. *Social process.* This perspective emphasizes knowledge of the social and cultural patterns that provide the social context for development and behavior. Such understanding is essential to social planning, but omits the uniqueness of the individual, and distinctiveness of patterns of living.

Each of these perspectives and others have served as a structuring theme for ordering knowledge of human behavior. Each enables scrutiny of various theories and hypotheses. Each, however, has limited applicability to the broadening base of human services. There has been an exponential increase of social science knowledge, which varies greatly in its quality and reliability. This increase requires a more comprehensive integrative framework than that provided by any of the previously employed organizing schemes. What is now required is an approach that will foster an integration of psychoanalytic, psychological, and developmental perspectives with the burgeoning discoveries from the many disciplines that study human behavior. We have found that the social systems theory is that approach.

Social systems theory may be described as a "way of thinking," a "theory about theories," a "hypothesis about theories," which has evolved into a loosely knit body of theory. It is a particular form of *general systems theory*, which crosses physical, natural, and social sciences. Emerging findings in many disciplines buttress the validity of general systems theory.

Social systems theory has these characteristics:

1. It is comprehensive. It offers greater potential for description and integration of seemingly disparate theories into a single framework than any other framework we know.

2. It provides suggestive leads for all sectors of human behavior, even though it does not map all sectors adequately or equally.

3. It has the potential to provide a common language to various disciplines, both within and across disciplines. Students interested in psychotherapy, education, community development, and administration may find social systems theory a useful common framework. The psychotherapist may not be vitally interested in community development, believing that significant changes occur within individuals; the community developer may believe that significant changes occur only when groups act; while the administrator may believe that change is real only when it is structured and solidified in an institution or program. We believe that each is partially right and partially wrong. Like the proverbial blind men examining the elephant, each has part of the truth. Yet these three specialists can see relationships between and among their localities if they share a knowledge of social systems. They might prefer their "home territory," but would be aware that it was "part of the main." They can recognize that interactions of persons, groups, and organizations are integrally related in a common system.

4. Parsimony is the final characteristic. Social systems theory allows the student to reduce the "blooming, buzzing confusion" of theories of human behavior and methods of practice to a framework that can be mastered. Herein lies a danger, of course; through reductionism the student may be content with the global map, flying from continent to continent, coast to coast, without encountering the precipices, mudholes, and arid wastes upon which many a theory has foundered. The systems approach cannot replace detailed knowledge of at least some particular sectors of human behavior. After all, people live through the processes of human interaction, not on maps.

This book describes a systems "skeleton" and then locates important human behavior concepts upon it. The instructors and students who use this book must flesh out the skeleton so that the approach will be directly applicable to the practice of each respective profession.

HOW TO USE THIS BOOK

This book is a large-scale map, intended to be supplemented in each particular sector of human behavior by more detailed maps. We have used it this way with both undergraduate and graduate students. We have guided students through the courses in modular fashion, using selected theories and indicating where each more detailed theory meshed with the large-scale map.

The first two chapters acquaint the student with social systems theory. The essential systems characteristics are introduced and explained. These concepts, which serve to draw the map, reappear in the subsequent chapters. They are the key ideas that together form the social systems approach of this book.

The subsequent chapters are modules—they can be taught as separate units, with only the first two chapters as prerequisites. The present arrangement of the chapters is only one feasible way of ordering human systems, in descending order of magnitude. If instructors using this book prefer other sequences, the order can be changed, or even reversed. In this way, a course might be better integrated with other courses during the same term, or might better convey a particular theme being emphasized. For instance, instructors in colleges of education might decide to present the chapter on the person prior to chapters on group or family.

We have found it most useful to use other texts with this book to provide additional threads of continuity through the general map, to assure degrees both of latitude and longitude, and to provide a single small-map source for each human system examined. For continuity crossing all systems, we have used *The Autobiography of Malcolm X*, Tillie Olsen's *Tell Me a Riddle*, Ken Kesey's *One Flew Over the Cuckoo's Nest*, and Randy Shilts's *And the Band Played On*. For specific systems, we have assigned Erikson's *Identity, Youth and Crisis* (1968) for the chapter on the person; Billingsley's *Black Families in White America* (1988) and Erdrich's

Love Medicine for the chapter on families, and Hall's *Beyond Culture* for the culture module. Again, many choices are open to the instructor.

Suggested readings, with brief commentaries on their particular usefulness, follow each chapter. The readings actually used will depend upon the instructor and students and on the clock and calendar time available. If students are unfamiliar with particular social systems (such as family or groups), the supplemental materials should be selected with this in mind. For students acquainted with particular systems, supplemental readings can give deeper insights into theoretical writings and related research. The listed films and videos may also be helpful to convey particular ideas, or as an opportunity for students to apply the concepts in analyzing the situation that is portrayed.

The glossary is designed for easy reference to the key concepts used throughout this book. The reader should consult the glossary because these are the definitions used throughout.

The book is (metaphorically) an open system. We assume that each instructor will add and substitute books, articles, films and videos, or other learning aids. This flexibility allows the book to be used in graduate schools, four-year colleges, community and junior colleges, and perhaps in-service training programs.

In other words, this work comes to you incomplete. It not only suggests that students and instructors add their own input to this study of human behavior; the book *requires* it. We hope that social systems theory will be a step toward an integrated body of social science knowledge that will reflect both the complexity of social forces and the uniqueness of the individual person.

Social Systems Theory

No man is an island, entire of itself; every
man is a piece of the continent, a part of the
main. . . . [A]ny man's death diminishes me,
because I am involved in mankind; and therefore never send to know for whom the bell
tolls; it tolls for thee.
—John Donne, *Devotions XVII*

Everything flows; nothing remains. . . .
One cannot step twice into the same river.
—Heraclitus

INTRODUCTION: PROVIDING MEANING
TO THEORY

Reverend Donne's well-known passage expresses the theme of this
book's systems theme, *social systems theory*. As we say in the introduction
to this edition, it now seems appropriate to recognize it as theory as well
as metaphor. General systems theory (GST), which includes the narrower
field of *social systems*, is a cross-disciplinary body of scientific thought that
developed during the twentieth century. One systems theorist says:

For decades, and even perhaps for 100 years, social science has been trying
to describe, or hit, a moving target—nonlinear behavior. It has been scoffed
at as "soft science," but this may no longer be the case. Potentially, these
theories of nonlinearity indicate that is more difficult to study nonlinear
phenomena, tougher to pin things down. Entirely possible is the notion that
social science has been doing the most difficult work in science. (Bütz,
1997:xviii)

The advent of computers has allowed testing of scientific hypotheses (e.g., of fractal geometry and so-called "fuzzy" logic) suggested by GST. This has presented exciting (and frequently unanticipated) insights into commonalities among the natural (or "hard") sciences and social (or "soft") sciences.

We will also describe it as the social systems *perspective,* a philosophical viewpoint on the relationship of persons with their social environment, which we discuss in the epilogue. Occasionally, we will also refer to it as the social systems *model,* meaning that it is at the same time a hypothesis to be tested, primarily through its application to professional practice in various professions and disciplines. Since "person-in-environment" (or PIE, as it is abbreviated) is a central motif of social work and of other human services, the systems metaphor is particularly well suited to social work practice. Gordon Hearn first stated this connection:

> The general systems approach . . . is based upon the assumption that matter, in all its forms, living and nonliving, can be regarded as systems. . . . If nothing else, this should provide social work education with a means of organizing the human behavior and social environment aspects of the curriculum. But beyond this, if the general systems approach could be used to order knowledge about the entities with which we work, perhaps it could also be used as the means of developing a fundamental conception of the social work process itself. (Hearn, 1969:2)

This conception is useful to other professions as well, for example, psychology, nursing, education, communication, and medicine. Auger stated that a systems approach enables the nurse

> to evaluate the status of the person who is ill and the significance of changes that may or may not have occurred in patterns of behavior. This content will help the student to develop a broader concept of the relationship between health and illness, the wide variations of "normal" behavior, and changes that may occur as a consequence of illness and / or hospitalization. (Auger, 1976:x)

Monge argued that a systems perspective provides the best theoretical basis for the study of human communication: "That perspective which incorporates the others is, until at least more information is available, the one best suited to guide us in our quest for knowledge about human communication" (Monge, 1977:29).

This chapter will introduce the basics of the social systems approach to understanding human behavior. We will provide a brief overview of the scientific context that gave rise to systemic thinking and the particular version known as social system. We will define and discuss basic concepts, some of which include terms that may be new to you, such as *holon.*

We will also discuss familiar terms, such as *energy* and *organization*, but some of these terms will have new, important meanings.

The social system model that we present in these first two chapters provides organizing principles for this book. This model enables the reader to recognize similar or identical ideas (isomorphs) emerging from different scientific and philosophical ancestries and provides a scheme for classifying and ordering such related ideas. Most importantly, it provides a means to understand human behavior better and may point to new directions for professional practice.

A. Systems/Systemic Thinking

In most dictionaries the first meaning of *system* is "a set of things or parts forming a whole," "a complex unity formed of many often diverse parts subject to a common plan or serving a common purpose," or something similar. *Systemic thinking* then means using the mind to recognize pattern, conceive unity, and form some coherent wholeness—to seek to complete the picture. That which is called *system* consists of elements cohering in some intelligible way, that is, capable of being understood.

As humankind seeks to find order amid disorder, meaning in the intrinsically meaningless, and the quality of wholeness, thought is patterned and imposed on the world as experienced by the perceiver.

Systemic thinking includes those ways of thinking that seek to understand coherence and connectedness of all life. A recurrent phrase that conveys this quality of coherence is, "hang together." Here are two uses of that phrase from quite different sources (emphases added):

> [H]e who wants to have right without wrong,
> Order without disorder,
> Does not understand the principles
> of heaven and earth
> He does not know how
> They *hang together*.
>
> —Chuang Tzu, poet-philosopher of Taoism

> The doctrine that everything in the universe *hangs together*, partly by mechanical cause, but mainly by hidden affinities (which also account for apparent coincidences), provided not only the foundation for sympathetic magic, astrology and alchemy; it also runs as a *leitmotif* through the teachings of Taoism and Buddhism, the neo-Platonists, and the philosophers of the early Renaissance.
>
> —Arthur Koestler, philosopher (1979:265)

Comprehension of the *part/whole* nature of life is the central tenet of systemic thinking. From this core flow most of the propositions of our social systems approach.

I. ESSENCE AND ANCESTRY: THE ATOMISTIC / HOLISTIC CONTINUUM

A social system is a special order of system, within general systems. It is distinct from atomic, molecular, or galactic systems in that it is composed of persons or groups of persons who interact and mutually influence each other's behavior.

> [A] social system is a model of a social organization that possesses a distinctive total unity beyond its component parts, that is distinguished from its environment by a clearly defined boundary, and whose subunits are at least partially interrelated within relatively stable patterns of social order. . . . [A] *social system is a bounded set of interrelated activities that together constitute a single entity.* (Olsen, [1968] 1978:228–229)

A. Polar Positions

Systems exist at all "levels": persons, families, organizations, communities, societies, and cultures. It is important, both analytically and ideologically, to specify what should be seen as the "basic unit" of social systems. In order to explain adequately what we consider the "basic unit" of social systems, we must step back and review the theoretical positions that have emerged.

Within sociology there have historically been polar positions on the designation of the social unit of primary attention: "macro" vs. "micro," or whole vs. part. Macrofunctionalists, such as Talcott Parsons, tended to view the society as the primary focus and therefore to view the behavior of smaller human systems and their components as being determined by the society's needs and goals, i.e., the whole determines the actions of its parts. Simply put, people are determined by society. This is a *holistic* viewpoint.

At the opposite pole were social behaviorists and social interactionists, such as Max Weber, G. H. Mead, and Herbert Blumer. They began with the smallest unit of the system, the behavior of the individual person. In this view, the acts of the individual persons tend to cluster into patterns; therefore the social system is constructed out of these patterns; i.e., the whole is the sum of its parts. Again, simply put, persons determine the society. This is an *atomistic* viewpoint. The holistic (or wholistic) view implied "downward" causality, while the atomistic view implied "upward" causality.

These two positions are important and powerful when applied to the task of deciding how to (or whether to) intervene in human behavior, as well as to explaining how change is achieved in the realm of human endeavor. Within social work education and practice this duality has emerged as the historical distinction between "casework" and "community organization," or as "individual change" vs. "social change." The social change emphasis is grounded in the macrofunctionalist view that behavior is primarily determined by the larger social systems: macrosystems such as society, community, or organization. Emphasis on clinical or individual change derives its theoretical legitimacy from the belief that society is constructed from the behavior of its smallest unit, the person. This duality is inherent in other social/behavioral disciplines, most explicitly in the paradigm of "nature vs. nurture." This phenomenon of polarity will be a recurrent theme throughout the remainder of this book. Most significantly, it is this duality and its historical tension that gave rise to the necessity for such a view as the social systems approach.

B. Holon

We hold that both polar positions are relevant and must be considered when examining human affairs. There must be attention to both the whole *and* the part. Our point of view is that each social entity, whether large or small, complex or simple, is a *holon*. This term is borrowed from Arthur Koestler, who coined it (borrowing from the Greek language) to express the idea that each entity is simultaneously a part and a whole. A social unit is made up of parts to which it is the whole, the *suprasystem,* and at the same time is part of some larger whole of which it is a *component* or *subsystem*. Like the Roman god Janus, a holon faces two directions at once—inward toward its own parts, and outward to the system of which it is a part (Koestler, 1967a:112ff.; 1979:23–51). What is central is that any system is by definition both part and whole (see Figure 1.1).

The individual person constitutes the apex of the hierarchy of organisms and, at the same time, is the lowest unit of the social hierarchy (Figure 8.1) conveys this idea]. The concept of holon is particularly useful; it epitomizes a consistent theme in this book: *Any system is by definition both part and whole. No single system is determinant, nor is system behavior determined at only one level, whether part or whole.*

The idea of holon as used in this book extends Koestler's proposition of whole/part relationships to include certain corollaries:

1. The systems approach requires the specification of a *focal system,* which is the system chosen to receive primary attention. Another way of saying this: the choice of focal system identifies the perspective from which the observer views, and analyzes, the system and its environment (see *perspectivism* in the glossary).

2. The idea of holon then requires the observer to attend to both the components (*subsystems*) of that focal system and the *suprasystem* of which the focal system is a part (or the *significant environment* to which the focal system is related), in order to fully understand it.

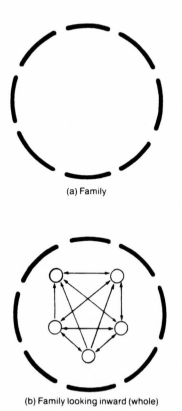

(a) Family

(b) Family looking inward (whole)

Figure 1.1. Diagrams of a family system. (a) Family. (b) Family as a whole: looking inward. (c) Family as a part: looking outward. (d) Family as holon (part and whole).

A family serves as a useful example to explain the concept of focal system. If family is viewed as a holon, attention must simultaneously be given to both the family's members and to its significant environment such as schools, community, work organizations, other families, and neighborhood. To focus only on the interactions among family members (family as suprasystem) ignores the family's interactions with larger systems (family as subsystem). A series of simple diagrams illustrates this (see Figure 1.2).

Social systems theory may be described as "contextual," "interactional," or *perspectivistic* (see the Introduction to this Edition). The latter term connotes that causation, or the significance of an event, is relative to the focus one has at the time of assessment; that the interpretation one places on events depends upon where and who one is and the perspective one has upon the focal system. As an example, recall in your own experi-

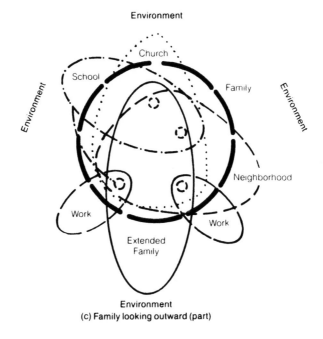

(c) Family looking outward (part)

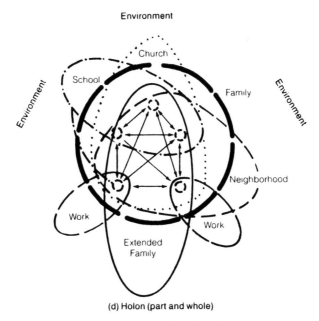

(d) Holon (part and whole)

Figure 1.1.   Continued

External
(environment)

Internal
(components)

Securing and
conserving energy

SE   SI

Goal-directed

GE   GI

Figure 1.2. Four energy functions (S: securing; G: goal; E: external; I: internal). See glossary for definitions of terms.

ence when you witnessed a situation and someone else who witnessed the same event formed a very different assessment from you (the classic film *Rashomon* portrays the same events as seen by four different people). So it is in the larger social/historical context: as events are viewed by other observers or at other times, meanings are likely to change.

Thus, social system theory is "holonistic," requiring:

1. specification of the focal system;
2. specification of the units or components that constitute that holon;
3. specification of the significant environmental systems; and
4. specification of one's own position relative to the focal system.

This process can be called *mapping*. One example is the use of "ecomaps" in family systems approaches to understanding and helping families. Components and environment find their meaning in their effects on the focal system and, conversely, the focal system finds meaning in its effect on its component parts and its environment.

Finally, to achieve an objective description of the focal system, one must state one's own position relative to the focal system, e.g., family's therapist, patient's nurse, community's organizer. Such a perspectivistic view is philosophically consistent with the basic metaphor drawn from Einstein's theory of relativity, that *perceptions of events are relative to the position of the observer.*

II. ENERGY/INFORMATION:
THE NECESSARY ELEMENT

Consistent with the atomic metaphor introduced earlier, we suggest the basic "stuff" of a system is *energy*. Metaphorically, as atoms and molecules are composed of energy, so also are social systems. The question becomes: Is energy an inclusive enough concept to denote the life of a social system? We suggest it is if, borrowing from physics, the broader meaning includes both *information* and *resources* as "potential energy." The nature of both information and resources includes the capacities to activate or mobilize the system and to serve as energy sources.

> While most readers would have no problem in conceiving of coal or petroleum as energy forms, the present argument requires that we also regard human beings, human behavior, social groups, and assemblages of social interactions as energy forms. Similarly, mental processes located in the brain, writing on paper, and soundwaves in the air are also energy forms. The inclusion of all these different kinds of things as energy forms is legitimate because all of them meet the definition. (Adams, 1988: 15–16)

Monane agreed: "System action can be understood . . . as the movement of energy/information (1) *within* a system and (2) *between* a system and its environment" (Monane, 1967:1–2). To disqualify information as energy is to deny its reality; information is nothing if it does not provide potential for action. Information *"is ingested as energy to the same extent that food fulfills biological needs"* (Bütz, 1997:136). The same author emphasizes that human beings use symbols to encapsulate their experiences and to communicate that experience to others—and that our symbols are "self-referential." That is, we constantly communicate our symbols not only to each other, but to ourselves (see Introduction to this edition), constructing reality and constructing self. Bütz (1997:131) ingeniously uses an illustration of the Möbius (or Moebius) strip, a strip of paper that is given a half-twist and then the ends are joined, so that it forms a continuous, one-faced strip—an unending loop. By this, he means that our experience is always simultaneously both internal and external, a continuous dialogue (or dialectic) between self and the world. Information is the content of this dialogue. This is a fundamental example of what we later describe as a *feedback loop* (in this case, a literal loop).

What occurs in and between social systems are "transfers of energy/information" between persons or groups of persons. The energy in this dynamic process is not directly observable; its presence is inferred from its effects upon the system and its parts. There is some disagreement among system theorists as to whether energy is a valid concept for social systems. Without getting into this intellectual debate now, we define energy as "capacity for action," "action," or "power to effect change."

It is important to understand that *energy* and *information* are not identical, but that they are complementary and inseparable in living systems: both are necessary although neither is sufficient. Energy must be structured in order to be useful; information, just as its root meaning implies, gives form to the energy. All systems carry information and instruction, in some form. We will occasionally use "energy / information" to convey the relation of the two or, rarely, just "information."

The exact nature of human energy is undetermined and depends in part upon the particular system being examined. Within a person, we refer to *psychic energy* (the energy of the psyche or personality); we could similarly refer to the social energy of a family, group, organization, or community. In both instances energy means the system's capacity to act, its power to maintain itself and to effect change.

Energy derives from a complex of sources including the physical capacities of its members; social resources such as loyalties, shared sentiments, and common values; and resources from its environment. Energy sources for personality systems could include food; the physical condition of the body; intellectual and emotional capabilities; emotional support from friends, family, or colleagues; cultural and religious sanctions for one's beliefs and activities; recognition of one's status by society and one's colleagues in an organization; and perhaps most important, one's own sense of worth and integrity.

A. Entropy and Synergy

1. Entropy. There are some fundamental concepts necessary to an understanding of energy as the term is used in social systems theory. The first is *entropy*, the tendency of an unattended system to move toward an unorganized state that is characterized by decreased interactions among its components; this is followed by decrease in usable energy. *Entropy* is a measure of the quantity of *energy not available for use.* Some common expressions that convey this concept are: "He's not performing up to his potential," and "What a waste of talent." The second concept is *synergy,* which refers to increasingly available energy within a system derived from heightened interaction among its components. Expressions of this might be: "She's got it all together, and look at the results," and *E pluribus unum* ("Out of many, one").

Entropy is a concept from physics that is applied metaphorically, not literally, to social systems. This limitation was recognized early by general systems theorists.

Physical processes follow the second law of thermodynamics . . . they proceed toward increasing entropy, that is, more probable states which are states of equilibrium, of uniform distribution and disappearance of existing differentiations and order. But *living systems* apparently do exactly the opposite. In spite of irreversible processes continually going on, *they tend to maintain an organized state of fantastic improbability*; they are maintained in states of *non*-equilibrium; they even develop toward increasing differentiation and order, as is manifest in both the individual development of an organism and evolution from the famous amoeba to man. (Bertalanffy, 1967:62; emphasis ours)

2. *Synergy.* An open system need not deplete its energy but, in addition to importing energy, may actually compound energy from increased interaction among its parts. *Synergy* (working together) occurs in open, living systems (and thus in social systems). Ruth Benedict, an anthropologist, first applied the idea of synergy to social interaction. She used it to denote the amplification of goal-directed activity where there was a fit between persons' individual goals and the goals of their culture. As with *entropy*, we again emphasize that the concept of synergy should not be used literally with regard to social systems, but rather as an analogy.

For example, it may be apparent that one organization is becoming increasingly static and predictable while another organization may be increasingly unpredictable and fluid, with internal shifts of concentration of energy and powers that result in "dynamic growth." The analogy we have introduced would be applied by describing the first organization described above as *entropic* and the second as *synergistic*. This same analogy could be applied to a person as well: rigidity and maintenance of psychological defenses could be evidence of entropy, while absorption of new stimuli and constant adaptation to the environment, with resultant stimulation of new attachments and ideas, could be evidence of either *synergy* or *syntropy*. This last term is new to this discussion and connotes the importation of both *energy* and *entropy* across system's boundaries: one system's (person's, town's, organization's, nation's) energy may be another system's entropy.

III. THE FOUR BASIC ENERGY FUNCTIONS

Systems require energy in order to exist. In our view, there are four basic energy functions that are essential to carry out a system's *purposes*. We simplistically diagram these four energy functions (see Figure 1.2) in order to illustrate the interrelatedness of energy functions and to demonstrate their applicability to all human systems.

A. Functions of Securing Energy (SE and SI)

The first pair of functions (cells SE and SI) pertains to *securing* energy (as opposed to the *use* of energy, cells GE and GI, discussed below). SE represents the function of securing energy from *outside* the system (negentropy, discussed later in this chapter); that is, from the environment. The

SE function inevitably involves GE as well, since the importation of energy occurs as a transactional process between the human system and the environment. SI denotes securing energy from *inside* the system, from one or more component parts of the focal system. A variety of outcomes is possible in the performance of SE and SI functions. The SE function is well-illustrated by the fossil fuel situation facing industrialized nations in the recent past and the foreseeable future. If less fuel is available externally (e.g., oil from the Persian Gulf) to supply national goals, more must be conserved and secured internally (SI function) through domestic oil, wood, coal, biomass, natural gas, or solar energy. An example in a social system is that if family members become unemployed, all must "pitch in" to pool resources. Fathers may provide child care while mothers work, children's earnings become family income, and everyone may have to "make do" with what they have.

If internal system energies are in short supply and energy from the subsystems is critically needed, energy-consuming frictions and conflicts among subsystems must be prevented or reduced. ("All right, break it up! We have work to do.") If, instead, the focal system has a surplus of energy available from its components, then the system can tolerate diversion of energy into subsystem conflicts. ("Oh, let 'em fight it out! They need to let off steam.") Such conflicts between components may be, in a choice between focal system goals, the lesser of two evils: diversion of energy to suppress one subsystem may be preferable to allowing the subsystem to go unchecked. One example of this process is the operation of defense mechanisms (see discussion of Freudian theory in Chapter 8): suppression of impulses or wishes may be preferable to allowing them free expression, which in turn could endanger the "survival" of the personality. On a larger societal scale, a national policy of racial domination is another example: the amount of available energy required to maintain segregation and second-class citizenship for a racial minority (United States) or a racial majority, as was the case in South Africa, is great and thus dysfunctional for the attainment of some goals. Continuation of the system as it is (*morphostasis*) may take priority for the privileged because of fear of the anticipated consequences of changing it (*morphogenesis*).

When a system is in danger of being destroyed or radically changed, system components may pool energies. Pulling together, tightening the ranks, and forgetting past differences may be found in the family, city, or nation when circumstances or events threaten continued existence. In foreign policy and war, the often-repeated mantra by members of Congress is "Politics ends at the nation's shores."

B. Functions of Goal Attainment (GE and GI)

The second pair of basic functions (cells GE and GI of Figure 2) pertains to the *use* of energy, that is, the *purpose* to which energy is applied. One of the characteristics of living systems is the purposefulness of activities. They operate in a goal-directed manner. This pair of functions together may be called *goal achievement* or *goal attainment*. As in the first pair of functions, this pair is performed both internally and externally; GE refers to goal-directed activity outside the system and is interrelated with SE, SI, and GI. The system must carry on transactions with the environment to achieve its own goals as whole and as part. It must achieve as much reliability and control over the linkages between system and environment as possible; this is the function of "intelligence" as Piaget describes it (see Chapter 8). One example is the "vertical integration" of corporations (like Microsoft), which purchase other companies to reduce competition, to assure supplies of raw material, or to control the market for their products. In the case of Microsoft, this has been a risky strategy that provoked antitrust actions by the federal Justice Department—an example of a suprasystem placing limits on the energy controlled by a system that seeks to control its own environment.

GI refers to goal-directed activity inside the system. Here energy is employed to subordinate the subsystems to the goals of the focal system in order to be consistent with the nature of the system and the environment. The declaration of a state of martial law in a nation is an example of goal-directed activity within the system. Because system survival is supposedly at stake, energies are directed inward to reduce or eliminate disorder. An example: professional organizations require their members to align their goals and behaviors with the goals and patterns of the organization; if members violate the rules, they are subject to expulsion or disciplinary measures. Social workers are regulated by a code of ethics and subject to sanctions by the National Association of Social Workers; psychologists are regulated by the American Psychological Association. A family system that holds a goal of educational achievement will direct energies to control a member who rejects education as a goal, for example, denying use of the family car unless grades are satisfactory.

C. Interrelatedness of the Four Energy Functions

It should be emphasized that these four functions (SI, SE, GI, GE) are not separate; a system performs all of these functions at the same time, although not equally at any particular moment. In any exchanges between whole and parts, all elements receive some energy and have some goals met. The reciprocal nature of the transactions and exchanges should be kept in mind. If one function is always dominant, the other functions are neglected, to the detriment of the total system. For example, the family system that concentrates energy only on the SE function through securing and importing energy from the external environment may experience internal disintegration. This might happen if a parent (or parents) devotes excessive time and energy to supporting the family, at the expense of internal family functions, not spending time with children, to support them, to play with them, or to discipline them. The phenomenon of "latch-key kids," children who arrive home after school to an empty house because the parent (or parents) work and have no other afternoon care, provides an example. A parent may not have a choice: survival of the family may depend upon the efforts she (or he) exerts at work; but all parties may pay a price (bear in mind the unpredictability of human systems, however; the children *may* be resilient enough to cope adequately). Here is an example with family as the focal system: President Clinton proposed subsidizing employers who provide day-care for employees' children, and subsidizing good day-care facilities at affordable prices at convenient locations (SE). This could reduce workers' stress and anxiety (SI) about their children's care and allow them to be more stable and productive (GE), and assure that children receive predictable, professional care that would allow them to become productive adults (GI).

IV. ORGANIZATION: THE SUFFICIENT ELEMENT

Just as energy is the basic "stuff" and the *necessary* element of a system, organization is the *sufficient* element. Even if energy is available in and to a system, if there is a total absence of organization then there is a total absence of system. Absence of organization equals entropy. To be a social *system* means to have some degree of organization; the word *organization* refers to the grouping and arranging of parts to form a whole in order to put a system into "working order." System organization secures, expends, and conserves energy to maintain the system and further its purposes.

The cybernetic concept of organization distinguishes between "high" and "low" organization. The degree of the system's intrarelatedness, that is, the degree to which components' actions affect each other, indicates the level of system organization. For example, in a highly organized system, such as the family portrayed in the novel *The Great Santini* (based on the author's own family and his father, who died in 1998), the components are strongly interdependent; what one member does is crucial for others. The founding of a social system, that is, the delineation of a new entity from its environment, can generally be expressed in the familiar phrases, "Let's get organized," and "Let's get it together." The first action of the components of a burgeoning system must be to order randomly distributed energies. If this task of energy organization is not accomplished, then the system will fail to develop.

The Constitution of the United States is a real-life example of the notion of organization and its necessity for ensuring systemic operation. In short, the Constitution is a document that organizes component systems in such a way as to create a suprasystem of both government structure and socio-political behavior. The Preamble sets forth the general purpose for forming a new system and then specifies system goals:

> We the people of the United States, in Order to form a more perfect Union, establish Justice, insure domestic Tranquility, provide for the common defence, promote the general Welfare, and secure the Blessings of Liberty to ourselves and our Posterity; do ordain and establish this Constitution for the United States of America.

Following this introduction, the various articles and amendments of the Constitution specify the conditions of intrarelatedness of the components (states and individual persons) to the larger system (federal government). The goals of the national system as specified in the Preamble are, and must be, congruent with the goals of its components. It was precisely this organization and interrelatedness that were at issue in the Civil War (or the War between the States, depending upon your perspective).

Organization is not synonymous with higher levels of complexity. That is, "A complex society is not necessarily more advanced than a simple one; it has just adapted to conditions in a more complex way" (Farb, [1968] 1978:13). A personality with complex defenses is not necessarily better or worse than an "uncomplicated" personality, but certainly the two function differently. Complexity or simplicity is not the issue; the measure of the effectiveness of organization is its capacity to fulfill the system's goals, as well as the goals of its components. (See discussion of "effectiveness" and "efficiency" in Chapter 5, under "Goal Direction"). Effective organization not only enables the internal energies of the system to be generated and purposefully used, but also enables the system to secure energy from the environment (i.e., SI and SE functions).

Disorganization of a system—whether person, family, or neighborhood—does not mean totally *un*organized; it means not *sufficiently* organized. The system's energies are not in working order; the components of the system do not stand in sufficient relatedness to one another. Energy is randomly distributed and expended; the system is tending toward a state of entropy. Vernacular terms for this process in a person are *spaced out* and *losing it*.

Organization is apparent in the human personality. It is present in Freud's personality subsystems of *id, ego,* and *superego*; as he envisioned it, this triad must work in harmony (with the ego being dominant) in order for a person to function effectively in a social context. Following Freud, Erikson's ([1963] 1993) formulation of *identity* is an expression of an *organizing* principle that enables the components of the personality to "get together" to fulfill the goals of the person. Central to Erikson's formulation is the notion of a person creating an identity for herself or himself, as opposed to experiencing *identity diffusion*. Identity is defined as personality components working together as a whole, while identity diffusion refers to lack of integration among personality components. A person who is schizophrenic is, in essence, a disorganized system.

We can also see the importance of organization when it is applied to the family system. Families with problems are generally disorganized families, and the reasons for this disorganization can emanate from internal sources and/or external forces:

1. The goals of one or more members are in opposition to system goals.
2. The elements of organization (e.g., communication, feedback, and role expectations) are disrupted or unclear.
3. Energies from within the system are not available or not sufficient for the demands on the system.
4. The family is not adequately organized to obtain additional energy from outside its own system.
5. The environment (the suprasystem) exercises a disorganizing influence on the family system (e.g., oppression).
6. Energy is denied or not available from the suprasystem (e.g., unemployment or having welfare benefits cut off).

The dimension of organization—the fact of organization—is characteristic of all social phenomena that can be designated as social systems. If there is no organization present, there is no system, and it is *un*organized. If organization is insufficient or dysfunctional for the goals of the system, the system is *dis*organized. Organization means the structuring of the organization in a system, the ordering of the energies of the component parts in some fashion that results in a whole.

V.   CAUSATION, FEEDBACK LOOPS, AND CHAOS THEORY

A social system contains a causal network that is not linear. Causation is multidirectional, multiple, and mutual. A change in any part of the causal network affects other parts, but does not determine the total network. In other words (as we said earlier), behavior is not determined by one holon but rather by the interaction and mutual causation of all (or many) of the systems and subsystems, that is, by holons of differing magnitudes.

It is not useful to seek to understand human behavior through searching for *linear*, one-directional cause-effect relationships. Consequently, it serves little purpose to ask "why" persons do what they do. A "why" question demands a causal explanation, a "because" response. A more useful inquiry is "how," or in what way something happened. An example of *nonlinear* causation is Forrester's "world dynamics" model, illustrated in *Limits to Growth* (Meadows, Meadows, Randers, and Behrens, 1972). The model recognized that factors interact in complex loops, avoiding an oversimplistic, linear, causal chain. That is, "A causes B causes C" is less likely than "A interacts with B to produce AB, which changes both A and B, and results in C, which is partly A, B, and AB." Certainly, this is a more complex description, but it also closer to reality, particularly the reality of human relationships, that is, *systemic* relationships. This more complex view of causality is the core idea in *nonlinear dynamic systems.* This retroactive influence on initial causal factors is called a *feedback loop* (see Glossary) and is characteristic of complex systems, including human systems at all levels.

Recent developments in the study of fractal geometry, in "fuzzy thinking," and in *chaos theory* place great emphasis on the role and importance of feedback for systems. Fractals are geometric shapes that resemble forms found in nature; the basic idea is that systems (and parts of systems) such as crystals, leaves, and coastlines proliferate in forms that are based upon "exquisite sensitivity to initial conditions." This means that each new form or development in a system is highly sensitive to the previous condition of the system, and to feedback as the new development occurs; so sensitive that the slightest variation will affect the evolving structure, making the outcome unpredictable. The classic expression of this is that the flutter of a butterfly's wings in Brazil affects weather in Texas; surely an overstatement, but it makes the point. This sensitivity to feedback confirms the principle of indeterminacy in systems: that only averages or aggregates can be predicted with any assurance. Weather forecasts are an excellent example of the use of systems theory in science (and of the fact that we can describe systems *theory* in the natural sciences). That is, local forecasts are less valid than those for an entire region or continent, and are frequently altered as unexpected developments occur. The analogy to social systems is that developments in human systems are unpredictable also and highly sensitive both to the system's history and to current feedback as new developments occur.

The term "fuzzy thinking" (Kosko, 1993) is not meant to describe what students do (or professors, either). It describes the application of feedback to industrial and scientific instruments and machines. The basic idea is that instead of simple binary decisions ("on or off," or in computer terms, "1 or 0"), gradations of judgment can be made automatically by the device itself: for example, "cold-cool-medium-warm-hot" for stovetops, "intermittent-slow-medium-fast" for windshield wipers, or a combination (slow-warm then fast-warm then slow-hot, for a furnace, e.g.). Japanese corporations have been particularly innovative, and hold most of the United States patents on fuzzy logic applications in electronic and household equipment, e.g., washing machines that use constant feedback to adjust water temperature, to sense the type of dirt in clothing, to choose the amount of detergent and softener to use, and to monitor the length of time needed to clean the fabric. The relevance here is that the theoretical and practical significance of the feedback cycle in systems, and the uses of it, have become much more sophisticated during the past decade.

Chaos theory is a confusing name for complex ideas. Its importance to human systems, however, requires that we make an effort to understand the fundamentals of the theory:

> [I]n works like Gleick's *Chaos* (1987) and Prigogine and Stengers' *Order out of Chaos* (1984), feedback loops are emerging at the heart of the phenomena of complex nonlinear dynamics and unpredictable deterministic systems. Thus psychotherapy, psychology, sociology, anthropology, social psychology, economics, political science, and management have all been touched and changed by the discovery of the potential significance of the feedback loop in human affairs (Richardson, 1991:3).

The fundamental concept in chaos theory is *order* vs. *disorder*. As discussed earlier, entropy describes a condition in which energy is completely dispersed (randomly distributed) and is not available for use by the system or its components. That is *disorder*: completely flat, unorganized, and undifferentiated, in other words, *chaos*. This use of the word chaos is somewhat difficult for most of us, because we think of piles of refuse, like the aftermath of a tornado or hurricane (or a typical dormitory room). But in chaos theory, chaos is better pictured as a pile of sand, or a beach, or a bag of marbles, made up of inert, disconnected particles. Living systems exist at the opposite extreme; they lump and clump (and sometimes bump) energy into concentrations: systems and subsystems, which are maintained only by great effort and only by intense energy exchange internally and with their environments. In chaos terms, this is *order*: "order [is] departure from maximum entropy" (Bailey, 1994:243). The effort required by living systems to maintain order means that they constantly live "on the edge of chaos" (Capra, 1996).

The leading theorist on entropy in living systems is Ilya Prigogine, a Russian-born Belgian chemist who won the Nobel prize for his work on the subject. He is founder of the "Brussels school," which has analyzed the dynamics of complex nonlinear systems. During forty years of research, Prigogine determined that living systems are able to maintain their high level of disequilibrium by importing energy and exporting entropy. Importing energy is, in the arcane language of GST, *negentropy*, or negative entropy. Another way to describe this process is that living systems are *dissipative* structures (Prigogine and Stengers, 1984); they dissipate, or export, entropy from the system. In the vernacular, they "get the lead out." An example would be a person whose internal conflict drains energy, or ties up energy, who resolves the conflict by interacting with a therapist or a treatment group; this then releases the person's emotional (psychic) energy for freer, more productive living. Another example in an organization would be restructuring of a department so that employees who were "dead-ended," unstimulated, unhappy, and unproductive interact with other units; the department's entropy would be replaced by new flows of energy in the form of new ideas, new alliances, and new challenges.

The way in which systems accomplish negentropy, or dissipation, is through feedback. As part of the feedback cycle, the system and its components modify their relationships to each other; in other words, they adapt their structures to accommodate (see Glossary, and discussion of Piaget's theory in Chapter 8) this feedback. In this sense, exchanges between the system and components are more determinative than the system's exchange with the environment; this is a modification of earlier thinking about systems (and of this book since the previous edition), and is largely attributable to Prigogine's work. This does not change the fact that *both* the components and the environment influence the system, however.

CONCLUSION

Social systems theory emerged during the twentieth century as an effort to bring more coherence among the disparate theoretical fields in the social sciences. It is a way of thinking and ordering theory and knowledge with the goal of "putting the pieces back together," rather than continually to pare social phenomena into ever smaller units of inquiry. It permits the observer or analyst to recognize different levels within the same phenomenon at the same time, and to understand the workings of the whole as well as the parts, as they occur. While this may make analysis more difficult, it also makes it more likely to be accurate, and closer to life.

Arthur Koestler, one of the pioneers of system thinking and the originator of the term *holon* provided the final words of this chapter:

> Looking inward, the person is a self-contained, unique whole, looking outward as a dependent part. No man is an island, he is a holon. . . . His *self-assertive* tendency is the dynamic manifestation of his unique wholeness as an individual; his *integrative* tendency expresses his dependence on the larger whole to which he belongs, his partness. (Koestler, 1979:303)

SUGGESTED READINGS

Adams, Richard.

1988   *The Eighth Day: Social Evolution as the Self-Organization of Energy.* Austin: University of Texas Press.

"A study of human society," "an exercise in applying to human social evolution concepts that have originated elsewhere." Compatible with our systems approach.

Bailey, Kenneth D.

1994   *Sociology and the New Systems Theory.* Albany: State University of New York Press.

Ambitious attempt to reconcile sociological and systems concepts as they developed in the last twenty years. Some of the algebraic formulas and acronyms are not easily interpreted, and he repeats too often that the two fields are compatible, but it is an admirable attempt to prove that systems ideas are back in fashion (obviously, we don't think they were out).

Bütz, Michael R.

1997   *Chaos and Complexity: Implications for Psychological Theory and Practice.* Washington, DC: Taylor & Francis.

Recommended for the advanced student of systems theory who wishes to apply the concepts to professional practice. Bütz provides extensive examples of application. This book should be the basis for any further developments in developing practice applications based on systems theory.

Capra, Fritjof.

1996   *The Web of Life: A New Scientific Understanding of Living Systems.* New York: Anchor.

Capra further develops his systemic thinking; we are struck by Capra's revelations and their congruence with our own thinking in this and earlier editions of this book. Clear, understandable, thorough, and engaging. Theory is applied at all levels, atomic, physiological, social, and terrestrial.

Jervis, Robert.

1997   *System Effects: Complexity in Political and Social Life.* Princeton, NJ: Princeton University Press.

The author is professor of international politics at Columbia University. He applies systems ideas to political processes, with clear perception of their congruence, or lack thereof. The chapters can be read separately. Chapter 4, "Feedback" is an excellent review of this concept. Recommended as a map of the "macro" level of national and international systems.

Koestler, Arthur.

1979   *Janus: A Summing Up.* New York: Random House.

Here is Koestler's final conception of holon and expansions of its applications.

Richardson, George P.

1991   *Feedback Thought in Social Science and Systems Theory.* Philadelphia: University of Pennsylvania Press.

Superb history and critique of the concept of feedback in the natural and social sciences: thorough and well-argued; for those who are already somewhat familiar with systems, not for the beginner. A landmark in the discussion of systems ideas, it should be read by any serious (and determined) systems student.

Van Geert, Paul.

1994   *Dynamic Systems of Development*. New York: Harvester Wheatsheaf.
Detailed, complex exploration of a model of "nonlinear dynamic systems," with extensive use of diagrams and mathematics, intended for the advanced student of systems. He presents current thinking about the centrality of feedback to systems thought, including thorough comparison of dynamic systems with stage theories of human development. This Dutch author's humor lightens this dense, challenging subject; how *do* you make wooden shoes out of concrete?

LITERARY SOURCES

Forster, E. M.

1989   *Howard's End*. New York: Vintage Books.
This symbol-laden novel with its oft-quoted theme, "Only connect," beautifully describes the systemic properties: "Only connect the prose and the passion, and both will be exalted, and human love will be seen at its height. Live in fragments no longer. Only connect, and the beast and the monk, robbed of the isolation that is life to either, will die."

Mailer, Norman.

1993   *Executioner's Song*. New York: Modern Library.
Mailer's biography of executed murderer Gary Gilmore, in novel form, is an excellent portrayal of the complexity of a person's part / whole aspects interacting across the range of systems: family, group, organizations, communities, and society.

FILMS AND VIDEOS

At the end of each chapter, we recommend appropriate resources. We know of none that directly address the content of this chapter. However, we suggest that it would be useful to view several variations of computer programs that demonstrate fractal geometry, e.g., the Mandelbrot set, to observe the general idea from systems theory that fantastically complex systems can evolve from simple premises (in this case algorithms), and that systems are "exquisitely sensitive" to small variations in their starting conditions and later development. The sheer beauty and complexity of the "design" will prepare you to envision systems in a different way.

Aspects of Social Systems

> Man is related to everything that he knows. And everything is both cause and effect, working and worked upon, mediate and immediate, all things mutually dependent. A bond that is both natural and imperceptible binds together things the most distant and things the most different.
> —Blaise Pascal, 1658

> La théorie c'est bon, mais ça n'empêche d'exister. (Theory is good, but it doesn't prevent things from happening.)
> —Attributed to Sigmund Freud

INTRODUCTION: ENERGY— EVOLUTIONARY, STRUCTURAL, AND BEHAVIORAL

As introduced in the previous chapter, *energy* and the *organization* of energy are the prime characteristics of social systems. We now discuss in more detail aspects of social systems that follow from these prime characteristics.

All systems are composed of energy interchange. One way to describe this basic energy interchange is to employ the constructs of *evolution*, *structure*, and *behavior* of social systems. *Structure* refers to those processes of energy interchange in which change is slowest and of longest duration and thus appear to the observer to be static. Those processes that change slowly over time but are not apparently static (that is, they move faster than structural but slower than behavioral changes), we label *evolutionary* aspects. *Behavioral* processes are of relatively faster tempo and shorter duration. For example, a structural change in the family may be from extended family to nuclear family over centuries; evolutionary change may be from traditional nuclear family to single-parent families over decades in the twentieth century; and behavioral change includes a particular family's functioning during its life cycle. This distinction between energy interchanges is important as we explore the "stuff" of social systems. Our focus will begin with the evolutionary process basic to all viable social systems.

I. EVOLUTION OF SOCIAL SYSTEMS: THE INTERPLAY OF CHANGE AND MAINTENANCE

Change and maintenance are not, in reality, diametrically opposed. Systems never exist in a condition of complete change or complete maintenance of the status quo. At any given time, systems are both changing and maintaining themselves. The balance between change and maintenance may shift drastically toward one pole or the other, but if either extreme were reached, the system would cease to exist. As philosopher Alfred North Whitehead said, "The art of progress is to preserve order amid change and to preserve change amid order." This is similar to Erikson's "bipolarities" of personality growth and Piaget's "assimilation" and "accommodation" (discussed in Chapter 8).

A. Steady State and Transition State

1. *Steady state*, a systems concept borrowed from physics, appears to be the most adequate term available to describe a "particular configuration of parts and relationships which is maintained in a self-maintaining and repairing system. . . . It is a state in which energies are continually used to maintain the relationship of the parts and keep them from collapsing in decay" (Laszlo, 1972:37). This is consistent with our discussion of living systems maintaining themselves in a state of high *dis*equilibrium.

Steady state occurs when the system is "in balance"; the system maintains a viable relationship with its environment and its components, and its functions are being performed in such fashion as to ensure its continued existence. The concept of steady state applies to all social systems. The word *steady* is somewhat confusing because it implies some kind of fixed, static balance, but in this usage it is a *dynamic* balance and always changing to some degree. Von Bertalanffy called it a "flowing balance," perhaps the most accurate description; it conjures up the metaphor of a river, similar to Heraclitus' view, at the beginning of Chapter 1.

We realize that the use of the word *state* in its singular form also is confusing. However, the concept involves a series of states in which the system, as a complex of components, adapts by changing its structure. It is somewhat the same, but not exactly the same, from one time to the next. The steady state is modified, perhaps along with the system's goals and the system's purposive, self-directed efforts (*syntropy*) to maintain the system's integrity. A social system that is in steady state is characterized by a sufficient degree of organization and complexity, and by openness to the environment.

Steady state is introduced here as an addendum to the more familiar term *equilibrium* and perhaps the less familiar term *homeostasis*. The two latter terms have meanings similar to steady state but with important differences. In both instances, they denote a fixed balance in which some particular adjustment is maintained, and the structure of the system is unaltered (or is not altered significantly). An example might be a person during a particular period of life, e.g., late adulthood, in which change is relatively minor, but there is still some change. Steady state does *not* include a fixed balance: the system may find a new balance and new structure; in some instances the new steady state might be radically different from the previous one.

The three terms may be illustrated by analogy to transportation, using the human body and the means of transportation to represent a system. Equilibrium is like a teeterboard: balance can be achieved, but the limits of being in balance are narrow. Very little movement is possible on a balanced teeterboard, and the balance is sensitive to changes in the environment, such as wind or movement by the occupants.

Compared to equilibrium, homeostasis denotes a somewhat more variable balance; that is, the system's balance may change within narrow limits; balance is maintained by movement and includes encounter with the environment. Homeostasis may be illustrated by a motorcycle. The motorcycle rider has some latitude in controlling his or her vehicle's movements and remains upright by leaning against centrifugal force (leaning into a curve) or by altering the machine's center of gravity on a banked curve by tilting the machine. Within some limits, which are determined by the weight of the machine, wind velocity, speed, and road angles, the bike is maintained in balance.

The various states of movement and balance experienced by the space shuttle dramatize what is meant by the notion of *steady state*. The shuttle is transported slowly, by feet per hour, to its launch pad; then hurled into space by huge rockets at increasing velocity; held in space by centrifugal force, traveling 17,000 miles per hour relative to the earth; and finally descending to earth in a long, controlled fall. It changes its configuration during each of these periods: first, simply cargo to be transported, then an appendage of the huge fuel tanks, then a space ship and cargo carrier, and finally a glider. It is a vehicle for moving people and machines throughout, but significantly (and radically) changes its mode of movement and its function.

The two tendencies involved in balance are *morphostasis* (structure maintaining) and *morphogenesis* (structure changing). Again, no system reaches either extreme, although it may tend toward one pole or the other. In order to continue to survive, all systems must maintain a shifting balance between status quo (morphostasis) and change (morphogenesis) and likewise a balance between order and disorder.

Another important distinction between steady state, equilibrium, and homeostasis is the significance of *stress*. Equilibrium demands a minimum of stress and disturbance and seeks minimal interchange with the environment. Homeostasis also requires minimal stress and disturbance but does admit moderate interchange with the environment. Steady state may involve a high degree of stress; social systems may prosper from stress and disturbance; they are maintained in a condition of high *dis*equilibrium, "on the edge of chaos." In fact, human systems tend to *seek* situations that are stressful as a means to achieve synthesis and wholeness. You may be experiencing stress as you are studying these systems concepts. Surely, you often experience stress as you pursue your studies, but you *choose* to expose yourself to this stress, presumably because you believe that it will ultimately lead to a more positive future. More than likely, you have encountered this book as a consequence of actively seeking to acquire information/energy as you seek a steady state for your system.

Interchange is essential to the existence of steady state. Equilibrium implies closed and static systems, homeostasis implies open and static systems, and steady state denotes open and changing systems (see Table 2.1). In essence, what we mean by steady state is the "identity" of the system, its continuity with the previous states through which it has passed, its newly emerged elements, and the states through which it will pass in the future. This is analogous to the human personality, as it progresses through stages, but remains identifiable. A familiar French saying can be translated as "the more things change, the more they remain the same." If one explains that from a social systems perspective, the idea of steady state will be clearer.

Table 2.1 Comparison of Equilibrium, Homeostasis, and Steady State

	Equilibrium	Homeostasis	Steady state
Stress	Least possible	Minimal	Optimal and necessary
Structure	No change	No change	Wide possibility of change
Interchange with environment	Least possible	Minimal	Optimal and necessary
Openness	Closed	Minimal	Open

2. *Transition (or transformative) state.* It could be said that *transition* states occur more often than steady states—our personal lives might testify to that! One of Prigogine's major points is that open systems "at the edge of chaos" react to stress or to new stimuli that require adaptation by transforming themselves to significant degrees; he called this *bifurcation*, meaning "branching"; other theorists identify such change as *phase transformation*: "*a system moves from a previous order to a new and more complex order by virtue of a chaotic transitory period*" (Bütz, 1997:16).

> At times, a single fluctuation [may] shatter the preexisting organization. At this revolutionary moment . . . a "singular moment" or a "bifurcation point"—it is inherently impossible to determine in advance which direction change will take: whether the system will disintegrate into "chaos" or leap to a new, more differentiated, higher level of "order" or organization. (Prigogine and Stengers, 1984:xv)

A restatement of this is that "some models teach that life is not order, but flux, and that stability lies somewhere between bifurcations, the edge of chaos, and chaos" (Bütz, 1997:113). Capra elaborates the same point:

> According to Prigogine's theory, dissipative structures not only maintain themselves in a stable state far from equilibrium, but may even evolve. When the flow of energy and matter through them [this is the meaning of "dissipative"] increases, they may go through new instabilities and transform *themselves* into new structures of increased complexity. (Capra, 1996:89; emphasis ours)

Prigogine's work has virtually revolutionized systems thinking in many respects. He and other systems theorists no longer regard steady state as the most natural or desirable condition of living systems—indeed, change / flux / bifurcation / transformation / transition is now seen as the "normal" condition of complex systems. For example, in describing the self, clinical psychologist Michael Bütz says, "The transitory self represents those briefly ordered periods of an individual's life, such as steady states. This self is the consummation of a *self-organizing* process that occurs at the edge of chaos or following chaos, and precedes another encounter with novel stimulus [*sic*] that would call for a new adaptation" (Bütz, 1997:114; emphasis ours).

Another, crucial aspect of bifurcation or phase transformation is that systems' adaptation is accomplished by *altering relationships between components of the system*; another way to say this is that the *components* alter their relationships to each other and to the suprasystem. Here is a description of personality system that conveys this:

> emergent properties arise through reciprocal interactions (coactions) among already existing constituents. . . . [I]*ndividual development is characterized by an increase of complexity of organization—that is, the emergence of new structural*

*and functional properties and competencies . . . as a consequence of horizontal and vertical coactions **among its parts** including organism-environment coactions.* (Cairns, Elder, and Costello, 1996:68; emphasis in bold ours)

Examples of this are families in which parents and children modify their relationships as children marry and establish their own families, and organizations that "restructure" or "repackage" in response to changing markets, sometimes merging or transforming themselves into producers of other goods (e.g., most tobacco companies have become conglomerates, with tobacco as a small part of their business). Another example is the adolescent who encounters the "identity crisis" and becomes a much different person (as Erikson describes it; see Chapter 8). Again, recent systems thinking stresses that minor changes may have profound effects on an entire system; further, that change in a system is accompanied by a change in the environment (see *coevolution*, later); and that such changes are unpredictable both in their timing and their outcomes.

Systems transform themselves; it is their *own components* that reorganize to accomplish the transformation. This is the meaning of *self-organization* and *self-development*. "Change is not controlled or imposed by a source outside the system. Rather it is the connection of the elements in the system or their interaction with the environment that create [*sic*] a different composition" (Bütz, 1997:16).

II. STRUCTURAL CHARACTERISTICS

This discussion of structural characteristics is related to the preceding sections, especially the discussion of holon and organization in Chapter 1, and to the immediately preceding section regarding change in structure as a means of adaptation to bifurcation or phase transformation.

A. Boundary, Linkage, and "Open" and "Closed" Systems

In order to be identified as distinct from its environment, a system must have some limits, that is, locatable boundaries. Consistent with our view that energy or activity is essential to social systems, we define a boundary as being located where the intensity of energy interchange is greater on one side of a certain point than it is on the other, or greater among certain units than among others. The intensity of energy transfer between units within the boundary is greater than the intensity of exchange across the boundary. For example, members of a family are distinguished not only by blood relationships, but also by frequency and intensity of personal contact. A neighbor would usually be considered outside the boundary, but may become "a member of the family" by participating in family activities and sharing emotional ties of the family. A household pet may be "like one of the family." An adopted child is another example of a person not related by blood who crosses the boundary and is incorporated by the family (or creates a family by being incorporated).

Boundaries can be identified only by observation of the interaction of the parts of the system and the environment. Some boundaries are visible because of their impenetrability, for example, the rigid personality that permits little modification by the environment. Some religious orders have boundaries defined clearly by behaviors such as dress, marital status, and allegiance to group beliefs. The Old Order Amish are set apart by dress, modes of transportation, and styles of beard. The fact that boundaries may change is evidenced in the Roman Catholic church by changes in nuns' habits and by changes in some members' beliefs about, e.g., birth control, and roles of women in some aspects of ritual. That women may not become priests is an example of internal boundary.

It is important to distinguish between the location of a boundary and its nature. Boundary does not necessarily mean barrier. A social system may have a readily discernible boundary and yet be very open to transfers of energy across its boundary (e.g., the boundary of male-female). Some social agencies survive by drawing clear boundaries (e.g., they serve teenage pregnant women, but do not provide abortions). Another example is the boundary between generations that has become an important tenet in systems approaches to family therapy.

Other boundaries are difficult to identify because interchange is frequent and intense across the boundary. An important concept here is the *density* of the boundary: the degree to which energy and information penetrate the boundary, that is, its permeability.

No single interaction defines a boundary; more than one criterion is involved in being "American," for example. Such behaviors as paying taxes, voting, and acknowledging "American" values and responsibilities are some criteria to be considered. The distinction between "illegal immigrant" and "legal immigrant" is important regarding eligibility for some welfare and medical services, as well as the right to remain in the country. During the Vietnam war, the issue of amnesty for draft evaders raised the question of such boundaries in a tangible and dramatic form. President Carter later attempted to resolve the issue by granting amnesty under a broad construction of the boundaries of "American," similar to President Lincoln's attitude toward secessionists after the Civil War.

When systems exchange energy across their boundaries they are *linked* or have *linkage* with each other. Their linkage may be for a very limited and peripheral purpose or may constitute a vital linkage, e.g., a family's association with a work organization. A family's memberships in social clubs and civic groups may be important links to community activity and resources. Their religious affiliation may be a vital social, emotional, and ideological link as well.

Energy transfers by way of linkages are rarely, if ever, one way: *reciprocity* of energy, or true exchange, is present in virtually all linkages. The church, club, or industry draws energy from its linkage to the family, hence industry's willingness to contribute to families' welfare through Social Security, United Fund drives, mental health campaigns, or ecological improvements. Some companies provide services directly in support of family welfare (e.g., day-care, social services, and retirement preparation), and President Clinton encouraged others to do so, with the incentive of government subsidies. (See discussion of organizations' relationships to other systems in Chapter 5.) Similarly, religious organizations maintain their role as prime defenders of family and marital stability because these linkages are considered vital and central to the organizations' purposes and to ensure the continued existence and relevance of the organizations.

Open and *closed* are largely self-explanatory terms: a system or its significant environmental systems can be receptive or nonreceptive to the movement of energy across their boundaries. In actuality, no system is completely open since it would then be indistinguishable from its environment, nor is a system ever completely closed. If a system were to be completely closed, it would cease to exist. The following describes the importance of openness:

> [W]hen a novel situation arises that the system does not have an appropriate response for, it must open up again to incorporate enough energy and information for a transformative adaptation to occur. Different aspects of the system will have to begin searching for new information to accommodate these new changes in the system. (Bütz, 1997:119)

We must clarify our usage of open and closed: what we really mean is "relatively more open" or "relatively more closed" than some other system or than some standard by which we are judging the system. A person is an open system but, from a teacher's or counselor's point of view, may be less open (or more so) than is desirable for the person's growth. For example, a child may be less open to interaction with peers than he or she "should" be and more open to interaction with parents than is expected at a certain age. Community organizers might wish for a social agency to be more open to ghetto residents and less open to interchange solely with white middle-class clientele. These examples illustrate that it is often not sufficient to generalize that a system is open or closed; it is frequently crucial to specify one's point of view (perspective) and to specify "open to what" or "closed to what." For example, systems theorists now state that a system is simultaneously open with regard to energy exchange, and closed with regard to its structure; that is, it maintains its integrity by regulating energy flow.

B. *Hierarchy*

Parts of systems are related to each other in various ways. One of these kinds of relationships is vertical or hierarchical, meaning that parts are arranged in the order in which energy is distributed, or the degree to which it is distributed. For example, parents in a family ordinarily have greater access to the family's income than do the children. Because they receive larger shares of public goodwill and public resources, state universities have an advantage over welfare and penal institutions in receiving public funds.

Another hierarchy is that of *power* and *control*: some parts control others by regulating access to resources or by regulating communication. For example, the executive officer of an organization has rank not only by title (status) but by virtue of controlling the allocation of responsibilities and resources. Another example is the power wielded by members of the White House staff who control presidential appointment schedules and screen incoming information. The "gatekeeper" function is of central importance to a system; it is the locus of control of the flow of information and the crossing of system boundaries from both inside and outside.

A third form of hierarchy is that of *authority*. Some parts serve as sources of sanction and approval through acting as "defenders of the faith" (a phrase applied to the monarchs of England, whose status far exceeds their actual power). Religious institutions and schools serve this function. Within a family, part of the mother's role has traditionally been that of imparting and representing certain values of the society—hence Mother's Day has been observed with a certain prescribed reverence and respect.

A fourth form of hierarchy is a *fixed sequence* in which development must occur. Some events or functions must occur before others can be attended to. One example of this is Maslow's hierarchy of needs within the person:

> Needs or values are related to each other in a hierarchical and developmental way, in order of strength and of priority. Safety is a more prepotent, or stronger, more pressing, more vital need than love, for instance, and the need for food is usually stronger than either [a person] does not know in advance that he [*sic*] will strive on after this gratification has come, and that gratification of one basic need opens consciousness to domination by another, "higher" need. (Maslow, 1968:153)

The physiological development of the human organism follows a hierarchical sequence of emergence and integration. Similar forms of hierarchy are found in Erikson's developmental tasks and Piaget's cognitive stages, discussed in Chapter 8.

There are, then, several varieties of hierarchies. We will discuss hierarchy in one of the forms just described. We will discuss instances in which the hierarchy is one of control and power and in which the parts are dependent upon other parts for some vital resources. The relationship in these instances will be that of *subordination-superordination*, or *submission-dominance*. The hierarchies most often examined will be those in which control is exerted in a "chain of a command" (e.g., bureaucracies or communities with elected leadership) or the personality, in which ego functioning provides control and direction.

C. *Autonomy: Autopoiesis and Self-Development*

1. Autonomy.   Literally, *autonomy* means living by one's own law, being self-governing, or independent. Living systems are distinctive by virtue of having a significant degree of autonomy from their environments; there is an interactional boundary between the system and environment. There are feedback loops of energy/information exchange, communication, and organization that are exclusive to the system; that is, they exclude those "outside" the system. Capra's recent description of networks applies to all social systems:

> Whenever we encounter living systems. . . . Whenever we look at life, we look at networks. . . . The first and most obvious property of any network is its nonlinearity—it goes in all directions. . . . In particular, an influence, or message, may travel along a cyclical path, which may become a *feedback loop*. . . . Because networks generate feedback loops, they may acquire the ability to regulate themselves. (Capra, 1996:82)

Autonomy is achieved and maintained by feedback cycles that are continually initiated by the system. A developing child is encouraged to develop autonomy by parents, and the feedback cycle is positive; the child responds with independent behavior (e.g., in the toddler stage by saying "No!" and by refusing to control its eliminative functions). Succeeding positive feedback cycles encourage the growing child to practice the behaviors that our society, especially, expects of autonomous, self-governing adults. Some limits are placed on this, however, again, through the feedback cycle. Driving a car is a signal of adult status; but recklessness results in a curbing (literally and figuratively).

We should note that every system has some degree of autonomy (otherwise it wouldn't have an independent existence), but at the same time is constrained by its environment, by other systems at its own level, and by its own subsystems. This repeats what was said earlier about holonistic relationships and the fact that causation is mutual; each system is both a superordinate whole and a subordinate part.

2. *Autopoiesis.* Recent research and writing on systems, especially by Prigogine, stress the autonomous, self-initiating behavior of living systems. Humberto Maturana at the University of Chile at Santiago (his ideas are labeled the "Santiago theory") coined the term *autopoiesis* to designate this autonomous behavior, combining Greek words that mean "self-made." In Prigogine's book, *Order out of Chaos* (co-authored with Isabelle Stengers) the term is translated as "self-organization"; other authors refer to it as self-regulation; it could be translated as self-creation or self-control. We prefer to translate it as "self-development," which allows us to engage in a bit of wordplay that conveys two meanings:

1. self-*development* connotes both self-origination and ongoing self-modification by the system; and

2. *self*-development, or development of the self, connotes that a major ongoing task of the system is the establishment of its *identity*, its steady state(s), its character, and the traits that are characteristic of the system, and that are observed to be relatively constant during its evolution.

This "paradigm shift" (a hackneyed phrase that even its creator tired of) in systems thinking toward emphasizing self-development does not vitiate the mutual interaction and interdependence of part and whole. Instead, it deepens our understanding of the nature of systems and their relations to suprasystems and subsystems. Instead of focusing our attention at the boundary of a system at which transactions take place, it focuses attention within the system, to identify the purpose and effect of such transactions. The change in focus is consistent with our experience: that persons and groups of persons are experienced as autonomous entities, not merely as flows of interactions. There is a "there" there; an initiator and shaper of experience that does not simply respond to flows of energy and information, but that selects and evaluates in order to create a self. This brings systems theory closer to phenomenology, to our experience of ourselves and others; perhaps to an existential or "self" psychology as discussed in Chapter 8. One definition of phenomenology is:

A method of exploration that primarily uses human experience as the source of data and attempts to include all human experience without bias. . . . Phenomenology is the basic method of most existentialists. (Corsini and Wedding, 1989:597)

This shift in focus permits systems theory to "come down from its ivory tower," to deal in direct experience, and not only in "bloodless categories." It is consistent with our position in Chapter 7, "Families," that "a family is to be construed as patterns of relatedness as they converge in a person." (page 183). From a phenomenological or existential viewpoint, this could be said of all systems. This is consistent with postmodernism, of course.

D. Differentiation and Specialization

The terms *differentiation* and *specialization* are similar but not identical. As we use it, differentiation means "dividing the functions," that is, assigning functions to certain parts and not to others. Specialization adds the further stipulation that a part performs only, or predominantly, a particular function. Differentiation is not the same as, but is always related to, allocation or distribution of energy. For example, assigning particular societal goals (GI function) to the federal Department of Health and Human Services is not the same as providing the necessary appropriations. Income maintenance for the elderly, as provided for in the Social Security Act, cannot be realized without the collection and allocation of necessary revenues; the sharp debate over Social Security funding illustrates this very well.

Differentiation may apply to any of a large number of aspects of system functioning. There is differentiation by age, with regard to earning income for the family. Typically, in middle-class families, adults are expected to earn, teenagers are expected to provide their own spending money, and the elderly and children are not expected to be self-supporting.

As society becomes more complex, it becomes necessary to differentiate functions. Modern professions such as nursing, home economics, social work, psychology, and law enforcement have come into being as part of the evolution of particular societies, to deal with problems of social welfare, health, and problems in social relationships.

There are several other aspects of differentiation that merit discussion. As a social system becomes differentiated, at some point the need arises to integrate and to establish communication between the differentiated parts. The greater the degree of differentiation, probably the higher the degree of internal exchange of energy/information that is necessary.

Differentiation may be reversible; a system may reorder its structures to adapt to new information from its environment, e.g., tainted food from another country may lead to tighter screening of imports; a community may create new programs for immigrants, like Hull House in Chicago, or programs to assist Asian immigrants, in Vancouver, B.C. The medical "community" acts similarly by creating specialties, e.g., family practice or the nurse practitioner. Social work has also differentiated by licensing clinical social work.

There are levels of differentiation according to the stages of development of the social system; the more complex, the more fully the functions are differentiated among the parts; this leads to discussion of specialization. As noted earlier, specialization means exclusivity of function—as a popular song puts it, "I can handle this job all by myself." Professions stake out their boundaries; who shall administer medication, who shall give legal advice, who shall approve adoptions, who is an expert witness in court. In that sense, professions are specialties, but they are not completely specialized, in that all of them are performing integrative SI and GI functions in the society.

The extent of occupational specialization in modern society has become problematic. As Darwin and later scientists demonstrated, the usefulness of specialization is always dependent upon particular environmental conditions. When these conditions shift, highly specialized adaptation may no longer be functional. Similarly, if technology replaces or supersedes a specialized occupation, the previous workers are no longer valued or needed (e.g., telephone operators, service station attendants, and, increasingly, bank tellers).

As with differentiation, specialization is necessary to perform functions, but certain dangers also arise. One such danger has been referred to as "tyranny by specialists," when people are divided into expert and ignorant, able and unable. As the physician may tyrannize the patient, so may the auto mechanic or the electrician tyrannize the physician. An indication of such tyranny is found where the expert assumes the matter is too complex for the nonexpert to make decisions. There is another danger of overreliance on specialization, which is that as specialties proliferate, so do areas of ignorance by others; ignorance then, increases commensurate with specialization.

Others have stressed that greater specialization leads to greater dependence on the products of other groups and the greater importance of systemic linkage It is risky to specialize completely. Systems may have to rely on other systems that do not perform adequately: the family upon the school, or the school upon the family; some persons choose not to risk engaging in family life, for example. In order to reduce risk, systems integrate vertically, both upward and downward. Thus we come full circle to hierarchy as an aspect of structure.

III. BEHAVIORAL ASPECTS OF SOCIAL SYSTEMS

Behavioral aspects are those interchanges that are of shortest duration and fastest tempo. Three of these seem to us most significant: They are related, but not identical, to the basic energy functions, and they are the subfunctions that seem to be most important for this book.

A. Social Control and Socialization

Social control and socialization occur in all systems and can have the purpose either of securing energy for the system from its components (SI) or of achieving goals (GI, GE). This process of securing energy or expending it to achieve goals can be done in either a coercive or cooperative fashion. The system can secure energy or achieve goals coercively either by threatening the component's survival and functioning or its goal achievement, or cooperatively by supporting the component's goal and encouraging its harmony with the system's goal. An example of this is the "gentle persuasion" that a religious organization can apply to its members to summon their efforts in supporting the system's goals, such as a building fund, yearly budget, or attendance at a revival. Or the religious organization may employ coercive means—excommunication or expulsion from membership—if the member interferes with its goals by refusing to rear children in the faith, failing to contribute financially, or violating its ethical standards.

Coercive control is usually labeled "power" (see the discussion of power in Chapter 5, under "Power and Control"). Traditionally, the helping professions have espoused cooperative approaches, holding up the value of "self-determination," but in practice, decisions are sometimes made for clients. When these decisions are forced upon the client and fulfillment of the client's own goals or the client's access to needed resources is threatened, the professional person is using power and is an agent of coercive social control.

Socialization is the induction of persons into the social system's culture or way of life, whether the system is a family, group, community, organization, or society. A bargain is struck: the system offers support or noninterference with the person's goals as long as they are consistent with the system's goals. The purpose of socialization is to get the work of the system done; the more successful the socialization, the less control is necessary because the person's goals will be harmonious with or identical to the system's goals. A certain degree of aggressiveness is tolerated and sometimes valued in our society if it is expressed in approved ways (football, military action, or self-defense, e.g.); but if we interfere with society's functioning by threatening people's lives, disrupting transportation, or preventing police or firefighters from performing their jobs, we are liable to be controlled in some manner consistent with our "offense."

B. Communication and Feedback

Communication is discussed in Chapter 3, "Language," in regard to symbols and language and in the appropriate chapters for functions of communication in communities, organizations, and families. Here we only wish to point out the necessity of communication and energy transfer in systems. As described above, when a system undergoes bifurcation or phase transformation, the relationships among its components are restructured; this is accomplished by exchanging information (communication) and energy. One of the results is altered communication; so communication is both cause and effect of the change.

Organization depends upon effectiveness of communication. We often think of communication as conveying emotional warmth and bringing components together. It may, but it may also alienate and separate people by its content. The point is that *communication* is the transfer of energy to accomplish system goals. The effect of communication depends upon the context in which it occurs. For example, "You're under arrest!" hardly seems likely to encourage affection; it expresses control. Professionals who say they "communicated" with clients usually mean that positive affect was conveyed. But the professional and the client also communicate when the communication exerts control.

Systems develop means to send and receive information. Feedback is the primary means by which systems accomplish self-direction and seek goals. Feedback is a term that has been bankrupted in popular usage. "Give me your feedback" or "I really want your feedback" are corruptions that, at best, deal with only one side of feedback. Feedback is not, as the popular definition suggests, merely the echo received in response to one's actions, like a radar blip. In cybernetics and systems thought, feedback includes not only the echo but the adjustment made to the echo. It is "feed" and "back"; a newer way to put it is "feed forward."

In social systems thinking, feedback is the means by which systems accomplish adaptation and self-direction. Feedback has been referred to as the secret of natural activity, that is, adaptation and self-direction in natural systems. It refers to the process of interaction whereby information is received and processed; behavior is validated or changed. Feedback enables a system constantly to monitor and adapt its own functioning, which is the means to steady state.

The use of the terms *positive* and *negative* in describing the nature of feedback varies among systems authors. Some view positive feedback as that which impels behavior in desirable directions and negative feedback as discouragement. Others describe negative feedback as characteristic "of homeostasis (steady state) and therefore [it] plays an important role in achieving and maintaining the quality of relationships; positive feedback, on the other hand, leads to change, i.e., the loss of stability or equilibrium" (Watzlawick, Beavin, and Jackson, 1967:31). Still others, including the authors of this book, label feedback as positive if it confirms or encourages existing behavioral patterns. Negative feedback, then, discourages or invalidates current behavior; it encourages change, and the adaptive response is one of change (accommodation).

Feedback operations and mechanisms are familiar to people in the human services. Some commonly encountered concepts are "reaction formation" and "overcompensation"; "looking-glass self" and "generalized other"; "positive reinforcement"; "unconditional positive regard"; "cycle of poverty"; dynamic modeling; and deviation-amplifying, deviation-counteracting, and deviation-reducing mechanisms.

An example of deviation-amplifying feedback is the following: a boy from an immigrant family speaks English poorly, and his teacher concludes that he is probably not very intelligent. He is treated as though he is not, and he responds to this with lowered performance, confirming the teacher's view, in order to "get along." His behavior confirms the teacher's opinion, and so the teacher provides him with less attention and simpler, less demanding material. He performs at this level and, when he is tested, his scores confirm that he does not perform as well as other children. His teacher continues to regard him as less capable than other children, and he continues to fall behind. Eventually, he withdraws or is expelled from school.

This example serves to illustrate the differing uses of "positive" and "negative" labeling of feedback. As this boy is confirmed in and accepts the position of "poor student," this status becomes a central element of his conception of himself. Each time he receives further recognition of being an inadequate or unwanted student, that is "positive" feedback. It is "positive" since it validates his self-conception. In this instance "negative" feedback would be information that impels him to reappraise himself and change sufficiently to cause others to revise their expectations of him. Since such change is more difficult than remaining the same, the first adaptation to this sort of negative feedback is to accentuate the familiar patterns of adaptation. Thus with the boy in the example, a teacher or counselor may ambitiously attempt to use strategies to manipulate the feedback cycle through informing the youth that he really is capable of better performance, and then becomes discouraged when the boy's response "proves" he is indeed a poor student. One example of this feedback cycle is Malcolm X's encounter with Mr. Ostrowski, who discouraged Malcolm's interest in becoming a lawyer (Malcolm X, 1966). Again, the point is that feedback processes are not simple causal chains; they are complex cycles of mutual interactions.

Feedback is an integral part of all teacher-student relationships or all counselor-client relationships, as it is of all human relationships. In part, therapy consists of interpreting signals from the client and "feeding back" (or forward) carefully chosen responses that are neutral, positive, or negative to stimulate behavior that is consistent with the goals of the two-person therapeutic system (or group treatment system, or milieu). Usually, the client similarly interprets and feeds back to the therapist.

C. *Adaptation*

The feedback cycle could be considered identical to adaptation, but adaptation is discussed separately here to emphasize two points. First, adaptation is viewed by some theorists as being of paramount importance because systems must adjust to their environment. While it is true that there must be adjustment between systems and environment, adjustment must be made by both system and environment, not by only one of them. Capra (1996) calls this *coevolution* of the system and its environment; this concept is a major revision in thinking about Darwinian evolution.

Second, adaptation takes two forms: *assimilation* and *accommodation*. These are discussed in Chapter 8 in the section on Piaget. These two terms indicate whether the system accepts or rejects the incoming information without any change on the part of the system (assimilation), or whether it modifies its structure in response to the incoming information (accommodation). In reality, systems do both of these at the same time in some mixture; as with other polarities, no system does one or the other exclusively.

CONCLUSION

This chapter introduced those concepts that are essential to a social systems approach to understanding human behavior. These are fundamental ideas that will be developed further in subsequent chapters. A few other key concepts will be introduced in later discussions of particular systems.

In conclusion, it is important to note that evolutionary, structural, and behavioral aspects are three ways to slice the same apple; they are not separate, but complementary dimensions of a system. A board that is long, wide, and thick is not three separate boards; nor can one dimension exist without the others.

SUGGESTED READINGS

Carse, James P.
    1994   *Finite and Infinite Games*. New York: Ballantine Books
        An interesting and entertaining inquiry into the nature of closed and open interactional patterning.
Ford, Donald H., and Richard M. Lerner.
    1992   *Developmental Systems Theory*. Newbury Park, CA: Sage.
        This is *the* book to begin with to construct a complete theory of systems practice in the human services. A thorough review of systems concepts with promising leads for practical applications. For our present purposes, we

recommend Chapter 4, "The Person as an Open, Self-Regulating, Self-Constructing System" (that about says it all!).

Kauffman, Stuart.

1995   *At Home in the Universe: the Search for Laws of Self-Organization and Complexity*. New York: Oxford University Press.

Pioneering discussion of chaos (or complexity) theory, in particular the emergence of order, self-organization, and phase transitions. Assumes basic knowledge of systems theory.

Kosko, Bart.

1993   *Fuzzy Thinking: The New Science of Fuzzy Logic*. New York: Hyperion.

The author is described as one of the leaders of "fuzzy logic" in systems. This book is in part autobiographical and anecdotal, relating the process by which he and others recognized the need for, and developed, fuzzy logic. Very useful as an introduction to the subject and its use in various fields, including manufacturing.

Luhmann, Niklas.

1995   *Social Systems*. Stanford, CA: Stanford University Press.

The author says: "This is not an easy book. It does not accommodate those who prefer a quick and easy read, yet do not want to die without a taste of systems theory." He's right, of course; it's also over six hundred pages. The introduction is entitled "Paradigm Change in Systems Theory," an accurate description of what Luhmann accomplishes here. He is undeniably one of the most original systems theorists.

Mingers, John.

1995   *Self-Producing Systems: Implications and Applications of Autopoiesis*. New York: Plenum.

The foreword describes this book as "a much-needed reference on autopoiesis. . . . It took me stage by stage through a clear and easy-to-grasp understanding of the concepts and ideas." This is the definitive book on the subject, intended for advanced students.

LITERARY SOURCES

Malcolm X (with Alex Haley).

1966   *The Autobiography of Malcolm X*. New York: Grove Press.

This moving autobiography exemplifies all levels of human systems and a person's interactions with them. It demonstrates how systems affect the person and how a person can influence wider systems. The authors have used this as a major text in the course.

Warren, Robert Penn.

1946   *All the King's Men*. New York: Harcourt, Brace, Jovanovich.

Written by a former poet laureate of the United States, and loosely based on the later years of political boss and governor Huey Long of Louisiana, this novel has as one of its fundamental themes the "web" of consequences that follow from human actions. "What goes around comes around"—or one can view it systemically: all actions reverberate, and affect the rest of the system, in unpredictable ways.

FILMS AND VIDEOS

Mindwalk (1990)

This unusual video is pure systems philosophy, voiced by three fine actors: Liv Ullmann, Sam Waterston, and John Heard. The setting is Mont-Saint-Michel, the mystic castle and island on the French coast. They explore the setting along with the ideas. Thought-provoking and highly recommended. Directed by Bernt Capra, it is a showcase for the ideas of his brother, Fritjof Capra, author of *The Turning Point*, and *The Web of Life*.

Culture and Society

Men commonly feel according to their Inclinations, speak and think according to their learning and imbibed opinions, but generally act according to custom.

—Sir Francis Bacon

The appearance of a crisis can be read as not simply noise in the system but as the signal of emergence to the next level of historical order.

—William Irwin Thompson

INTRODUCTION

As we arrive in the twenty-first century (of the Christian or Common Era), we are faced with a cultural crisis and a crisis of cultures. From the viewpoint of our own culture (whichever it may be), we face the necessity of adjusting to the presence and the power of other cultures to which we must relate in new and unaccustomed ways: as economic partners and competitors, as societies in which many of us live, study, and work for periods of time, and as places that are depicted (however briefly) in international news stories as locations of events that profoundly affect us. From the viewpoint of all cultures, technology presents us with pictures (both still photos and live television) of a small planet in a vast space, and poses the question, Can't we all live together? How to preserve the highest values of each culture (whether of a society, community, ethnic or racial group, or a family) while recognizing the validity of others is perhaps the major question facing us. The answer will almost certainly be given within the next century.

With these crises as background, this chapter explores human behavior at the broadest, most general level—that is, as a species. We will examine ideas from a number of disciplines, ideas that seem particularly pertinent to human services and social systems theory. These disciplines include biology, sociology, linguistics, psychology, ethnology, communications, and especially anthropology.

A. Definitions

First, we should explain how we use the terms *culture* and *society*. To be consistent with social systems theory, we use the term *culture* in two ways. First and generally, culture refers to those qualities and attributes that seem to be characteristic of all humankind. Culture denotes those things unique to the species *homo sapiens* as differentiated from all other forms of life. Humans, by contrast to all other species, evolve and adapt primarily through culture rather than changes in anatomy or genetics. We employ this general usage of culture to underscore the notion that the human evolutionary timetable is unique in that it is through culture that the human is immediately affected by and subject to the evolutionary principle of natural selection. As an ethnologist put it, "[H]istorians will have to face the fact that natural selection determined the evolution of cultures in the same manner as it did that of the species" (Lorenz, 1963:260). Sociobiologists have derived formulas of cultural diffusion and demise based upon maximization of selected cultural traits through breeding and mate selection (Boyd and Richerson, 1985). This approach is hotly disputed as lending itself to a theory of cultural (or racial) superiority. In general, we can say that a culture survives if it can accommodate to changing conditions. One reason for the decline and near disappearance of some Plains groups of American Indians is that the buffalo were exterminated by white hunters and there was no adequate substitute. Another example might be the demise of Western, industrial cultures as we know them, should supplies of cheap petroleum disappear midway through the next century—would *our* culture survive the demise of the private automobile and cheap electricity?

Humans are social beings, uniquely possessing culture. Cultural forms—not the species—are changed, synthesized, radiated, and extinguished. This does not preclude the possibility of the human species being subject to the laws of species survival as well, but the time scale is much different for biological evolution. Consistent with this broad definition, we view culture as a macrosystem, for purposes of discussion and speculation.

A *society* refers to a group of people who have learned to live and work together. Society is a holon, and within the society, culture refers to the way of life followed by the group (society). This, then, is the second usage of culture—that which binds a particular society together, and includes its manners and morals, tools, and techniques. To repeat, culture may refer to either of two levels: that which is characteristic of the species, and that which is characteristic of some specific group within the human species.

B. *The Nature of Culture*

Culture is a group phenomenon. While individual persons may originate ideas or behavior, they do not create cultures alone. Cultures evolve from the interactions of persons with others, and a person's belief or behavior becomes part of a culture when it is *externalized* and *objectified* (Wuthnow, Hunter, Bergesen, and Kurzweil, 1984:24ff.). Externalization is the process by which ideas are presented to others and become accepted as part of the culture. Once the ideas are built into a culture, and act upon the people within the culture, they have been objectified as part of the external world: "This world as an objective reality manifests itself most unmistakably in its coercive power, in its capacity to direct behavior, impose sanctions, punish deviance and at the extreme, destroy human life" (Wuthnow et al., 1984:39).

Television is an excellent example of externalization and objectification. The television set itself is an objectified conception of human communication, and the concepts (in picture or word form) presented on its screen are another layer of objectification. There is yet a third layer of objectification. Having become reality, television acts upon us, emotionally and physically:

> Recently, Toronto media critic Morris Wolfe created the concept of "jolts per minute"—or JPM's—to describe how TV shows hit us. . . . [W]e interpret gestures, postures and expressions on TV with a kind of sub-muscular response, expressed in muscle tone and stress factors. . . . [W]e store their relevant effects in our neuromuscular system . . . precisely what Hans Selye called stress. (De Kerckhove, 1995:11–12)

Does it have "coercive power" or "capacity to direct behavior," and so forth? That is precisely the question posed regarding the effects of television (and movie) violence on children. It is the "Frankenstein" question, here applied to culture (or "cyberculture"): Does that which we create have the power to destroy us? One tentative answer is that by Robert Putnam in Chapter 4, on community.

A culture evolves as each person encounters four "poles":

1. *One's own body,* or somatic process, which includes the biological constitution and genetic endowment.
2. *Other persons, or society;* this encounter can be described in such terms as the feedback cycle, "looking-glass self," and "generalized other,"

discussed later in this chapter. This includes the behavior of others as mediated by symbols and interpretations.

3. The *material world of nonhuman objects,* experienced as Piaget described them (see Chapter 8); this world exists independent of each person (although some philosophers might disagree), but must be interpreted by each. It includes tools and other objects created by humans, as well as the natural environment.

4. The *universe of socially constructed meanings,* which must be interpreted by each person. This includes language, customs, and institutions. Berger's is a generally accepted view:

> The very heart of the world that humans create is socially constructed meaning. Humans necessarily infuse their own meanings to reality. . . . In concert with others, these meanings become objectified in the artifacts of culture—ideologies, belief systems, moral codes, institutions, and so on. In turn, these meanings become reabsorbed into consciousness as subjectively plausible definitions of reality. . . . Culture, then, is at base an all-embracing socially constructed world of subjectively and inter-subjectively experienced meanings. Without the intended and subjectively meaningful actions of individuals, there would be no such thing as culture. (Wuthnow et al., 1984:25)

These "poles" are similar to Erikson's description of the three processes of organization: ego processes, somatic processes, and social processes (see Chapter 8). This can be diagrammed as a spiral, in which the self evolves within a field that has the four poles just described (see Figure 3.1). This conception can, by analogy, be pictured as an atom evolving in a dynamic field. As one atom evolves in interaction with its environment, it changes, as does the environment; simultaneously, other atoms interact with the first, and with their environments, of which this atom is a part. Thus, cultures evolve simultaneously with their components, the persons who inhabit them. In this process, objects, artifacts, conventions, and language (layers of meaning) accumulate, but some are dropped or modified; these elements are part of the culture only as long as they are employed by someone who inhabits the culture.

The spiral in Figure 3.1 might be seen like the path of a pinball as it caroms across the playing surface of the pinball machine, bouncing from one pylon to another, sometimes "hung up" at one spot and sometimes suddenly hurled toward another. Is a person similarly determined by the forces of society? Berger denied this:

> Though Berger would acknowledge society is the stronger partner . . . he also contends that the individual is not passively shaped by his [sic] world. He is a participant in the process, co-producing with others not only the social world but himself as well. More important is Berger's repeated insis-

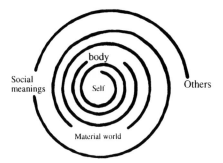

Figure 3.1.   Evolution of Self in culture.

tence that individuals can say "No" to the institutional imperatives. The consequences in the end may be grim, but . . . the individual, while a product of society through socialization, is, according to Berger, capable of genuine acts of freedom. (Wuthnow et al., 1984:447)

How free? Can a person transcend the playing field, escape culture and its poles? Can a person be "beyond systems"? Apparently not. Contrary to Abraham Maslow's conception of the person who transcends culture as "self-actualizing," and Lawrence Kohlberg's similar view of the most advanced stage of moral development, Erikson's psychohistories of persons such as Gandhi, Luther, and Jefferson indicated that these creative people externalized and objectified (and internalized) the most universal values of their respective cultures, but did not escape them (see our discussion in Chapter 8). At most, they experienced other cultures sufficiently to internalize significant values of those cultures also.

As in the examples Erikson analyzed, cultures change through the actions of persons whose ideas and behavior "fit" the culture, and were adopted by the culture because (as Erikson said) these new ideas and behaviors solved a problem for the culture (see Chapter 8) and hence were adopted.

Change can also occur as a result of cataclysm, either physical as in famine, war, epidemic, or disaster (the "four horsemen of the apocalypse"). It can also change as a result of a "paradigm shift" (Kuhn, 1970) in fundamental understandings by those in the culture; one example is secularization as occurred in Western societies; another is scientism as believed in the "modern world," and discussed later in this chapter. The acceptance of Freud's views constituted such a "paradigm shift" in Western cultures, grounded in the two examples just given.

The two major sections following deal with, first, those aspects of culture that are uniquely human; and second, dimensions by which culture can be analyzed.

I. SPECIES AND CULTURE: UNIQUE ASPECTS OF THE HUMAN SPECIES

Human beings have certain attributes in common regardless of time or place. These common attributes can be parsed and explicated in a number of ways. For our present purpose, we will generalize these attributes under four headings: (A) the capacity to think, (B) the family as a human universal, (C) language/communication, and (D) territoriality.

A. The Capacity to Think

The capacity to think is perceived as the most distinctive attribute as witnessed by our identification of the species as *homo sapiens,* "thinking man." Julian Huxley commented that "the first and most obviously unique characteristic [is the] capacity for conceptual thought, if you prefer objective terms, you will say his employment of the true speech but that is only another way of saying the same thing" (Huxley, 1964:8). The capacity to think and communicate thoughts sets humans apart from most other forms of life. From recent research, it appears that humans are not unique in this ability. Dolphins' language, e.g., is being decoded by means of computer; it appears whales have an elaborate set of sounds, consisting of songs and "whistles" by which they communicate over long distances; and higher primates can communicate in sentences by using signs for words.

Gross impairment of the capacity for thought in humans is a grave matter. Much of child rearing is devoted to the refinement and development of this capacity (as is apparent in the discussion of cognitive theory in Chapter 8). Perpetuation of tradition and use of tools is dependent upon members of the culture having the capacity to think.

Humans are unique in that not only can they think, but that they can externalize the thought process itself, possibly in three ways. One implication of the viewpoint expressed earlier about culture is that each thing created by humans is an externalization of human thought and, in some particular way, reveals some aspect of the human thought process. As discussed later, tools are amplifications of human capacities, and the tool that comes closest to fully externalizing human thought is the computer. We can discuss the human brain as a computer, but this is backward; the computer is an externalization of the brain and nervous system, and a relatively poor copy, at that. Scientists have constructed computers from mechanical switches, vacuum tubes, transistors, silicon chips, and magnetized film, and are experimenting with living cells as material from which to construct computers. Should this prove successful, human beings will have externalized human thought through the creation of human biocomputers in the second way available to them. The first way is through human reproduction; every baby is, in a very limited sense, a human biocomputer. The third way for humans to externalize their thought processes would be through cloning. The implications and possible dangers to human culture have been expressed by science fiction writers, notably Mary Shelley (again in the novel *Frankenstein*), who raised the fundamental question: What is distinctively human about human thought?

B. The Family as Human Universal

We devote Chapter 7 to the family, but discuss it briefly here as part of culture. Family is both cause and result of culture. It is the basis for transmission of cultural attitudes toward caring, as discussed later in this chapter.

The family is biologically based and is the primary social (and socializing) unit. The *fact* of the family is a constant; the *form* of the family is variable. Anthropological studies have demonstrated convincingly that although the family as a primary socializing unit is a universal phenomenon, there is no "normal" form. As ethnologists have learned about the mating, reproducing, and rearing patterns of a range of species, they have uncovered a number of factors that seem to influence the pairings and groupings of various species. These factors include:

1.   The number of offspring per mating—the reproductive rate.
2.   The length of the gestation period, which influences the number of matings.
3.   The length of the period of the immaturity of the young, expressed in ratio to total life span.

As the first factor reduces (smaller number of offspring per mating) and the other two factors lengthen (gestation and length of time of immaturity), pair bonds and family rearing of the young increase. Among humans, the existence of the family is, of course, a necessary element for the development of culture because culture is transmitted from one generation to the next through education, not through the genes.

The cultural form of family must never be confused with the biological norm of the family; the cultural forms vary tremendously between cultures and between subcultures within the same culture. The nuclear family, consisting of the biological parents and their offspring, is only one of these forms and not the most prevalent at that. The city of San Francisco, in the spring of 1989, became the first governmental unit in the United States to recognize the union of a same-sex couple as legal. "In San Francisco, nearly 2,000 companies now offer benefits to nontraditional couples because of a new law requiring that of city contractors" (Price, 1998).

In 1993, the Supreme Court of Hawaii ruled that the state must show a "compelling reason" that justified refusing gay and lesbian couples the right to marry, and remanded the case to a lower court, which ruled in 1996 that the state had not proven its case. Hawaii's "Reciprocal Beneficiary (RB) Law" became effective on July 1, 1997; it provides "at least 50 benefits of marriage (such things as hospital visitation rights, the right to inherit property from one another, etc.)" (Marriage Project Hawaii, 1997). But the Attorney General of Hawaii stated in August 1997 that employers were not compelled to provide health benefits under the RB law. As of July 1998, the Supreme Court had not yet made a final ruling. In November 1998, "Hawaii's voters will decide whether to empower the legislature— already on record as opposed to gay marriage—to amend the Hawaii Constitution to restrict marriage to male-female couples" (Price, 1998); the Supreme Court rejected the state's request to delay its ruling until after the election.

If gay or lesbian marriages are legally sanctioned, recognition of new family forms presumably must follow, with new definitions of filial responsibility, inheritance rules, and custody provisions for any minor children (e.g., it is becoming more common for lesbians to choose artificial insemination in order to bear children). The form of the family is influenced by the culture in which it exists; in turn, the family form influences the culture. The human family, then, is a system, a holon, and it has a simultaneous existence as part and whole. Its form organizes the energies of the family members, and it must engage in transactions with its supra-systems.

The following is an example of how cultural aspects influence the family system. Our economic system, with its accent on production and distribution of goods achieved through the standardization of organization of energies, requires a mobile work force. Adaptation to this single cultural artifact has been extremely stressful to the form of the family during the past generation and has been amply discussed in both popular and technical literature. (See our discussion of this subject in Chapter 7.) The cultural bind experienced by emigrants from Appalachia and by African-Americans from the South are prime examples (Stack, 1996). To seek and find gainful employment required a move to an industrial city. The nature of the mutual obligations between the emigrants and those who remain behind, especially those obligations to family, required the emigrants' presence at certain times of need. As these occur, the emigrant may decide to "take time off" to "go down home." This is a phenomenon also noted among American Indians, many of whom return to their home reservations to be with family and tribe, periodically and for varying lengths of time.

C. Language/Communication

Etymologists broadly define language as any transfer of meaning, but general usage refers only to spoken and written messages. Appreciation of the universality in the broader sense—that is, any transfer of meaning—is particularly important to those who deal with persons rather than objects. Since persons with troubles often have their difficulties because they rely on other means of communication without conscious intent, it is essential to be attuned to unspoken and unwritten language. A person may express feelings and ideas with signals rather than with consensual symbols of communication. Consequently, such ideas as "body language" become important.

There are explicitly arranged language forms other than spoken and written verbal messages. A driver's exam for persons who are illiterate uses colors and sign shapes rather than the printed word. American Sign Language uses a combination of stylized gestures, and signals for specific letters and words, which are a significant part of what is increasingly recognized as "deaf culture." Transients ("hobos") developed a more or less standardized set of signs that were chalked, painted, or scratched on walls, posts, or fences to inform others about what to expect at particular homes or businesses; a stick-figure cat meant, "Kind-hearted woman lives here"; a hieroglyph resembling a broken-leg chair with a cross on top meant, "Food here if you work" (Richards and Associates, 1974). The key to nonverbal language is the consensus of meaning attached to symbols and their manipulations. An important aspect of socialization into a new system is to become acquainted with such symbolization and learn the attached meanings. Excellent examples are the sometimes subtle and complex, silent or audible signals exchanged at auctions, and the elaborate motions employed by baseball coaches.

There are also implicitly understood conventions and symbols that require even more consensual agreement than the explicit symbols. The initiation of a social transaction between equals can be signaled by the shaking of hands, an embrace, or mutual acknowledgment of deference, such as bowing or the removal of hats. The culturally conditioned "embracer" learns very quickly in a "handshaking" culture that the meanings of gestures are culturally relative and are not universal.

Communication seems to be present in other life forms, as noted earlier. The dancing flight of the bee and the singing of birds to announce territorial prerogatives to other members of their species are well-known. Such phenomena seem distinguishable from human language in respect to the thought and meaning signified. The evidence thus far is that bees and bird signals, operating from instinct, evolved for purposes of species survival.

Etymologists have an interesting time with cross-cultural comparisons of word meanings and in the process provide interesting insights. For example, in his fascinating book *The Story of Language* ([1966] 1984) Mario Pei dealt with the symbolism of color and how symbols vary from one language to another and one culture to another. Why are we "blue" when depressed, "yellow" when cowardly, "red" when radically inclined? In

Russia, red is beautiful, and both "red" and "beautiful" have the same word root. White is the color of purity and innocence (and surrender) to most European cultures, but to most Asians, it is the color of mourning and death. In the Russian civil war, the Reds had a gigantic psychological advantage over the Whites because of the symbolic overtones. This kind of information carries implications for attempts to understand racial conflicts. Those who launched the "Black Is Beautiful" campaign in the 1960s were attuned to the cultural importance of color symbolism. How much racial prejudice is attributable to the cultural artifact of color symbolism is unknown, but it appears to be an important factor. In considering language and thought as species characteristics in humans, the thesis propounded by Whorf and Sapir is worthy of note. Their hypothesis was that language structures reality; the form and variability of the language determine how members of the culture will view reality and structure their thoughts (Whorf, 1956). This hypothesis is generally accepted. In developing his thesis about territoriality and its importance to people, E. T. Hall analyzed the words listed in the Oxford Pocket Dictionary and found that 20 percent of them referred to space and spatial relations (Hall, 1969:93).

There is a close, demonstrable relationship between culture and language. This relationship is not necessarily causal in either direction. As often cited, modern English and American language structures attend closely to the passage of time, and to gender. Tenses are of utmost importance, since time is so essential to aspects of these cultures, and gender distinction is considered essential. Some cultures and languages make no provisions for tenses or gender—the precise measurement of time is of little importance to them, and gender is interpreted from the context of the sentence.

La Barre presented intriguing facts and speculations about language as symbolic communication. He accepted Whorf's hypothesis and stated that the structure of reality is, much of the time, merely imputed to reality by the structure of our language. As soon as the human infant learns to speak any language at all, it already has a "hardening of the categories," or "they are different, this we know, for our language tells us so" (La-Barre, 1954, Chapter 10).

La Barre developed the idea that language is so flexible that a word can put into semantic equation any two disparate objects in the universe. If the society accepts the equation by consensus, semantically it becomes reality; if the individual does this without societal consensus, the person may be labeled schizophrenic and thus not attuned to reality (the person may, alternatively, be a creative genius, of course). Another alternative is the deliberate use of "plastic words," words borrowed from science, but that denote little in factual content (Schwartz, 1997:37); they are the "hamburger helper" of conversations: words such as project, function, model, system, needs, information, and communication. The popular way to describe these words is "buzz words," often intended only to convey that the speaker is "with it," "hip" to cultural trends, "cool." We hope that after reading this book, you will use such words in more productive ways. "A psychotic's truth is one 'I' make it, and cultural truth is what by unwitting vote 'we' make it; but ultimate truth still remains in the outside world of that which is" (LaBarre, 1954:266). Robert Merton expressed the same idea in his Thomas theorem, "If [persons] define situations as real, they are real in their consequences" (Merton, 1957:421). Hence the significance of "politically correct" language, an effort (occasionally strained) to eliminate conscious or unconscious bias such as sexism, racism, or classism from the culture by altering perception.

D. Territoriality

Territoriality refers to the tendency of people, in their social systems, to seek and maintain a territory. Some authors deal with territory as primarily spatial (Ardrey, [1966] 1971; Hall, 1969), while others stress the interactional aspects (Lyman and Scott, 1967). The definition of spatial and interactional territories is a paramount feature of any culture.

One simple example is the definition of territorial elements as squared or rounded. It seems that this choice is simultaneously determined by other features of the culture and is a determinant of culture, as well. "Home territories" within a given culture give clues to other aspects of the culture. A sedentary and specialized culture with much differentiation of function tends to organize living and work spaces in squares with specialized uses. The square house has its bedrooms, bathrooms, kitchen, living room, den, and so forth. The nomadic, unspecialized culture lives in round houses (igloo, wigwam, cave, or round hut) without specialized compartments. Arranging territories in squares tends to close boundaries. A newspaper columnist reports that a "cube farm" is slang for cubicles, work spaces created by the temporary and movable partitions used in many organizations (Wilbers, 1998). The squares are mutable as necessary; some have curved walls, to avoid squareness. "Prairie dogging" is "when someone yells or drops something loudly in a cube farm, and people's heads pop up over the walls to see what's going on." Some workplaces are large, open spaces without walls, "industrial" or "warehouse" in style, in which workers have areas, rather than enclosed spaces; the usual intent is to convey an atmosphere of creativity and fluidity; a sort of "workplace in the round."

The spirit of equality, fidelity, and camaraderie embodied in the King Arthur legend is symbolized by the "table round." Formal dining tables are usually rectangular, while tables in small, intimate bars are round. Youths' expressions of dissatisfaction with the impersonal, highly structured role relations and specialized functions of bureaucracies were expressed in the 1960s epithet "square," which had been used in African-American culture even earlier, to denote someone who wasn't "hep" (which later became "hip"). Dictionaries show that the meanings attached to "square" by immediately preceding generations were "just," "fair," and "honest," as in a "square shooter" or a "square deal." These meanings reflected the primary purpose of the impersonal bureaucratic system—to protect the person from unjust and arbitrary decisions. Negotiations at the end of the Vietnam War were delayed for months over whether the talks would be conducted over a rectangular table or a circular one. In part, this symbolized crucial differences in cultural traditions and beliefs.

Relationships are symbolized by diagrams intended to concretize interactional territories (Figure 3.2). The components in Figure 3.2a are arranged in a vertical hierarchy and each component (person or department) is designated by title or role rather than by name. These labels designate specialization and differentiation. In Figure 3.2b, the components would be labeled by name (or number, to protect the innocent); the hierarchy here is represented in the horizontal plane and conveys positive, negative, and absent patterns of relatedness. Each diagram is illustrative of interactional territorial arrangements and relationships.

It is hypothesized, then, that all systems have a territorial dimension. This territory may be spatial or interactional; it probably is a "sense of territory," and is congruent with the particular culture. Territoriality refers to the cultural ways people locate themselves in their universe and establish the boundaries of their various human systems.

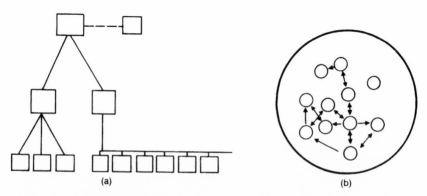

Figure 3.2. A typical representation of a bureaucratic structure is depicted in (a). A typical sociogram is represented in (b).

II. ANALYTIC DIMENSIONS OF CULTURE: QUALITIES OF A SOCIETY

Definitions of culture abound and frequently conflict. Kroeber and Kluckhohn (1952) devoted an entire book to a listing of definitions of culture and concluded that the definition given by Edward Tylor in 1871 was as good as any: culture is that complex whole that includes knowledge, belief, art, law, morals, custom, and any other capabilities and habits *acquired by a human being as a member of society.* The italicized words represent an important qualification occasionally overlooked by enthusiastic culture determinists. Konrad Lorenz considered this qualification to be of the utmost importance, and stated that "human behavior, and particularly human social behavior, far from being determined by reason and cultural tradition alone, is still subject to all the laws prevailing in all phylogenetically adapted instinctive behavior" (Lorenz, 1963:237).

Rather than choosing a definition of culture from the myriad that have been offered, or trying to formulate another, we will discuss six dimensions of culture. The first five of these dimensions are expansions on what Jerome Bruner termed "the five great humanizing forces" (Bruner, 1968:75ff.): tool making, social organization, language, management of the prolonged human childhood, and the human urge to explain the world. We add another: social relationships. These dimensions are definitive aspects of any culture. One can approach the analysis of culture through examining these dimensions regardless of the time, place, or kind of culture being studied. In regard to a *subculture* within a culture, such as a peer group or professional culture, certain of these dimensions may seem less applicable; but each of the five seems applicable to some extent. We are then viewing culture as the ways of doing, being, and explaining, as they exist in each particular system.

A. Tools

Tools are amplifiers of human capacities, whether the tools are invented or synthesized. They fall into three classes:

1.   Amplifiers of *sensory capacities;* for example, microscopes, telescopes, telephones, television, clocks, spectacles, radar, conch shells, and "mind-expanding" drugs (such as peyote in some cultures).
2.   Amplifiers of *motor capacities,* for example, hammers, wheels, the lever, rockets, and automobiles.
3.   Amplifiers of *reasoning and thinking capacities,* for example, mathematical systems, logic, the abacus, the computer, and the chalkboard (a major educational invention).

Tools include devices, objects, and procedures that are extensions of human natural capacities. The crucial, most important aspect is not the tool itself but rather its function, that is, the use to which the tool is put. A hammer is generally assumed to be of use to pound nails and, if it is a claw hammer, to remove nails as well, but it can also be used as a lethal weapon or to prop open a door or window. Books generally are assumed to be for the purpose of reading, but they can also be used to press flowers, impress people, or level the short leg of a table. Understanding the tools of a culture includes, therefore, not only understanding their seeming intrinsic or built-in purpose but, more importantly, their purpose for the user. Some years ago, one of the authors worked in a small Indian reservation where electricity was available and each household had been given a refrigerator, but preserving food by refrigeration was not then part of that culture's way of life. The refrigerators were used for other purposes—for decoration in a few instances—but mostly for storage. They were perceived as attractive boxes with a door; the "built-in purpose" was not the purpose of the users. A current example is the function of unused exercise equipment as clothing racks or end tables; they function to maintain an air of potential, if not actual fitness.

Peter Farb, a cultural anthropologist, analyzed the evolution of cultures in a remarkably readable book. One of his theses was that a new tool or technique must have a counterpart in social organization or knowledge to become functional. He used the example of the introduction of the horse into two quite different cultures. The first of these cultures, a hunting tribe, mounted the horses and used them to pursue the bison. This amplified human motor capacities, making them much more efficient hunters, and the horse rapidly became central to the culture. The second culture merely slaughtered and ate the horse; it had no function in this culture (Farb, [1968] 1978:129). A more homely example might be the personal computer in many homes, unused by adults because they were reared in a pre-computer-literate society, and have found no function for it in their lives. Their children, however, may find uses for it, for games, net-surfing, or word-processing, having been born into a computerized society.

Tools, then, are a key dimension by which a culture may be analyzed. They extend the uses of energies within the cultural system toward fulfillment of the system's goals. It may be equally significant and analytical of a culture that certain tools do not exist. For example, the absence of written languages, or of the wheel, was significant in some North and Central American Indian cultures.

B. Social Organization: Society and Roles

All cultures, being social systems, have organization. As previously stated, the structure is not fixed, and any analysis of structure is like a still photo. At the moment of analysis, the social organization of a culture is not what it has been nor what it will become. It is structured in the sense of a system of interacting elements, and any change in one element or single pattern of relationships affects all other elements directly or indirectly.

The theory of evolution, in its essence, describes the increase of complexity, whether from simple to complex biological organisms or from simple to complex cultures. The social organization of an evolving culture becomes more complex because of an increased volume of relationships among the various elements of the culture. A "stagnant culture" is one in which the relationships are static and interaction of the cultural elements is unchanging. Some have postulated that bureaucracy appears as an organizational structure when society reaches a given state of complexity, regardless of the form of government. The bureaucracies of ancient China, Rome, the Roman Catholic church, the Russian monarchy, and most recently Western democracies and communist states can all be cited as illustrations. Bureaucracy seems to have as a major function the reduction and containment of forces that may lead to change. As such, bureaucracy is probably used as a "buffering" device by all complex societies. The systems term *equifinality* (see glossary) applies to this phenomenon; Beer defined it as "the proven ability of certain open systems to reach the same characteristic result, despite differences in initial conditions, and despite different rules of conduct along the way" (1981:191).

Certain important concepts related to social organization are commonly employed. These are the interrelated ideas of *social class, status,* and *role.* All societies have schemes of ordering human interaction and ways of defining and communicating expected behaviors. As with definitions of culture, many theorists have proposed hypothetical social class structures. Perceptive observers have identified life-styles, socioeconomic indices, and values that differ among social classes.

English sociologist T. H. Marshall believed that there are three aspects operating to define social class: economic status, social status, and political power (Marshall, 1964). When the groupings of these three coincide (multibonded), then social class is visible. If the boundaries between the social classes are clear and closed, the result is *caste.* The idea of social class suggests a group consciousness on the part of members, both of their own social groups and other groups, and of their general position in the social hierarchy. However, in the United States, the existence of social classes is largely denied; in such an instance, Marxist theorists would presumably suggest that this is a "false consciousness," which obscures class members' real positions in the societal hierarchy.

Some researchers and writers suggest the emergence of a permanent "underclass" in American society, made up of those who persist in poverty for several generations (Murray, 1984; Wilson, 1987; Zinn, 1997).Of the

38 million persons in poverty in the United States in 1994, 30 percent were African-American and 30 percent were of Hispanic origin (which may be of any race) (U.S. Census Bureau, *Current Population Reports*). The unemployment rate for African-Americans (age 16 and over) in 1995 was double that of Caucasians (10.6 percent, compared to 4.9 percent); the same was true for single, never married African-Americans (17.6 percent, compared to 8.7 percent) (U.S. Department of Labor, *1995 Annual Averages*). Median annual income for African-American households in 1994 was about $21,000; for Hispanics, $23,400; for Caucasians, $34,000. Of prisoners sentenced to death in 1993, 42 percent were African-American. Such figures lend support to the existence of an "underclass."

Role relates to and derives from status. Role is the total of the cultural expectations associated with a particular status, including the attitudes, values, and behavior. The complexity of a status is manifested partly by the complexity and differentiation of role expectations. Bureaucracy is one of the organizational forms devised to reduce this complexity. In a bureaucracy, the role often becomes more important than the person occupying the status, but it is only through occupying the status that the person can assume the role. In systems larger than the family, continuity depends less on the characteristics of the person and more on the role being occupied.

Role expectations, then, are defined by the culture and its components, and incorporated by the persons filling the role. A culture may allow greater or less latitude in deviations from the expected behaviors. Certain cultures rigidly define role behavior, but more often the rigidity or flexibility of role definition is dependent on what else is transpiring within the system.

In a dynamic, open cultural system, role occupants constantly seek flexibility of role definition with or without the encouragement of the culture. As the cultural system is threatened from either internal or external quarters, strings are drawn more tightly on the expected role behaviors. One dramatic example is the behavior of students in Beijing's Tienamen Square in May and June 1989; their behavior was proscribed so severely that many were killed, and others hunted by means of nationwide searches. This was part of a series of student demonstrations beginning in 1985, and is part of a pattern of cultural change involving a contest for power between the Communist party, the army, and a new managerial middle class (Woodruff, 1989). Students, some of whom have traveled or studied abroad, represent this new class.

All persons occupy a complex of roles: parent, child, worker, voter, and worshipper, for example. The total number of roles is influenced by the quantity of networks they are involved in. At any given moment, a person is likely to be more actively fulfilling one role than another but carries them all at once, nevertheless. When a person experiences excessive conflict in fulfilling varying role expectations, or if society judges the person to be failing in this respect, the person and the society both have troubles.

A contemporary example is the strong expectation for the work role. Work is quite narrowly defined as contractual employment, profession, or own business, and it is expected that each adult, unless certifiably disabled or past an arbitrary age, will fulfill such a role. The work role is fused with the economic role. Even though members of the society accept the prescribed role expectations, a significant number are not able to fulfill the agreed-upon role if there are insufficient jobs, or if they have insufficient qualifications for the jobs. The culturally prescribed remedy is to attempt to generate more jobs (i.e., work roles). Another culture might seek to broaden the definition of work (e.g., paying women for "mother's work") or to separate work from economic participation (e.g., Social Security or a guaranteed income).

If any significant minority of the members of a society (some have suggested 10 percent is sufficient) do not do what the consensus requires for a length of time, the system is in difficulty and the survival of the culture is in question; or it may undergo phase transformation. In such instances, energies of the system must be devoted to maintaining the organization and redefining the expectations of those in the particular status. In the latter years of the Vietnam War a significant minority refused to fulfill the expectation for military service. Subsequently, the draft was terminated and expectations modified. It may not be clear for a generation what effect the revolt of Beijing's young educated elite against the regimentation and militarism of China's culture will have; almost certainly it will have a profound effect.

C. Language

Here again we refer to language in its broadest sense, that is, as *transfer of meaning* between systems and between subsystems. The structures of language strongly influence the content conveyed. Knowing what a culture considers important enough to symbolize and communicate is as important as knowing the methods of communication.

Language is composed of symbols and the meanings are learned and transferred through social interaction. *Symbolic interaction* refers to this process. The communication of symbols and their meanings represents the major form of transaction between human systems. Most of the work of the symbolic interactionists is built on the insights of George Herbert Mead and Charles Horton Cooley. Mead stated that we do not simply respond to the acts (including speech, of course) of others; rather, we act on *our interpretations* of their intentions and judgments. Gestures are an important kind of symbolic communication, and we respond to the meanings not necessarily as they are intended but as we interpret them. When a gesture has a common meaning (some measure of consensus), Mead termed it a linguistic element—a significant symbol. Common examples include the kiss as an expression of affection; the drawn-back, clenched fist as threat of aggression; the smile as an expression of pleasure; and the frown as an expression of displeasure. Because of the consensus of meaning, we attribute the quality of pleasure to the smile of a baby even though it may be an expression of gas in the stomach.

The term *generalized other* is central to Mead's formulation. This refers to a generalized stance or viewpoint imputed to others that one uses to evaluate one's own behavior. A person responds not only to others who may be present, but to the general expectations of one's reference group (that is, a group to which one belongs or wishes to belong).

Another key concept is *self*. An individual may act socially toward self as toward others. The self is composed of the *I* and the *Me*. The *I* is the impulsive, spontaneous, and unorganized part of the self. *Me* is the incorporated other. The *I* energizes and provides propulsion, whereas the *Me* provides direction, in other words, controls function. These are similar to, but in important ways different from, id and superego. The emphasis is on social rather than intrapsychic functioning.

The *looking-glass self* is Cooley's construct and refers to the idea that we interpret what others think of us. It involves the following sequence: (1) the imagination of our appearance to others; (2) the imagination of their judgment; and (3) a self-feeling in response to this imagined judgment (e.g., pride or mortification).

The symbolic interactionists go far toward explaining the process of transfer of meaning. Their formulations demonstrate that meaning derives from interaction between the sender and receiver, both verbally and nonverbally. These are forms of the feedback cycle. If there is insufficient feedback from outside the focal system, then an assessment of one's appearance and judgment of it must be projected from inside. For example, the paranoid person is not able, or is not allowing self, to participate in this feedback cycle with outside systems and must rely on his or her own imagined judgments. As Philip Slater put it, "Without air we die, without love we turn nasty, without feedback we go crazy" (1974:49). The same can occur in nations that are cut off, with feedback projected from within, and therefore become isolated and chauvinistic. This may have been part of the dynamic of China in 1989, as its army killed its own citizens; it may have been reacting to its own internal feedback, due to millennia of cultural norms of order and centralized control.

Language is a means of setting and maintaining cultural boundaries, as well as a major means of organizing the energies of the system. Subcultures universally employ their own jargon and argot, and one of the major tasks of socialization into a subculture is to become acquainted with the special language. Certainly the subculture of social work is an example with such jargon as "person in environment," "personal-social needs," "relationship," and "intervention." Another example is the American Psychiatric Association's standardized nomenclature, in the Diagnostic and Statistical Manual (e.g., in the fourth edition, DSM-IV), which other professions may use to communicate with psychiatrists and with each other. The special language of a subculture may serve to exclude others from participation in the culture. Because it prevents interaction, this "linguistic collusion" is an effective way to close a boundary. (Incidentally, we hope that social systems theory helps prevent such boundary closures between helping professions, although we do recognize the initial difficulty in learning the jargon of systems thinking!)

The importance of screening and interpreting symbols in working with people is abundantly clear. Much of the literature of the helping professions, for example, is devoted to making the reader sensitive to the possible meanings of symbols received from the person being helped. Reik's idea of "the third ear," in which the therapist's own emotional reactions give clues to unspoken messages being sent by the patient, is a time-tested example (Reik, 1948). Another example is psychological testing, especially "projective" tests such as the Rorschach, Thematic Apperception, or House-Tree-Person tests. In these tests, the responses of the subject are interpreted in order to provide clues about the subject's personality structure and what treatment methods may be most useful. In these instances, between the professional person's reception (input) of the symbols and response (output) to them, the interpretation (processing) that occurs is formalized and takes on the character of scientific problem-solving—or at least, this is what professional schools hope their graduates are capable of doing.

In each profession, some standardization of language and symbols is necessary, and thus each theoretical approach, such as psychoanalysis, transactional analysis, behavior modification, or family therapy must devote much energy to training professionals in some standard terminology (and so must social systems theory). This is necessary so that the results of professional efforts and the theoretical elaboration of them can be conveyed in some common language. Certainly the history of psychiatry is replete with examples of attempts by Kraepelin, Freud, and others to standardize terminology (Menninger, 1963:Chapters 1 and 2, and Appendix). A major problem for each of the developing helping professions has been the training of professionals to apply the same labels to similar phenomena so that terms have some consensual meaning—that is, so that one psychiatrist's "schizoid" is not another psychiatrist's "passive-aggressive." Despite such efforts as the American Psychiatric Association's standard nomenclature (DSM), however, serious disagreements on interpretations of symbolic behavior do occur within that profession. Consensus of meaning with a high degree of precision is difficult to achieve; if it were not so, probably books like this would not need a glossary.

D. Child Rearing: Management of the Prolonged Human Childhood

Anthropologists, sociologists, and psychologists have exhaustively researched forms of child rearing in various cultures. Although most of these studies focus on the family system, many deal with other educative and socializing social systems as well. The management of the human's prolonged childhood is a major task of any culture and, as such, must fit with other aspects of the culture and interact with these. As a culture becomes more complex and differentiated, so too does child rearing, and other social provisions appear. There are numerous examples in the recent evolution of United States society. As the economic system required greater mobility, the extended family began to dissipate (see the discussion of this in Chapter 7). This was accompanied by the advent of the baby-sitter. Currently, the demands of the economic system and shifts in role definition of women are leading to rapid growth of day-care centers, the emergence of the "househusband" (in two comic strips, e.g.), and demands for federal legislation to support wider availability of day-care centers.

New social institutions such as day-care facilities for children and elders are accompanied by changes in family functions, but this is not necessarily equivalent to family breakdown. These new systems arise to realize more effectively the complex of values of a culture. Usually, certain values are in conflict with certain other values, leading to tension and strain within the culture. The historical development of the public school is an excellent illustration. The belief that a certain amount of formal education should be the right of every person developed over centuries in a number of places, particularly Western Europe. This was related to values such as "equality" and "the importance of knowledge." An informed citizenry became a national system goal in the first half of the nineteenth century. As the belief became a cherished value held by a significant portion of the components of the system, provisions were implemented such as the "common school" in the 1850s. The public school as a child-rearing social subsystem (if not a subculture, almost) has continued to evolve, becoming more complex and differentiated. The current controversy over the transmission of culture, manners, and morals through education about sexual behavior and AIDS, and whether this should be a family or school responsibility, exemplifies the process of culture change and the inherent value conflicts. Concern about portrayal of violence in television and movies, and its effect upon children, as well as the issue of prayer in the public schools, are other examples.

E. The Human Urge to Explain the World

Berger said that there is "a human craving for meaning that appears to have the force of instinct. [Humans] are congenitally compelled to impose a meaningful order upon reality" (quoted in Wuthnow et al., 1984:26). This major dimension of culture is often overlooked or minimized when explicating the concept of culture. Much of the energy of a culture system is expended in this effort to find meaning and to institutionalize it. Religion, philosophy, science, and superstition are some of the means. This quest to explain the unexplained can be viewed as an integral aspect of the adaptation of a system to its environment. In our present-day culture, science continues to be the dominant means of exploring, explaining, and changing our world (the scientific method, empirical observation, and inductive reasoning are, of course, highly valued only in certain cultures). It is dogmatically believed that the scientific method or technology can solve all important problems. Major religious organizations in this culture have been responsive to the currently accepted way of explaining the world and have engaged in social problem-solving in the "scientific" way. One denomination, of course, refers to "Christian Science."

The arrival of the Millenium (in the Christian calendar) has spurred a renewal of interest in other, nonscientific ways of knowing and explaining the cosmos. Popular manifestations include astrology, numerology, meditation, "talking with the dead" (the title of a best-selling book), and communing with angels; many of these interests have been labeled "New Age" thinking. Adherents of creationism continue pressing to juxtapose their explanation with scientism in the curriculum of the public schools.

F. Social Relations: Caring

Cultures are marked by the style in which they conduct social relationships. For example, Japanese culture is marked by a high degree of formality, and specificity about interactions and obligations between roles. Confucian ethics were based on the concept of *jen*, translated as "human-heartedness," "love," and "magnanimity"; the Chinese character denotes what is common, or shared, between human beings. "Filial piety (*hsiao*) begins as the natural and early exercise of the *jen* sentiment, leading to a cultivated attitude of respectful affection toward one's parents" (Mei, Pulleyblank, and Chan, 1987:693). Relationships between parent and child, family and community, and ruled to rulers were spelled out in detail.

A game that has been widely used to sensitize persons to cultural differences separates participants into two "cultures" and then requires them to interact; one culture is exclusively oriented toward acquisition, the other toward sharing and communication. The results are often confusing to participants and hilarious. Perceptive analyses of Western cultures, particularly that of the United States, suggest that ours is a "commercial" culture in which material gain is foremost and people are treated instrumentally, that is, as means to an end. Buber's philosophy described the difference between an *I-Thou* relationship, a complete, open, and mutual relationship between persons, and an *I-It* relationship, in which the other person is treated as an object (Buber, [1937] 1947, 1965). "Thou" is intended to convey the sacredness of the other person's being, a reflection of the divine.

> An animal does not need to be confirmed, for it is what it is unquestionably. It is different with man. Sent forth from the natural domain of a species into the hazard of the solitary category, surrounded by the air of a chaos which came into being with him, secretly and bashfully he watches for a Yes which allows him to be and which can come to him only from one human person to another. (Buber, 1965:17)

Many writers have observed that our culture is largely characterized by *I-It* relationships, and a lack of validation of each other; a more recent observation by feminists particularly, but not exclusively, is that our culture generally lacks *caring* among its members.

Caring "involves both an emotional disposition and caring labor. [It] is a practice in which both thought and action are integrated around central aims or goals" (Kimball, 1995:153). Care has been defined as "*a species activity that includes everything that we do to maintain, continue, and repair our 'world' so that we can live in it as well as possible*" (Joan Tronto, quoted in Kimball, 1995:153). Caring, then, is a dimension of culture as much as tools and language; it preceded them both. Illich defined culture as "the sum of rules by which the individual came to terms with pain, sickness and death, interpreted them, and practiced compassion toward others faced by the same threats. Each culture set up the myths, the taboos, and the ethical standards needed to deal with the fragility of life" (Ivan Illich, quoted in Schwartz, 1997:84).

A feminist critique states that caring is largely delegated to women by a male-dominated society. Wood agrees, but adds that caring arises from a situation of subordination which is not confined to women:

> Perhaps the most persuasive support for the idea that caring grows out of culturally constructed subordinate status rather than sex-role socialization would be empirical demonstration that caring is practiced by people in subordinate positions who are not female. . . . [W]e find there is indeed some intriguing evidence of precisely this. (Wood, 1994:99)

Wood cites studies of ethnic groups, and in particular African-Americans, that support this thesis: "[R]egardless of sex, individuals and groups who occupy subordinate status display a responsive orientation to others characterized by deference, attentiveness, awareness of needs, understanding of perspectives, moods and intentions, and responsiveness" (ibid.:100). However, she cites examples in which caring occurs outside subordinate statuses. From this, she proceeds to suggest two other, more constructive ways in which caring may become part of men's behaviors, as well, and become a fundamental style of our culture: first, psychologically as part of a "dynamic autonomy" of individual persons, defined as "an awareness of one's own desires, plans, motives, and viewpoints and those of others . . . being comfortable thinking and acting independently and thinking and acting cooperatively or in relationship with others" (ibid.:109); it is "fluid, secure, and able to be both with and apart from others with equal comfort and equal security in one's own selfhood . . . a person may recognize and accommodate someone needing care without 'losing self.'" In part, this describes moral, cognitive, and identity development at a mature level, as they are described in Chapter 8. Also, as noted in discussing Gilligan's ideas in Chapter 8, this emphasis on autonomy as a basis for caring may be more acceptable to men.

The second means to inculcate caring as a cultural ethic is described in Woods's Chapter 7, under the heading "The Cultural Imperative: Creating a Culture That Values Caring." She describes in some detail a program of "discursive struggle," including government actions, innovations in business and industry, educational institutions, and parenting, which through "synergetic change" (ibid.:156) could "restructure how our society evaluates and teaches its members to think about caring, men and women, and the essence of public life" (ibid.:157). She describes what is called in Chapter 5 a "patch" approach: "An inventive idea that works in one community may function as a model for other communities until, grassroots fashion, what was originally an innovation may become standard practice throughout the United States" (ibid.).

In the same vein, Schwartz describes the Peckham Experiment in a London suburb previous to World War II (Schwartz, 1997:79–81), an experiment in "retribalization" and "social network intervention" (ibid.:76–77). The experiment began with two physicians who explored why people did *not* become ill: "they made the great leap of going beyond individual factors to examine the characteristics of a community and to try to do something about individual health by focusing on the strength and viability of the community" (ibid.:80). They founded a health center with a range of services, similar to a community center, which encouraged wide interaction among members of the community. They documented the improved health of individuals, and the concept gained attention; however, the war intervened, and the experiment was not repeated.

CONCLUSION

All professions and disciplines concerned with human behavior now recognize that culture must be attended to and understood. The concept of culture has become politicized as an instrument of change in the past two decades by, e.g., feminists, racial minorities, ethnic groups, and organizations for deaf persons; they have called attention to the vitality and integrity of their own cultures and have influenced "mainstream" culture. A powerful example of a redefinition of our culture is this indictment:

> What is a rape culture? It is a complex of beliefs that encourages male sexual aggression and supports violence against women. It is a society where violence is seen as sexy and sexuality as violent. In a rape culture women perceive a continuum of threatened violence that ranges from sexual remarks to sexual touching to rape itself. A rape culture condones physical and emotional terrorism against women *as the norm.* (Buchwald, Fletcher, and Roth, 1993:vii)

Obviously, changes in our thinking about culture have implications for the human services. "Diversity" has become the key word in attempting cultural change to reflect the experience of less powerful groups and individuals; to reflect the mosaic of cultures that is the United States. Without an awareness of the power and legitimacy of culture, it is very difficult to assist, care for, teach, or learn from anyone whose cultural experience is different from one's own.

The pioneering anthropologists tended to study cultures markedly different from their own; these were so-called "primitive" cultures. Lack of familiarity allowed them a measure of objectivity in reasoning from symbolic behavior to related meanings, but even so, they were frequently confounded by what they observed, or inaccurately inferred meanings derived from their own cultures. Margaret Mead (1972) said that her field studies were conducted so that Americans might better understand *themselves.* This is consistent with Hall's contention that to be able to see one's own culture, it is first necessary to experience a foreign culture (E. Hall, 1977). This is true for the simple reason that one's native culture becomes "normal," "sensible," "natural," and "right." Moreover, it *feels* natural; it feels natural to shake hands, to smile when pleased, to bathe frequently, and to be informal; but, of course, all these conventions are peculiar to particular cultures.

How one applies the concept of culture depends on one's vantage point, what one is prepared to see, and perhaps most important, the knowledge used (see Piaget's "schemas" in Chapter 8) to interpret one's observations. Visualize the three-dimensional atomic model as a system and then consider the study of culture. If you are somewhere within the cultural system you can see some components well, others less well, and others not at all. If you are outside the system your perspective may help you better see the "big picture," but the further out you are, the more danger there is of reductionism and oversimplification.

To understand best a culture in any of its forms (e.g., a tribal society, an ethnic group, a peer group, or a profession), observers must strive for objectivity if they are themselves components of the system, or strive for involvement if they are outside the system. Social work, nursing, and other professions have increasingly emphasized the need for greater understanding of and greater involvement in the "client system," be it family, organization, neighborhood, community, or culture.

SUGGESTED READINGS

Cohen, Bernice.
　　1988　*Global Perspectives: The Total Culture System in the Modern World.* London: Codek.
　　　　She says "culture is a system," and we are now in a worldwide culture, a "total culture system," which we must understand.
Farb, Peter.
　　1968　*Man's Rise to Civilization as Shown by the Indians of North America from Primeval Times to the Coming of the Industrial State.* New York: Dutton.
　　　　In this very readable book, with its foreboding title, Farb illustrated how cultures evolve.
Hall, Edward T.
　　1977　*Beyond Culture.* Garden City, NY: Doubleday Anchor.
　　　　Hall's synthesis of his own research and the research of others, and his theorizing about culture.
De Kerckhove, Derrick.
　　1995　*The Skin of Culture: Investigating the New Electronic Reality.* Toronto: Somerville House.
　　　　The author is director of the McLuhan Program in Culture and Technology at the University of Toronto, and colleague of Marshall McLuhan. The title is from McLuhan's comment, "In the electric age, we wear all mankind as our skin." His ideas are provocative and while descended from McLuhan, are perhaps more accessible.
LaBarre, Weston.
　　1954　*The Human Animal.* Chicago: University of Chicago. (The 1968 edition has minor differences.)
　　　　The author, an anthropologist, examined human culture from an evolutionary viewpoint. He combined findings from anthropology, psychiatry, linguistics, and human biology into a controversial thesis. His arguments are particularly thorough as he deals with family, symbolic communication, and deviant behavior.

Van Maanen, John.
   1988   *Tales of the Field.* Chicago: University of Chicago Press.
      A practitioner's guide to methodological and conceptual issues in ethnogra-
      phy, the study of culture in the field. Witty, wise, and useful to the student
      of cultures. It surveys most of the major works of cultural field studies.
Wuthnow, Robert, James Davison Hunter, Albert Bergesen, and Edith Kurzweil.
   1984   *Cultural Analysis: The Work of Peter L. Berger, Mary Douglas, Michel
      Foucault, and Jurgen Habermas.* Boston, London: Routledge & Kegan Paul.
      Clear, concise analysis and comparison of these preeminent theorists. Pre-
      sumes familiarity with basic concepts of sociology. The chapter on Berger is
      virtually a summary of mainstream thought on the nature of culture, and
      highly compatible with social systems theory.

LITERARY SOURCES

Dorris, Michael.
   1987   *A Yellow Raft in Blue Water.* New York: Warner.
      A novel of American Indian culture related through the experiences of
      grandmother, mother, and daughter, who move through life together. Vine
      Deloria, Jr., said it "shows us the humorous, ironic side of reservation life as
      it has rarely been portrayed."
Erdrich, Louise.
   1985   *Love Medicine.* Toronto, New York: Bantam.
      This is a powerful novel of a complex American Indian family and rich
      culture, in which meanings become evident only after the fact, in the under-
      standings of others. The stories of some of these characters have been con-
      tinued in subsequent novels.

FILMS AND VIDEOS

The Cutting Edge: Portraits of Southeast Asian Adolescents in Transition (1983)
   Portraits of three Asian refugees: Hmong, Vietnamese, and Lao. Each describes
   the survival of his culture in the new United States setting. Music, instruments,
   costumes, and rituals are part of the background.
Dreams on Hold (1986)
   This documentary examines the growing gap between rich and poor in the
   United States, and the shrinking middle class. Underemployment and the need
   for two paychecks in a family are examined. The implications of employment of
   mothers of young children are discussed. The dream of security, growth, and
   upward mobility seems to be fading.
Farewell to Manzanar (1976; made for television)
   Superb portrayal of the internment of Japanese-Americans during World War
   II. Pictures well their plight as acculturated Issei, Nissei, or Sansei (first, second,
   or third generation) Americans; their humiliation by their chosen country, and
   their dignity.

Gandhi (1982)
British and Indian cultures, and the transformation of both by a powerful set of ideas embodied in one person, vividly portrayed. The dramatic events convey well a sense of how cultural change occurred.

Maids and Madams (1986)
Apartheid in South Africa viewed in the relationship of the black household worker and the white employer. More than a million black women were economically bound to such jobs. The psychological battle for dominance was waged in intimate settings in white homes.

Powwow Highway (1989)
A small, unpretentious film that is a gem. Believable characters, plausible plot. A unique film in that contemporary American Indian cultures are presented accurately, sympathetically, and with humor.

Communities

The triumph of the industrial economy is the fall of community. But fall of community reveals how precious and how necessary community is. For when community falls, so must fall all of the things that only community life can engender and protect: the care of the old, the care and education of children, family life, neighborly work, the handing down of memory, the care of the earth, respect for nature and the lives of wild creatures.

—Wendell Berry (quoted in Schwartz, 1997)

Somewhere is better than anywhere.

—Flannery O'Connor

INTRODUCTION

As one perceptive writer put it, "Yearning for community seems to have become a modern preoccupation. It is as if everyone were thirsty and always dreamed of water" (Schwartz, 1997:43). A text on community illustrated its current condition by printing "community" with a large X through it, and called community a *catachresis*, meaning "there is no literal referent for [it]; that its definition comes apart, as it were, as soon as we begin to articulate it. . . . We can neither say what we mean . . . nor mean what we say" (Godway and Finn, 1994:2). *Is* community dead?

I. COMMUNITY AS SYSTEM

Probably the most difficult systems to define with precision are community and small group (which will be discussed in Chapter 6). The term *community* has become overly used, with broad and vague applications. It is frequently employed to impute commonality of interest to what in fact are disparate groups of people, e.g., the "intelligence community," the "community of elders," and the "faith community." Possession of one common defining quality does not in and of itself form a community. For some, a definition of human community must include nonhuman and nonliving elements as well. Over fifty years ago, conservationist and ecologist Aldo Leopold "proposed enlarging 'the boundaries of the community to include soils, water, plants, animals, or collectively, the land.' The implication of this deceptively simple shift is that humans must change their role from conqueror of the community to citizen" (Lind, 1994:128).

Both communities and organizations are macrosystems as contrasted with the microsystems of persons, families, and small groups. Both are intermediate (or "mediating") systems between society and the small groupings in which intimate affective transactions occur. Sociology has found it difficult to define and distinguish among community, organization, and society. The major distinction between community and organization, historically, is: "A community is held together by feeling and sentiment, primarily, while an organization is sustained by 'rational' considerations, usually explicit in formal contracts, usually written" (Tönnies, 1957).

Because the community is at the interface between society and microsystems, it is of concern to all social disciplines and professions. The family is a person's primary field of interaction during childhood; in adulthood, the other major field of interaction is community, or at least significant sectors of community. Such sectors include the financial, commercial, religious, educational, social, and legal institutions (among others) in which the person participates. Community is simultaneously a subsystem (or component) of society and *is* the society itself. To the individual, the community represents the culture and shapes persons' lives; at the same time, it is affected by individual persons who can change the community. Consistent with our stance on adaptation and accommodation (Chapter 2) we place importance upon mutual causation here; the citizen and the community influence each other with family, small group, and organizations as intermediaries.

A. Kinds of Communities

Communities differ in several respects. First, Tönnies described them as being held together by two sorts of bonds—*gemeinschaft* and *gesell-*

schaft. A *gemeinschaft* community is characterized by implicit bonds that relate all community members to the others. These bonds include common values and beliefs, mutual interdependence, respect, and a shared sense of status hierarchy. Rules regarding relationships are not formalized but rest in cultural traditions and complementary social expectations rather than written codes or contracts. An American Indian tribal community may be an example in that behavior often is greatly influenced by tradition and culture; however as tribes have "modernized," they too have become somewhat more formalized with Reservation Business Committees (as required in the 1934 Indian Reorganization Act) and parliamentary structures. Yet, there remains for many a *gemeinschaft* feeling of place, as for Roland Lussier, who wrote this as a sixth-grader in Northern Minnesota:

> There is no place better than the Indian reservation. It's so beautiful, the land is covered with dark green pine trees and other kinds of trees. At dawn we can watch the sun, and we will see beautiful colors around the sun. We are proud of our reservation and we thank God for giving it to us. (Brill, 1974:56)

A *gesellschaft* community is characterized by bonds that are both formal and specific. Community members relate to each other through formally structured relations within community institutions such as work organizations, professions, and civic organizations .

A second way that communities differ from one another is in the degree of attachment to a specific location. This variable can also be used to determine specific types of communities, but the reader should keep in mind that these categories, like all typologies, are ideal and not real. In reality, attachment to place or location is more or less present in all communities. Tönnies described *place* and *nonplace* communities:

1. *Place communities.* Tönnies also called this kind of community a "locality." One form of community organization has been called "locality development" (Cox et al., 1987). This type of community has also been called a geographic or spatial community. It is based upon a common habitat and occupation of adjacent (or nearby) properties. Examples of place community are neighborhoods, reservations, villages, towns, and cities.

2. *Nonplace Communities.* Tönnies also called this community a "mind" community, which "implies only cooperation and coordinated action for a common goal," without reference to "place" (Hillery, 1968:77–78). Examples of nonplace communities include religious communities and professions. A spirited debate continues among sociologists as to whether "social networks" are nonplace communities.

Beginning with Barnes's study of the social structure of the fishing community in Norway, researchers have found social networks a fruitful topic of study. His definition of social network is most useful:

> Each person is, as it were, in touch with a number of other people, some of whom are in touch with each other and some of whom are not. Similarly each person has a number of friends, and these friends have their own friends; some of any one person's friends know each other, others do not. I find it convenient to talk of a social field of this kind as a network. The image I have is of a set of points some of which are joined by lines. The points of the image are people, or sometimes groups, and the lines indicate which people interact with each other (Barnes, 1954:127).

The diagrams in Figure 4.1 represent Barnes's ideas. The fact that it was a fishing village may have influenced Barnes's choice of the term *net*work rather than other possible terms, such as web. In Barnes's view, a network consists of the relationships between pairs of people (or dyads), an atomistic view. Later theorists have applied network concepts to larger social groupings. Barnes's definition is perspectivistic: each person has a unique social network defined by the person's dyadic relationships. In most current usage of the term, social network is synonymous with non-place community: it "implies only cooperation and coordinated action for a common goal, without reference to place" (Hillery, 1968:77–78). This is the sense in which it is used in discussing "networking" as a technique for changing the personal and work conditions of women.

In a social work context, Eilene McIntyre defined a social network as consisting of "a set of people all of whom are linked together, but not all of whom know one another. This inclusion of indirect links differentiates a network from a group" (1986:422). All such networks are not necessarily socially desirable. For example, illegal drug distribution is often carried out through such a social network.

The late Virginia Hine, who studied social change, noted the emergence of "segmented, polycephalous, ideological networks" (abbreviated to SPIN), which were loosely organized alliances with bonds based on strongly held ideological bonds (Hine, 1982:4–5). She believed this was a

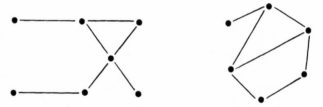

Figure 4.1.   Diagrams of unbounded networks.

new form of nonhierarchical organization: it functioned effectively, did not collapse in the face of opposition (in fact became stronger). The model she observed has in fact become common in "movement" organizations such as gay rights, feminist associations, and the Promise Keepers, e.g., E-mail and the Internet permit distribution of information to large numbers of people simultaneously and at low cost, a necessary factor in most such organizations. Such ties are referred to as "loose coupling"; at the same time, observers discuss the "strength of weak ties" in such loose couplings. Our discussions of boundaries in Chapters 1 and 2 are relevant here, in that linkages can be intense for short periods of time, for specific purposes. This is very similar to the descriptions in feminist literature of women's mutual support groups or networks. To the extent that they are stable and function as significant environments for their members, such networks clearly qualify as nonplace communities.

3. *Kinship.* As Tönnies described it, this third kind of community is one in which members have blood relationships. An example might be an American Indian reservation, a barrio or community as portrayed in the movie, *The Milagro Beanfield War*, or an Amish community. It might also include immigrant groups that, though geographically dispersed in the new country, still support each other; examples include Chinese communities that comprise members in Hong Kong, Vancouver (Canada), and San Francisco, and Vietnamese (or Lao or Hmong) communities that include Los Angeles, Minneapolis–St. Paul, the Philippines, and Vietnam. It is common for more affluent members of such communities to remit money to their less prosperous relatives in the "home" country (e.g., Jamaica or China). Barnes's definition of social network includes both a "networking," goal-oriented social system (which might also be viewed as a loose-knit organization) and kinship networks.

As mentioned, these categories are not exclusive. Nonplace communities and social networks have some geographic connection, even though members may never convene in one location at one time (indeed, cannot, in the case of refugees and those left behind) and do not consider physical location to be a primary or constant factor. For instance, the "academic community" does not reside in a single location, but it does have ties to college campuses. Similarly, the "scientific community" and the "medical community" have ties to laboratories and other research facilities. A "community of believers" usually has connections with temples, synagogues, churches, or shrines, but exists independent of these, as well.

Other examples of nonplace communities, such as the traditional occupation of barbering, are protected from intrusion by custom or by law, as symbolized by the striped pole and the barber's license (although hair stylists, among others, have gained legal status performing many of the same tasks). Another example is the academic community's jealous protection of academic freedom, as when a professor went to jail rather than reveal a vote on giving another professor tenure. Academic freedom, also, is a highly abstract and symbolic territory that some persons will defend with their liberty, if not their lives.

A third way in which communities differ is in the breadth of activities, interests, and needs that they encompass. The place community encompasses virtually all human interests and needs; the nonplace community is usually concerned with one, or few, of these. Almost every kind of human activity, in one form or another, is to be found in Chicago, for example, or nearly any small town, while the nonplace "business community" or "academic community" concerns itself with a narrower range of interests and needs.

II. DEFINITION OF COMMUNITY

We suggest the following composite definition. Community is a population whose members:

1. consciously identify with each other;
2. may occupy common territory;
3. engage in common activities;
4. have some form of organization that provides for differentiation of functions, which allows the community to adapt to its environment, thereby meeting the needs of its components.

Its components include the persons, groups, families, and organizations within its population and the institutions it forms to meet its needs. Its environment is the society in which its exists and to which it adapts (and which it also modifies) by energy exchange, and other communities and organizations outside itself that impinge upon its functioning. We discuss the energy functions in the following section.

A. Energy Functions

1. For Components/Subsystems. The functions the community performs include the maintenance of a way of life or culture (in the second usage of "culture" in Chapter 3). Wallace Stegner described this in *Where the Bluebird Sings to the Lemonade Springs:*

> A place is not a place until people have been born in it, have grown up in it, lived in it, known it, died in it—have both experienced and shaped it, as individuals, families, neighborhoods and communities, over more than one generation. Some are born in their place, some find it, some realize after long searching that the place they left is the one they have been searching for. But whatever their relation to it, it is made a place only by slow accrual like a coral reef. (1992:p. 201)

Another important function is the satisfaction of common needs, interests, and ambitions. A striking example of the recognition of common interests and needs was Malcolm X's redefinition of the community to which he belonged. He found common interests and needs unexpectedly in a new community:

> That morning was when I first began to reappraise the "white man." It was when I first began to perceive that "white man," as commonly used, means complexion only secondarily; primarily it described attitudes and actions toward the black man, and toward all other nonwhite men. But in the Muslim world, I had seen that men with white complexions were more genuinely brotherly than anyone else had ever been.
> That morning was the start of a radical alteration in my whole outlook about "white" men. (Malcolm X, 1966:333–334)

Further, the members of a community must be aware of its "we-ness" (French, 1969); there must be a social consciousness or "sense of community." This assists the community to meet the social identity needs of the persons who are its components. The community must provide for them "full opportunities for personal development through social experimentation. . . . This conception falls close to Erikson's views on ego identity and ego integrity as well as to Sullivan's emphasis on a full repertory of interpersonal relations" (Stein, 1960:335–336).

Erik Erikson and Karen Horney, both psychoanalysts, and Harry Stack Sullivan, a social psychiatrist, recognized the importance of the social environment (as discussed in Chapter 8), including the community, in providing a medium for the evolution of the person. They were a distinct minority among early psychoanalytic theorists in the importance they placed upon the social environment. Stein elaborated, "A community must . . . provide its members with, at the least, meaningful sexual and work identities if it is to ensure its own continuity as well as the psychic integrity of its members"

Many communities are unable to provide opportunities to develop work identities because of lack of jobs, e.g., some inner-city ghettos, many American Indian reservations, the "rust belt" of industries related to steel production from Gary, Indiana, to Pittsburgh, Pennsylvania, or the Appalachian region. Some persons in these communities may fail to develop ego integrity since they are prevented from viewing themselves not only as productive members of the community but also as worthwhile persons individually. While some social theorists and policymakers accept this as an inherent risk in a capitalist industrial society, others regard this as unjustified damage to the community as a system and to its members.

We do not yet know the effects of such failure by society and the community to provide adequately for their members' identity needs, although the effects of previous economic depressions are known to some degree. Some suggest that we now see the effects of economic marginality in a sharp rise in violent criminal behavior, and in the institutionalization of an illicit drug trade whose participants number in the hundreds of thousands. Some writers have suggested that the effect of such societal neglect may be to produce severely alienated persons and groups who turn to authoritarian ideologies for security and as a means of participation in some form of community. Erich Fromm, Hannah Arendt, and other writers on "alienation" stated strongly that such alienated groups are breeding grounds for fascism (Arendt, 1962; Fromm, 1942, 1955; Giner, 1976:138–144). The burgeoning of "skinheads" and paramilitary militia groups in the United States, and violent incidents such as the Oklahoma City bombing of a federal building may reflect a societal turn toward absolutist or extremist or anarchist ideologies.

Other components such as families, organizations, and groups must also be able to identify with and find common cause with the community's way of life in order that their energies may be used to meet the community's needs. Alexis de Tocqueville, the French nobleman who so accurately described the United States and its future in 1831, identified three characteristics of community groups who came together to solve problems they held in common: "First, they were groups of citizens who decided they had the power to decide what was a problem. Second, they decided they had the power to decide how to solve the problem. Third, they often decided that they would themselves become the key actors in implementing the solution" (McKnight, 1995:117).

The term *common cause* was adopted as the name of a national citizen's action organization that explicitly recognizes the necessity to involve citizens and to draw upon their energies. This organization mobilizes energy in the form of funds and lobbying activity from its citizen-members to attain agreed-upon goals. It meets the definition of a system, specifically a social network, or nonplace community, in this respect.

2. *For Environment/Suprasystems.* A community must also meet the needs of its environment in order to survive. It is clear from "central place" theory in geography and economics that place communities function as parts of hierarchical, relatively stable economic and political systems, and that alterations in one community affect other parts of the region as well (Christaller, 1966; Dunn, 1980). The rise of Chicago ("that toddlin' town, the town that Billy Sunday could not shut down") as a major industrial and railroad center affected the commercial and social development of communities within its region. It became, as Carl Sandburg put it,

> Hog butcher for the World,
> Tool maker, Stacker of Wheat,
> Player with Railroads and the Nation's Freight Handler . . .
> —Carl Sandburg (1955:442–443)

Smaller communities nearby adapted, sometimes unwillingly, to Chicago's emergence as a trade center, both supplying and being supplied by Chicago's services and industries. Communities unsuited to adapt to new economic and transportation networks, or unable to compete with new centers of power, declined or ceased to exist. In the American West in the last few decades, "boom towns" arose as the demand for minerals or new sources for oil increased; some have failed to prosper.

Religious communities, as examples of nonplace community, have also been confronted with the need to adapt to their environment. Within the Roman Catholic church, some orders that formerly were relatively removed from society have become socially active, performing less specifically religious tasks, such as teaching and social service. A few orders have disbanded as their members have returned to lay status, some members in order to marry and others to carry on secular work as part of their religious commitment. The Roman Catholic "community," however, maintains some clear boundaries. Priests and nuns are still forbidden to marry (except when released from their vows), and procreation is still the purpose of marriage. In another example of boundary-setting, the pope banned priests from holding elective office, which caused strong reactions from some Latin American priests who subscribed to Liberation Theology, which calls upon priests to participate in the civil community to fulfill their responsibilities in the religious community.

The history of utopian communities is replete with examples of those who attempted to isolate themselves from the social environment and thrive as closed systems, unsuccessfully. Without energy exchange with the environment, a system is certain to become entropic and die. Amish communities in Pennsylvania, Indiana, Iowa, and other states have survived by maintaining energy exchange with the environment in certain carefully limited ways; this is an excellent illustration of boundaries that are relatively more closed than other communities but still open to exchanges of energy.

American Indian reservations are examples of communities that were excluded from the general society and suffered entropy. In recent years, economic and social development by the tribes (in part funded by casinos operated by about a quarter of the tribes) have opened the boundaries. While white society may wish to remove the boundaries entirely (the "assimilation" or relocation policies, particularly in the 1950s), American Indians have consciously encouraged maintenance of open, but clearly recognizable cultural boundaries, especially during the past three decades. From a systems perspective, the assimilation policy was unworkable because it would have required only the Indian societies to accommodate (to change their *schemes*—see Chapter 8), after which white society would assimilate them. A systems perspective would indicate that mutual accommodation would be necessary, and each culture would have to both *accommodate* and *assimilate*. The Indian Child Welfare Act of 1978 is an example of accommodation by the general society, by recognizing the rights of tribes to control adoptions and foster care placements of their children.

In general, the functions that a community performs for its environment are the energy functions described in Chapter 1, *giving, getting,* and *conserving* energy. The community supplies energy to its environment and its components in the form of persons and products to be used by those systems. For example, a community may supply students for higher education who become leaders while also supplying political support for organizations outside the community and taxes for state and national governments.

President Reagan's "new federalism" explicitly stated that communities and states were required to supply too much of their resources to their suprasystem, the federal government, handicapping their efforts to meet the communities' own needs and those of its components: organizations, families, and persons. Presidents Reagan, Bush, and Clinton agreed that too much has been taken by an overgrown federal bureaucracy. The position of many liberals is that only the federal government can be trusted to redistribute these resources equitably because communities and states are more vulnerable to pressure groups and more likely to deny resources to the powerless and disadvantaged. This liberal-conservative debate will continue for the foreseeable future; it illustrates the need for an energy exchange that meets the needs of each, among suprasystem, system, and components, if all system levels are to function satisfactorily. A large part of the debate also, of course, is over the definition of "satisfactory" functioning, and which functions should be performed at what system levels. It seems likely that the community system will be the arena in which a great deal of this controversy will occur during the new century.

B. Aspects of Community Systems

1. Evolutionary Aspects. The first cities were burial places to which wandering tribes returned at certain times to perform ceremonies that ensured the stability of the universe. From that symbolic beginning, place communities evolved to encompass all human needs and functions. Max Weber, Hans Paul Bahrdt, and others contend that the city had its genesis in the market. Thus, a city is a settlement with a resident population that regularly satisfies economic and social (including spiritual) needs for energy exchange through the device of a local market. We could combine these speculations by saying that cities began as locations that were sites of seasonal rituals, which became permanent market sites as agriculture evolved.

The character of a particular community is determined by its relationships to other communities and the society within which it exists, by the characteristics of its components, and by its own preceding steady state. The Lynds' Middletown (Muncie, Indiana) evolved toward being a satellite in the regional system of New York City, because decisions about industries were increasingly made outside Middletown (Lynd and Lynd, 1929, 1937). When Theodore Caplow and associates reexamined Middletown fifty years later, they found the major change to be the degree to which the federal government determined economic and social conditions. By 1979, "about one-third of all the income received by Middletown families came out of the federal treasury" (Caplow, Bahr, Chadwick, Hill, and Williamson, 1982:26).

Doxiadis described the evolution of large cities through five stages, differentiated by "kinetic fields," that is, the distance a person can travel within a certain span of time (Miller, 1972:117–118):

A-level organization: The city encompasses 2 by 2 kilometers and has a population of no more than 50,000. No more than ten minutes are required to walk from the center to its periphery.

B-level organization: The city encompasses 6 by 6 kilometers and has a population of more than 50,000. Examples are capital cities of empires such as Rome, Constantinople, and Beijing. Walking time in these cities at this stage of development was no more than half an hour; paved roads and horse-drawn carts moved people (and in Beijing still do). Such cities were difficult to govern, slums grew, and mobs frequently controlled the city.

C-level organization: These cities depend upon subways or elevated trains to extend the "kinetic field." This is satisfactory only briefly, as cities evolve and freeways are built to accommodate automobile traffic. It is entirely possible, of course, that cities may return to this mode of transportation, but if so, the largest cities would probably use high-speed subways to compensate for distances.

D-level organization: This is the "modern" metropolitan city, beset by the myriad urban problems with which we are all too familiar. The urban population exceeds the capacity of the freeways, resulting in the now ubiquitous gridlocks and air contamination. Modes of public transportation must be augmented or new ones developed, such as the Light Rail system in Portland, Oregon. Examples include Mexico City (soon the world's largest city), Beijing, Bombay, and Los Angeles.

E-level organization: This is the megalopolis, the modern urban complex that comprises several cities with a total population of several million. In the United States, the so-called "BosWash" (Boston to Washington) megalopolis is almost a single, continuous urban area. This urban level is marked by the pathology that remains from having failed to solve problems at the D-level.

The "universal city" or "ecumenopolis" would be the ultimate city and would require highly centralized planning. Presumably, technology would solve the problems of transportation, distribution of energy supplies, and waste disposal, although many are not convinced. Some believe that microchip technology, most importantly the computer, will enable us to continue to participate in advanced technology working at home, even in relatively isolated communities. Many people today, including the authors of this book, compose on computers at home, utilize libraries via computer, correspond with workmates in other parts of the country and overseas via e-mail and satellite, and research subjects on the (literally) World Wide Web. McLuhan's (1965) "global village" is a "virtual reality"; another way to describe it would be a nonplace or "mind community."

How a sense of community will be maintained is not clear. Divisions of social class or status, ethnic or racial heritage, religion, or ideology, continue to frustrate efforts to strengthen a sense of "the commons" shared by all inhabitants. The shape taken by cities of the future is being determined by experiences and crises in cities today. Many wonder whether the continuing exodus from central cities to the suburbs is a permanent trend, especially given a long-term shortage in petroleum fuels. Like other systems, cities are subject to multiple factors that influence growth and decline.

Today, ghost towns that were formerly company-owned mining camps, small farming villages, or fishing villages attest to the alternative of disintegration for the community that does not have, or does not use, resources to adapt. Currently, in both Canada and the United States, the future of the family farm is in doubt; according to a member of Congress, "In North Dakota and parts of northern Minnesota, it is feared up to *half* the farmers will close their operations. The ag sector is a vital part of our region's economy, not just for farming families, but for residents of our towns as well" (Minge, 1998). The Midwest lost 3 percent of its population in the first half of the 1980s. In the eighties, half the small-town gas stations in Iowa closed; nationally, over 150 hospitals in small towns closed, and at least that many more were threatened; smaller school districts closed throughout rural areas; in Kansas, 33 rural banks closed. Churches closed; retail stores were replaced by shopping malls, WalMart, and K-Mart. A farmer in Saskatchewan, Canada, told a researcher:

> Tell the people that they're going to have to start supporting the family farm. Make sure you put *family* farm in there. We don't want corporate farms. Co-ops are okay but we don't want huge corporations in here. Let the families stay out there. We want the community to stay there. (Lind, 1994:120)

The late Harry Caudill's classic book, *Night Comes to the Cumberlands* (1963), painfully illustrated the process by which rural Appalachian communities became the lowest level in a hierarchy of industrial power, subject to decisions made by corporations in Pittsburgh, Detroit, and New York. One study analyzed the history of Coos Bay, Oregon:

Immediately after the Second World War, the timber resource was extensive and there was still time to develop a long-range resource-management strategy. However, as this study has made clear, the market prevailed and the social and economic stability of the region was never a major consideration in private and public decision making. Now that the resource base has been severely depleted and nineteenth-century social theories are fashionable in state and federal capitals, there is even less likelihood that those communities will escape from the strategies and investment decisions of the private corporations who control much of the land. (Robbins, 1988:167–168)

Some communities have turned to tourism as a major source of revenue (e.g., Central City, Colorado; Bayfield, Wisconsin; Gatlinburg, Tennessee; Victoria, British Columbia; Kyoto, Japan; and the Portuguese colony of Macao). Still other localities are seeking survival through developing a "retirement industry," specializing in housing, goods, and services for the expanding population of active elders. The same principle of adaptation applies to nonplace communities. Certainly the history of Christian and Muslim sects or denominations illustrates the evolutionary process of such nonplace communities.

2. Structural Aspects

a. Boundaries. The boundaries that separate communities from larger and smaller social units—the so-called vertical hierarchy—are often difficult to establish precisely. Minnesota's Red Lake Reservation is, by treaty law, a sovereign nation. By tribal law one must have a Red Lake passport to enter legally. As one enters the reservation, one encounters signs like this:

Warning. This is Indian land. No trespassing. No fishing, hunting, camping, berry picking, peddling or soliciting without authorized permit from Red Lake Tribal Council Office. Violators and trespassers will be prosecuted under Federal Law 86-634. (Brill, 1974:22)

The sign indicates that the interactional boundary between the reservation and the federal government is open. The sign further indicates that the geographic boundary is relatively closed, but in reality is closed only in certain ways:

Red Lakers are not isolated from the outside world. I am always amazed when someone asks me, "Can the Indians leave the reservation?" There are no fences around the reservation; the roads to Bemidji and other cities in the area are well traveled. . . . It is common for Red Lakers to drive to larger cities to shop in the supermarkets and discount stores; to bowl with the league on Tuesday and Thursday evenings. . . . Some commute to classes at Bemidji State College. In addition to the Redlake Neighborhood Centers Newsletter . . . many people subscribe to the Bemidji *Pioneer* and the Min-

neapolis *Tribune*. Television is popular and reception is generally good.
(ibid.)

Increasingly, as noted earlier in this chapter, communities are subordinate to larger, regional networks and to industrial and communications
centers in their economic and social affairs. Recent corporate and stock
market reversals in Indonesia, Hong Kong, and Japan affected production
and employment in "middle America" as well as larger commercial centers. In some communities, the internal structure may comprise relatively
autonomous bodies such as corporations that function as private, independent governments. Rochester, New York, is the home of Eastman
Kodak; Detroit to Ford, General Motors, and Chrysler; "silicon valley" to
high-tech industries in California; and Redmond, Washington, to Microsoft Corporation.

Boundaries within the community include those between institutions
that differentiate tasks. These horizontal boundaries include, for example,
the uniform worn and the choice of specific colors and tasks. Firefighters'
gear is adapted to their task, but it also distinguishes them from police.
Their distinctive gear says, "We fight fires. We don't baptize children with
our hoses, pick up garbage with our trucks, or fight off mobs with our
axes and poles!"

Sometimes the boundaries between differentiated institutions are not
so clear: Are parochial schools entitled to public funds? Should schools
provide sex education? Should police conduct drug education programs?
Should health clinics do AIDS testing and should they be required to
report the results to state or federal agencies? These continue to be controversial questions in many communities.

b. Institutions. Differentiation of functions by assigning them to specialized subsystems leads to the emergence of institutions within communities. Such institutions usually originate in several communities in
slightly different forms. Since the community is a holon between society
and microsystems such as families and ethnic groups, it contains fundamental system processes such as socialization and social control, embodied in religious institutions, schools, and police; these institutions are
prescribed in modern, industrialized cultures. The form the institution
takes in a particular community depends upon the community's components, its previous steady states, and its environment (an institution is a
holon also). Our society prescribes that education shall be performed by
formal schools, but the form of the school varies from community to
community. It may be a one-room country school or an urban elementary
school; it may be single-sex or coed, private or public, and may be a
"magnet," "charter," or "home" school. The mode of instruction may be
the Montessori method or the traditional "3 Rs"; the instructional equipment may be slate blackboards or satellite television and lasers.

Certain communities evolve distinctive institutions. Pine Mountain Settlement School in Kentucky began the "Little School," a forerunner of the national Head Start program. Significant portions of the War on Poverty of the 1960s were modeled on the Mobilization for Youth program in New York City; hot lines and youth crisis centers originated in a number of cities at about the same time; in California, Berkeley's Shanti Project was a model for services to AIDS patients (Shilts, 1988:123). Internationally, several Austrian communities are known for their Children's Villages, a unique response to the need to care for orphans. The process originates as a recognized need that is unmet by existing institutions; the community (or some influential component) differentiates a new institution to incorporate the new service.

Some institutions almost escape our notice because they exist in most communities, but their functions are overlooked. Examples are taverns or bars (pubs are more visible in England's society), e.g., Small's Bar, which Malcolm X protected by confessing; this was an important institution in Harlem's social structure, as were the nightclubs Malcolm frequented. Think of bars as settings for radio and television shows, e.g., "Cheers" (based on an actual bar in Boston). The laundromat serves a socializing function in many neighborhoods. Restaurants and coffeehouses serve a similar function, as portrayed on television series such as "Friends," "Frasier," and "Seinfeld." One author points out, "In the eighteenth century, some of the most basic discussions about the formation of the government of the United States and its Constitution occurred in inns and taverns" (McKnight, 1995:118).

Community institutions pose special challenges, as well as support, to social workers and other professionals acting as change agents, because institutions are social systems and seek to maintain themselves. This may be done by modifying structure and function to better fulfill community needs (*morphogenesis*). However, as systems they also seek to remain the same (*morphostasis*). Thus, institutional provisions generally lag in meeting emergent community needs. As Thorstein Veblen wrote in 1899, "institutions are . . . adapted to past circumstances, and are therefore never in full accord with the requirements of the present. . . . This process of selective adaptation can never catch up with the progressively changing situation in which the community finds itself at any given time" (Boguslaw, 1965:150–151). Thus it is that we are always preparing for yesterday, believing it is tomorrow.

   c.   Social class and caste.   Studies of social stratification have substantiated social class or status groupings in most communities. Hollingshead's *Elmtown's Youth* is among the most ingenious of these studies and has been a fountainhead for other community studies. Differentiating characteristics found by researchers are income, life-style, and access to services. The recent history of the United States indicates a widening gap in in-

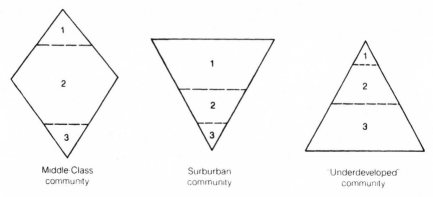

Middle-Class   Surburban   "Underdeveloped"
community   community   community

Figure 4.2. Diagrams of class structure (1: higher, 2: middle, 3: lower socioeconomic class).

come (and presumably in social class): "wealth in the United States is
even more concentrated than income. . . . [T]he richest 1 percent of households held 36 percent of the nation's wealth in 1989, and . . . this percent-
age had increased phenomenally by some 70 percent over a six-year
period" (Gus Hall, quoted in Rothman, Erlich, and Tropman, 1995:7).

As noted in Chapter 3, communities differ in their cultures. Diagrams
of class structure (or, more usually, socioeconomic status) vary from a
diamond-shaped structure, with most persons in the middle class, to an
extreme pyramidal structure, with either very few poor in some wealthy
suburban communities or very few wealthy in some Appalachian communities (see Figure 4.2).

Another differentiation between communities may be that of *caste.*
Most would deny that caste exists in the United States. If it is defined as
an impermeable boundary, a status assigned by virtue of some characteristic beyond a person's control (e.g., skin color, gender, national origin,
or age), it may be an accurate description for the status of some Latinos,
Asian-Americans, African-Americans, and American Indians.

d. Social networks. We have placed this discussion of social networks
between the sections on structural aspects and behavioral aspects of community systems because in reality it is difficult to describe social networks
(see Vaux, 1988:especially pp. 11–15).

> Conceptually, social network analysis entails no cultural or psychological
> prejudgments beyond the minimal ones that there are individuals who have
> repeated contact with each other, and that there is some cumulative nature
> to these contacts. . . . The distributions of these links around an individual
> or within a population then constitute the networks of social linkages.
> (Salzinger, Antrobus, and Hammer, 1988:3)

Some theorists maintain that neighborhoods (and by implication, communities in general) are simply social networks that have a base in a particular locality. Opposing theorists maintain that neighborhoods are not synonymous with social networks and have different dynamics. The opposing positions are similar to the distinctions between place and non-place communities—that is, must a community (or a social network) be based in a particular location? One test of the answer is whether computer "bulletin boards" or networks through which people exchange information can be considered real networks; the important criteria being the significance the exchanges have to the participants, the breadth of the content of the messages (especially whether content is personal), and duration of the relationship.

Social networks have become popular as a vehicle for "consciousness raising" among disadvantaged populations such as women, gays and lesbians, and racial or ethnic minorities. Such networks emphasize awareness of commonality among the members and often stimulate awareness of their disadvantaged status and the societal dynamics that underlie it. Further, the network provides support (the networks are often called "support groups") to members that consists of both emotional support and suggestions for immediate action. Support groups for rape and assault victims, and feminist groups in general fit this description. The more organized the groups become and the more specific their goals (e.g., the National Organization for Women), the less they resemble networks and the more they become formal organizations. Probably most movements, including civil rights, antidraft, antinuclear, antiwar, and right-to-life, can be defined as networks rather than organizations. This is true even though many are large and connected (though perhaps loosely) with formal organizations that share particular instrumental, limited goals of the movement.

In addition to social causes, networking can be a means of career development:

> Networking is just another name for making friends. It's contacts building contacts. It's getting yourself known and getting to know people in your field. Networking is exchanging information, exchanging contacts, and exchanging resources. It helps you create your own accidents. (Juario, 1989:7)

Networks can be highly useful to human service professionals who want to secure support for a client or patient. The client may need support, enlightenment, and guidance for specific action and may accept it best from a group whose members are in similar situations. Alcoholics Anonymous (AA) is probably the most successful of these social networks. Social networks often cross economic and social lines in their common identification as victims, or people with problems. For the environment, they function as agents of change and, for their members, as "escape valves" and nurturing environments.

Networks have infiltrated therapeutic services more directly. Vaux examined the efficacy of "network therapy":

> the goal of network therapy is to reestablish the individual's network as a functioning unit, in order to enhance closeness, supportiveness, and the helpfulness of members to one another and to the disordered individual. . . . These goals are achieved through convening the network, connecting members, and shifting responsibility and control to the network. Network therapy is a time-limited, goal-oriented approach that focuses on mobilizing the network as a collaborative support system in times of crisis. (Vaux, 1988:278)

3. *Behavioral Aspects.*   We will discuss the three central aspects: *social control, socialization, and communication.*

a. *Social control.*   The overall purpose of social control is to maintain the system, not necessarily to maintain the status quo. Social control may be exerted by the entire community through its network of values and goals, which are embodied in one or several of its institutions. These institutions may act on behalf of the entire community or they may, as sometimes happens, act on behalf of some group or special interest. For example, neighborhoods with relatively high concentrations of ethnic or racial minorities (particularly African-American) frequently charge that police do not act in their behalf to protect their property or lives but protect only white businesses and white property owners. The "web of urban institutions" that operates to enforce racial discrimination has been convincingly described and analyzed (Knowles and Prewitt, 1969).

In nonplace communities, social control may be exerted by formal or informal sanctions. In a professional community such as nursing or teaching, sanctions may include temporary loss of license or a public notice that the employer is sanctioned, which means that no member of the profession should work for that employer.

Overlapping memberships of community members can mitigate social control. Power structure and decision-making studies have revealed that some persons in the communities hold interlocking positions: The same family may be represented on the public library board, the planning and zoning commission, the board of directors of a bank, and also may operate a large business. Such overlapping memberships may lessen the effect of centralized social control or may aggrandize it. The Lynds' *Middletown* study indicated that whatever the formal arrangements might have been, the commercial leaders of the community exerted a great deal of social control; Caplow and his associates (1982) found that this continued to be true fifty years later. The same has been found in most communities that have been studied.

A related aspect of community, and one that has received increasing attention during the past thirty years, is that of "community power." A "social Darwinist" description would recognize that persons simply represent their interests and form subsystems; that communities are an ecology of such subsystems that cooperate or compete as the occasion arises; that power is not distributed evenly among these subsystems, which rise and fade. If they continue, they must represent interests that endure.

The classic and most frequently imitated study is Hunter's *Community Power Structure* (1953) in Atlanta. He found that the most powerful persons in the community were heads of large commercial enterprises, especially banking and finance; and that other leadership was composed of professional men and a few representatives of government and labor. Hunter found that within the group of those who were powerful, a relatively small number were policymakers, or the "power elite" of the community.

The dispute continues between "elite" theorists and "pluralist" theorists as to whether there is any single, dominant power group. In part, the question is one of identifying the focal system since some theorists focused on the local community and others on the national, societal system. Domhoff attempts to tie the two together with results that have been criticized with regard to methodology; nonetheless, his conclusions are intriguing. Domhoff and Dye (1987) summarize the three methods by which the networks of community power structures can be constructed—the positional, the reputational, and the decisional. Together, these can be viewed as "naturalistic," or "ethnographic" methods (Lincoln and Guba, 1985:7).

A Positional analysis uses printed public information available in libraries and other archives to establish the leadership interlocks among profit, nonprofit, and governmental agencies as well as to trace the flows of money, information, and other resources among the same organizations.

A Reputational study, in contrast to the positional method, is based upon the personal opinions of a wide range of people who are interviewed about who the key people and organizations in the power structure are. This method was developed by Hunter, who later characterized it briefly by saying it was equivalent to arriving in a previously unknown tribal society and asking the natives to take you to their leaders.

A Decisional mapping of a power structure is based on case studies of the people, organizations, and pressure groups that become involved in trying to influence the outcome of specific policy initiatives in a range of issue-areas. In effect all three methods generate a list of people and their connections to each other and to organizations and issues. (Domhoff and Dye, 1987:9–12)

Community researchers have described models of decision-making that range from the bureaucratic, pyramid model in which decisions were made "at the top," to "mutual adaptation" models in which decisions were made by consensus in a participatory, decentralized fashion. These two models are related, of course, to the argument between "elite" and "pluralist" theorists. In these decision-making studies, it was found that the political subsystems played important, but not necessarily dominant roles. Instead, decisions were made by informal or private subsystems differentiated by social class, organizational position, or the kind of institution being represented. The informal decision-making structure was often as influential, or more so, than the formal (including political) structures.

b. Socialization. Socialization is essential to the life of a community. If new members are not socialized into the community to supply new energy (*negentropy*), it becomes entropic. Enculturating the newcomer is often a community concern. Some communities have attempted to socialize deviant subcommunities that reject established community values, specifically norms of productivity, health, and dress. In the face of such deviations, communities attempt to apply social control in the form of jail sentences, compulsory socialization (e.g., enforcing truancy laws or mandatory work programs for welfare recipients), or expulsion. Expulsion took the form of "warning out" as early as the sixteenth century in England and was perpetuated in the United States. Persons likely to become recipients of public assistance were told to leave the county. In 1950, one of the authors was "warned out" of a county in a western state for being in a condition of limited means. The practice continued until recent times; one of the authors found people who had previously been warned out when he took over a caseload in 1960.

New institutions arise to perform new functions, just as public schools were created to socialize millions of European immigrants and Project Headstart was intended to socialize racial minorities. In Vancouver, British Columbia, e.g., new organizations, funded by the Canadian government, were created to socialize immigrants, particularly refugees, who entered the society and who now constitute significant minority populations in Canada's largest cities. Their presence has added to a rich diversity of the Canadian population.

There are less formal means of socialization: parades and Fourth of July or Victoria Day celebrations socialize citizens into wider patriotic values. Formal ceremonies may mark induction to the community: the Jewish Bar or Bat Mitzvah, Christian baptism, freshman hazing, the "capping" ceremony for new nurses, the "hooding" of new Ph.D.s and naturalization ceremonies are examples. Such rites of passage symbolize the socialization of a person into a new status within the system. Another example is drumming and singing in Ojibway (Anishinabe) culture:

A small boy may grow up standing at the edge of the drum circle. A circle of three or more intense, somber, sweating men. . . . There are times, in the afternoon or early in the evening, when a young boy may be permitted to kneel between the men and beat on the metal edge of the drum with a stick. Then one day when it is time, he will have the courage and the confidence to drum on the white surface, straighten his body, lean forward, and make the sound. It is time to become a man. (Brill, 1974:82)

Social networks can be highly significant in socialization in organizations and communities. Newcomers usually find that the most important task is to join a social network that reliably describes the norms, mores, and sanctions of the system. Everyone who has entered a new school, new job, or new community, or who has changed status within a system can probably remember the process of finding such a network (or failing to find one).

As noted earlier in this chapter, networks function primarily as sources of information and as efficient distributors of information. Nonmembers of networks have less information than members of the network about matters that are equally important to both. Networks are typically more fluid and have fewer fixed roles than groups, organizations, or communities; thus, it is easier to fit into a network and both to give and get energy (in the form of information). Networks often serve as "welcome wagons," assisting newcomers to find niches for themselves in new systems and to learn the "lay of the land." Frequently, information exchange is the primary (or sole) reason for the existence of a network, and network members abandon the group, or disband it, when their needs for information are more adequately met in the new system they have joined. Networks are less demanding than organizations or institutions, since they are partial and cannot offer either a full set of societal roles or complete roles. As illustrated in Chapter 6, "Groups," centrality in the flow of information is often synonymous with leadership roles; thus networks are often the "farm teams" or "out-of-town tryouts" for more established systems. On occasion, a network functions as the embryo of a developing system in which network participants are the charter members. This has been the pattern for organizations that socialize, develop, and induct women into leadership roles in their communities, e.g., Junior League, university women's clubs, women's health clinics, and Children's Defense Fund. United Way is a common training ground for the socialization of community leaders of both genders. The Masonic Lodge and the Knights of Columbus also perform such functions for their members and communities.

   c. *Communication.* Communication is a highly important aspect of community system behavior in communities. Certainly, institutions such as churches, businesses, and schools carry on some communication, but

both inside and outside these institutions, the most frequent and significant communications activities occur between persons face-to-face and
through public media such as newspapers, television, and radio. In early
British, United States, and some Sioux (Dakota and Lakota) communities,
this function was performed by the town crier or its equivalent. Bill-
boards, soapboxes, loudspeakers, sirens, pamphlets, and classified adver-
tisements are all means of communication used and controlled by
segments of the community to impart symbols of the community's way of
life. In contrast, bumper stickers, T-shirts, stylized hand movements by
gang members, and modular telephones in automobiles tend to be communication devices used for individual expression.

"The essence of community," as John Dewey suggested, "is communication, for without communication there cannot be that interaction by
which common meanings, common life, and common values are established" (quoted in Ross, 1955). In that communication is one form of
energy exchange, it is a vital process, and cannot occur if components are
isolated or are unable to interact. The result would be entropy or
disintegration.

Social networks, discussed earlier, have communication as their major
function. They have both *instrumental* (goal-oriented) and *affective* (emotional) functions, but networks perform primarily as conveyors of information, rather than suppliers of material needs, or intermediary systems
that negotiate survival. That is, social networks identify groups, families,
neighborhoods, or even communities within which primary needs can be
met; but the networks themselves do not meet the needs. However, to the
extent that a network evolves a culture in which members meet each
others' needs (e.g., a women's group in which members become "family"
to each other), it may *become* a system, better identified as a group, organization, or (in the sense we use it later) family. This distinction may seem
petty, but it is necessary to clarify focal systems and whether or not
something is a system. In this respect, a network may be seen as an
interlocking set of roles with relatively specific functions, compared to
groups or communities that are broader in their functions. In other words,
social networks resemble groups and communities in some respects while
resembling organizations in other respects.

C. Professions as Nonplace Communities

An established profession claims for itself, and is recognized by society
as having, responsibility for a symbolic territory or domain. Almost by
definition, when a group carves out for itself a societal function or some
part of the society's stock of ideas, it becomes established as a profession.
When the societal function of instructing the young was delegated to and
assumed by teachers, the next logical step was the formation and protec-

tion of territory by professional teachers' organizations. The same is true of medicine, law, and the clergy, the three so-called classic professions. It can be said as well of the newer, developing professions of law enforcement, nursing, engineering, and social work.

The major commonality among the professions is that they are formally legitimated by society to bring about change that is beneficial to the society and its components, as well as to maintain the society. Despite their seeming conservatism on occasion, professions do promote change as well as maintenance. If a profession refused to allow change, that could be harmful to a society and could signal that the profession will lose its societal sanction. An example might be a refusal by physicians to accept changes in the provision of care to elderly or the poor, to defend their incomes; or a refusal of college professors to accept public accountability through evaluation of their students' performances.

Professional licensure symbolizes societal acceptance and sanction for a professional territory: "Each profession has a specific or core function and in a sense holds a monopoly on this function. . . . However each profession shares with all other professions in society what Hiltner has called a village green, a common area that is peripheral to each profession" (Boehm, 1965:642). Clearly, social work, nursing, psychiatry, education and law enforcement, among other professions, share a "village green" that is socialization and social control.

Historically, social work has concerned itself more with change among microsystems (persons, families, and small groups) than with change among macrosystems (organizations, communities, and society). But it has dealt with societal and community change as well, although these have also been the domains of other professional groups such as political scientists and sociologists. Social work has enlarged its territorial claims in the past half-century, and boundary disputes between professions within the same institution are common. Examples are social work and law within the juvenile court, social work and psychology in mental health institutions, and social work and educators in the schools. There are boundary disputes between home economists and family counselors, between nurses and physicians' assistants, and between teachers, guidance counselors, and school psychologists.

There are other characteristics of community that distinguish a profession: a common system of values and ethics (way of life, or culture); a group identity that holds the allegiance of the members, and social control and socialization within the profession. All of these characterize professions as nonplace communities. However, in practice, professions sometimes fail to meet all of these criteria (e.g., group identity or common values). The most accurate way to define a profession may well be to define it as a social network, that is, a set of interlocking roles organized for relatively specific goals that are set within expressly stated, idealized goals of "service to society" and the sanctity of the persons being served. Professions are organized for specific purposes, with limited bonds between members, and largely dependent upon affiliations between a limited number of members who are loosely connected to some larger system (looser, presumably, than their connections to family or friends). Professions often lack a sense of "community" that is sufficient to mobilize their members to joint action, and usually resemble organizations as much as communities. Some professions exercise a significant degree of social control typical of organizations, with power to disbar or "defrock" practitioners; but do so only rarely. Most professions have relatively weak powers of enforcement.

III. THE COMMUNITY IN CRITICAL CONDITION

The community is the subject for sharp (and productive) debate, and the outcome of the debate is crucial for community theory. It can be viewed in systems terms as a systems crisis, with two fundamental systems questions to be answered: (1) What is the focal system: the society, the community, the family, or the person? (2) What should be the relationships of subsystems to the community; what should be the balance among them?

There is, of course, general agreement that communities in the United States are threatened, and many are in decline, or defunct: "Gloomy tendencies toward social entropy are all too visible in wide areas of American life today" (Sullivan, 1995:180). Observers blame many factors. Robert Putnam and his associates studied local communities in Italy; they found that the communities that thrive are "civic" communities, with strong traditions of citizen participation, with vital subsystems in which residents are deeply involved, including choral groups. In "The Strange Disappearance of Civic America" Putnam isolated the factor most responsible for the decline of community:

> The culprit is television. . . . Most studies estimate that the average American now watches roughly four hours per day (excluding periods in which television is merely playing in the background). . . . Controlling for education, income, age, race, place of residence, work status, and gender, TV viewing is strongly and negatively related to social trust and group membership, whereas the same correlations with newspaper reading are positive. Within every educational category, heavy readers are avid joiners, whereas heavy viewers are more likely to be loners. In fact, more detailed analysis suggests that heavy TV watching is one important reason *why* less educated people are less engaged in the life of their communities. (Putnam, 1996:46–47)

Putnam believes that we should "consider how technology is privatizing our lives . . . to ask whether we like the result, and if not, what we might do about it. Those are questions we should, of course, be asking together, not alone" (Putnam, 1996:48; see also Putnam, 1995).

One ideological solution to the problem is offered by *communitarianism*, a philosophy of community that stresses the "social compact" or "social contract" between persons and the society, and the mutual obligations that community members have to each other. "Communitarians think of themselves as searching for solutions that go beyond both the market and the state" (Wolfe, 1995:128). Communitarianism attempts to avoid the extreme individualism and lack of social obligation of classic liberalism and, at the same time, to avoid some of the oppressive features of community.

The communitarian viewpoint is attractive, in that it reestablishes community as the focal system in the effort to bring a sense of belonging to the atomized society of the United States, and to emphasize mutual obligation among its citizens. However, there are three counterpoints to the communitarian conception. First, there is a preoccupation with self in our society; Bellah, Madsen, Sullivan, Swidler, and Tipton (1985) described individualism as the society's "first language." Lasch (1979) labeled ours a "culture of narcissism." Lichterman described "personalism" as seeking "self-fulfillment and individualized expression, 'growth' in personal development rather than growth in purely material well-being. . . . The self lives with ambivalence towards, and often in tension with, the institutional or communal standards around it" (Lichterman, 1996:6).

A feminist critique (Weiss, 1995) maintains that this personalist or individualistic conception is directly at odds with women's experience, which is more commonly characterized by connection to multiple systems and caring, as described in the writings of psychologist Carol Gilligan (1982) and others.

Second, a feminist critique says that the community espoused by communitarians overlooks the presence of disadvantaged groups, and the effects that recognition of these groups would have on the definition and behavior of communities. Gays and lesbians, for example, often suffer community disapproval (Bawer, 1996; Bull, 1994).

[C]ommunitarians fail to note that the separated self of liberalism reflects the reality of men more than women [and] may also be more reflective in many Western cultures of those who are white and / or heterosexual than of those who are Black and / or homosexual . . . feminists not only recognize a broader range of social forces that influence identities than do communitarians, but they also find that these forces have a deeper impact than is generally acknowledged by communitarians. . . . [F]eminists stress how social context affects everything from personal characteristics, emotions, beliefs, capacities, and motives to human nature itself. (Weiss, 1995:166–167)

Further, according to this critique, the communitarian conception of community neglects the family in its various forms, and in doing so, implies that the heterosexual, patriarchal family is the norm (Weiss, 1995:174). At the same time, children are absent from the census of this community; this is a critical omission, from a feminist viewpoint. They want a redefinition of community that recognizes women's lives and their concerns, including their children, as "public" and not merely "private" issues. One way to put this is that women want a place at the conference table, not just the kitchen table.

A third counterpoint is, "There's little that anybody could find fault with [in communitarianism's] basic theme of social responsibility. Its weakness lies not in its intentions, but in its misreading of what is going on in the world. . . . [N]o amount of moral exhortation can recreate the idealized existence in intimate and familiar connection to a single town or neighborhood" (Anderson, 1995). Most Americans are "multilocality," relating to two or more geographic communities: the city in which one works, and the suburb or ghetto in which one lives, e.g.; or the community in which one lives with a new partner and children, and the community in which one's older children and former partner live.

The Internet has become a "virtual community" for some computer users via "chat rooms" as well as one-to-one simultaneous or "time-shifted" conversations. This pseudointimacy sometimes blossoms into face-to-face friendship—or its opposite; there is also the danger to children who are contacted by predators. The "Net" is a powerful tool for activists of all political and ideological persuasions: conservative groups mobilize thousands of messages to Congress overnight. A longtime community activist says:

> It's about being able to keep track of government programs and pending legislation. . . . It's about emailing a message to a Congressperson on Tuesday and getting a response by Wednesday afternoon. It's about creating networks among organizers in their own neighborhoods and communities who go online to maintain contact with each other even when they're not in a position to meet (E. Schwartz, 1996:176).

CONCLUSION

A community

1. is a system intermediate between society and "Microsystems;"
2. has a consciously identified population characterized by a sense of belonging, that is, it is aware of itself and is part of its members' identities;
3. is organized and engaged in common pursuits;
4. has differentiation of functions;

5. adapts to the environment through energy exchange; and
6. creates and maintains organizations and institutions to fulfill the
needs of both subsystems and suprasystems.

To find or keep a place for themselves in a "postmodern world," persons and groups of persons seek to create or maintain communities in many ways, including the use of electronic media. The following perceptive comments appeared in a local newspaper:

> All these developments create a confusion of new connections, new identifications. . . . In an era when communication is no longer rooted in place, sermonizing about voting or serving on juries offers no solution. The real question is how to develop and sustain lasting ties in the absence of proximity, how to find intimacy in a world where borders no longer exist. (Anderson, 1995)

SUGGESTED READINGS

Fellin, Phillip.
    1995   *The Community and the Social Worker,* second edition. Itasca, IL: Peacock
    The author uses a systems approach to analyze community and to describe processes within it. The book could be used as a "large-scale" text for this chapter.
Flora, Cornelia Butler, and Jan. L. Flora.
    1996   "Creating Social Capital." In *Rooted in the Land,* edited by William Vitek and Wes Jackson. New Haven: Yale University Press.
    Excellent discussion of the concept of social capital and the necessity of meeting human needs in social systems.
Fowler, Robert Booth.
    1991   *The Dance with Community.* Lawrence: University Press of Kansas.
    Fowler identifies the crucial elements of the debates regarding community: feminist, communitarian, new age thinking, and contemporary Christian ideology. He identifies with existentialism: Community is "a calling, a struggle, a journey."
Hardcastle, David A., Stanley Wenocur, and Patricia R. Powers.
    1997   *Community Practice: Theories and Skills for Social Workers.* New York: Oxford University Press.
    This is a masterwork, all 450 pages. If it isn't here, you probably don't need to know it. Chapter 5 on documenting the life of a community and Chapter 10 on using networks are exceptional. Their "Field Force Analysis" of community is highly useful.
Putnam, Robert.
    1996   "The Strange Disappearance of Civic America." *American Prospect,* Winter.
    Putnam identifies the sources of the decline of community. His is currently among the most cogent thought regarding recovery of community.

Selznick, Philip.
   1996   "In Search of Community." In *Rooted in the Land,* edited by William
   Vitek and Wes Jackson. New Haven, CT: Yale University Press.
      Selznick, along with Robert Putnam, is an indispensable resource regarding
      the current state of community and what may reverse its decline.
Vaux, Alan.
   1988.   *Social Support: Theory, Research, and Intervention.* New York: Praeger.
      An exhaustive review of the theory and literature of social support. The
      conclusion is that social support is an ecological (systemic) process. Social
      networks are examined as a specific form of social support.

LITERARY SOURCES

Keillor, Garrison.
   1985.   *Lake Wobegon Days.* New York: Viking.
      Created in the fertile mind of one of the nation's finest humorists, this
      fictional community portrays "Midwestern," small-town values, subtly and
      sometimes hilariously. The community is a vehicle for social criticism and
      subtle observations about contemporary America.
Lee, Harper.
   1960.   *To Kill a Mockingbird.* Philadelphia: Lippincott.
      Now nearly forty years old, the novel is truly an "American classic." The
      interwoven strands of community are seen through the eyes of a young girl.
      Secrets that bind the townspeople together are gradually revealed. The rigid
      rules of racism in the southern town were well portrayed. The movie is
      powerful, but omits the subtler aspects of community.

FILMS AND VIDEOS

The Amish: Not to be Modern (1985)
   Rare film of a community that separates itself from the world. Photographed
   over four seasons, capturing the daily life of people who preserve rural tradi-
   tions. Narrated by Amish themselves, with four-hundred-year old Amish
   hymns, handed down orally, as soundtrack.
High School (1968) and *High School II* (1994)
   Frederick Wiseman's documentaries are always profound and provocative.
   These two, a generation apart, are revealing studies of community through one
   of its institutions.
The Hutterites: To Care and Not to Care (1984)
   The Hutterites have preserved a completely communal life-style for nearly five
   centuries. While they live simply, they employ modern technology such as
   computers, but not for personal comfort.
The Last Picture Show (1971)
   Set in a small Texas town in the 1950s, it is very well acted. The lives of the
   residents are interwoven in ways that only gradually reveal themselves. Bit-

tersweet and poignant. The demise of the movie theater is a metaphor for the loss of a *gemeinschaft* way of life in small towns.

Matewan (1988)

A union organizer enters a mining community. His methods are a case study of organizing tactics. Portrays elements of community and conflict.

The Milagro Beanfield War (1988)

Rituals and binding ties in a Mexican-American community are well portrayed in this film, based on the novel. Cultural pride and vitality sustain them in their battle with the large landowners who control the water supply.

Organizations

Given the expectation that organizations will take a relatively narrow band of interests and pursue them unremittingly, our reluctance to enshrine organizations as the social and moral centers of the new society may seem more intelligible.
—Scott Adams, *The Dilbert Principle*

So pervasive is the power of the institutions that we have created that they shape not only our preferences, but actually our sense of possibilities.
—David B. Schwartz, *Who Cares? Rediscovering Community*

INTRODUCTION

Modern societies are organizational societies. Human service professionals have been slow to recognize and take this into account in their appraisals of human behavior. We notice the effects that the organizations that employ us have on our practice and our own lives, but tend to overlook the influence that organizations have on the persons we serve. Organizations constitute the fabric that connects the person and the society and have, to a significant degree, replaced communities and families as mediating (or intermediary) institutions in society. Social systems theory enables the reader to appraise and evaluate the influences that organizations have on human behavior (see Oshry, 1995).

The nature of organizations has been insufficiently understood, and even the most knowledgeable organization theorists readily admit that there is no single definitive theory. However, Scott (1998) reviewed current theories of organizations, and concluded that there has been substantial change in recent years:

> Early research on organizations was conducted almost exclusively at the social-psychological level. The structural level of analysis became prominent in the 1960s and continues to be heavily utilized by sociologists. The ecological [systems] level was the last to develop, emerging in the late 1960s, but it is this level that is associated with much of the intellectual excitement and energy that have characterized the field during the past three decades. (Scott, 1998:16)

We begin with a workable definition of organization. The sociologist Talcott Parsons's statement is clearer than most:

> Organizations are social units (or human groups) deliberately constructed to seek specific goals. Corporations, armies, schools, hospital, churches, and prisons are included; tribes, classes, ethnic groups, friendship groups, and families are excluded. Organizations are characterized by: (1) divisions of labor, power, and communications responsibilities . . . ; (2) the presence of one or more power centers which control the concerted efforts of the organization and direct them toward its goals . . . ; [and] (3) substitution of personnel. (Parsons, 1960:17)

Each of the characteristics Parsons cited is true to some degree of societies and communities as well. The differences between these systems "levels" are not in the presence or absence of these characteristics but rather the degree to which they are present, and the form they take. Consistent with Parsons's view, the characteristics we discuss in Section II of this chapter are goals, differentiation, power, control, leadership, and communication.

Sociologist C. Wright Mills defined an organization as "a system of roles graded by authority" (cited in Presthus, 1962:4). Members of organizations are not expected to exhibit their full range of behaviors, but only those that are necessary or useful to the purposes of the organization, that is, goal achievement. In other words, persons are to perform according to their assigned roles, not according to their personal wishes. These roles must be *coordinated* so that they can combine to achieve the system's goals. They must be *differentiated, hierarchical* (in power, or sequence, or both), and have some functions taking priority over others, although the ranking in the hierarchy can change from one occasion to another.

Taken together, Parsons's and Mills's definitions form a relatively complete description of organizations that includes the following elements: (1) an organization is a social system whose purpose is the achievement of specific, explicit goals. In order to accomplish this, its members must (2) confine themselves to a relatively narrow range of behaviors intended to fulfill this purpose. The members (3) exercise power over each other in the form of authority and hierarchical control, to (4) assure compliance with the system's goals and adherence to the members' prescribed roles.

I. THEORIES OF ORGANIZATION

There are three major types of organization theory, to which we add a fourth—systems—in the next major section. The typology that we used in the previous edition of this book has been modified, in part due to Scott's (1998) analysis. We combined the "classical model" of organizations and the "decision-making" model under the heading of "rational systems," since they share a general orientation. We hope that anyone familiar with our previous editions would agree that this is theoretically justifiable.

The order of presentation here is deliberate; in our view there is a continuum, if not a progression or sequence, that runs from the abstract principles that underlie the *rational systems perspective* through the more complex *natural systems perspective,* in which the organization is personalized, to the *open systems perspective,* which embraces complexity. The latter stresses intensity and mutuality of the organization's relationship to its turbulent environment while it also incorporates the main aspects of the other two perspectives. Another way to state this is that in the rational systems perspective, the organization itself was the focal system; in the natural systems perspective, the components (members) were the focal system(s), and in the open systems perspective, both of the other perspectives are taken, along with the organization's relationship with the environment: it is *holonistic.* That is, the difference between the perspectives is the *level* of the focal system: the open systems view allows the analyst to shift the level of analysis from one focal system to another. A third way to state the differences is that the first perspective treated the organization as a relatively closed system; the second treated the organization as having permeable interior boundaries (internal openness); and the third treats the organization as open to both components and environment.

Section I of this chapter presents an overview of kinds of theories of organizations: (A) the rational systems perspective and (B) the natural systems perspective, followed by a section in which we discuss the present bureaucratic situation. Section II comprises our presentation of the third kind of organizational theory, the open systems perspective.

A.   Rational Systems Perspective

Scott's definition of this rational systems perspective is: "Organizations are collectivities oriented to the pursuit of relatively specific goals and exhibiting relatively highly formalized social structures" (Scott, 1998:26). Both models discussed under this heading share these characteristics. One difference is that the classical model focused on the *structure* in which decisions and actions were taken, while decision theory focused on the *goals* being sought within the structure. The two are interlaced: they are warp and woof of the fabric that is an organization, two dimensions of the same entity. Another difference is that the classical view aimed at complete rationality, while decision theory is realistic enough to recognize the impossibility of complete rationality, and aims for maximum feasible rationality at a given time, regarding a given decision, and within a given set of circumstances. Nonetheless, the general perspective is the same: organizations operate with rationality as their prime directive, and strenuous effort should be made to achieve it.

1.   The Classical Model.   The classical model is sometimes called the "machine theory" because the organization was viewed as a machine with interchangeable parts and clearly identifiable operations, and members were treated as cogs and gears in that machine. The emphasis was on mechanical regulation, control, and rationality, which are characteristics of this model. Principles of this formal organization include (1) *division of labor,* with each unit performing certain tasks; (2) *pyramid of control,* with each unit subordinate to one above it in the hierarchy; and (3) *unity of command,* that is, centralized control emanating from the top of the pyramid (see Figure 5.1). We will discuss this model further in Section I,C, The Bureaucratic Situation.

This has been the most visible model, from the Roman army to the modem bureaucracy. The fact that this form of organization (e.g., the Roman Catholic church) has survived thousands of years indicates how effective it can be at achieving goals and ensuring compliance. However much we denigrate "bureaucracy," in fact it freed societies from traditional

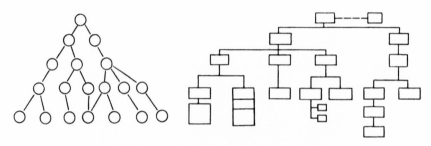

Figure 5.1.   Diagrams of the classical model.

patriarchal, autocratic rule; bureaucracies (ideally) embodied just rules, based on merit, administered impartially. Henry Ford based his assembly line on the rationality of this model. Social historian Lewis Mumford said that organizations arise from the human need to create regularity in the world (see the discussion in Chapter 3, Section II,E, The Human Urge to Explain the World):

> Behind every later process of organization and mechanization one must . . . recognize primordial attitudes, deeply ingrained in the human organism— indeed, shared with many other species—for ritualizing behavior and finding satisfaction in a repetitive order that establishes a human connection with organic rhythms and cosmic event. Organization Man is the common link between the ancient and modern type of megamachine: that is perhaps why the specialized functionaries, with their supporting layer of slaves, conscripts, and subjects—in short, the controllers and the controlled—have changed so little in the last five thousand years. (Mumford, 1970:277)

This probably explains the inscription on the Great Pyramid of Egypt, presumably scratched by one of the original workmen, which (translated) says, "Khufu is a drunk."

2. *Decision Theory.* Decision theory is concerned with the achievement of rational decision-making *whenever possible.* This theory recognizes that there is, in addition to the horizontal differentiation by task, a vertical hierarchy or differentiation by "levels of decisions" that are made. This differentiation is made on the basis of *power* (i.e., whose decisions are binding upon whom), and distinguishes between policymaking and policy implementation. In this theory, power consists of access to, and control of, information that is sufficient to formulate policy, and the ability to get others to carry out the actions necessary to implement the policy. Perhaps most important is the qualification "whenever possible."

This theory holds that human behavior in organizations is best described as "intendedly rational" (Simon, 1945:196). It recognizes the nonrational aspects of decision-making in organizations. It also emphasizes "search behavior," the concept that an organization does not seek endlessly for perfectly rational behavior but instead seeks satisfying (sometimes called "satisficing") solutions that are "reasonably good" or "acceptable" (Etzioni, 1964:30–31). If tension or conflict between components and the organization cannot be completely resolved to everyone's satisfaction (and it rarely is), the organization may need to find another solution. The solution may be to coerce members into agreement, or to modify the organization's behavior, to accommodate the difference, in order to arrive at a compromise that does not fully satisfy anyone, but permits continued movement toward a mutual goal.

Decision theory recognizes the inevitability of tension and conflict; it states that tension and conflict occur not only over personal factors but also over organizational issues. That is, conflict is sometimes nonrational, but it is often rational and concerned with decision-making. Further, decision theory recognizes a necessity for organizational differentiation in order to make decisions and accomplish tasks. Differentiation need not lead to a fixed hierarchy, since organizational structure, leadership, and decision-making can change according to task.

B. Natural Systems Perspective: Human Relations Theory and Conflict Theory

Rational systems theorists emphasize the normative structure and so focus on decision—designs or proposals for action—as if they were the principal outcomes. Natural systems theorists stress the behavioral structure and are more interested in examining what is done rather than what is decided or planned. Commitment and motivation loom as more salient variables. (Scott, 1998:58)

Scott identifies two varieties of natural systems theory: *social consensus,* "a view of collectivities as composed of individuals sharing primarily common objectives," exemplified by *human relations* theory; and *social conflict,* which "views social order as resulting from the suppression of some interests by others. Order results not from consensus, but from coercion, the dominance of weaker by more powerful groups" (ibid.).

1. Human Relations Theory.   Human relations theory arose in reaction to "machine" theory. It is exemplified by Elton Mayo, Kurt Lewin, and, indirectly, the philosopher John Dewey. It stressed the *informal* structure and the emotional, nonrational motivations that operate in organizations. It emphasized such processes as communication, participation, and leadership. Japanese organizations' motivational programs for workers, such as saluting the company flag, singing the company song, and other means of encouraging a corporate spirit and corporate identification, are variations of human relations theory. They increase productivity and decrease alienation through greater participation and involvement in corporate by workers. Another means used by some American corporations to encourage a sense of participation is employee stock option plans (ESOPs), which supposedly permit employees to see themselves as owners.

The best known studies issuing from human relations theory were the Hawthorne studies, including the Bank Wiring Room study (Mayo, 1945; Olmsted, [1959] 1978; Roethlisberger and Dickson, 1947). The results of these studies showed conclusively that the classical theory was inadequate to explain behavior in organizations. Clearly, other factors besides rational, impersonal calculation determined the workers' production.

These studies found that the highest motivation for one group of workers was neither money nor working conditions but rather what is now known as the "Hawthorne effect"—the fact that they were a special group being researched! The general conclusion that sets this theory apart from the machine model is that workers do not function as separate, distinct units organized in linear chains, but rather as members of groups to whose norms they adhere. The influence of the small group became readily apparent.

Adaptations of human relations theory included Maslow's "hierarchy of needs" to explain motivation and behavior in organizations (Maslow, 1968). In this view, needs are hierarchical, with "safety" needs (adequate food and physical protection, e.g.) and "security" needs (medical care, income assurances in case of illness, e.g.) being fundamental; psychoanalyst Karen Horney had earlier anticipated this description of needs. If these needs are filled, a person progresses to fulfill "higher" wants/ needs: "social" needs including contact with others and membership in groups; "esteem" needs for positive regard by others, and one's own positive feelings about self. If all other needs are satisfied, a person then progresses to the "highest" need, which is *self-actualization*, the fulfillment of one's potential as an individual (ibid.).

Scott places human relations theory within the "natural systems perspective," in which the "goals pursued become more complex, diffuse, differentiated, and subject to change; participants are viewed as motivated by their own interests and as seeking to impose these on the organization" (Scott, 1998:26). His definition of an organization from this perspective is:

> Organizations are collectives whose participants are pursuing multiple interests, both disparate and common, but recognize the value of perpetuating the organization as an important resource. The informal structure of relations that develops among participants provides a more informative and accurate guide to understanding organizational behavior than the formal. (ibid.)

2. Conflict Theory. Conflict theorists, who include Karl Marx and Max Weber, represent in some respects a synthesis of theories; they recognized both formal and informal structures, and their interaction, as significant. They agreed with the classical theorists that the attempt to achieve goals through rational, impersonal structure is important; they also recognized a necessity for the organization to meet the human, personal needs of its components. However, conflict theory does not place primary emphasis on the human, emotive factors; instead, this view stresses the importance of the work setting and the influence of the technology that is used, not the human, emotive factors. This gave rise to the study of the "sociotechnical" aspects of industry, the interaction of persons with technology (often called cybernetics). In contrast to the classical, machine theory, conflict theory pictures organizations as open systems; that is, the structure of the organization varies according to the environment and the technology employed.

The major difference from the previous theories is that conflict theory declared that conflict within an organization is inevitable. Etzioni said that conflict theory "sees the organization as a large, complex social unit in which many social groups interact. . . . The various groups might co-operate in some spheres and compete in others, but they hardly are or can become one big happy family as Human Relations writers often imply" (Etzioni, 1964:41). Conflict theory resembles social systems theory because it recognizes the components within the organization and the tension that inevitably exists between components, and between components and the organizational suprasystem. Like systems theory, conflict theory does not view conflict as a "problem," the resolution of which will restore equilibrium. Conflict is an inherent characteristic of organizations; indeed, one administrative or organizational development strategy may be to induce conflict deliberately in order to stimulate change (analogous to the use of paradoxes in psychotherapy, or stimulating patients' awareness of inner conflict through psychoanalysis).

Coser (1964) cited positive effects of conflict—for example, that it may force a confrontation that leads to a test of power and the possibility of significant change. The history of nearly any organization reveals successive tensions and conflicts whose resolution (or nonresolution) contributed to its present condition. Some of these conflicts could be viewed as "healthy" because they restored vitality or resolved issues that had retarded the organization's development. Conflict theory, then, like social systems theory, portrays organizations more realistically than either the classical or the human relations theory alone.

C. The Bureaucratic Situation

Presthus coined the term *bureaucratic situation* to describe the "total environment" provided by large organizations (Presthus, 1962:4). This is the same as Handy's role culture, referred to later; we use it in the same sense, knowing that not all organizations are characterized by what is often derogatorily referred to as "bureaucracy." Bureaucracy is a phenomenon that has its roots in ancient societies, as said earlier. It underwent morphogenesis with the emergence of the modern nation state, and contemporary with industrialization. Its primary theorist was Max Weber, whose major concern was power: the distribution of power, control of power, legitimization and uses of power, and the satisfaction derived from membership in the organization. Weber was clear that organizational structure is intended to permit and regulate the use of power. The principles of bureaucracy are:

1. *division of labor* and specialization of tasks;
2. *hierarchy of position*; each officeholder or employee is supervised by a higher authority;
3. a consistent *system of generalized rules* to assure coordination of tasks and uniform results (that is, effectiveness), through, e.g., a manual of policies and procedures;
4. *impartiality* toward members of the organization as well as those being served, in the conduct of the organization's activity, at all levels;
5. *secure employment* within the organization, based on objective criteria and impartial evaluation;
6. machinelike *efficiency*; and
7. *separation of career and personal life*, so that the organization's control is limited to work-related matters;
8. positions are filled by persons *qualified* by training and / or experience specifically for that position; and
9. transactions are *reported* in a form that can be recorded and properly stored.

These bureaucratic principles are intended to protect the integrity of the offices and the officeholders at all levels; like the feudal contract between lord and vassal, which spelled out mutual obligations, these bureaucratic prescriptions detailed the rules for interactions. Blau said that "authority is strictly circumscribed and confined to those directives that are relevant for official operations. The use of status prerogatives to extend the power of control over subordinates beyond these limits does not constitute the legitimate exercise of bureaucratic authority" (1956:29). It is not so easy to limit the power of one's superiors in bureaucracy, however. We have the examples of Nazi Germany, the Soviet Union, and Watergate to remind us of the potential for abuses of bureaucratic power. In the Watergate, Iran-Contra, and Whitewater investigations during the Nixon, Bush, and Clinton administrations, respectively, bureaucratic power was also employed to prosecute crimes. The bureaucracies of the Justice Department, the Office of the Independent Counsel, the courts, and legislative committees were brought to bear.

Such rationality as is demanded by rules and regulations is, as the human relations school pointed out, unrealistic. There are limits to rationality. The basic commitment to the organization is only partially rational. It inevitably involves emotive factors such as loyalty and sentiments about the worth of the organization and about oneself as part of it. Such commitments, values, and feelings do not originate with the organization.

They must begin in other systems, with the socialization provided by family, school, and community: socialization toward such qualities as reliability, commitment, sacrifice, and the ability to subordinate oneself to larger systems. It is also true that personal integrity and the courage to confront organizational pressures have the same origins.

Many writers have described the effects of bureaucratic organizations on the personalities of their members. Some have suggested a "bureaucratic personality." Etzioni (1964) described the features of this personality: it (1) is accustomed to shifting between social units, especially the family and the organization, (2) has high tolerance for frustration and the ability to defer gratification, and (3) has the urge to achieve material and symbolic rewards (achievement orientation). Etzioni added this note about the relationship between organizations and other social systems:

> The major credit for this convergence of personality and organizational requirements . . . must go to the modern family and the modern educational system, both of which produce the type of person who will make a good organization man [sic]. The middle-class stress on the values of punctuality, neatness, integrity, consistency, the accent on conformity, and above all achievement, are the foundation. . . . The organization's effectiveness . . . is due more to the social environment which provides the "right" kind of participants than to any deliberate efforts by the organization to shape personalities according to its needs. (Etzioni, 1964:110)

An organization rewards the kind of personality that puts the organization's goals above its own. To the extent that the organization can enforce this, it has power over its members. Fromm (1962) and others have shown that this may be unhealthy behavior that encourages alienation because it is manipulative. Presthus warned against "a subtle corrosion of integrity" (1962:18).

Scott (1998) cites feminist criticisms of bureaucracy: that it "feeds the dualism of private-expressive and public-instrumental selves and worlds" (Glennon, 1979) and that "[t]he organizational forms and discourse of bureaucratic capitalism institutionalize modes of domination that recreate the very patterns of oppression that feminism arose to combat" (Ferguson, 1984:203). These critics point to the priority that bureaucracies give to "masculine" virtues and values (see discussion of Horney's and Gilligan's views in Chapter 8): inequality, hierarchy, impersonality, aggressiveness, competition, and independence. These differ from "women's values," which are egalitarian, personalized, nurturant, and relational (Scott, 1998:5). On these bases, feminist critics assert that the fundamental characteristics of bureaucracy as Weber described them are

> gender-biased not only in their application for criteria for appointment and promotion but, more fundamentally, in their choice of criteria—in their

conception of what is entailed in creating a rational system for supporting collaborative action. Contemporary organizations are said to be modeled on military systems and sports teams (ibid.).

Whether this is less true of human services or social work organizations is debatable; medical settings typically demonstrate "masculine" traits. The criticism may be most applicable to large, public social welfare and health bureaucracies; whether it applies to smaller, or private health and welfare organizations depends on the particular organization and its environment.

Much writing (both popular and academic) and research has been devoted to describing the dehumanizing influences of our institutions and organizations. In the effort to structure human interactions in large organizations to conform to criteria of efficiency, objectivity, and merit, the needs of individual persons have been relegated to the background. *Alienation,* referred to at various points in this book, is a product of dehumanization. This is also an example of conflict between goals of component and system, and of system and suprasystem. Consequences of such conflict are many, and manifest themselves in shoddy products and negative attitudes, whether at the fast-food counter or in professional services.

> I can just look at a car and see all kinds of things wrong with it. You can't do that because you didn't see how it was made. I can look at a car underneath the paint. It's like x-ray vision. They put that trim in, they call it. The paint and all those little pretties that you pay for. Whenever we make a mistake, we always say, "Don't worry about it, some dingaling'll buy it." (Laughs.) (Terkel, 1975:229)

Classical organization theory assumes that rational behavior in organizations prevents alienation. Human relations theory perceives alienation as inevitable; this is similar to entropy, in that organizations will degenerate into randomness and disorganization if the members' personal needs are not tended to. Both conflict and decision system theorists seem to suggest that some degree of alienation is inevitable.

> Outrageous as it may seem, the fact is that a new value system dominates America. The organizational imperative, while originally a subset within the context of the overarching social value system, has now become the dominant force in the homogenization of organizational America, displacing the more individualistic values of the past. (Scott and Hart, 1980:52)

One of the authors of this book described corporate domination of our society as "the new feudalism," a quarter-century ago. If these warnings are correct, we face a crisis in the degree to which organizations are responsive to the needs of human beings within them and the degree to which these persons are manipulated for the good of the organization.

Further, there is a great deal of concern about whether organizations are responsive to social needs, for example, Exxon's handling of the catastrophic oil spill in Alaska's Prince William Sound, and the behavior of tobacco companies in promoting the sales of tobacco and in withholding information about the dangers of smoking. There are, of course, examples of corporate responsiveness to concerns about public health and safety: voluntary recalls of defective products, and introductions of safety features that are not required by law. In another example, some corporations in Minnesota cooperate in pledging 5 percent of their profits to charitable causes, and other corporations and foundations support public radio and television programs. A significant number of companies participate in programs to train welfare recipients and the unemployed.

1. *Burnout.* Many theorists and organizational specialists have studied the phenomenon of burnout among members of organizations. Burnout is defined as:

> a debilitating psychological condition brought on by unrelieved work stress, which results in:
> a. depleted energy reserves;
> b. lowered resistance to illness;
> c. increased dissatisfaction and pessimism;
> d. increased absenteeism and inefficiency at work.
>
> (Veninga and Spradley, 1981:6–7)

Burnout may be considered a particular form of alienation. Clearly burnout is a serious and, in some extreme cases, life-threatening condition. Women are susceptible to burnout because they (1) are often placed in monotonous jobs with little opportunity for promotion, (2) have no leisure time because of domestic chores and child care in addition to their full-time jobs, and (3) have limited social contact off the job because of work and family demands and sometimes feel isolated and lonely because of demands on their time.

Veninga and Spradley (1981) identified five stages of burnout, beginning with an initial period of satisfaction with the job ("the honeymoon"), followed by a second stage in which the characteristics previously listed (energy depletion, etc.) begin to be evident. The worker is not necessarily aware of the symptoms in this stage. In a third stage, the symptoms become chronic and begin to interfere with the person's functioning at work and at home. In a fourth stage, crisis, the worker becomes obsessed with the problem and burnout dominates his or her life. If the worker progresses as far as the fifth stage ("hitting the wall"), it is impossible to function on the job and the person's life deteriorates in significant ways. There is no inevitable progression through the stages. People have highly individual patterns, sometimes moving in and out of burnout depending upon their own resources and the resources available to them from the environment and upon whether they find ways to relieve the chronic stress contained in the job. Change can come about in true systemic fashion by altering the job, the environment, or the person's perception of the job or of themselves. At times, however, the only available course is to find another, more compatible organization.

We should note that satisfaction among employees appears to be higher than dissatisfaction according to most polls. Most workers appear to be relatively satisfied with the tangible and intangible benefits of their jobs. Membership in labor unions, e.g., has declined to about 15 percent of the work force, although major unions currently are making strong efforts to recruit groups that are traditionally nonunionized, e.g., women, professionals such as physicians and professors, secretaries, and low-wage manual laborers. The purpose is, of course, to redistribute power in work organizations.

Another means of altering the job, the environment, or the perception of self is networking. A worker may find other workers experiencing similar problems, and they may be able, through group action, to generate mutual support or, further, to effect change in the organization. These were elements that fostered the development of labor unions. Among other benefits of unions, they may combat a sense of isolation and powerlessness. The movie and television series *Nine to Five* showed not only some hilarious means of achieving change (including tying up the boss as a prisoner) but also some serious efforts at reduction of burnout including "flextime" (allowing workers to vary their hours), more individualization of work space ("flexiplace"), and day care for employees' children. These are sometimes supported by corporations and federal legislation and strongly advocated by President Clinton and Mrs. Clinton. Often, efforts to humanize organizations take the form of decentralization: less emphasis on specialization by workers, reducing units to smaller scale, or restructuring decision-making processes to allow employees to have more influence in determining their own fates and that of the organization. Quality circles, discussed later in this chapter, exemplify a constructive use of feedback cycles.

II. THE OPEN SYSTEMS PERSPECTIVE: THE SYSTEMS MODEL

An open systems perspective is less concerned with distinguishing formal from informal structures; instead, organizations are viewed as a system of interdependent activities. Some of these activities are tightly connected; others are loosely coupled. All must be continuously motivated—produced and reproduced—if the organization is to exist. The arrival of this perspective has triggered the elaboration and elevation of levels of analysis. (Scott, 1998:28)

Large organizations are similar to society as a system: they have specialization, hierarchy, and authority, and they socialize their members in similar ways. The systems model avoids some of the limitations of the preceding models; it agrees with decision theory that the goal is not perfection. It goes one step further by stating that goal-seeking behavior (GE, GI) is not always the primary behavior of a system since exclusive attention to goal attainment leads to neglect of other essential functions of the system (see discussion in Chapter 1). The systems model stresses a wider context of decision-making and organizational behavior than is pictured in other theories; like conflict theory, it takes into account environmental influences as well as the influence wielded by components. Conflict is better explained by the systems model in that it recognizes the inevitability of conflict not only within and between components and subsystems, each of which holds to the legitimacy of its own goals, but between a system and its environment. James Miller a premier systems theorist and former college president, stated the systems point of view:

> No decision is entirely rational or satisfactory, a fact which can give administrators some solace. There is no perfect, rational solution to most administrative problems. The higher the echelon, the truer this is of the issues which confront it. The dimensions along which many decisions must be made are incommensurable. Human lives are incommensurable with money. Money is incommensurable with time. Time is incommensurable with professional excellence. Yet all of these are in scarce supply to a given organization and trade-offs among them must be decided upon. (Miller, 1972:79)

Control is also pictured differently in the systems model. Like goal attainment, control is exclusively pursued only to the detriment of other functions and, at times, other functions do take precedence. The fact that power, control, and the influence of the environment may vary from time to time requires the use of a flexible model of organization. The systems model accounts for such variant adaptive forms.

A. Behavioral Aspects of Organizations

1. Communication. In his influential book on executive functions, Chester Bernard stressed the importance of communication (appropriately, since he was president of a telephone company): "In an exhaustive theory of organization, communication would occupy a central place, because the structure, extensiveness, and scope of the organization are almost entirely determined by communication techniques" (Barnard, 1938:91). A recent text also emphasizes communication: "Organizations are information-processing systems. One of the most vivid metaphors or images sees the organization as a *brain*. . . . This imagery captures the idea that organizations capture and filter information, process it in terms of what it has already learned, interpret it, change it, and finally act on it" (Hall, 1996:169).

In order to focus people's attention on specific goals and activities, organizations must monitor and set parameters for communications. This may become as detailed as prohibiting personal phone calls and use of E-mail for private correspondence, or as broad as requiring that all correspondence with external systems be reviewed (and perhaps censored), e.g., during secret military operations or in prisons. One means of controlling content and intent is the practice of submitting drafts of documents to committees or superiors for review before issuing them. Supposedly, organizations are exemplars of efficiency in communication, because they control the channels through which information flows. This is done hierarchically and by restricting the range of content; that is, information passes through various gatekeepers (supervisors, editors, legal advisors, and policy analysts, and sometimes "spin doctors") before it is allowed to flow onward or outward to its intended audience.

Researchers have identified certain standard patterns of communications networks: These are recognizable in general systems theory as feedback loops. Each network formation may be functional in a particular organizational setting, for a particular purpose. If centralized decision-making is important, then unidirectional communication, restricted times, and controlled volume may be the preferred modes. If open participation with widely shared decision-making is the organizational style, then bidirectional communication, accessibility at all times, and uncontrolled volume might be the appropriate choices. Many other variations are, of course, possible.

In addition to the general shape of the communication network, there are at least three other dimensions: (1) the *direction(s)* in which information may flow, (2) *when* flows may occur, and the (3) *volume* of information permitted to flow.

The nature of the organization is a factor in the style of communication chosen. Hall says, "Communication is most important . . . in organizations and organizational segments that must deal with uncertainty, that are complex, and that have a technology that does not permit easy routinization. . . . The more an organization is people and idea oriented, the more important communication becomes" (1996:171). However, technologically sophisticated organizations require precision in communication also: replacing a "thingamabob" in a computer or handing a surgeon a "whatchamacallit" probably won't do. Learning the "lingo," cant, or jargon of an organization is another way of mapping the territory. Systems thinking may help to cut across disciplinary fields, in this respect, even though it has jargon of its own.

Probably the most common means of communication in organizations is the infamous and universal *meeting*. Hall comments:

> Meetings have the potential for yielding common meanings among participants, particularly when the intent of the meetings is to achieve consensus. While meetings are quite valuable, it is obvious that time spent in meetings is time not spent on other activities. When I have a day filled with meetings, I have a day when I will not get any research, writing, or preparation for classes accomplished. (ibid.:186)

It is a rare member of an organization who will not sigh in agreement; one organizational expert seriously suggested that all meetings be conducted standing up, in order to shorten them. Much depends upon the goals for the meeting. Solidarity or consensus may be achieved, but precise communication may be a less likely result—hence another infamous, universal device: the memo, whether on paper or in digital form. The ability to write clearly and concisely is highly valuable in organizations; columnists in newspapers' business sections regularly suggest methods to accomplish this. On occasion, it is perhaps equally valuable to write ambiguously and with circumlocution, but one is not likely to find a guidebook for it; done skillfully, this can communicate that the author is wise in the ways of bureaucracy.

2. Goal Direction. Goals have various functions, as described by Scott (1998:286–287): (1) *cognitive,* to guide decision-making and action; (2) *cathectic,* to psychologically "hook" members and external systems into participation; (3) *symbolic,* to gain support by capitalizing on people's views of the organization, and to secure legitimacy and resources; (4) *justification* for organizational actions; and (5) bases for *evaluation* of organizational functioning.

What *is* an organizational goal? One definition is that a goal is a particular characteristic of a steady state that the organization attempts to realize. In this sense, a goal may be expressed by an ideal or myth (sometimes expressed by an advertising slogan: "Better living through chemistry" or "See the USA in your Chevrolet") or by a rational, projected set of specific objectives—that is, it may be "highest quality service to the client" or "caseloads of 20, using short-term treatment, that will increase agency clientele by 15 percent." The goal expressed by either of the latter statements is a desired future condition (steady state) of the organization in which its declared purposes would be fulfilled. These goals guide the organization in its activity; they either encourage or discourage specific actions undertaken or contemplated by the organization. This is similar in some regards to the "ego ideal" of the person, and to the self toward which one strives in Sartre's form of existentialism, or Maslow's self-actualization; this has been described as the *syntality* of an organization, similar to a personality. An emerging theme within this past decade has been "organizational learning," which is analogous to ego functioning in the person: the ability to adapt by securing information both outside and inside the organization and sharing it among all components (Argyris, 1994). Winter, an economist at the Wharton School at the University of Pennsylvania, described current events as "disintegration of the vertical organization of firms. . . . We are downsizing. It is all captured by a common theme: repackaging. We are shifting packages of economic activity into new smaller units. The folk model of organizations as top-down and centralized is out of date" (Kauffman, 1995:245). Decision-making is being decentralized and desynchronized, as well, into "patches":

> The basic idea of the patch procedure is simple: take a hard, conflict-laden task in which many parts interact, and divide it into a quilt of overlapping patches. Try to optimize within each patch. As this occurs, the couplings between parts in two patches across patch boundaries will mean that finding a "good" solution in one patch will alter the problems confronted by the neighboring patches, and the adaptive moves made by those patches in turn will alter the problem faced by yet other patches, the system is just like our model coevolving ecosystems. . . . Patches, in short, may be a fundamental process we have evolved in our social systems and perhaps elsewhere, to solve very hard problems. (ibid.:252–253)

Two aspects of goal attainment should be distinguished: *effectiveness* refers to the degree to which the organization achieves its goals; *efficiency* refers to the manner in which it is done, specifically the amount of energy and resources necessary to achieve a goal. The former is part of the GE and GI functions of systems; the latter is part of the SE and SI functions. Efficiency in an organization requires reduction of conflict ("friction," in slang) within the organization; thus some internal control of the utilization of energy is necessary for goal attainment. One example would be a coach's encouragement of team spirit with its implied reduction of intrasquad animosities in a football team so that points (or goals) may be scored.

Goals are not static. Goals can be *displaced* (i.e., other goals can be substituted for them); the most frequent form of this is making ends of means. For example, efficiency in public welfare expenditure is purported to be a means to effective service to clients and society, but all too often efficiency by cutting welfare spending becomes an end in itself. "Social workers may be directed by their supervisors to provide therapeutic casework services but be evaluated primarily on the basis of the number and timeliness of their visits to clients and the correctness of their calculation of budgets" (Scott, 1998:347). Another example is the accusation by many university students, especially undergraduates, that universities have displaced education with publication and research, resulting in absentee professors and lower-quality instruction.

There are other forms of goal change. One is *goal succession*, in which an organization achieves its initial goals and establishes new ones; or the goal disappears and the organization turns to new goals. Examples of this include those private welfare agencies that began as adoption agencies in an era when there were more children available for adoption than now, and whose successive goals have become the treatment of emotionally disturbed children or family treatment. Definitions of social problems shift with startling rapidity; this is one result of "the turbulent environment" (Hasenfeld, 1983) in which social service agencies exist, and to which they must rapidly adapt. Both Christmas Seals and the March of Dimes established new goals after attaining their original goals, the supposed elimination of tuberculosis and polio as major health hazards.

There may also be *goal multiplication*. The Red Cross, which began as a service to soldiers on the battlefield, broadened its goals to include services to soldiers' widows and orphans, then to disaster relief and to visiting political prisoners. The Boy Scouts have, in recent years, broadened their former goals of camping, crafts, and character development to include ethical leadership for adult leaders, and family support through family life education; 4-H has expanded to urban settings. There are, of course, advantages and disadvantages to such goal multiplication. Among possible advantages are that synergy of goals may increase the effectiveness of an organization; that staff recruitment may be easier because they enjoy variety; and because a wider range of contributors may be motivated to support the organization. Possible disadvantages include shortage of energy to accomplish tasks, conflict between goals, and a dilution of focus.

Any discussion of organizational goals must realistically qualify the power of organizations to inspire their members or to synergize their efforts, however; social systems theory takes the environment into account:

> Open systems theorists emphasize that individuals have multiple loyalties and identities. They join and leave or engage in ongoing exchanges with the organization depending on the bargains they can strike. . . . [F]rom this perspective, participants cannot be assumed to hold common goals or even to routinely seek the survival of the organization. (Scott, 1998:27)

3. Differentiation. Differentiation is the prime sociological characteristic of modernization. Modern societies are societies of differentiated organizations, and these organizations differentiate internally to carry out their purposes more effectively. For example, education has become the domain of organizations grouped under the rubric of "schools." These in turn have differentiated along dimensions of age and function: preschool, elementary, middle, and high school. Secondary schools have differentiated into technical, vocational, college preparatory, and general. Postsecondary education has community colleges to prepare students for specific occupations, colleges for general higher education, and universities for occupations designated as professions. The most recent differentiated form is elder hostel for the elderly, often on colleges campuses.

Differentiation of tasks within an organization may have disadvantages. If workers do not see and understand others' activities as complementary to theirs and horizontally related to them, each employee may become nothing but an isolated, "inert piece of machinery." They must "keep in constant relations with neighboring functions . . . not lose sight of [their] collaborators, that [the worker] acts upon them and reacts to them" (Durkheim, 1968:43). Differentiation may lead to isolation of the components of an organization (e.g., in offices and factories where there is little exchange between clerical and professional staff or between workers and management, or a university with rigid departmental boundaries). Some factories, e.g., Volvo and Saab in Sweden, have employed "autonomous work groups" in which a group of workers produces a car, and each worker performs a variety of tasks; the outcome is a shared group product, with less differentiation or specialization. United States industries originated "quality circles" fifty years ago; the idea was then adopted by Japanese industry, and reimported to the United States during the 1980s. It is estimated that about one of every nine Japanese workers is involved in a quality circle (Handy, 1985:333).

> The quality circle consists on average of a half-dozen employees, headed by a supervisor, who constitute a natural work group. As group members, they are charged with pinpointing quality problems and developing effective solutions to them. . . . For example, the fourteen members of a quality circle at the Kariya plant of Nippon Denso examined leaky auto radiators and determined how to produce a 100 percent leak detection rate. Nippon Steel sliced its liquefied petroleum gas consumption by 5.3 percent over a four-year period as a result of quality-circle suggestions each year. (Larwood, 1984:402)

However, "quality circles depend on circles members' believing that they can make a difference" (ibid.:403). Spenner noted that persons "in self-directed jobs become less authoritarian, less self-deprecatory, less fatalistic, and less conformist in their ideas while becoming more self-confident and more responsible to standards of morality (Spenner, 1988:75).

4. Power and Control

Organizations generate power; it is the inescapable accompaniment of the production of goods and services; it comes in many forms from many sources; it is contested; and it is certainly used. (Perrow, 1986:265)

Organizations must ensure compliance in achieving specific, narrow goals and therefore must apply some kind of control—the use of power. One characteristic of organizations as distinct from other systems is the explicitness of power: it is largely visible and institutionalized.

Robert Dahl defined power: "A has power over B to the extent that he can get B to do something B would not otherwise do" (1957:201–215). Emerson elaborated this: "A's power over B is (1) directly proportional to the importance B places on the goals mediated by A, and (2) inversely proportional to the availability of these goals to B outside the A-B relation" (cited in Scott, 1998:304). Such power is based on "manipulating rewards and punishments important to the other person" (ibid.).

Force should not be taken to mean only physical force: moral force or Gandhi's "Truth Force" qualify as well. Since power is an energy function, it is finite; energy expended (through GE or GI functions, for example) to influence the behavior of others may deplete the system's power potential.

Power is the system's *potential* to achieve its goals by the application or deprivation of energy to another system or component. The degree of effectiveness of power depends upon the extent to which the focal system is affected and the extent to which the goal is achieved. One example is the use of federal funds for Appalachian development during the War on Poverty. The stated goal was social and economic change; the result was an improved highway system and some new courthouses, which benefited the residents of the county seat towns and the politicians (in the opinion of one author, a resident of the area). A great deal of energy (funds and propaganda) was expended, but although there were some substantial achievements, they were not the ones originally stated. In this instance, the federal government's power to achieve its goals was shown to be minimal. If the federal government's covert goal was political, its power to achieve its goal through the political system of Appalachia was quite effective. Power must thus be measured by its objectives, not merely by the magnitude of its effects.

Power and control are similar except that control suggests narrower and more precise goals than does power. Further, power may have effects other than control. The application of power could release control ("the truth shall set you free," e.g., is a good psychoanalytic principle). One example is education, which is the application of the teacher's and school's power (and, we hope, the student's) so that the student is freer to perform the necessary tasks of adulthood (an idealistic view of education, we admit). Etzioni stated the importance of control:

> The success of an organization is largely dependent upon its ability to maintain control of its participants. All social units control their members, but the problem of control in organizations is especially acute. Organizations as social units that serve specific purposes are artificial units. They are

planned, deliberately structured; *they constantly and self-consciously review their performance and restructure themselves accordingly.* (Etzioni, 1964:58; emphasis ours)

Control is a central concept in cybernetics, together with related concepts such as "steering" and "regulation." The question, To what extent can social systems be steered? was investigated by Felix Geyer and Johannes Van der Zouwen in their book, *Sociocybernetic Paradoxes* (1986). They concluded that systems steer internally in their closed aspects, and are responsive to external control in their open aspects. In other words, internal control is primarily a function of the system as a *whole* and external control is the system's function as a *part* of a larger system. This is consistent with newer systems thinking, as described in Chapter 1.

The objective of power and control is *compliance*, the cooperation of a system or component in achieving the goals of the system that applies power and control. Organization theorists have focused primarily on two aspects of organizations: structure and compliance. Understandably, managers of organizations devote more attention to compliance than to any other aspect of organizations—how to assure the desired results. The problem of compliance is apparent in the following analysis of the destruction of the space shuttle *Challenger* on January 28, 1986:

> The Commission concluded that the failure was not in the design of the launch decision structure or in the procedures followed in arriving at a decision, but rather in actions (or nonactions) of key decision makers within the system [who] (1) ignored the warnings of . . . engineers regarding the potential dangers presented by the low temperature and ice buildup at the time of the launch, and (2) failed to communicate those concerns to [other] key decision makers. . . . [A] proper accounting of that decision requires us to adopt a more comprehensive and systems-oriented perspective. [This] requires us to examine the interaction and joint influence of various cognitive, psychological, and social factors. (Hirokawa, Gouran, and Martz, 1988:414–415)

One powerful factor was the "perceived pressure" from NASA officials, which led the engineers to set aside their own misgivings about the launch:

> Another psychological factor that apparently exerted a powerful influence on the decision to launch the Challenger concerns the "launch commit criterion" in operation during the deliberation process. Traditionally, NASA decisions involving the launch of manned space vehicles were governed by a very conservative rule that dictated that a launch *should be canceled if there is any doubt of its safety.* . . . In the case of flight 51-L, however, it seems clear that a very different decisional rule was in operation. Specifically, it appears that Level III managers operated under the rule that a scheduled launch

should proceed unless there is conclusive evidence that it is unsafe to do so. (Hirokawa et al., 1988:423)

With whom would the engineers comply? Their own corporation and its professional standards, or with what they perceived to be NASA's (or perhaps political) pressure not to postpone the launch? What did compliance mean in this instance? Compliance with what and with whom?

There are three forms of control, as Etzioni describes them, each of which fits with a particular kind of organization: (1) physical control, employed by *coercive* organizations, which use threat and punishment that may result in alienation among members of the organization; (2) material rewards such as goods and services, used by *remunerative* organizations, in which members calculate the benefits they will receive; and (3) symbolic rewards, employed by *normative* organizations, which use moral involvement and social acceptance as means of control, which tend to encourage high levels of commitment to the organization by its members (Etzioni, 1964:47–59; House, 1975:74–78). Symbolic or normative rewards are in many ways the most significant, because one's sense of identity and the value one has, is derived from symbolic interaction with others (as noted in Chapter 3, Section I,C, Language). Symbolic rewards are most likely to be used by the systems with the least physical control or material rewards—religious institutions are the prime examples. In this light, professions such as nursing, social work, or education can be regarded as means of social control: through the deliberate use of symbols, they assist organizations such as schools, hospitals, prisons, or the military to secure compliance (SI and GI functions). Of course, these institutions have other forms of control; but in order to maintain positive linkage with their environment (the general public, parents, or legislators, e.g.), they seldom use physical control, and may be unable to use material rewards because of fiscal, ethical, or legal restrictions.

Organizations whose primary purpose is social control are examples of "total institutions," a phrase coined by Goffman in his classic work, *Asylums* ([1961] 1973). He described a total institution as an organized agency of society in which a large number of like-situated persons, cut off from the larger society for an appreciable length of time, together lead a formally administered round of life. These systems are composed of two groups variously called staff and patients, guards and inmates, keepers and kept, or faculty and students. This is descriptive of such organizations as workhouses (remember *Oliver Twist*?), prisons, mental hospitals (for example, the movie *One Flew Over the Cuckoo's Nest*, based in part on a Veterans Hospital in California), the military (the movie *A Few Good Men*), and, in some instances, boarding schools. The experience of American Indian children who were reared in federal boarding schools is particularly relevant: socialization into "American" culture was the primary goal. They were often denied contact with their tribal cultures: denied the right to speak their own language, denied their customary dress, and denied contact with their families and tribes for extended periods of time.

Generally, the purpose of a total institution is to socialize or resocialize the population with which it works. This is done by the staff through a two-step process designed to change the "structure of self" of their charges. The process begins by changing the person through external definition, usually by (1) divesting the person of socially defining symbols and characteristics (e.g., the "GI" haircut in army basic training and personal clothing); (2) using clothing to symbolize distinctions between inmates and staff, e.g., separate uniforms for guards and inmates, and "street clothing" for administrators; or hospital gowns for patients, as opposed to the green or white clothing of the medical staff; and (3) severing links with outside systems that tend to support and validate previous identity (again, the experience of American Indian children in boarding schools is an example). Thus, depersonalization and dehumanization are often the initial phase of experience within a total institution. Once a new, imposed definition has been established, the second step in the process is to see that the definition is internalized by the inmate (or patient, prisoner, or student) thus changing that person's "selfhood." In the case of American Indian children, forced socialization was often unsuccessful. Many children often rejected the imposed "American" identities and were denied their own personal and tribal identities; many suffered identity problems, along with difficulties in being reabsorbed into their own tribal cultures. The objective of power and control, again, is to ensure compliance with the organization's goals; but power has limits, even in total institutions.

The term "greedy institutions" was coined to denote organizations that make a totalistic claim on their members' time and energy: "They seek exclusive and individual loyalty and they attempt to reduce the claims of competing roles and status positions on those they wish to encompass within their boundaries" (Coser, 1974:4). Coser differentiated greedy institutions from Goffman's total institutions on the basis that the latter were physically separate and used isolation as a means of control. Greedy institutions rely on voluntary compliance and loyalty. Status rewards are heavily relied on and the higher the status the higher the personal commitment of time and energy; a current example is the extreme commitment of some personnel in the computer industry, for example, at Microsoft or at Dell computers, who worked eighty or more hours per week for long periods, developing new products. Some of the latter became "Dell-ionaires," amassing fortunes in company stock, then left to pursue their dreams as auto racers or independent entrepreneurs.

5. *Leadership. Leadership* may be either formal or informal, and it includes power and control used to achieve organizational ends and to make means effective. *Command* is defined as the use of power to ensure

compliance, and leadership is defined as a "continually creative function involving constant appraisal." "Authority of position depended upon centrality in the organization's communications system—it was determined by a structural decision—while authority of leadership was dependent upon the superiority of the leader" (Zaleznik and Jardim, 1967:217). In other words, command derives from the organizational position, from the role and status, while leadership derives from the personal characteristics of the leader. But leadership is not solely dependent upon these personal qualities: it also depends upon the context (the environment) in which it occurs.

Here is a simple, elegant formulation, which forms a typology of leadership:

1. The person *ahead* of the system through special accomplishment or creativity, e.g., Gandhi, Einstein, Lenin, Freud.

2. The person who is *the head* of the system, given leadership through formal structural procedures such as election or delegation of authority, e.g., the president of the United States or a corporate chief executive officer (CEO).

3. The person who is *a head* of a system, one who situationally emerges with particular talents or qualities for determining and attaining systemic purposes. (Ross and Hendry, 1957:13–36)

In actuality, most situations of leadership will be some combination of two or three of these aspects. These three correspond to the dimensions of systems we use throughout this book, i.e., evolutionary, structural, and behavioral.

Leadership, like power, may be horizontally as well as vertically hierarchical. Leadership occurs at all levels; organizations contain groups, and leadership emerges from these. In some organizations, such emergence of leadership at lower levels is deliberately cultivated; the usual manner in which this is done is to decentralize decision-making.

B. Structural Aspects of Organizations

Parsons identified three levels of structure in organizations: (1) the *technical system,* which is the production level; (2) the *managerial* system, which maintains the linkage between the organization and its suppliers and manages the organization's internal subsystems; and (3) the *institutional system,* which is the link between the organization and the societal system. In some respects, this is analogous to Freud's triad of id, superego, and ego.

Handy (1985, 1993) presented four "cultures" of organizations; in this context, it would be more accurate to describe them as "microcultures," or "organizational cultures," since they are specific to individual organizations. Each microculture or organizational culture mirrors the societal culture in which it exists, to some degree, but may also differ from it. Multinational corporations (or "transnational") may have branches in several, very different cultures (e.g., the United States, Japan, and Saudi Arabia); clearly, the organizational culture cannot simply mirror each and every culture in which it is located.

The term *organizational climate* defines a narrower aspect of the organization's functioning, including the morale of its employees, the degree to which effort is rewarded, and the aggressiveness with which the organization pursues its goals. "Climate" also includes attitudes toward women, in at least two respects. First, as employees or executives, e.g., the "glass ceiling," meaning that women can see the upper levels of the organization, but are barred from rising to them. Second, as victims of sexual harassment, which the Supreme Court defines not as "intersexual flirtation" but as "'behavior so objectively offensive' that it creates a hostile work environment for the victim" (El Nasser, 1998). Sexual harassment lawsuits frequently describe such "hostile work environments" experienced by women who are object to sexual harassment or who file complaints: they are subjected to insults by the aggressor, their work is unfairly evaluated, or they are shunned by other personnel (all means of social control) (see Reardon, 1995).

Many women entrepreneurs leave corporate positions to start their own businesses:

> Professional women say they're leaving corporate jobs because of advancement barriers, scant help balancing work and family, and a desire to pursue an entrepreneurial goal. . . . An unprecedented number of professional women are taking the same initiative. The number of female-owned businesses is growing at nearly twice the national average. . . . The number of female-owned businesses grew by 78% from 1987 to 1996, according to the National Foundation for Women Business Owners (NFWBO). There were about 8 million female businesses in 1996, or 36% of all businesses. . . . Female business owners employ about 18.5 million people, which means that one out of every four company workers in the USA is at a female-owned firm. "The rise in women entrepreneurs is one of the big demographics changing our society," says Lynn Neeley, president-elect of the United States Association for Small Business and Entrepreneurship. (Armour, 1998)

Handy's four cultures are each embodied in a typical structure: (1) role culture, (2) power culture, (3) task culture, and (4) person culture.

1. Role Culture. In Handy's conception, the role culture is a bureaucracy. Its structure is a "Greek temple," with a relatively shallow pyramid of control at the top, and supporting vertical columns (see Figure 5.2). This culture is based on rationality and specialization. Each "pillar" or

Figure 5.2. Role culture. From Charles B. Handy, *Understanding Organizations,* third edition, 1985 (Hammondsworth: Penguin Books,), copyright © Charles B. Handy, 1976, 1981, 1985. Reproduced by permission of Penguin Books Ltd.

department has its assigned function, and reports to the triangle of power at the top. Coordination is performed by the triangle, made up of a relatively small number of people. "Role prescription," as described by Weber below, is more important than individual personalities. The major source of power in this culture is *position power,* the status the person holds. Rules and procedures are the major elements of the culture. This structure operates well in a stable environment—its role occupants can feel secure; however, its adaptability is limited. This culture is clearly compatible with the classical model previously described, and with the "bureaucratic situation."

2. Power Culture. Here power derives from a powerful person, often the entrepreneurial founder. Rules and procedures are less important than employees' connections with those who are powerful at the center. The organization depends upon trust and face-to-face relationships. Handy pictured this as a web (see Figure 5.3).This kind of organization is flexible and can react quickly to threat or opportunity, but it is limited in size, since *gemeinschaft* qualities may be difficult to maintain in a larger organization. It is frequently a competitive, "tough" climate, and judgments about effectiveness or worth can issue quickly from the center; staff must be very alert to changes in the environment because of the organization's reliance on other organizations for resources, both finances and clientele, and perhaps upon government (another organization) and the public for goodwill and support. Examples include a treatment facility begun by an entrepreneurial social worker to serve developmentally disabled clients, and a clinic founded by a medical specialist to serve Alzheimer's patients. In this type of organization, staff must be very alert to changes in external resources or clientele.

3. Task Culture. This culture is exemplified by the development of the space program by NASA, which was accomplished by "modular" work structures and assignments. Units were formed as needed and dis

Figure 5.3. Power culture. From Charles B. Handy, *Understanding Organizations*, third edition, 1985 (Hammondsworth: Penguin Books,), copyright © Charles B. Handy, 1976, 1981, 1985. Reproduced by permission of Penguin Books Ltd.

banded as particular subprojects were completed. This can perhaps best be represented by a grid (see Figure 5.4). The "matrix" organization embodies this culture. The organization assembles the appropriate resources and expertise at the appropriate intersections of the grid. Expertise is placed at the intersections where projects occur and, since a premium is placed on expertise, power flows from these temporary locations. The organization (and its temporary subunits) are united by specific tasks, in the short term, and by a sequence of tasks accomplished, in the long term. This is a highly adaptable organization. Examples might include an emergency response unit in a hospital, a crisis intervention unit in child protective services, or an "external resources" team that writes grants to secure outside funding, with a very short "turnaround time."

4. *Person Culture.* The person culture is similar to the power culture in that both are based upon personalities, but the person culture is decentralized. It is best represented by an aggregation of independent professionals who share a single location, whether law firm, medical practice, or university department. Here each individual is a central point: thus there may be no single center (see Figure 5.5).

Handy said the structure is as "minimal as possible," and that a "cluster" may be the best description, or perhaps "a galaxy of individual stars" (Handy, 1985:195). Control is minimal or nonexistent, except by mutual

Figure 5.4. Task culture. From Charles B. Handy, *Understanding Organizations*, third edition, 1985 (Hammondsworth: Penguin Books), copyright © Charles B. Handy, 1976, 1981, 1985. Reproduced by permission of Penguin Books Ltd.

Figure 5.5.   Person culture. From Charles B. Handy, *Understanding Organizations,*
   third edition, 1985 (Hammondsworth: Penguin Books,), copyright © Charles
   B. Handy, 1976, 1981, 1985. Reproduced by permission of Penguin Books Ltd.

consent. Individuals have a great deal of autonomy, either because of their
expertise and the demand for their services elsewhere, or because they
are tenured in their position (as with teachers or professors). Handy said:

> The kibbutz, the commune, the cooperative, are all striving after the person
> culture in organizational form. On the whole, only their original creators
> achieve any success. Too soon, the organization achieves its own identity
> and begins to impose on its individuals. It becomes, at best, a task culture,
> but often a power or a role culture (ibid.:196).

He added that there are many persons who prefer a person culture, but
find themselves in other settings. For example, the stereotype of professors is that they are person-oriented, working in a role culture; that
they do what they must (e.g., committees), and teach when they must, to
retain their positions in the organization, but that they view the organization essentially as a base upon which to build their own careers and carry
out their own interests (ibid.). To the extent that the stereotype is true, this
behavior has been supported by the increasing reliance of universities
and colleges on faculty to secure outside resources, largely through research grants. But this phenomenon is two-edged: as the institutions'
dependence upon entrepreneurial faculty increases, so does the institutions' need to monitor and control their performance, using the forms of
control discussed above. Accordingly, there are efforts throughout the
nation (and internationally) to abridge the independence of professors in
the name of "accountability" and "fiscal flexibility," through posttenure
peer reviews, fixed-term appointments, and an increasing proportion of
"nontenure track" and temporary appointments.

The resolution of issues of "intellectual property," that is, whether a
professor's or researcher's ideas belong to that person, or to the institution, are also vitally important; the issue is being pressed in the name of
securing financial resources for the institution. The traditional person
culture (and perhaps role culture) of universities may be ending as universities become "corporatized," that is, as they become power cultures
(under centralized control by a university president or state governor,

e.g.) or task culture (as departments are dismantled and faculty are shifted into *ad hoc* research or instructional units). The implications of this for universities as "knowledge organizations" are enormous; and unknown. The issues illustrate the power of organizations and institutions, and the nature of our organizational society.

C. *Evolutionary Aspects*

1. Patrimony. Are there realistic alternatives to large-scale bureaucracies? Weber thought the alternative was *patrimony,* that is, control by persons (apparently males; notice that *matrimony* has a much different cultural meaning) rather than by laws and regulations. Patrimonial control is one in which decisions are the leader's prerogative. The leader appoints friends and loyal supporters and delegates patrimonial powers to them. Although Weber favored bureaucracy because of its norms of equity and impartiality, he recognized that bureaucracies are likely to become cumbersome and immobile, that means tend to become ends, and that such organizations tend to be self-perpetuating.

As Weber observed, perhaps all organizations are a combination of bureaucracy and patrimonialism, formal and informal. The Constitution of the United States established ground rules enabling the coexistence of the two. The presidency exemplifies the patrimonial aspect. A president appoints those loyal to him and his cause, those who have aided in his attainment of the office. For example, John Kennedy appointed his brother to the office of attorney general. Richard Nixon appointed his campaign manager to the same position. Jimmy Carter appointed loyal supporters (referred to as "the Georgia Mafia"); presidents Reagan, Bush, and Clinton followed the same pattern, which will, in all probability, continue through succeeding administrations.

A strong symbol of the patrimony of the elected executive is the presidential pardon (state governors have a similar power), which allows the officeholder to make an independent, legally binding decision that does not require legal precedent or any justification. President Lincoln pardoned deserters. President Ford pardoned Richard Nixon, and President Carter granted amnesty to those who fled the country to avoid the draft during the Vietnam War.

The "new entrepreneur" business owner is another example of patrimonial organization (even if a woman). The business is operated with authority remaining firmly in the hands of owner(s). Promotions, bonuses, and status are the vehicles used to foster employee loyalty. The owners employ and discharge employees as they see fit without recourse or appeal (except as a court may find illegalities). This contrasts with the bureaucratic situation, in which procedures for hiring and firing are thoroughly detailed, often complex, and slow; and conditions for promotion and salary advancement are carefully spelled out.

Again, most contemporary organizations are mixtures of patrimonial and bureaucratic, based on both personal factors and structured procedures. An organization's movement from bureaucracy to patrimony may be exemplified by General Electric's chairman, "an intense, powerful man" who "spearheaded a gut-wrenching change" in the company, slashing thousands of jobs:

> Like him or not, Jack Welch has succeeded in sweeping a major American company clean of the bureaucratic excesses of the past and transforming a paternalistic culture into one that puts winning in the marketplace above all other concerns. Like it or not, the management styles of more U.S. companies are going to look a lot more like GE. (*Business Week*, 1998)

2. *Other Alternatives.* Alternatives to large-scale bureaucracies have been attempted by some organizations, with decentralized structures such as autonomous work groups that allow freedom and control to line workers. Such attempts have drawn heavily on research done following World War II by the Tavistock Institute in England; these studies indicate that greater productivity and reduced alienation are best achieved by autonomous work groups. Other efforts have focused on redesigning jobs ("job enrichment," "job enlargement") and restructuring to permit greater self-determination by workers. In a few instances, U.S. companies have permitted workers to participate in management decisions. In Europe, this has long been practiced as "codetermination" or "industrial democracy."

In the Japanese model ("Theory Z"), trust is fostered by companies' commitment to lifetime employment for each employee (although this has been modified in recent years); in case of recession, companies aggressively look for new markets or new products while workers perform other duties (including janitorial services) until the financial situation becomes better, meanwhile keeping their jobs. However, faced with serious recession and international competition, Japanese corporations have transferred employees to other cities or countries, causing hardship for employees' families. One couple sued the husband's employer for nearly a quarter-million dollars for "emotional pain of separation and traveling expenses" (Coleman, 1998).

> Companies say transfers—with or without families in tow—are a necessity. As companies have diversified and expanded overseas, branch offices and subsidiaries have proliferated. Bosses say they need to move trained employees around to spread their expertise and give them wider experience. The trend, which is increasing as juvenile delinquency is rising and Japanese youth seem more troubled, has some people alarmed that companies are breaking up families at the expense of children and society. The moves

usually look voluntary, but workers know a stint at a branch office can be an important step up the corporate ladder. (ibid.)

The "groupness" of the work situation is encouraged by workers sharing space without walls; interaction is not only encouraged, it is demanded, consistent with Japanese culture. Permanence of employment and group solidarity result in absence of (or at least lessened) alienation, since "people committed to long-term relationships with each other have strong commitments to behave responsibly and equitably towards one another" (Ouchi, 1981b:34). This resembles a community, clan, or tribe, with strong communal ties. In this instance, organizational culture mirrors the wider culture. There is some question as to whether the society and culture are changing, and whether the organizational culture must change, accordingly.

Decision-making in Japanese corporations is often a group process governed by consensus. It apparently is disturbing to Westerners who are accustomed to more authoritarian decision-making and who perceive the Japanese as slow to decide and their decision process difficult to fathom. The Japanese reply that it may take longer to arrive at consensus, but that once achieved, it is quicker to implement with little dissatisfaction with the decision.

> Intimacy, trust and understanding grow where individuals are linked to one another through multiple bonds in a wholistic relationship. . . . The Japanese show clear evidence that wholism in industrial life is possible. (Ouchi, 1981b:54–55)
>
> It is a consent culture, a community of equals who cooperate with one another to reach common goals. Rather than relying exclusively upon hierarchy and monitoring to direct behavior, it relies also upon commitment and trust. (ibid.:83)

Humanization and improving the "quality of work life" are complex undertakings, involving recognition of more facets of the person than simply the employee's role as a production unit in the industrial system. Paradoxically, it may well require the person to give up some freedom and independence (randomly distributed energy that tends toward entropy), to assume new obligations of mutuality (negentropy or synergy) with management and other workers. Some observers suggest that we are witnessing the breakdown of bureaucracy and that it will be supplanted by a task culture of temporary, regularly shifting structures, an organizational scheme congruent with an era of accelerated change, wherein people are brought together to accomplish a specific task and disband once that task is completed.

One hypothesis is that larger size generates a greater variety of subsystems. Organizations, unlike families, may outlive the original members (though, of course, extended families may outlive organizations). Because organizations can replace components and learn from experience, it may be true that the longer an organization lives, the better its chance for survival.

Many have observed that the changes previously discussed (decentralization, or humanization of the workplace) are more cosmetic than real, and that organizations tend to perpetuate their ways with as little change as possible (morphostasis). When pressed, governmental organizations "reorganize"; industry becomes "lean and mean" and "downsizes." Hundreds of thousands of workers have suffered this fate in the last two decades; some analysts suggest that organizations are being short-sighted by reducing their productivity to the point that it may be difficult to recover.

For significant organizational change to occur, there must be modification in both internal and external aspects, especially goals. Contentions over plant closings during the last generation provide an instructive example (see Michael Moore's movie, *Roger and Me* for a humorous take on a very serious subject). Corporate industry, in its pursuit of its profit goal, may determine that a particular production facility is not contributing to profit and decide to close that facility to move production to another location in which labor and raw material are cheaper, often to a "third world" country. Other interests and organizations, such as labor unions, may be strongly affected by the relinquishment of the secondary goal, i.e., the provision of employment that enables the purchase of goods and services. Efforts are made to block the plant closure and / or develop other ways to maintain employment. Similar dynamics operate with the closing of a prison or a hospital, as regards the impact upon the surrounding community or neighborhood.

The pace of change in an organization is nearly always controversial. The last several presidential elections, for example, indicated public dissatisfaction with the speed of change in the federal bureaucracy; civil rights reforms were occurring too quickly for some and too slow for others; tax reforms were occurring too slowly. Centralization of power in the executive branch was feared by many, who cited revenue sharing as desirable. Elections since 1968 have been interpreted as "mandates" against centralized federal bureaucracy.

One reason for organizational change is the rapid diversification and expansion of major corporations and a rapid acceleration of "megamergers" recently. According to a highly regarded management expert, the new multinational corporation (MNC):

> does not fit the traditional organization structure of the multinational corporation, with a central top management to which management of subsidiaries reports. It requires, rather, a *system* approach, in which one body coordinates autonomous managements that do not report to one another.

A major requirement is the ability and willingness to adapt to different culture and to work with people of different habits and traditions. [It] is not only transnational, rather than multinational; it is, above all, transcultural. And it is an idea whose time has come. (Drucker 1982:192; emphasis ours)

Thoughtful analyses including some by science fiction writers (notably the late Isaac Asimov in the *Foundation* series) suggest that governments of the future may not be nation-states. Instead, international conglomerates may rule, and perhaps more rationally. It may well be that unless national governments become equally adaptable, other organizations may absorb what we now recognize as "governmental" functions. The United Nations recognized the insufficiency of information on multinationals and their activities and formulated a code of ethics for multinational enterprises.

CONCLUSION

Organizations present significant problems for our society, as well as providing means to deal with other, serious societal problems. Large business organizations may provide a model for federal programs, when they decentralize and allow local administration of services. However, it is an open question whether corporations will develop a "social conscience" sufficient to allay some of the very problems that their activities create: pollution, large-scale layoffs, removal of plants to other countries, inequitable tax write-offs, unsafe products, monopolizing local capital, and competing with smaller-scale, local businesses that have sustained communities for generations.

In the field of human services, the effects of privatization are yet to be determined. Decentralization is an attractive idea; its implementation has an uncertain future. Returning responsibility for delivery of social services to local agencies may sound attractive, but it is clear even now that funding at local levels is inadequate to meet increasing needs.

SUGGESTED READINGS

Adams, Scott. *The Dilbert Principle.*
    1996   New York: HarperCollins.
        Always a delight, and often too close to the truth, the daily "Dilbert" cartoon lays bare the inner torments of corporate America. Some ideas are inspired by submissions from the cubicles, probably using the company's E-mail.

Branch, Taylor.
1988   *Parting the Waters: America in the King Years: 1954–1963.* New York: Simon and Schuster.
This historical account of the roots of the modern civil rights movement exemplifies the transitory shifts between community and organization.
Hall, Richard H.
1996   *Organizations: Structures, Processes, and Outcomes.* Englewood Cliffs, NJ: Prentice-Hall.
This is a comprehensive, accessible text, organized in "reverse order," placing aspects of organizations first, and theory last, a useful approach. Well-organized and conceptually sound.
Handy, Charles B.
1985   *Understanding Organizations.* Harmondsworth, England: Penguin.
1993   *Understanding Organizations.* New York: Oxford University Press.
"Jam-packed" with information; also entertaining due to Handy's selection of illustrations and excerpts. The "Guide to Further Study" is unique, a selection of the author's comments and musings on the subject. Highly recommended in paperback.
Hasenfeld, Yeheskel.
1983   *Human Services Organizations.* Englewood Cliffs, NJ: Prentice-Hall.
This has been the most useful text for a course on human services organizations. It is comprehensive and thought-provoking. One of the authors has used it as a text; it is entirely compatible with our approach.
Hasenfeld, Yeheskel, ed.
1992   *Human Services as Complex Organizations.* Newbury Park, CA: Sage.
A highly valuable sourcebook; a companion text to Hasenfeld's earlier text, just described.
Hirokawa, Randy Y., Dennis S. Gouran, and Amy E. Martz.
1988   "Understanding the Sources of Faulty Group Decision Making: A Lesson from the Challenger Disaster." *Small Group Behavior,* 19 (4):411–433.
Excellent, balanced analysis of decisions and processes that led to the destruction of the shuttle and its crew. Despite the objective, scholarly tone, the tension of the NASA environment is palpable.
Lauffer, Armand, et al.
1984   *Understanding Your Social Agency,* second edition. Beverly Hills: Sage.
An excellent way to introduce students to a systems view of social agencies. It is a slightly different set of systems ideas from ours, but the two books are compatible.
Miller, James G.
1978   *Living Systems.* New York: McGraw-Hill.
Chapter 10, "The Organization," pp. 595–745. Very productive of stimulating ideas for the serious student of systems; it continues to be regarded by writers on organizational theory as a primary source of systems ideas.
Scott, W. Richard.
1998   *Organizations: Rational, Natural, and Open Systems,* fourth edition. Englewood Cliffs, NJ: Prentice-Hall.
A remarkable book; this is the definitive overview of theories of organiza-

tion; he regards an "open systems" theory of organizations as the most useful and comprehensive viewpoint. It includes detailed history and critiques of organization theories. It is a gold mine for applications and isomorphisms of social systems ideas at all levels, not only organizations. We highly recommend this as the primary resource for this chapter.

Senge, Peter M.

1990   *The Fifth Discipline.* New York: Doubleday.

While this is a management text, it is also a systems approach to organizations. He makes a convincing case that the "fifth discipline," which is systems thinking, underlies all aspects of management. It is very readable, and well illustrated with examples and the author's experiences.

Shilts, Randy.

1988   *And the Band Played On: Politics, People, and the AIDS Epidemic.* New York: Penguin.

The "must" book on the AIDS crisis, it portrays in rich detail the behavior of federal, municipal, and gay organizations through mid-1988. One of the authors uses it as a casebook on organizational behavior and social policy. Shilts was the first national reporter to concentrate on the epidemic, and died of AIDS in 1994.

LITERARY SOURCES

Kesey, Ken.

1962   *One Flew Over the Cuckoo's Nest.* New York: The Viking Press.

The modern classic story of the round of life in a total institution. Also available on video starring Jack Nicholson. Loosely based on a real Veterans Hospital in California.

Solzhenitsyn, Alexander.

1963   *A Day in the Life of Ivan Denisovich.* New York: Praeger.

[1968] 1969   *Cancer Ward.* New York: Farrar, Strauss, and Giroux.

1973   *Gulag Archipelago.* New York: Harper & Row.

Any of Solzhenitsyn's novels/documentaries are worth reading as examples of "total" institutions and the survival of the human spirit within them.

FILMS AND VIDEOS

Barbarians at the Gate (1993)

A humorous, tongue-in-cheek true tale of the attempt by the CEO of RJR Nabisco to take over the company, with the help of American Express, based on the book. Made for television; it won Golden Globe awards.

Roger and Me (1989)

Michael Moore pursues the elusive chairman of General Motors, to discuss the closing of an automobile plant in his hometown of Flint, Michigan. Moore is a populist *agent provocateur*, satirizing and lambasting corporate America. The video vividly portrays community response to social disaster, and community decline. He pursued this theme in his 1997 Film, *The Big One,* also.

Welfare (1975)

One of Frederick Wiseman's series of documentaries, it is among the best materials for the study of organizations, even though it is more than a quarter-century old. It portrays an unending purgatory for welfare recipients and staff in a Manhattan welfare office, a Kafkaesque environment in which clients and staff are both caught. One of the authors used it in an organization course.

Groups

Nothing is harder to stop than a freely and fully united band of human beings.
—Milton Mayer, *On Liberty: Man vs. the State*

Feminist groupwork delabels, deconstructs boundaries, expands a sense of personal vision and makes the connections between these and wider socio-economic forces. The changes in women's personal lives have irreversible repercussions. Sustaining social change in the face of resistance and ridicule is nurtured by the bedrock of the group . . .

Every time this happens, the world does not remain the same.
—Butler and Wintram, *Feminist Groupwork*

INTRODUCTION

The social group is a critical system to each person and, in particular, to the helping professions. As an arena of social interaction, the group has potential to provide for a range of human needs, which include:

1. a need to belong and to be accepted by others;
2. a need to be validated by others through feedback processes;
3. a need to share common experiences with others; and
4. opportunities to work with others on common tasks.

The human group is a social system that has received, and deserves, extensive investigation. The term "group" comprises those patterns of association and activity in which persons engage most of their "selves" from day to day. Its components are individuals and small constellations of persons (e.g., dyads and triads) and it is, in turn, a component of its environment. A group is more than simply an aggregate of individuals: it has a unique wholeness of its own. As Kurt Lewin phrased it, "The whole is *different from* the sum of its parts; it has definite properties of its own" (cited in Marrow, 1969:170, emphasis ours). (Note that we use the words "different from," not "more than.") The human group is a system distinguishable from its environment, has the characteristics and functions of a system, and provides the connection between its components and its environment. Like other social systems, groups are characterized by energy/information exchange to promote *synergy*; this term, originated by anthropologist Ruth Benedict, was applied to groups by psychologist Abraham Maslow. The following passage is one application of the term, in "sensitivity training":

> Synergy involves the resolution of the selfish/unselfish dichotomy by making the enhancement of the Other the precondition or result of personal enhancement. . . . Further evidence for synergy came from the supervisors' reports on their work groups. There was a substantial increase in groups which reached decisions by mutual agreement and in reports that "differences in opinion are directly confronted and discussed to productive solutions." (Golembiewski and Blumberg, 1970:51–52).

From a social systems perspective, a cluster of persons can be considered a group only if it fulfills certain specific criteria of systems. Instead of assuming that aggregations are systems, each aggregate should be empirically examined to determine whether they do, in fact, have the properties of systems. If the subject of such examination is not found to possess such properties, that is, cannot be established to be a holon, then the analysis should properly be carried out at the next lower level (Campbell, 1958). Thus, a group with a *high level* of systems properties might be analyzed largely with group concepts; a *moderate level* with group and individual concepts; and a *low level* with individual concepts.

An example might be the ensemble of characters in the two popular television series "Friends" and "Cheers": in each series, the characters interact as a whole group on occasion, but some interact as dyads or triads; one couple were lovers and interact as a subset of the whole; and each interacts intimately at times with others who are not members of the usual "cast of characters." Do they constitute a group? A loose network? A fluidly structured aggregation? In other words, a gathering together of persons does not make a group. The expression "the group jelled" conveys a point in time or process when an aggregate of persons became an entity, a group, distinguishable from its environment (that is, it had an interactional boundary), and different from the sum of its parts.

This obviously leads to the questions: What kinds of groups are there, and what are the significant properties of a group as system? The remainder of this chapter answers these questions.

I. TYPES OF GROUPS

Small groups are distinctive among social systems examined in this book in that a group system can be created for particular purposes by human service professionals (as could an organization, although this occurs less frequently). Groups can be created for purposes of therapy, self-actualization, support, problem-solving, goal achievement, or to influence larger systems as in community organization and social action. In practice, groups often fit into more than one of the types described below, simply because groups are such powerful instruments for change, and have a wide range of effects, both intentional and unintentional. Out of the incredibly wide range of types of groups, we have selected those that seem most common and useful for the human services.

A. Growth Groups, or Human Potential Groups

Growth groups, or human potential groups, are organized to further purposes of their members, usually *personal* growth, through provision of "intensive group experience" over a limited time span. Examples include T-groups, sensory awareness groups, encounter groups, sensitivity training groups, and marathon groups. Other varieties of groups may also be considered in this general category, however: hobby groups, theater groups, art groups, book groups, recreation groups (swim clubs, softball teams, and bowling teams might even qualify, on occasion, if the physical activity is secondary to personal development; it is an elastic category). Reid says: "Growth-oriented groups have as their focus the facilitation of an individual's passage through the normal developmental stages. There is no assumption of pathology. Rather, the person is interested in becoming more aware of himself or herself as a struggling human being" (1997:11).

Growth groups tend to focus on expressive functions, to emphasize feelings and impersonal transactions. The norms include mutuality of support, openness, and disclosure. The group's powers of acceptance and validation are employed. However, it is essential that group leaders be competent to deal with the hazards of intensive group experience.

B.   Therapeutic Groups, or Remedial Groups

Reid divides "remedial groups" (which we consider to be the same as therapeutic groups) into three kinds:

(1) *supportive treatment groups,* which "generally emphasize restoration, enhancement, or maintenance of each member's level and mode of function or problem solving";

(2) *interpersonal growth groups,* which "focus on helping members gain insight, growth, and change in their relationships"; and

(3) *intrapsychic growth groups,* which emphasize development of insight into one's own personality. (1997:12)

Therapeutic groups are structured to serve as vehicles for persons struggling with intrapsychic concerns. Often the group is open-ended and long-term, with members cycling in and out. In describing the efficacy of therapeutic groups, Kovel says, "[I]n a therapeutic situation an individual's problems often become clearer when expressed in a context of interaction with, or in reaction to, several others. Sometimes behavior in the group stimulates or surfaces problems which an individual has not dealt with in . . . interviews with a therapist" (1976:52). Therapeutic groups usually have an expressive focus with leaders clearly differentiated from the group. Socialization and communication are emphasized. Group process may be subordinated at times to the need of an individual.

C.   Self-Help and Support Groups

Over the past fifty years, there has been a phenomenal increase in the incidence of persons who come together around a common personal concern; groups exist for virtually every such concern. Self-help and support groups differ primarily in the degree of direction provided by the leader or facilitator.

The role of the worker is to encourage sharing, risk taking, and mutual problem solving. He or she may ask members to speak directly to one another, may focus the discussion, and may limit story telling. . . . The worker helps members explain their situations, offer suggestions to others provide support, and learn from each other. (Reid, 1997:11)

Self-help and support groups differ from therapeutic groups in that members of self-help and support groups are not seeking (at least overtly) personal psychological insight or growth. Sharing experiences and ways of coping are vehicles for mutual help—self and other, helping and accepting help. In self-help groups, professional direction is usually not wanted, although in some circumstances, a professional helper may convene a group or sponsor it. The focus is either on participants working on a kind of personal problem they share with the other group members or joining together to influence external systems to provide resources or recognize members' needs and rights (e.g., a divorced women's group, or a group of neighbors in a community who seek better policing, or better housing). Feminist groups fit this description:

If we peel off the layers of academic and agency sophistication, we are left with women's own powerful and fundamental statements. For them the group is:

1. a source of immediate support, where the knowledge that the meeting will take place every week provides a safety net in itself;
2. a place to recognize shared experiences and the value to be derived from these;
3. a way of breaking down isolation and loneliness;
4. the source of a different perspective on personal problems;
5. a place to experience power of personal situations with the capacity to change and have an effect on these;
6. a source of friendship (Butler and Wintram, 1991:17).

Although some self-help groups may be largely task-oriented, sentiment is an ever-present factor. There are several types of self-help and support groups:

1.   Groups that are primarily focused on self-fulfillment, self-development, or growth in specific aspects of personal functioning, e.g., in handling anxiety;

2.   Groups that meet in sheltered environments under close supervision by peers or others who have experienced similar problems, e.g., Alcoholics Anonymous, that may meet in community settings or in prisons; and

3.   Groups for those who care for others in both senses of that term: either care about them, or provide services to them. This includes family members of persons with Alzheimer's disease, family members of persons with HIV / AIDS, and Alanon and Ala-Teen for families of alcoholics.

Some self-help groups originate locally, whereas others are national organizations with local face-to-face chapters. Alcoholics Anonymous and Weight Watchers fit the cultural penchant for mobility, in that members who migrate to different geographic locales can immediately affiliate with a local chapter in their communities.

Such groups evolve their own leadership in order to pursue specific goals, often the protection of civil rights or social and cultural prerogatives. The latter includes groups such as Skinheads, survivalists, and white supremacists, whose avowed purposes are to preserve themselves and their values, by violence if necessary, against those whom they define as enemies.

D. Consciousness-Raising and Social Action Groups

Consciousness-raising has its roots in radical social/political philosophy, e.g., the use of Paolo Freire's (1983) *conscientizacion* philosophy in which literacy training among low-income groups was accompanied by discussions about political structures and personal involvement in social change. One objective of such groups is *cognitive restructuring*, self-examination of one's behavior and reactions.

> Given that identity is both personally held . . . and, in addition, is social-
> ly constructed, cognitive restructuring can play a key role in helping group
> members to gain control over their environment. . . . A feminist gloss on
> each thought or behavioural pattern can have a liberating effect by encour-
> aging women to:
> 1. recognize patterns of self-protection, self-blame and self-effacement
> from the past, and to articulate the reasons behind the need for such
> behaviour;
> 2. express distress and anger at the extent to which direct, honest self-
> expression has been denied them . . .
> 3. recognize such behaviours and cognitions as survival mechanisms,
> rather than pathological disturbances (Butler and Wintram, 1991:66–67).
> [O]ne of the most striking messages which women's groups convey is
> the need for women to take power for themselves. The realization that each
> interaction point is an exercise of power negotiation can energize women to
> tread the rocky path towards self-control. What develops is an internal
> legitimation of the constructive use of authority and influence. (ibid.:78)

Groups that fit this category include:

1. *Social advocacy* groups, which promote and support activism, e.g., gay rights groups, HIV/AIDS patients groups, feminist groups, or tenants rights groups.

2. *Empowerment* groups, which combine elements from other types of groups (e.g., self-development, advocacy, and specific problem) while focusing on increasing each member's self-awareness, confidence, and capacity to gain control of their lives. Examples include groups for victims of domestic abuse, childhood sexual abuse, sexual harassment, and for persons who are overweight, anorexic, or bulimic, as well as self-discovery groups:

> The small-group structure of consciousness-raising groups has been partic-
> ularly suitable for the exploration of personal identity issues . . . growing
> out of the sense of "restless constraint" . . . felt by women whose lives are
> circumscribed within narrow confines. (ibid.:31)

These authors also describe examples of members of women's groups who exercised personal power: "One group participant . . . dissatisfied with the work her solicitor was doing . . . appeared at the lawyer's office without an appointment and refused to leave until matters had been organized to her satisfaction, berating the lawyer all the time." In another instance,

> one participant who was faced with eviction for rent arrears . . . demanded legal representation and a proper check of the records. . . . She met considerable resistance but remained undaunted, and ultimately was proved correct. When recounting the episode in a group session, she said that the strength and self-confidence gained from attending the group had given her the faith in herself that she had needed to survive. (ibid.:159–160)

E. Task Groups

Task groups most often are part of organizations, but may exist independently. They assume, or are assigned, specific tasks to accomplish, within a specified time period. Task groups include committees (appointed for a fixed term or for as long as needed), work teams (e.g., the autonomous work groups described in the preceding chapter), and volunteers who accept responsibility for completion of a specific goal (e.g., fund-raising). Reid (1997:12) points out that "While not normally thought of as a form of treatment, task groups can have significant therapeutic value," but this is rarely their intent, of course. As a community organization text states it, "all group interactions have a *task* and a *process* dimension, and *task groups of all kinds must attend to both in order to succeed*" (Hardcastle, Wenocur, and Powers, 1997:264).

Aside from individual persons carrying out their assignments, task groups are probably the most common means of accomplishing tasks in our society and in organizations, particularly. It is a rare organizational participant who is not a member of at least one task group at any one time. Productive participation requires sufficient personal development to initiate ideas and defend them, to maturely consider others' contributions apart from one's personal relationship to them, to assume leadership if necessary, and to be able and willing to subordinate oneself to the general will of the group if necessary. Thus task groups are adult enterprises that children learn by themselves participating, usually in school or in youth organizations and clubs.

F. Cliques and Coalitions

This topic is an example of the difficulty in choosing a level of analysis when defining and analyzing systems. Some groups operate within organizations without legitimation, as cliques, coalitions, or cabals (depending upon one's viewpoint). Most administrators or managers can provide examples of such groups, which challenge the formal leadership of the organization and coalesce around one or more issues. They may have a base of *legitimacy* as members of a committee, or by virtue of their positions (as supervisors, or lower-level administrators, e.g.); or, instead, they may have *power* by virtue of controlling certain resources internally (the majority of votes on an important committee; knowledge of Robert's Rules of Order; or the minutes of decisions made in the past) or through connections to external sources of energy (funding sources, or as members of the labor union that represents the organization's work force).

Such groups usually are time-limited: they dissolve with their goal satisfied (or unsatisfied); achieve power and become the leadership themselves; or simply fade as circumstances change (the current leader departs, the organization changes, or members of the clique drop out or leave the organization, e.g.). There is no likelihood of predicting or generalizing about the evolution of such groups.

Most people who work in organizations have observed such cliques, participated in them, or opposed them. We do not imply that such groups are necessarily wrong or unjustified; e.g., they may champion the cause of an employee (or group of employees) who has been wronged, like the once-famous *Willmar 8* (the name of a movie about them), a group of women employees at a bank in Minnesota who, for several years, protested the treatment they received. Groups might also protest illegal practices or inept management in the organization; or, e.g., a group of faculty members might advocate unionization as a means of "saving the soul" of a university from a "corporate mindset."

The question remains, of course, whether the group is properly regarded as a system in its own right or as a subsystem of the organization.

II. DIMENSIONS OF GROUPS

There are as many kinds of groups as there are group leaders, observers, and therapists (and perhaps members, since each has a unique personal perspective on the group). Rather than attempt a comprehensive taxonomy, we will discuss a few important dimensions that have been used to classify groups. These dimensions are here discussed as polarities. Any given group, at any given time, theoretically could be placed at some point on each continuum.

A. *Instrumental versus Expressive*

This continuum is similar to others that are frequently used: "task vs. sentiment," "goal achievement vs. group maintenance," "task-oriented vs. group-oriented," and "guidance behavior vs. sociable behavior." The distinction is usually understood as being between a particular, articulated, time-limited objective and a diffuse, unarticulated, enduring and supportive group climate. Further, the distinction is usually taken to imply that a "goal" or "task" is adaptive, that is, related to the environment, whereas "expressive" or "sentiment" is related to interactions among components of the group. The distinction is best understood as a distinction between two desirable steady states toward which the group could move. The first steady state is one in which some fairly clear, specific objective would be accomplished, with specific results for "vertical" relations (that is, with the group's suprasystem or environment). The other state is one in which the objectives are fairly diffuse and nonspecific, with the general result of integration of components (i.e., "horizontal" relations). Consequently, instrumental or expressive activities are intended to move the group toward one of these two steady states. Perhaps "adaptive versus integrative" would be equally accurate: "The social system, in its organization . . . tends to swing or falter back and forth between two theoretical poles; optimum adaptation to the outer situation at the cost of internal malintegration, or optimum internal integration at the cost of maladaptation to the situation" (Weisman, 1963:87).

These are polarities and are not mutually exclusive. The "adaptive" steady state focuses more attention on goals and tasks but also deals with integration, although to a lesser extent. The "integrative" steady state, similarly, does not exclude some adaptive activity. For example, the U.S. Supreme Court (indeed a powerful group) must spend some time mediating between the Justices' personal feelings at times (Woodward and Armstrong, 1981; Lazarus, 1998). A sensitivity group must make decisions about meeting dates and when termination should occur. Another example is Reginald Rose's play (and movie) *Twelve Angry Men*, which illustrates the successive steady states of a jury as it alternately focuses upon the court's demand for a verdict and the members' needs (Rose, 1955). It is this variability that makes "group" difficult to characterize, in contrast to the family, which is predominantly integrative, and the organization, which is predominantly adaptive.

Groups resemble both communities and organizations. The community is largely made up of groups and shares their indeterminate character; indeed, it is sometimes difficult to distinguish between communities and groups. We suggest this guideline: the greater the breadth of influence that a group has upon its members and the more diffuse its goals, the more it resembles a community. Groups resemble organizations to the extent that they are aimed toward specific goals. Many such groups are components of organizations and can be called "work groups."

B. Primary versus Secondary

This polarity describes the importance that the group has for group members. The afternoon (or morning) neighborhood coffee klatch is a good example. It is predominantly (if not purely) expressive. If it is highly significant to its members, it is a primary group; but if it has relatively little importance to them, it should be considered secondary (one shouldn't forget, of course, that the group may be more important to one member than to another). This criterion is the breadth of influence the group has upon its members and particularly its influence upon their affective functioning. Another way of saying this is that if members react to each other as role occupants rather than as persons, it is a secondary group. As these roles become more formalized, the group becomes more goal-specific and narrows its range of influence; thus, the closer the group comes to being an organization.

C. Narcissistic versus Generative

This polarity applies to the *self*-gratification of one or more members versus a wider commitment to the *group's* goals; this is similar to Freud's pleasure and reality principles, and related to Erikson's crisis of "generativity *vs.* stagnation" (see Chapter 8). The importance of this dimension of groups is that it explains the ability (or inability) of some groups to survive; that is, a concentration solely upon members' needs violates the principle that no single function can be concentrated upon to the complete exclusion of others. If members are unwilling to adapt, the results might be an inability to alter relationships (and therefore structure), resulting in a closed, morphostatic system. By contrast, a generative system, like a generative person, would engage in mutually constructive interchange with its environment and among its components. The polarities discussed above indicate that groups have important properties of systems: adaptation, integration, goal-seeking, structural maintenance, and structural change.

III.   ASPECTS OF GROUP AS SYSTEM

A. Evolutionary Aspects

Analysis of any specific group requires much attention to its evolution. This is true because groups and families are more dependent upon specific persons than are other systems and are thus more likely to be affected by changes in personnel. By contrast, organizations are usually deliberately designed to minimize dependence upon individual persons. Formation and disintegration of a group are more likely to occur during a single member's lifetime, and therefore can be observed and analyzed by a single observer. Accordingly, in literature about groups, more attention has been paid to "process" (behavior) and to problem-solving (goal attainment) than to structure; and in research on groups, the dynamic balance (or steady state) of the group has received most attention. In group work practice, it has been almost a dogma that all aspects of groups are subordinate to the maintenance of steady state. In our discussion of other systems, we have had to establish that they are systems and that steady state is a valid term to apply to them. With groups, the problem is the converse; so much has been researched and written on the group as a system, and on group equilibrium or steady state in particular, that the task is instead to establish that any other aspect of the system is of equal importance.

1. Steady State

The group is like an organism—a biological organism. It forms, grows, and reaches a state of maturity. It begins with a set of constituent elements— individuals with certain personalities, certain needs, ideas, potentialities, limitations—and in the course of development evolves a particular pattern of behavior, a set of indigenous norms, a body of beliefs, a set of values, and so on. Parts become differentiated, each assuming special functions in relations to other parts and the whole. . . . As a group approaches maturity it becomes more complex, more differentiated, more interdependent, and more integrated. (Mills, 1967:13)

This is a detailed way to describe a group's steady state. More general ways are to describe its "identity," or its "culture." Mills described groups as having some of the same qualities that Erikson described in persons. Groups have "personality," similar to the personalities of individuals, according to some writers. This was labeled "syntality" by Cattell as early as 1948 and defined as "the personality of the group, or, more precisely, as any effect that the group has as a totality. . . . Syntality traits are inferred from the external behavior of the group and may include such behaviors as decision making, aggressive acts, and the like" (Shaw, 1981:20). It might also be accurate to say that each group possesses its own culture, a microcosm of the larger culture; without its own culture (or microculture) the group would not be a system but merely an aggregate of individual persons.

   a. *Norm, consensus, and bond.*   A group establishes norms through consensus. One definition of *norm* is:

a generalization concerning an expected standard of behavior in any matter of consequence to the group. It incorporates a value judgment. It is a rule or standard to which the members of a group are expected to adhere. A set of norms introduces a certain amount of regularity and predictability into the group's functioning. (Northen, [1969] 1988:33–34)

"Regularity and predictability" are obviously relevant to steady state. In groups, if successful, individual persons' norms tend to converge into a group norm. This was illustrated in the classic Bank Wiring Observation Room study, in which workers had explicit expectations about the production norms and pressured others to conform (Roethlisberger and Dickson, 1947). Another example is the group norm of supporting their "buddies" among soldiers or their "partners" among police officers. As cartoonist Bill Mauldin stated in *Up Front*, combat units "have a sort of family complex."

> New men in outfits have to work their way in slowly, but they are eventually accepted. Sometimes they have to change their way of living. An introvert or recluse is not going to last long in combat without friends, so he learns to come out of his shell. Once he has "arrived" he is pretty proud of his clique, and he in turn is chilly toward outsiders. (Cartwright and Zander, 1960:165)

The norm is cooperation; the underlying consensus is survival, whether in World War II, Vietnam, or the Gulf War.

Consensus is agreement regarding goals, norms, and roles. When such agreements and need satisfactions bind members to the group, the group has "attractiveness" or "valence," and the result is cohesiveness of the group. Such cohesiveness gives rise to solidarity, "the stabilized mutual responsibility of each toward the other to regard himself as part of the other, as the sharer of a common fate, and as a person who is under obligation to cooperate with the other in the satisfaction of the other's individual needs as if they were one's own" (Bales, 1950:61). The Polish labor union Solidarity obviously included this meaning in its name. For a decade after the union was declared illegal, Solidarity's members exhibited sufficient cohesiveness to prevail over the government of Poland, to be declared legal again, and to function as part of the government; the union's head, Lech Walesa, became the leader of the country.

With the establishment of norms and consensus, a group is well on its way to having forged a *bond* between its members. Grace Coyle described group *bond* as having three levels:

> 1. conscious purpose, for example sociability or friendship;
> 2. assumed or unavowed objectives, such as achievement or status, ego expansion, courtship (especially among adolescents), and class rise;
> 3. unconscious purpose, including sanctioned release of aggression, escape from reality, and sublimation of erotic impulses. (Coyle, 1948)

Consensus and cohesiveness, then, are *expressive, integrative,* and *primary* aspects of the group and are essential to supporting goal direction.

b. Goal direction. The other component of steady state that should be discussed is goal direction or goal pursuit. In contrast to consensus and cohesiveness, goal attainment is *instrumental, adaptive,* and *secondary.*

Group "purpose" means any ultimate aim, end, or intention or, as we define it in the glossary, a desired steady state of the group. Group *objective* or *goal* usually refers to a specific end that is instrumental to the purpose. We use "goal" to mean both those ends the suprasystem assigns to the group and those ends sought by the group itself.

"Locomotion" is the name given to group goal pursuit by Kurt Lewin and the group dynamics theorists. It means that a group moves within its environment to achieve goals; the goals are mutually defined by the group and its relevant environment. Goal-directed behavior affects group consensus and cohesiveness. It may disrupt expressive, integrative norms and force members to choose between instrumental and expressive behaviors. In some instances, groups may disband because of the divergence.

2. *Stages of Evolution.* As a group seeks to establish its steady state, it moves through various stages of dynamic evolution, as discussed in the following section. As Reid says, "Social scientists have, for decades, grappled with the issue of sequence and order in a group's development. While theorists and clinicians agree that groups go through these stages, there is no agreement as to how many stages exist and what these stages actually look like" (1997:56). Here is one very general, abstracted view:

1. The group adapts to its environment; in response to this adaptive behavior, members develop activities, sentiments, and interactions. These adaptive components are the group's external system.

2. The group develops activities, sentiments and interactions beyond the necessary adaptive behavior, through its goal-oriented behavior; these become the internal system.

3. As the internal system elaborates, it develops bond, cohesiveness, norms, roles and statuses.

4. In feedback fashion, adaptation is affected by the environment and the developing internal system.

5. The group, in turn, modifies the functioning of its members. (Weisman, 1963:87)

Another general scheme of stages of group evolution is the following, with captions for each stage, and a one-word description of what occurs in each stage (Glassman and Kates, 1990):

Stage 1: "We're Not in Charge"   Preaffiliation
Stage 2: "We Are in Charge"   Power and Control
Stage 3: "We're Taking You On"   Power and Control
Stage 4: "Sanctuary"   Intimacy
Stage 5: "This Isn't Good Anymore"   Differentiation
Stage 6: "We're Okay and Able"   Differentiation
Stage 7: "Just a Little Longer"   Separation

Table 6.1 Synthesis of Stages of Group Evolution[a]

Phases	Cognitive aspects	Affective aspects	Behavioral aspects
I. E. pluribus unum Components' goals predominate Affiliation (approach-avoidance) Commitment	Discussion of symbols, meanings Attempt to find common meanings, symbols Limited agreement on symbols, meanings, norms	Checking for feelings, values of others; "valence" Expression of feelings Development of group bond; satisfaction of individual's feelings; group values emerge	Observes behavior of others; tentative participation Interaction and reaction in overt behavior; territory shared Beginning of modification of behavior to conform; mutual accommodation; locomotion
II. Control phase Group goals predominate Socialization Social control ↘a Stability (internal)	Internalization of developing group culture; accommodation of schemes Standardization; acceptance of group views; subordination of idiosyncratic views Enforcement of group views, codes and stated purposes; "right thinking" and developed symbol systems	Same as cognitive Subordination of idiosyncratic feelings; reinforcement of those that "match" others' Enforcement of group values; statements expressing solidarity and allegiance; traditions	Roles defined and agreed to Group prescription of behavior; reduction of deviance; differentiation of roles and territories Rituals, offices, hierarchy

Group goal direction (external) ↘a Intimacy; cohesiveness	Problem solving; decision making; thought exclusively focused on goal and means to achieve it; "brainstorming" Exchange with each other to the exclusion of non-members; "private" group views, beliefs, actions	Elevation of values that support goal; devotion to them, excluding other values, both personal and group Devotion to each other, to exclusion of ties with "outsiders"	Focus on specific group goal; sacrifice and joint effort Group rituals and culture concretized and protected
III. Conflict phase Components' goals predominate	Dissensus on norms, goals, evaluations; selectiveness of evidence used against group members	Disaffection; return (or maintaining) to predominance of individuals' sentiments; "hidden-agendas" predominate	Antagonistic behavior; violation of roles, territories, boundaries; violation of rituals, hierarchy

Loop to earlier phase or move to terminal phase

IV. Terminal phase Disintegration (into subgroups or complete disassociation) Termination (planned or by agreement)	Maintenance of divergent views; ideological combat Reinforcement of belief of worth of group; attempt to analyze "meaning" of the group	Hostility; defensiveness; feelings of betrayal, anger *OR* Feelings of guilt, rejection because of termination; warmth toward other members	Alliances; power struggles; 'splitting' from the group; 'betrayal' to outsiders Open communication about termination; displays of sentiment; approach or "flight" behaviors

aArrows indicate that these subphases may be reversed in sequence.

These stages seem roughly to correspond to the general stages in Table 6.1, in which we present our own, highly generalized scheme of group development. Our scheme focuses on the internal development of the group; little reference is made to the environment, since it is difficult (if not impossible) to generalize about the myriad environments in which groups exist. It is designed to acquaint the reader with a wide range of aspects of group development—in reality, no single group exhibits all these aspects or this exact sequence of stages. We encourage the reader to apply this scheme to actual groups to determine its applicability, bearing in mind that a systems view of groups includes "looping back" to other stages, and not necessarily a strictly sequential set of stages.

In the literature on group evolution, three major phases of system development emerge, with several subphases. A fourth phase, termination, may or may not occur. The most frequently used description of stages is that of Tuckman (1965): the stages of *forming, norming,* and *storming,* to which he later added *adjournment.* Our scheme can be seen as somewhat similar, although we attempt to present the stages in greater detail, and in a different theoretical context.

None of these phases is presented here as discrete or absolute. Ours is a highly general synthesis that—to refer again to the introduction of this book—corresponds to reality of groups in the same way that a map corresponds to mud, rocks, and a turbulent stream.

a. *Phase I: E pluribus unum.*   During this first major phase, exploration of each other occurs among the members. Members probe each other, testing for security and support. In this phase, members look primarily to the leader for direction, rather than to other members. Eventually, in successful groups, members agree to tolerate each other's thoughts, feelings, and behaviors although there may be some reluctance initially. Such tolerance permits open discussion of the group's emerging culture, i.e., the way we do things. Some sense of "we-ness" must emerge: *"Until that collection of autonomous individuals begins to feel some allegiance to the collectivity and finds some way to work together on a common goal, a group has not yet formed"* (Hardcastle et al., 1997:265).

Carl Rogers identified and described the phases of encounter groups. His phases are similar to our generic outline here. Rogers described "patterns or stages," the first five of which fit within our first major stage. They are (1) "milling around," (2) "resistance to personal expression," (3) "description of past feelings," (4) "expression of negative feelings," and (5) expression of personal feelings (Rogers, 1970:15–20). Discussion of symbols and meanings may take the form of tentative exploration of what structure is possible for the group, what "freedom" means in this group, and how others interpret what the leader says. The interpretation that members arrive at determines the group's valence or attractiveness. Members begin to share their life space (Lewin's term) to permit others to enter their interactional, personal territory, their "bubbles." Leaders of women's groups reported that

> women's groups should experiment with as many different pursuits, activities and exercises as possible, in order to connect with the totality of women's lives and selves. . . . Our own trials and errors, and statements that women have made, have taught us that trips out and visits, the opportunity for fun, laughter and enjoyment, are just as central as psychotherapeutic exercises and sociopolitical discussions. (Butler and Wintram, 1991:42)

This first phase is similar to Tuckman's stage of *forming.*

   b.   *Phase II: Control phase.*   In our second major phase, the emphasis shifts from "inclusion" to "control." In the control stage the member asks: Now that I have decided to be a member of the group, what power will I have in it? Who is in charge and how do I find this out? What does the group want of me?

One text (Corey, Corey, Callanan, and Russell; 1982:91–93) describes a stage following the preliminary testing of each other by members, a stage in which members are engaging in productive, mutual activity. This is called the "working stage" and has the following characteristics: (1) a focus on the immediate interactions; direct and meaningful interaction, including confrontations; (2) free communication among members; the group becomes an "orchestra," listening to each other and working productively together; (3) self-disclosure is the norm; (4) members know each other through feedback and learn to trust the feedback; and (5) group cohesion is increased as they become "a trusting community." This second phase is similar to Tuckman's stage of *norming,* which he places as his third stage.

Rogers' stages 6–10 are not applicable to all types of groups but illustrate evolution in encounter groups. In these stages, immediate interpersonal feelings are disclosed; a "healing capacity" develops; members are willing to risk, resulting in self-acceptance and change; "facades" begin to be discarded, and the member receives feedback, both positive and negative. Rogers described in these stages the elements that we include in the subphase, "socialization," in Table 6.1. Members have taken the group norms "to heart"—they have internalized them. They have begun to sort out roles of "facilitator" (not always group leader), "conciliator," and so forth. They heal each other and restrain other members who violate the group norm of caring for each other. Those members who express caring or negative feelings validate the group's norms of behavior. Intimacy and cohesiveness are achieved as thoughts, feelings, and behavior are expressed among members, which are not expressed to others outside the group. The notable difference between our scheme and Rogers's is that he deals little with group goal direction. This is understandable since his encounter groups were oriented toward relatively diffuse goals, and achievement of goals beyond group process were of minor importance.

   c. *Phase III: Conflict phase.*   Phase III can occur at any point in group process. It does not necessarily follow Phase I or II. It is similar to Tuckman's stage of *storming,* which he places second in sequence; in our view, conflict can occur at any point. When it occurs, however, it is a crisis in the life of the group: the group will either loop back to an earlier stage (similar to regression in individual persons) to resolve the issue or at least deal with it in some fashion so that the group can proceed (analogous to Erikson's description of the resolution growth crises—see Chapter 8). Rogers described well some of the most intense encounters that can take place in groups, in his stages 11–15:

> *Confrontation.* There are times when the term feedback is far too mild to describe the interactions that take place . . .
>   *Norma:* (loud sigh). . . . Any real woman I know wouldn't have acted as you have this week, and particularly what you said this afternoon. That was so *crass!!* It just made me want to puke, right there!!! And—I'm just *shaking* I'm so mad at you—I don't think you've been real once this week! . . . I'm so infuriated that I *want to come over and beat the hell out of you!!* (1970:31–32)

After this, this group could have disintegrated or reverted to an earlier stage. However, if norms are established permitting resolution and continuation, positive resolution can occur. One example is the full expression of negative feeling to another member, which may lead to a deeper understanding and acceptance between the two members. Rogers called this "the basic encounter." Butler and Wintram described values in women's groups that promote integration even through confrontation:

> a belief that all contributions should be considered and if not used, then appreciated;
>   a belief that mutual support is an effective buffer against stress and oppression;
>   a belief that confrontation should be communal;
>   the validation of efforts by members to change their behaviour, attitudes or lifestyle;
>   a belief in sisterhood and collective action. (Butler and Wintram, 1991:85)

   If norms have not developed, and positive outcomes are not forthcoming, however, conflict may result in disintegration and termination. Coser raised the question, "If conflict unites, what tears apart?" (1964:73). He observed that "not all conflicts are positively functional for the relationship, but only those that concern goals, values, or interests that do not contradict the basic assumptions upon which the relation is founded" (ibid.:80). If members of one of the groups Rogers described did not take a healing role or offer mutual support, the conflict could indeed affect the basic function of encounter groups (i.e., to provide an experience of confrontation and caring). The group might terminate or break into subgroups as indicated in the disintegration subphase of our Phase III.

Northen described several attempts to resolve conflict that include:

> *elimination,* that is, forcing the withdrawal of the opposing individual or subgroup, sometimes in subtle ways. In subjugation, or domination, the strongest members force others to accept their points of view. . . . Through the means of *compromise* . . . each of the factions . . . give up something to safeguard the common area of interest. . . . An individual or subgroup may form an *alliance.* . . . Finally, through *integration,* a group may arrive at a solution that is both satisfying to each member and more productive and creative than any contending suggestion. ([1969] 1988:42–43)

The latter is an example of *synergy,* of course, and an example of integration as a basic system function. Ødd Ramsoy (1962), a Norwegian sociologist, investigated the conflict inherent between system and subsystem in social groups. He observed that a group as an entity must tend toward adaptation and integration if it is to survive. The members must always decide between choices that favor system, subsystem, or suprasystem. Ramsoy postulated that conflict between part and whole decreases as the integrative problems of the common inclusive system outweigh each subsystem's adaptive problems and goal problems. Ramsoy, and others including Coser (1964), concluded that *conflict can be reduced through concentration on a superordinate problem* (e.g., manufacturing a war to allay internal conflict, as satirically presented in the 1997 movie, *Wag the Dog*). In the presence of a stranger there are no subgroups. Such conflict may provide an occasion for restoring a balance between adaptation and integration in the system's steady state. As an outcome of group process, it means that the components (individual members) and the system (the whole group) may have synergistically satisfied needs and goals. That, indeed, is the height of achievement for any system. We do not intend to minimize the existence or the (sometime) usefulness of conflict in systems, but no system endures with conflict alone, rather than cooperation (synergy), as its predominant mode of activity.

   d.   Phase IV: Terminal phase.   As indicated in Table 6.1, Phase IV represents a terminal phase, which may have one of two general outcomes: (1) disintegration or (2) a planned, or agreed-upon termination in an affirmative manner. Disintegration is essentially a loop back to an earlier phase in which components' goals predominated over those of the group: either to the beginning (Phase I) if fundamental issues were unresolved at the start, or to Phase III, in which conflict predominated.

   Reid's description of group evolution is based on the life stages of individual persons, and this phase is, of course, "death." He uses Kübler-Ross's stages of death and dying to identify group members' reactions to group termination. While these seem appropriate enough (denial, rage and anger, bargaining, depression, and acceptance), they seem to omit the most positive outcomes of group process: celebration, a sense of fulfillment and accomplishment, satisfaction, and sometimes merely relief. Our Phase IV is more similar to Tuckman's *adjournment* stage, which, like ours, contains both affirmative and negative possibilities.

Reid says of the worker's role in this final stage:

> [T]he worker needs to help each member examine his or her responses. The worker also needs to help the members evaluate how the group has evolved and how they have grown. . . . And the worker needs to encourage the members to look to the future and apply what they have learned to the other systems in their lives. (Reid, 1997:72–73)

B. Structural Aspects

1. Boundary and Autonomy. As with all systems, the boundaries of a group are determined by the structuring activity of the group and its components through interaction among the members and with the environment. Persons define themselves as members, and are defined by others as being members of the group (boundaries are reinforced both internally and externally). For example, separation into religious denominations is largely a matter of individual choice in many societies (though not all, certainly) but segregation by race, age, or gender, along with assigned characteristics, is usually prescribed by society. Here is a discussion of the boundaries of women's groups:

> There are . . . times when women's group process *reflects* what happens in society by way of jealousy or competition between women. Women learn not to value each other, are threatened by each other, are deeply afraid of being seen to be dependent on each other, and resort to manipulation to get some leverage in personal relationships. All of this demonstrates the profound internalization of oppression. How can this well-established pattern be broken down among women's groups? (Butler and Wintram, 1991:93)

Groups have greater or less degrees of autonomy from their environment. A delinquent group such as Whyte's ([1955] 1981) Norton gang was relatively autonomous from its environment, with few direct controls or supports. In 1987, the Los Angeles city attorney stated concern about the lack of societal controls on gangs (i.e., their autonomy): "In a mood of frustration, you feel like the only effective way to deal with street gangs is with a flame thrower" (Vigil, 1988:x). The group of workers in the previously mentioned Bank Wiring Observation Room study was much less autonomous, being subject to a high degree of control by the Western Electric company (Roethlisberger and Dickson, 1947). The boundaries of both groups were clear: the Norton gang's boundary was much less permeable. Another example of permeability of boundaries is Mauldin's description of combat units cited earlier in this chapter. A group, as any other system, must have discernible, locatable boundaries in order to exist.

2. *Differentiation, Hierarchy, and Role.* As previously noted, differentiation of roles occurs as part of elaboration in the evolution of groups. These roles are ranked by the group according to the usefulness of the roles for adaptation and integration. In addition, the person who fills the role is evaluated; members of the group may respond to either the role or the person, or to both. As noted, in secondary groups, members tend to respond more to roles than to persons. When group members agree on rankings, the group may be said to be stratified.

Some roles become standardized among groups and persist regardless of the person occupying the role. Some roles are common to most groups: the scapegoat, who is the recipient of group hostility; the clown or joker, who may be either the butt of humor or the donor, and who serves an important expressive function; the peacemaker, to whom the group turns for conflict reduction, an important integrative or social control function; the idol, who sets some moral or social standard for the group; and the critic, who carries out social control by voicing group ideals and negative judgments.

A recent article cites Fritz Redl's concept of *role suction,* the strong invisible power in a group wherein the group unconsciously selects certain members to fulfill particular functions that meet some of the group's covert needs. The term *suction* indicates that group forces operate in powerful ways to "suck" a given member into an emotionally needed group role. (Gemmill and Kraus, 1988:301)

Some members perform "covert roles":

In a covert role, a member functions to absorb or contain the emotion that the remaining members of a group have difficulty expressing or accepting about themselves. Once a covert role is assumed, it is difficult for group members to discuss how the role has been covertly assigned, since it happens outside their awareness. (ibid.:300)

These authors suggest that groups' syntality includes (in Carl Jung's terminology) a "group shadow":

Like an individual, a group in the process of doing its work develops a shadow of its own, composed of the unexpressed emotional negativity occurring within and between members. Attributes group members find difficult to accept in themselves and in one another constitute the group shadow.

. . . These covert fragments form one basis upon which members are differentiated within a group. (Gemmill and Kraus, 1988:301)

The subject of most research on groups is leadership in its various forms. The two most commonly identified forms are the *task* (instrumental or adaptive) *leader* and the *social-emotional* (expressive or integrative) *leader*. The latter is sometimes called the sentiment leader. In his study of groups, Homans observed several rules for leadership:

1. The leader will maintain the primary position.
2. The leader will live up to the norms of the group. The higher the degree of conformity, the higher will be the member's rank.
3. The leader will not give orders that will not be obeyed; "losing face" would result.
4. In giving orders, the leader will use established channels.
5. The leader will listen.
6. The leader will be self-aware. (1950:440)

While this seems to be a recipe for leadership, the rules describe common expectations for the leader role, for example:

The fact is that leadership in a group may be at one time abrupt, forceful, centralized, with all communications originating with the leader, and another time, slow, relaxed, dispersed, with much communication back and forth between leader and followers. Each mode is acceptable, appropriate and authoritative, but each in different circumstances. (ibid.:419)

Gemmill and Kraus suggested that

a group, when faced with the inevitable uncertainty and ambiguity regarding its initial direction, creates the role of "leader" in order to avoid confronting feelings such as helplessness and fear of failure. In other words, a group unconsciously colludes to create a leader role upon which its members can collectively project threatening feelings and impulses. . . . Once this role is created, the person occupying it becomes, in the view of other group members and himself [sic], the primary person responsible for successful accomplishment of group goals. (1988:304)

In other words, interaction between the leader and the group members and between the group and its environment determine (through activity that creates structure) which form of leadership is most functional for the group at any particular time. The leadership role need not, and usually does not, reside in only one person. Leadership tasks are usually, if not always, distributed among the members. Perhaps leadership is best defined as "the set of functions through which the group coordinates the efforts of individuals" (Katz and Bender, 1976:117).

C. Behavioral Aspects

1. *Adaptation.* This has been discussed under the section on steady state, earlier in this chapter. It remains here only to restate that all group behavior has some bearing upon securing and expending energy externally (SE and GE functions) whether explicitly designed to do so or not. All systems must provide some service or product to their suprasystems or environments, but systems cannot concentrate exclusively on the adaptive function to the exclusion of integration.

An important component of adaptation is leadership, specifically the problem-solving and decision-making activities inherent in the leadership role. These activities have received much attention in research on groups and in research on organizations, in particular. As noted earlier, problem-solving has received prime attention in social group work practice. Mills described task leadership and decision-making

> as an *executive system;* i.e., the set of executive orientations and processes as they are distributed and organized among and performed by group members. Any member, regardless of position or office, who performs executive functions . . . participates in the executive system . . .
>
> The executive system is the group's center for assessment of itself and its situations, for arrangement and rearrangement of its internal and external relations, for decision-making and for learning, and for "learning how to learn" through acting and assessing the consequences of action. . . . The executive system is the partly independent, autonomous center where information about the role-system . . . is processed. (ibid.:93)

More accurately, it is an executive *subsystem* that primarily serves the function of goal attainment. This is isomorphic to the ego functions of the personality system, as Freud described them.

2. *Socialization.* Socialization is, of course, integrative behavior within the group intended to furnish energy to the group and to reduce the likelihood of conflict. The use of small groups to facilitate socialization is widespread, e.g., the pledge group in a sorority, basic training in the military, groups to prepare schizophrenic persons for employment and to resocialize former cult members (who were previously socialized into the cult group). Much like the family, the small group can readily serve as a transition into wider systems. Socialization into the group itself is based upon some match between the person's needs and the group's offering; a good example is the frequent use of groups by adolescents for security, opportunities to make friends, and to learn the cultures of both youth and adult life stages.

The process of socialization may be of three kinds:

a. *compliance*, in which the person conforms, but does not agree with the group's view;

b. *identification*, in which members adopt the group's view because the group becomes part of their own identities;

c. *internalization*, in which the group's view is adopted because it meets some personal objective, or resolves a member's internal or external conflict; that is, the group's view agrees with the member's view.

The adaptation of the person and the integrative behavior of the system must reach some mutually acceptable "bargain," or the process of socialization will fail.

3. *Social Control and Social Conflict.* The process of standardization is related to social control. A group achieves consensus or steady state by shaping its members' behaviors in certain ways. The application of sanctions in one form or another is social control. As noted earlier, social control is exercised by the entire group through various means. The major means of control is energy applied to, or withheld from, a member. One example is the traditional Robert's Rules of Order in formal meetings; if members do not conform to its usage, they may not be recognized (i.e., allowed any oral interchange with the entire group) or may be ejected from the group. An extreme example would be forcing group members to accept certain roles such as worker, hunter, or mate in order to survive. A more subtle example is that new members of the U.S. Congress are expected to "be seen but not heard." The play *Twelve Angry Men* illustrated the various forms that social control can take in a group, from threat of violence to ridicule and "putting down" a member.

An important part of social control in groups is conflict, discussed earlier in this chapter, and the management of conflict.

> Group experience is conflict . . . a response to the reality that there is a shortage of what people need and want. . . . To organize, a group must coordinate one part with another, and in doing so must limit the freedom of some parts. . . . And further, groups accept and reward some members more fully than others, and this inequality creates yet another type of conflict. . . . Change, which occurs at every moment, is determined both in direction and in quality by the manner in which conflicts are resolved. Response to conflict determines the new state of the system. (Mills, 1967:14–15)

As noted earlier, probably the most complete statement of the dimensions and uses of conflict in groups is found in Coser's *The Functions of Social Conflict* (1964).

4. *Communication.* We previously defined communication as "transfer of meaning or energy" by any means. According to this definition, virtually all group activity could be considered communication, render-

Groups

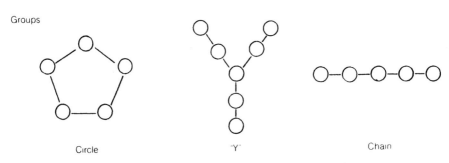

Circle   "Y"   Chain

Figure 6.1.   Diagrams of communications networks.

ing the term so broad as to be meaningless. Rather, we mean communication intended to accomplish adaptation, integration, social control, or goal attainment (in other words, the SE, SI, GI, and GE functions) for the system.

Bales's interaction process analysis theory of groups (Bales, 1950) is based upon the analysis of units of communication into a few categories, such as "shows solidarity," "shows tension release," "disagrees," and "shows antagonism." Tabulating the number of units exchanged during a given time and their distribution by categories allows some index of group process to be derived. This has been a popular means of group analysis. Other theorists, especially those with backgrounds in information theory, have also focused on communication as the basic process in groups. Satir's conjoint family therapy and Berne's transactional analysis both focused on communication. Small group communication became a field of study in its own right, with a rapidly increasing body of literature that included descriptions of communication nets in groups, including the diagrams in Figure 6.1 (Shaw, 1981; Handy, 1985).

> Literally hundreds of studies have been conducted using the communication net approach. The main findings . . . can be summarized rather directly. First, centralized communication nets are more efficient in transmitting messages. Hence, when the task only requires transmission of information . . . the highly centralized wheel is the most efficient net. . . . The *circle*, on the other hand, cannot route all information to any one node as efficiently as the wheel, but the information can be routed to, and the nonroutine aspects of the group's task . . . can be done by, *any* group member equally. (McGrath, 1984:167)

Research confirms that autonomy and the demands of one's task and role in a group are more important than centrality of location (McGrath, 1984). Communication is best carried out when members have significant freedom, and are not overwhelmed by the demands of communication.

Communication between group members is one powerful element of leadership. In addition, one purpose of communication in groups is to allow the group members to improve their communication skills within the group and then transfer these skills to other systems. An example is a group of single, pregnant young women and their parents. This group provided

> the means whereby families may learn new, more appropriate communication behavior. . . . In some instances, family members learn how to communicate better when the therapists and the group decode messages that are sent and inappropriately received in a family system. In other instances, good communication among the therapists in the group's presence serves as a positive model. (Papademetriou, 1971:88)

One means of assuring that all members have opportunity to speak, and to be listened to, is the use of "speaking turns," periods of time during which each member is "given their own space," and other members give support and empathic responses. Among American Indian tribes, passing around a "talking stick" has been a sophisticated means to achieve the same end, the recognition of every member's contribution.

CONCLUSION

It is clear from a wealth of research that groups are social systems. Furthermore, it is apparent that most group theory is based in systemic thinking. Since group experiences are both natural and essential to social living, purposeful use of groups offers opportunity for people to come together to pursue mutual interests and goals. Those who work in human services must understand group phenomena and develop competence in working with groups in order to use wisely the fundamental and immense power contained in the human group.

SUGGESTED READINGS

Butler, Sandra, and Claire Wintram.
   1991 *Feminist Groupwork*. London: Sage.
      Excellent presentation and discussion of group work with women, thorough and insightful. They describe the social and psychological situations of women with precision and sensitivity. The English authors describe themselves as "generic social workers within two County Council Social Services Departments," one in a rural area, one in an inner city. The book is based on their experience conducting women's groups; and provides excellent analyses and great detail.

Donigian, Jeremiah, and Richard Malnati.
1997 *Systematic Group Therapy: A Triadic Model.* Pacific Grove, CA: Brooks/
Cole.
   This little book focuses on "the systemic nature of groups within the framework of general systems theory." It is clear, cogent, readable, compact, and
   (presumably) affordable; it is an excellent supplement to this chapter on
   groups. Its description of group process is generalizable to other groups.
Durkin, James E.
1981 *Living Groups: Group Psychotherapy and General Systems Theory.* New
York: Brunner/Mazel.
   Excellent attempt to reconcile social systems theory and other group treatment theories. Highly useful for the practitioner or teacher looking for
   stimulating ideas. Includes some case examples of the fit between the two
   bodies of thought.
Glasser, Urania, and Len Kates.
1990 *Group Work: A Humanistic Approach.* Newbury Park, CA: Sage.
   The authors protest "the existence, nature, and activities of authoritarian
   groups that develop social and professional situations for controlling social
   milieus and individuals, and for suppressing differences." They emphasize
   democratic values in the goals and conduct of groups. Their discussion of
   group stages is useful, and compatible with social systems theory.
Handy, Charles B.
1985 *Understanding Organizations.* Harmondsworth, England: Penguin.
1993 *Understanding Organizations.* New York: Oxford University Press.
   Chapter 6, pp. 154–184, "On the Workings of Groups," is a fine, brief summary of knowledge about groups in organizations. As noted in Chapter 5,
   this a unique book in its organization and excerpts.
Johnson, David W., and Frank P. Johnson.
1991 *Joining Together: Group Theory and Group Skills,* fourth edition. Englewood Cliffs, NJ: Prentice-Hall.
   This book is truly impressive in its comprehensiveness and its inclusion of
   examples and exercises. Perhaps too large for a supplementary text, but it
   contains a wealth of material for students. A delight to read.
Miller, James Grier.
1978 *Living Systems.* New York: McGraw-Hill.
   We refer here to Chapter 9, "The Group," pp. 515–593. Useful for examples
   of processes in groups. It is Miller's massive application of systems processes to groups and is useful as an example of the lengths to which a
   systems theorist may go in elaborating the ideas. Useful to the serious
   student of systems ideas. Miller studied under Alfred North Whitehead, a
   noted "process" (systems) philosopher.
Northen, Helen.
1988. *Social Work with Groups,* second edition. New York. Columbia University Press.
   A newer edition of a classic text. Our comments on Roberts and Northen,
   below, are applicable here.

Reid, Kenneth E.
  1997   *Social Work with Groups*. Pacific Grove, CA: Brooks/Cole.
  This book is subtitled *A Clinical Perspective*, so does not address all groups that social workers or other professions might encounter. Reid provides historical context for general group work, however. Much of what he describes *is* applicable to other kinds of groups. This is highly valuable, and is probably the best text currently for beginning group workers regarding group dynamics and process.
Roberts, Robert W., and Helen Northen, eds.
  1976   *Theories of Social Work with Groups*. New York: Columbia University Press.
  Excellent sections on historical development and thoughtful evaluation of current status of group work theories. They demonstrate explicitly that a systems approach is fundamental to virtually all theories of group work.

LITERARY SOURCES

Golding, William.
  1959   *Lord of the Flies*. New York: Capricorn Books, Putnam.
  Are human beings evil? Are we basically savage? These are Golding's questions in this famous novel, which portrays a Freudian triad of leaders. Provocative and disturbing.

FILMS AND VIDEOS

The Full Monty (1997)
  A small group of unemployed men in England find a unique way to cope with their common situation. Stages of group development are identifiable. Funny, and poignant in conveying their sense of loss. (We suggest viewing it before deciding to use in class!)
Twelve Angry Men (1957; originally on television's "Studio One" in 1954)
  Illustrates the interactive processes among jurors deliberating a capital case, and the shifts between individual and group goals; it demonstrates that a group is indeed different from the sum of its parts. The film was rated by the late Henry Fonda as his best (we agree). There is also a recent up-dated version.
The More We Get Together (1986)
  This video is primarily about working with very old, disoriented nursing home residents. Part II, "Three Stages of a Validation Group," demonstrates how to form a group with the goals of anxiety reduction, regaining social controls, and recovering sense of well-being.

Families

> All happy families resemble each other; each
> unhappy family is unhappy in its own way.
> —Leo Tolstoy, *Anna Karenina*

> As families go, so goes the nation.
> —Margaret Mead,
> United States Senate Hearing

INTRODUCTION

"Family systems theory" has been the predominant mode of analysis
in family research and family treatment over the last generation. As
Burr says,

> Many of the concepts in family-systems theory are the same as in general
> systems theory—for example, terms like input, output, feedback, rules of
> transformation and boundaries. In addition, however, a number of concepts
> are primarily limited to the family-systems theory: individuation, mystifica-
> tion, paradoxical bonding, double bind, complementary and parallel rela-
> tionships, metacommunication, rules and metarules, boundaries, openness,
> pseudomutuality, coalition, and triangulation. (Burr, 1995:85)

Since social systems theory lies between the "suprasystem" of GST and
the "subsystem" of family systems theory, it uses some terms from both
of the other levels, as was apparent in Chapters 1 and 2.

The family system is centrally important in defining social expectations
and in providing resources necessary for growth, in every phase of the

person's life cycle. Family is the only system that is inextricably interwoven with all other systems. As noted in Chapter 3, Section I,B, "The
Family as a Human Universal," the family assumes, or is delegated, primary responsibility for socialization into the culture and major responsibility to ensure the survival of society and of humanity. However, it is
not a unanimous opinion that families are responsible for the traits of
their children. Rowe (1994) marshals research data to demonstrate that
the "fit" between genetic endowment and cultural characteristics explains
far more than family dynamics does. Whatever the outcome of this theory
of *coevolution*, we should be cautious about heaping responsibility and
blame upon families.

This chapter is entitled "Families" to emphasize that there is a wide
variety of family forms. Use of the singular "family" and its implication of
a single, normative form would perpetuate confusion and lack of precision when conducting "family analysis," "family policy," and studies of
"family impact." Further, it would abet unrealistic and sometimes ideological efforts to enforce that norm as part of a political agenda, to the
detriment of other families and children.

I. APPROACHES TO FAMILY ANALYSIS

We will briefly examine selected approaches to understanding the family. Our intent here is to summarize those approaches that are most congruent with social systems theory.

A. *Family as a System of Roles*

The family as a system of roles is the predominant theme in the literature of family analysis. Roles embody cultural expectations for behavior,
and the family is where these roles are learned and carried out. In classical
psychoanalytic theory, the resolution of the Oedipal conflict depends
upon the availability of constructive role models and the child's adoption
of these roles. Families function through the use of roles that change
during the "family life cycle." Members may exchange roles, or import
new roles to the family (children who are "computer literate," for example). Roles may be explicit or implicit, and *instrumental* (that is, goal
oriented) or *expressive* (that is, emotional). Healthy families carry out roles
that are appropriate to the members' developmental stages, their abilities,
personal characteristics, and social and emotional needs; these factors
change over time, of course. Disturbed families may have faulty perceptions of roles, may be incapable of performing appropriate roles, or may
(for internal or external reasons, e.g., racism or excessive demands by
employers of one or both parents) be forced to perform roles inadequately
or destructively.

The family system of roles must be analyzed both structurally and functionally. Parsons's description of the family as a social system differentiated between instrumental and expressive role functions by gender (male-father as breadwinner and link to the environment, female-mother as social and emotional provider who integrated the family's members) did not apply to all families fifty years ago, and certainly not to the majority now. Many of Parsons's critics point to the fluidity of these roles within the changing family in the United States. Billingsley (1968) viewed such fluidity in African-American families as a source of strength. Dowd agrees: "Black families characteristically demonstrate greater flexibility in gender roles, rely upon extended family and community support systems, and have strong work and religious orientations. Key characteristics . . . include collectivism, cooperation, obligation, sharing, and reciprocity" (1997:106). Recent writers about African-American families describe the strengths, responsibilities, and power of the mother's role (Burton, 1996; Dowd, 1997:105; and see our discussion of feminist viewpoints, later), but as Dowd points out, African-American mothers are blamed for the violence of young African-American men: "The target of [Vice-President] Dan Quayle's speech that included a single reference to [television's] Murphy Brown was Black single mothers. 'When there are no mature, responsible men around to teach boys how to be good men, gangs serve in their place'" (1997:10). Dowd takes strong exception to that viewpoint, describing it as a "myth": "There is no empirically based argument or developmental need for elevating the heterosexual, nuclear two-parent family, or denigrating the single-parent family" (ibid.:39).

Society has been slow to recognize the variety and adaptability of family roles, not only in families of color but in families headed by women, and gay and lesbian couples. Dowd (1997) provides a spirited defense of single-parent families, African-American in particular; Laird and Green (1996) and Slater (1995), provide evidence of the strengths of families headed by lesbian and gay couples.

African-American families also incorporate extended family, neighbors, or others [e.g., Shug Avery in *The Color Purple*; another example (in this case American Indian) is Louise Erdrich's *Love Medicine*; see also Stack, *All Our Kin*, 1974]. The role of the "aunt" in black families is well-known (e.g., Ella's role in *The Autobiography of Malcolm X*).

Parsons did later observe that roles for women broadened from the "pseudo-occupation" of mother-housewife to include role choices of "career pattern," "glamour pattern," and "good companion pattern" (Rodman, 1966). Within the preceding generation, society apparently accepted a feminine role combining these role patterns (see Margaret Adams's comment on this later in this chapter). Hillary Rodham Clinton was the first First Lady to exemplify the "career pattern" while in the White House; the public has held mixed opinions about this. These shifts in masculine and feminine roles occurred because of changes in work roles.

Traditionally, in most (but not all) societies, the family business or family farm consolidated the instrumental functions in the father and reinforced his paternal authority, primarily through inheritance laws passing property from father to son [see, e.g., Engels ([1884] 1902) on the importance of bloodlines in capitalist societies].

In "modern" societies, much of a father's authority derives from his economic contribution to the family, usually through employment in a work organization (Bernard, 1997). Relying upon this external system diffuses and dissipates the traditional authority of the father role, particularly when he is (or is perceived by family members, and perhaps himself) as a functionary in a bureaucracy. In addition, most married women in the United States are employed; the rate of employment increases with the age of the children. When the youngest child is between two and seven years of age, the rate of employment gradually increases to 60 percent as the age of the child increases; there is no further increase until about age seventeen (Sweet and Bumpass, 1987:148). Authority that derives from economic contribution is thus shared by both parents, in a two-parent family.

Single-parent families headed by women, many of which result from divorce, provide a model that has further reduced the legitimacy of father-husband dominance of families and reinforced a model of shared power and authority. Another source of the decline of males' authority is loss of employment, often due to "downsizing" and "restructuring" (Rubin, 1997; Newman, 1997; Wallulis, 1998). Lack of employment and loss of employment affect African-American males more frequently than Caucasian males (O'Hare, Pollard, Mann, and Kent, 1997).

The family's role as determinant and perpetuator of cultural expectations has long been controversial. Engels ([1884] 1902) argued that the family was a bourgeois device designed to enslave women: "The Modern individual family is founded on the open or concealed domestic slavery of the wife." More recently, C. Wright Mills stated: "In so far as the family as an institution turns women into darling little slaves and men into their chief providers and unweaned dependents, the problem of a satisfactory marriage remains incapable of purely private solution."

Far more attention is devoted to adults' roles in families as being necessary to family integrity and functioning than to children's roles, and these adult roles are largely parental roles. Popenoe suggested that inattention to children results from their subordination not only in the family but in society as well:

"Individual" means adults and not children; the rights of adults are given considerably more weight in this regard than are any presumed rights of children. One wonders how much of this in the modern welfare state . . . is due to the downgrading in the political shuffle of the interests of children;

children of course do not vote or normally even express their opinions. It is often pointed out that in virtually every welfare state the growth of benefits for the elderly has far exceeded that for children. If children were involved in formulating welfare-state policies, I have little doubt that the situation would be different. (Popenoe, 1988:336)*

One indication of this attitude toward children (and women, as well) is the lack of a national family policy, in Great Britain (Muncie, Wetherell, Dallos, and Cochrane, 1995:40) and in the United States (Hansen and Garey, 1998; Mason, Skolnick, and Sugarman, 1998).

1. Feminist Views of Women's Roles and Families. Feminist theory has profoundly affected academic and clinical analysis and popular views of family life. Our discussion of feminist views is indebted to Lynne Segal, a professor of gender studies in England, who describes herself as "a feminist psychologist and political activist who has attempted to map out the theoretical and political significance of different strands of feminist thinking around the nature of sexual difference" (Segal, 1995:295–316). She says the feminist perception of the family may seem to have come full circle; it began with a fundamental critique of women's "dependent, undervalued and frequently isolated and miserable existence inside the family" (ibid.:296). "Radical" feminists stressed the oppression of women in families, which was part of patriarchy, and was the basis for other hierarchies, such as race and class. Segal reports that "social feminists" like herself rejected (in some part, at least) the "radical" view, instead analyzing racism, sexism, and classism as "hierarchical axes of power currently serving the interests of a global 'patriarchal capitalism'" (ibid.:299). Male dominance of social science was challenged, and new concepts were called for that more capably interpreted women's experiences: "a women-centred orientation."

What this meant was that the family should no longer be viewed as an undifferentiated unit. Its subsystems and suprasystems, its wider economic, political and ideological environment, all needed to be analyzed ("deconstructed") to identify the ways in which men held power over women, and the effects upon women. "Feminist solutions . . . usually involved extensive social—as well as personal—struggle and transformation" (ibid.:300). In the 1970s an intense period of research and theorizing focused on the role of the state and of welfare policies, in particular, in subordinating women; this was accompanied by proposals for reforms of policies and programs, including women's work and wages, and reproductive choices. Men were encouraged to broaden their roles to include child care and domestic responsibilities (see Booth and Crouter, 1998). In contrast to the earlier feminist view, this aim in this period was to *reform* the family, not to replace it.

In the late 1970s, Segal says, a shift occurred: some feminists, began to celebrate the importance and significance of motherhood and of women's roles as mothers and wives, particularly stressing female bonding and "maternal thinking." This shift was led by Betty Friedan's rethinking of her position in *The Second Stage* in 1981, by Adrienne Rich's *Of Woman Born* in 1976, and Nancy Chodorow's *The Reproduction of Mothering* in 1978. These books "emphasized the overriding importance of women's maternalism" (Segal, 1995:303). Chodorow introduced the theory (later built upon by Carol Gilligan—see Chapter 8) that men and women had different relational styles, which depended upon their need to separate from or identify with *mothers*—that this fundamental fact that *mothers raised children* was centrally significant. Thus, in systems terms, individual women determined all larger social systems, a truly radical feminist viewpoint.

Segal cautions that this shift in thinking occurred amid disputes and theoretical divergences. One of the most significant factors that modified feminist thinking in the early 1980s was the "flowering of Black feminism" which had its own viewpoint on the family, and was critical of the views of white feminists. Other feminists' views evolved; some rejected the earlier negative views of nuclear families, and others advocated for more recognition of diversity among families. Some feminists rejected *any* generalizations about women or women's viewpoints.

> These feminist theoreticians were now questioning all types of fixed categories, identities and relationships, stressing what they saw as the complex, shifting and plural nature of the social meanings which construct, and allow us to speak of, our own experiences of gender, sexuality, parenting or any other aspect of our existence. (Segal, 1995:297)

The rethinking of women's roles led to reexamination of men's roles, as well, and of the psychology of men (this has been carried in the ideology of the Promise Keepers, as discussed elsewhere in this book). By the early 1980s, "'fatherism' was being reclaimed and celebrated by men influenced by feminism" (ibid.:306). Research since then tends to confirm that "fathers who are full-time caregivers display the same type of enhanced sensitivity to their infants as full-time mothers" (ibid.:307). If this is true, men's relational style may change when they are given cultural permission to be "fatherly," and not merely workers. "One study in Britain, for example, found that married men under thirty work four times the amount of overtime as childless men of the same age" (ibid.:307, citing her own work). There is accumulating anecdotal evidence that men as well as women are making choices to step out of the "rat race" and to replace the values of the marketplace with familial values: choosing to stay in smaller communities that are "family friendly" rather than climbing the corporate ladder (see the example of a Japanese family in Chapter 5, Organizations).

But so far, men's behaviors regarding child care and domestic chores have not changed significantly; and it is not clear "who benefits" (as Cato said millennia ago) from the new emphasis on fathering:

> At a time when men's hold on their traditional familial and paternal authority is becoming less secure than ever before, the new stress on fatherhood can thus serve very old familiar rhetoric [which] negates feminist insistence upon the actual contemporary diversity of households with children, whether co-habiting single people, lesbian couples, gay men, women on their own, or women living with friends or other relatives. (ibid.:309)

Family roles evolve, and not merely in grand terms. From the viewpoint of the family as subsystem, it makes changes almost daily in its social, marital, personal, and parental choices. Viewed from a role perspective, contemporary work provisions such as flextime, flexiplace (telecommuting, or working by computer from home, e.g.), maternity/ paternity/family leaves, and day-care at the work site are family choices designed to relieve role stresses and strains and to accommodate shifts in family structure and role allocations. Feminist theoreticians and activists have greatly influenced society's view of the roles of women (and men); and so have families, one by one, parent by parent, child by child, day by day.

2. *Families Headed by Lesbian or Gay Couples.* Until the 1990s, little was published regarding lesbian and gay families. Recently some remarkable books have appeared, including Slater's *The Lesbian Family Life Cycle* (1995), Laird and Green's *Lesbian and Gays in Couples and Families* (1996), and Drucker's *Families of Value* (1998). Weston describes gays and lesbians as "exiles from kinship"; a common stereotype is that they reject family and exile themselves from family life, but to assert that "gay people are destined to move toward a future of solitude and loneliness, is not only to tie kinship closely to procreation, but also to treat gay men and lesbians as members of a nonprocreative species set apart from the rest of humanity" (Weston, 1995:160). Benkov describes the process and the choices that are made by lesbians and gay men who want to have children, the nature of joint parenting, and how they "reinvent the family" (Benkov, 1997).

Slater says, "Starting from scratch, they look to themselves and to each other to construct their partnerships, devoting tremendous energy to imagining and experimenting with possible ways to proceed" (1995:231). She describes a life cycle of couples somewhat like Erikson's stages, particularly in the use of "generativity" to describe Stage 4. The stages are: (1) *formation*, in which the couple bonds and eventually tells others of their relationship; (2) *ongoing couplehood*, in which the couple makes a commitment and works out aspects of their dyad; (3) the *middle years*, in which the couple makes a deeper commitment, but encounters the possibility of disruption by separation or death; (4) *generativity*, which is similar to Erikson's adult stage, and involves a wider commitment to others (including parenting, perhaps); and (5) *couples over 65*, who are likely (because of women's longevity) to share old age—and to face the same crises of aging as other couples. "Lesbian widowhood" is similar to other spouses' survival, with the exception that "lesbian elders . . . frequently must do without most or all of the public component of the healing process. Funeral rituals, newspaper and other public announcements . . . and the public naming of the deceased person's next of kin are critical acknowledgements" (ibid.:223).

B. Family as Cause or Effect

The family as cause or effect is a second major approach. The family can be seen either as "dependent" variable or as "independent" variable. In the former, the family is responsive to the demands and dictates of larger social systems (macroperspective). It adapts or, more precisely, *accommodates* to the goal requirements of the society within which it exists. The nuclear, mobile family emerges because of the requirements of the economy; parents relinquish their functions to other social institutions. Governments influence families by prescriptions and proscriptions, for example, compulsory school attendance, abortion laws, Sweden's law against spanking of children (Popenoe, 1988:199; also see Davis, 1997), and court decisions that place the "welfare of the child" above the rights of the parents. In this way, society determines the family. Although few family theorists opt for either extreme, dependent or independent variable, most do see the family as determined by societal changes rather than the reverse. But, as noted earlier, this is not a universal opinion. Scholars increasingly recognize families as initiators of change.

In the opposing view, family as independent variable, family is seen to be cause rather than effect (microperspective). The family initiates change, and society accommodates; in other words, the family determines the society. Popenoe said that the "classical Western family died out in portions of Europe well *before* the Industrial Revolution and, indeed . . . the nuclear family is now seen to be as much a cause as a consequence of industrialization" (1988:58). Laslett (1971, 1974) concluded that the nuclear family preceded industrialization in Europe and thus may have "caused" it. Another example is sociologist Elise Boulding (1972:188), who believed that "the family is a potentially powerful contributor to the generation of alternative images of the future." In this sense of creating alternatives, the family is independent variable.

The role of women in creating social change through child-rearing and character-building activities has been greatly neglected, except in auto-biographies (usually of prominent men) that point out mothers' influences. The influence of the mothers of presidents of the United States, for example, has been noted episodically.

According to Boulding (ibid.), the family is also an independent variable in that it generates social change as a "play community." Play is one means by which culture is created, and alternative societal futures are imagined. The family's position between the person and the society allows it to perform this function. However, Popenoe noted that in Sweden, which he suggests may be the model of the future, contemporary families do less together, including play.

The controversy over abortion laws exemplifies families' initiation of social change that requires social accommodation. Family planning, in order to liberate the parents and maintain their desired living standards for themselves and their offspring, requires that society approve and provide means for birth control. The 1973 Supreme Court decision *Roe v. Wade* gave legal sanction to abortion as a means of birth control. In December 1988, Nancy Klein was pregnant, and comatose as the result of an auto accident. Physicians believed abortion might increase her chance of survival, and her husband requested an abortion, but prolife advocates sought to prohibit it. Two weeks later, a court affirmed the husband's right to make the decision, the judge remarking that outsiders had no right to interfere in this family tragedy. One columnist observed that Ms. Klein's situation had restored rationality to the controversy over the control a woman, or someone legally responsible for her if she is unable to make decisions, has over her own body (Goodman, 1989b). This is a vivid example of a family as initiator of change. Attempts continue to persuade the Supreme Court to overturn the *Roe v. Wade* ruling.

The family is, of course, both independent and dependent variable, since it is a holon. Mutual causation between families and society can be seen in all aspects of living. For example, shifts in family structure and roles that are responsive to changes in employment patterns lead to marketplace accommodations. Women are increasingly employed outside the home, and family living standards are increasingly dependent upon their incomes. Employment hours vary, which influences the time available to shop, prepare, and serve meals, and for family dining (feature articles often report that employed mothers rarely have more than half an hour per day to themselves, if that much). All of the following could be construed as societal adaptations to such family changes:

1. Extension of hours in which commercial and retail establishments conduct their business.

2. "One Stop Full Service" shopping at convenience stores.

3. Marketing of increased varieties of frozen prepared foods.

4. Fast-food restaurants that usually portray workers or families in their advertising.

5. Mass production of synthetic fabrics marketed as "wash and wear."

6. The use of fax machines and computers to order from grocery stores and restaurants.

C. Family as Evolving System

The family as evolving system is a dual approach to family inquiry. One focus is on the developmental cycle of *a family*, while the other is a focus on the evolutionary cycle of *the family* as a social institution.

Family life cycle has sometimes been adopted as an organizing theme in courses in human behavior. The usual conception of the family life cycle is from the point of marriage, to and through expansion stages, then to and through contraction stages. The more thorough formulations of family stages attempt to account for the related growth tasks for all family members, not just the children. Most of these formulations assume a nuclear family, the presence of biological offspring, and a marriage that will continue until the death of a spouse. These assumptions, in fact, describe *only a relatively small minority of actual families*, given the proportion of divorces and female-headed families, of "reconstituted" and "blended" (remarried couples with children of former marriages) families and the increasing number of single, never-married parents (both adoptive and biological).

Family evolution comprises a series of changes as family members of various ages simultaneously encounter transition stages in the life cycle. The preschooler may face becoming a kindergartner at the same time the parents are dealing with the recognition that the future is not boundless. The preteen enters puberty while parents are taking stock of their own adult identity and grandparents are moving toward retirement. The television series, "The Wonder Years" (now in reruns) presented this from the viewpoint of a sensitive youth. Conflicts between adolescents and their parents are legendary, and are the basis for numerous films (e.g., *Rebel without a Cause*; even 1997's *Titanic* had such a theme). One recent book addresses "how your child's adolescence triggers your own crisis" (Steinberg, 1994). As young adults seek a more fully consistent identity, their parents are adapting to the "empty nest" and the grandparents cope with the decline of physical functions. The most frequently cited events that signal role changes and new stages of the life cycle are: forming a couple, birth of the first child, departure of the children, and dissolution of the couple (by divorce or death of one partner, e.g.). Added to these are educational, residential, and occupational changes (which research indicates may be highly stressful events).

A related facet of family change that is being studied is *resilience*, the ability of families (and children) to cope successfully with stress (see Hetherington and Blechman, 1996, among others). Three dimensions of family dynamics that have been identified as relevant to stress and change are cohesion, adaptability, and communication. These three are combined in the "circumplex" model of marital and family types, which has demonstrated validity as a predictor of family success (Olson, 1983, 1993; Olson et al., 1988).

Carle Zimmerman, the best known advocate of a cyclical theory of family in society, began with the premise that family and society constantly interact and cause changes, each in the other. Other social institutions (particularly the church and government) vie with the family for control of family members. Drawing on historical data, Zimmerman proposed a three-phase family typology and suggested that it is a repetitive cycle (Leslie, 1967:223–230).

1. The *trustee* family—the living members are trustees of the family name, family property, and family blood. The family itself is immortal; there is no conception of individual rights, and individual welfare is subordinate to the family. To the extent that his type survives in contemporary society, it is most obvious in "royal" families such as the Windsors of England—and even there may be more apparent than real. Dramas have long used the tensions in such families: see Shakespeare's *Romeo and Juliet* and *King Lear*, and television's "Dallas," e.g.

2. The *domestic* family—an intermediate type that evolves from the trustee family. As the state gains in power, family control over its members is weakened. The state shares this power and control with the family and creates the concept of individual rights to be maintained against family authority. Popenoe said:

> The modern nuclear family was organized largely to serve the end of child rearing in an environment of stability and love between the married couple. Backed by the unique coercive powers of organized religion, as well as by the laws of the state, the nuclear family unit was culturally held up as the goal of human sexuality combined with romantic love; it was the only acceptable form of adult pair-bond. (1988:329)

3. The *atomistic* family—the power and scope of family authority is reduced to an absolute minimum: The family no longer mediates between its members and society. The state becomes a bureaucracy that deals directly with individual persons, without intermediary systems. "Family"

functions are shifted to community or societal institutions; e.g., hospitals and extended care facilities tend to ill family members; foster care and juvenile institutions provide for children needing care or control; domestic courts provide counseling for parents and children; schools educate with little involvement by parents; and the nation conscripts youth without consulting families about their beliefs.

Zimmerman judged the present-day American family to be well into the third phase, the "atomic age" in yet another sense. He did not find the "present decay of the family" unique. He documented similar family dissolution prior to the fall of the Greek and Roman civilizations. Popenoe suggested that, in Sweden, a new nuclear family has emerged, that of single mother and child (the child born "out of wedlock" but later adopted by the mother's husband). Such a pattern may be emerging in the United States, as well, as evidenced by public concern about public welfare expenditures for single (particularly teenage) women who bear children and by legislation intended to control the women's behavior.

Popenoe identified "the emerging value system of America as 'bureaucratic consumer capitalism,' in which expressive individualism overtakes moral commitment" (Popenoe 1988:289, citing Bellah et al., 1985). He speculated, "This style of life could be the wave of the future—the new, individualized, and autonomous individual making a suitable adjustment to a rationalized and affluent world" (Popenoe, 1988:327). United States census data revealed that

> Marriage and family relationships seem to be occupying a shrinking space in our lives. Marriage rates before 25 have declined markedly. . . . Parenthood is also being delayed. . . . [A] substantial proportion of today's youth may never become parents at all. The vast majority will marry and have children, but over half of those who do will experience the breakup of that marriage. Persons who are not currently married . . . have progressively chosen to live alone, rather than with other family members. (Sweet and Bumpass, 1987:391)

Zimmerman deplored the popular view of the family as ever evolving to higher and better forms:

> [modern] inhumanity lies close, in a basic casual sense, to the decay of the family system. Indeed the familial decline may well be the primary causal agent in the sapping of the universal capacity for human sympathy. Juvenal held this opinion when he wrote of "the decline in the capacity to weep." . . . The consequence then of a declining family system is that controls of society come more into the hands of men who, in the words of Bacon, have no "hostages to fortune," and who do not possess judgments biased by an immersion in fundamental humanism. (1947:77)

Zimmerman recommended open recognition and understanding of the current state of family decline and hoped that a "creative minority" would come forward to reassert the values of familism.

D. The Structural Approach

The structural approach to the family has received the attention of a host of investigators. Any attempt at family analysis addresses itself to certain family forms and excludes others; the majority of Western observers of the family accept the two-generation nuclear family as the norm (two parents and their children). This is particularly true of those interested in the child-rearing aspects of the family. As noted earlier, the nuclear family has been the norm in some parts of European culture for five or six centuries. It is this family structure that serves as the basis for societal policy in support of the family (e.g., welfare and tax structure). It should again be emphasized that this family form is no longer found in the majority of families in the United States, and that there is variation by ethnic group: "African-American children have been most affected by the changes in marital status and family composition. . . . The share of black children living with two parents declined from 58 percent in 1970 to 38 percent in 1990. . . . Black children are more likely to live with a grand-parent than are white or Hispanic children" (O'Hare et al., 1997:89).

Parsons characterized the present-day American family as "the isolated family," isolated especially residentially and economically from the extended family, which was a natural consequence of the specialization and differentiation of the complex social system of the United States today. He qualified the degree of isolation, however: "I think it very important indeed, that there is much accumulating evidence that the extended family is an exceedingly important resource to fall back on in case of emergency or trouble, for financial support and for emotional support and help in planning" (Parsons, 1964:17). The high cost of living in many areas of the country during the past two decades has impelled adult (especially young adult) children to return to live with their parents: the "revolving door" phenomenon (the "nest" contracts and expands parallel to the state of the economy).

The extended family may well go beyond the bounds of those related by blood or marriage. Billingsley drew on the formulations of Parsons, Bales, and Shils to establish a typology of forms for categorizing African-American family structures. The refinements he introduced through his three categories and twelve types have also been applied to the society generally (Billingsley, 1968:15–21):

1. The *nuclear* family includes three types: the *incipient*, consisting of only the marital pair; the *simple*, consisting of the marital pair and minor

children; and the *attenuated*, containing only one parent and minor children. The latter seems to imply that the family previously was a "whole" family and was reduced by some circumstance; another description, such as "single-parent family" might avoid this implication and include the single, never-married parent with children. Dowd notes that *"70 percent of children will spend some time in a single-parent family before reaching age eighteen; for women entering adulthood, the probability that they will maintain a single-parent family for some period of time is 40 percent"* (1997:5). Another form of attenuation is the "bean pole" family, in which there are more generations living at one time, and fewer members are born in each generation (Bengtson, Rosenthal, and Burton, 1995:347).

2.   The *extended* family includes types in which other relatives are part of the household. As noted elsewhere, African-American children are more likely than other children to be living with grandparents. "The rise of out-of-wedlock childbearing suggests yet another form of intergenerational family structure. . . . Older black women may be called upon more often by their daughters to serve as the 'other parent'" (ibid.:350).

3.   The *augmented* family includes types of families wherein unrelated persons are incorporated into the household, and function as family members. Dowd describes this type: "The model of single-parent families is of caretakers within a support structure—whether kin, friends, or paid care . . . simply one form of a support structure" (1997:113).

Boulding (1972) placed all family forms on a continuum from one isolated householder to a cluster of persons either biologically or voluntarily associated. She correctly pointed out that there is no clear line between an *expanded* family (which includes the last two of Billingley's types, above) and the "intentional community" (i.e., a community organized for specific social or ideological purposes). Given the present variety of forms of families and communities, such an elastic definition is very useful.

The study of kinship networks and relationships, particularly by social anthropologists, has yielded additional insights into the variety of family forms. Kinship responsibility in the United States is a neglected dimension in family studies. Cultural guidelines for determination of allegiance to kinsmen are ambiguous and often conflicting. Although the nuclear family norm would seem to dictate that one's primary responsibility is to spouse and children, conflicting claims do arise. The parent of today in an isolated nuclear family might have been the child of yesterday in a closely tied extended or nuclear family. For such a person, the transfer of allegiance and emotional involvement from the family of orientation to the family of procreation may be a monumental task, as indicated by frequent letters to "Dear Abby" from wives and mothers-in-law about the son/ husband's responsibilities to each.

Scholars have studied kinship relationships in "remarried families" and "blended" families and the perceptions of obligations and relationships within them (Hetherington, Law, and O'Connor, 1997; Ahrons and Rodgers, 1997). The term "binuclear" was coined to describe families in which a child is part of two separate nuclear families, formed by the child's divorced parents (Ahrons, 1987). Children must decide (often with strong guidance from one or both parents) who are "kin": Does a stepmother's mother become "Grandma"? Are the noncustodial parent and the new stepparent invited to graduation ceremonies? Parents must decide their relationships to their biological children with whom they no longer live: do they attend the funeral of the former spouse's parent who is, after all, the children's grandparent? These are often painful questions to resolve.

Overall, the present generation of elders in the United States is relatively fortunate compared to earlier generations regarding health and income, but many live in isolation and in situations of inadequate care. The unenviable status of these aged persons and the guilt felt by their adult children are products of the nuclear family and the nature of the society in which it exists. Women in their fifties often have parents who are over eighty, and with smaller families, these women are less likely to have siblings to share responsibility for care of parents (Bengtson et al., 1997:348).

Alternative family forms have been suggested as possible substitutions for traditional ones, especially to replace the nuclear family norm. In the latter half of the twentieth century in the United States, a new family form has emerged, most easily termed "living together," or cohabitation. Popenoe (1988:303) noted that in the Netherlands it has been carried one step further, and called "living-apart-together." In Sweden, he observed, there are separate names for persons with whom you have a sexual bond, and share a household with (a *sämbo*), or do not share a household with (a *särbo*).

Some thoughtful observers, including some feminist authors, argue that the family in its traditional forms is dysfunctional in modern industrial society, and that alternative forms are preferable. Endorsement of the ultimate nuclear form of family—mother and child—by a prominent celebrity indicates that it may have become an accepted social form: Academy Award–winning actress Jodie Foster, in disclosing her pregnancy, said she "plans to be a single mother, 'just like I was raised myself.'"

E.   The Functional Approach

This is another dominant theme in family studies. Usually, *functions* are looked at in tandem with *structures* because they cannot readily be separated, not even for purposes of objective study. There are inherent difficulties in functional analysis of the family, as in examining the functions of any other social system. The pitfall is, of course, to reason circularly that a pattern or value is "functional" to the given system and the proof of functionality is found in the fact of its existence.

Parsons explained the changing functions of the modern family as examples of differentiation and specialization of the family system. As the macrosystem (society) becomes increasingly complex, the family as a component system (or microsystem) becomes increasingly specialized in the functions it performs for both the larger system and for family components. The core functions remaining in the family are the maintenance of the household and the intimate personal relations of the members of the household, including child rearing and socialization into affective networks (of peers, friends, sexual and marital partners, and communities). Relinquishing of family functions particularly affects women. Margaret Adams, a social worker, commented on the transfer of women's "nurturant" roles from the family to professions. She described the process by which women are channeled into social work, nursing, teaching, secretarial work, and certain other professions, as "the compassion trap":

> The proliferation of the helping professions into a complex array of welfare services took many of the more highly specialized aspects of the nurturing and protective functions out of the home. . . . In addition, when one or both parents were out of the home for a substantial part of the day, they had to delegate their acculturating functions. Thus the synthesizing role traditionally discharged by women in the home was translated into a wider sphere and spread its influence through a broader range of activities. Instead of (or in addition to) keeping the family intact and maximally functional, women became involved in housekeeping tasks on behalf of society at large and assumed responsibility for keeping its operation viable. (Adams, 1971:72)

Lasch (1979) deplored this transfer of nurturance and parenting from the family to the burgeoning professional experts. He, as Parsons previously, noted the emergence of specialized peer groupings that evidently have assumed functions previously performed by the family. Popenoe's studies in Sweden showed that "many of these youth were lonely and had few, merely superficial, social contacts. The young people . . . inhabit an 'age-stratified world' in which they meet very few adults other than their parents" (1988:320–321). This is graphically portrayed in Hersch's A Tribe Apart (1998). Peer groups differentiate and remain separated on the axis of age: examples include senior centers and communities for the aged, adolescent clubs and gangs, and young adult bars and health clubs. A generation ago, Keniston proposed a "new" stage of life, which occurs outside either a family of orientation or a family of procreation, noting the emergence on a mass scale of a previously unrecognized stage of life . . . the stage of youth. . . . A growing minority of post-adolescents today . . . have not settled the questions whose answers once defined adulthood: questions of relationship to the existing society, questions of vocation, questions of social role and lifestyle. (Keniston, 1970:634–635)

The youthful followers of cults may be a manifestation of this new life phase; those who have received the most notoriety, because of their parents' efforts to regain their allegiance, have been in their twenties, opting for a calling devoid of any kind of family connection; however, not all such followers are youths. The Unification church (followers of Reverend Sun Yung Moon: disparagingly referred to as "Moonies") conducts mass marriages of hundreds of couples at the same time to partners selected by the organization; this is perhaps an example of deliberate attempts to create "family" within an organization and to negate family ties outside it.

Another example of youth organization during this life phase is neo-Nazi "skinheads" located in several cities in the United States. These groups evolved from alienated working-class youth in Great Britain who were notorious for their "bashing" of immigrants. Although not all skinheads are racist or violent, this appears to be a frequent characteristic. As with many organizations of alienated youth, historically, they are susceptible to exploitation by political manipulators (Coplon, 1988).

This "youth" stage is clearly related to Erikson's sixth "crisis," that of *intimacy vs. isolation* (see Chapter 8). If families are unable to assist in resolving this crisis, then a generation of young adults must look to other institutions or create new ones, or conceivably simply fail to resolve the crisis, in massive numbers. Currently, there are many "youth service" programs that would reward teenagers and young adults for participation in volunteer programs with vouchers for housing or education, as well as wages (the armed services offer similar inducements). The most obvious objectives are social control, socialization, and integration into the society in some significant way, either as workers, students, or consumers. Described another way, its purpose is to structure the adolescent (or young adult) "moratorium" (see Erikson's definition in Chapter 8) to reduce the possibility of deviance, when the family is not capable or sufficient of doing so.

Youth gangs are another form of socialization, in this case to a "deviant" subculture:

Dysfunctional families as the cause of gangs . . . is the theory Armando Morales (1992) uses to explain Hispanic gangs in Los Angeles. Morales maintains that adolescents turn to gang membership to achieve the nurturance, support, and protection denied them in their biological families. Invariably, their families are beset by drug addiction, alcoholism, chronic illness, impoverished housing, physical and emotional abuse, and parental discord. Morales says the gang provides members "affection, understanding, recognition, loyalty, and emotional and physical protection." (Balk, 1995:479–480)

Lidz found that the family performs three sets of discrete but interrelated systems functions: For the children, the family provides physical care and nurturance and at the same time directs their personality development. For parents/spouses, it furnishes the means to personal fulfillment and stability. For society, the family takes responsibility for enculturating new members. Lidz suggests "it is possible that these functions which are fundamental to human adaptation cannot be fulfilled separately at all and must be fused in the family" (1963:45).

Maruyama (1966) found the extent of family function specialization alarming. He coined the term *monopolarization* to describe the state of affairs in which the child's relationship to adults is confined to a mother or father or, more precisely, to one set of parents. This totality of children's relationships to their parents sets narrow parameters for development and places excessive responsibility in the parents. Maruyama said that this exclusivity was assumed as the norm by theories of personality and of many Western philosophies. He recommended dilution of this relationship through increased interfamily contacts and integration of persons who are not in the family circuit. This could be accomplished through the formation of voluntary adult-child communities without any necessity of major reforms in family structure; some religious congregations have attempted this, with mixed success. During the 1960s and 1970s, many communes attempted to create alternative family structures. One writer reported a generation ago that "today's communes seek a family warmth and intimacy, to become extended families. A 50-person commune in California, for example, called itself 'The Lynch Family,' a New Mexico commune 'The Chosen Family,' a New York City group simply 'The Family'" (Kanter 1970:54).

II. A SOCIAL SYSTEMS VIEW
OF FAMILIES

Most professional observers of family now view it as a system (Schutz, 1993). Family therapists are most notable among these, in their relevance to this book. One of the outstanding researchers and pioneers in family therapy, Jay Haley, optimistically stated that

> What family therapists most have in common they also share with a number of behavior scientists in the world today: There is an increasing awareness that psychiatric problems are social problems which involve the total ecological system. There is a concern with, and an attempt to change, what

happens with the family and also the interlocking systems of the family and the social institutions in which the family is embedded. The fragmentation of the individual into parts, or the family into parts is being abandoned, and there is a growing consensus that a new ecological framework defines problems in new ways and calls for new ways in therapy. (Sager and Kaplan, 1972:270)

The family is a holon that possesses the characteristics of a social system and is distinguishable from other social systems by its goals, functions, and climate of feeling (its microculture). The family is defined both by its members and by the culture and community within which it exists. A family systems theorists distinguishes three "levels of interaction" in families: *Level I,* "interaction is rather open to view and is focused on the everyday event. . . . These are the daily routines, responses and exchanges that characterize family interaction"; *Level II,* the *metaprocesses* that occur in families, "the unspoken rules and redundancies, the script-line miniplays that each family knows when a given situation arises. . . . Like the framing of the wallboard of a house, the studs . . . are unseen but hold it all together"; and *Level III,* which "describes the general context in which a family operates. It is more abstract and, unseen, like the foundation of a house" (Day, 1995:91–92). This may be also be analyzed as follows, perhaps: Level I is the system as system, "doing its thing"; Level II is the subsystems that react to scripts and roles that they have learned and are enforced by the system; and Level III is the environment of the family system.

The inclusions and exclusions of the family system must be from some particular perspective, that is, *from the perspective of some particular person.* If that perspective is to determine the legal status of a person for inheritance purposes, that is quite different from establishing who are the members of a household. Consistent with our comments about the feedback cycle and system structure, *a family system is to be construed as patterns of relatedness as they converge in a specific person.* This is (as discussed in the Introduction to this edition) compatible with a postmodernist view. These patterns may be similar or identical to those of another family member, or they could be unique to this one person. The characteristics of the family system will be grouped under our usual headings of *structure, behavior,* and *evolution.*

A. Structural Aspects

As with any social system, its organization is a fundamental concern. Family organization is distinguishable from other systems by a high level of relatedness among its components. Since it is the smallest social and interpersonal system, typically there is intense interdependence among its components. The effectiveness of family organization is the extent to which goals are fulfilled—the goals of its members and the goals of society. If societal goals are not fulfilled, the family may be dissolved by legal decree, as when children are removed or divorces granted. The family may persist as an interacting system. However, as Malcolm X clearly described after his family was dispersed by the court: "separated though we were, all of us maintained fairly close touch around Lansing—in school and out—whenever we could get together. Despite the artificially created separation and distance between us, we still remained very close in our feelings toward each other" (1966:22).

Society, the family, and its members may all share familial goals of economic independence, intimacy, and affection and yet be in conflict about the priorities to be assigned to each of these goals. These conflicts may occur when people find it necessary to leave familiar territory to find employment. A Kentuckian told this story to one of the authors:

> A man died and was being shown around Heaven by St. Peter. Off in one corner of Heaven they saw a group of people with suitcases. The man asked who these people were and St. Peter replied, "Oh, they're from Kentucky; they go home on weekends."

In the boom times of the 1970s the greatest "reverse migration" in American history took place as Appalachian coal mining revived and people returned from northern industries to work "at home." African-Americans "returned home" to the South:

> By 1990 the South had gained more than half a million black Americans who were leaving the North—or more precisely, the South had *regained* from the cities of the North the half-million it had lost to northward migration during the 1960s. The Census Bureau now predicts that the southward trend will continue "well into the next century." (Stack, 1996:xiv)

Stack says "What people are seeking is not so much the home they left behind as a place they feel they can change, a place in which their lives and strivings will make a difference—a place in which to *create* a home" (ibid.:199).

In order to achieve goals, the family must, through its organization, secure and conserve energy from both internal and external sources. The members of the family must contribute energy for the family system as well as import energy for their individual purposes. The following dialogue between mother and sons (about the husband-father), from the classic (and prophetic) play, *Death of a Salesman*, illustrates this dependence of family upon energy from its members and from the environment.

> LINDA: No, a lot of people think he's lost his—balance. But you don't have to be very smart to know what his trouble is. The man is exhausted.

HAPPY: Sure!

LINDA: A small man can be just as exhausted as a great man. He works for a company thirty-six years this March, opens up unheard-of territories to their trademark, and now in his old age they take his salary away.

HAPPY: (Indignantly) I didn't know that, Mom.

LINDA: You never asked, my dear! Now that you get your spending money someplace else you don't trouble your mind with him.

HAPPY: But I gave you money last—

LINDA: Christmas time, fifty dollars! To fix the water heater it cost ninety-seven fifty! For five weeks he's been on straight commission, like a beginner, an unknown!

BIFF: Those ungrateful bastards!

LINDA: Are they any worse than his sons? (A. Miller, 1955:56–57)

The boundary of a family is behavioral and is evidenced by the intensity and frequency of interaction among its components (see Day, 1995:95–97, for a discussion of family boundaries). The intensity of sentiment interchanges is especially distinctive as compared to other small groups. In the sixteenth century, the boundary was "porous" in that "the family was thoroughly embedded in the community. [It] had little normative structure apart from that of the community, and the community's scrutiny of family members . . . was a powerful form of social control" (Popenoe, 1988:64). It is within the interactional boundaries of the family that the member participates in a particularly close network of feelings, both positive and negative, with a minimal sense of "needing to put up a front." The common expression, "I feel at home," conveys something of this freedom to be oneself.

Family boundaries change as members come and go. Extended kin, close friends and neighbors, or foster children may be absorbed within the boundary of a given family. Research on "remarried families," especially those with children and stepchildren, found "boundary ambiguity" (Boss, 1987). Whether stepchildren living with an ex-spouse are members of the family, and whether young adults still function as members of the family after they leave home, for example, are important questions for many families. The boundaries are both physical and psychological, and it is particularly stressful when the two definitions do not coincide, for example, when a parent continues to view the adult child as part of the household, but the adult child does not. Boundary ambiguity is found to be highly related to family stress and overall family dysfunction (Pasley and Ihinger-Tallman, 1989).

Even physical presence is not a measure of participation within family boundaries. A person may be related by birth or marriage and living in the same household, yet not be within family boundaries and not part of the interactional network. On the other hand, the family member in the hospital, away at school or military service, or incarcerated may well remain within the family boundary as just defined. In the case of families of servicemen who are MIAs (missing in action), the difficulty is particularly poignant. Again a quotation from Malcolm X is illustrative:

> I'm rarely at home more than half of any week; I have been away as much as five months. I never get a chance to take her anywhere, and I know she likes to be with her husband. She is used to my calling her from airports anywhere from Boston to San Francisco, or Miami to Seattle, or here lately, cabling her from Cairo, Accra, or the Holy City of Mecca. Once on the long-distance telephone, Betty told me in beautiful phrasing the way she thinks. She said, "You are present when you are away." (Malcolm X, 1966:233)

Maintenance of family boundary occurs on both sides of the boundary. The family frequently excludes others ("this is a family argument," "the family vacation"). Society supports family boundaries by assigning the family priority on occasions highly charged with sentiment such as weddings, funerals, and holidays. Cultures decree special occasions to reinforce family sentiment and interchange, such as Mother's Day and Father's Day (the manufacturers of greeting cards added Grandparents' Day). Federal policy and the policies of many businesses permit employees leave to care for members of the immediate family who are ill, and for funerals of members of both immediate and extended family. Colleges and universities also recognize and support family boundaries of sentiment through allowing students to absent themselves for such family occasions (one book suggested that exams must be dangerous since there is such a high correlation between exam days and the deaths of grandmothers).

Within the family, boundaries are maintained by differentiation and specialization, as reflected in role allocations. So that the family can meet societal expectations and continue as an economic unit, particular family members are breadwinners by mutual consent of the family members. Differentiation is commonly determined by age and sex, but these are uniquely refined in each family system. There is also differentiation of expressive functions, e.g., a family may reposit much of its unresolved or unacknowledged tensions in one family member, who then specializes as the "problem" family member. The concept of the "family scapegoat" or "lightning rod" is a case in point:

> The parents are fraught with internal conflicts and ambivalence but each consciously expressed only one side of the ambivalence thus forming a set of overt polarization and mutual avoidance. A marriage cannot survive under these conditions so an appropriate object is selected to symbolize the conflicts and draw off the tension. The emotional disturbance of the child is simply the effect of internalizing the conflicting demands placed on the

child by [its] parents. In the short run [the child] receives rewards from [the] family when [it] accepts [this] special role. The scapegoating mechanism may be functional for the family group through enabling its continued existence but be dysfunctional for the child's development and [its] adaptation outside the family. (Vogel and Bell, 1960:382–397)

Another aspect of family structure is its *territoriality*. Family territory has both a spatial and behavioral dimension. The concept of home territory is especially descriptive of family territory since the occupants have a profound sense of "place" and of "belonging." The family consolidates around, and in part finds its identity through, achieving and maintaining territory. Behavioral territory was earlier described in the discussion of boundary; it is the interactional territory of feeling-closeness. Physically, the family also occupies territory. The architect, the contractor, the city planner, the mail carrier, the garbage collector, all exist as societally supported occupations to serve and maintain families within their spatial territory. This territory is signified by an apartment or house number, or by a distinctive name (the grandmother of one of the authors called the family farm "Doomsday"; seaside homes often have clever or "cutesy" names, prominently displayed); it may be further marked by posts, fences, and hedges. The family territory may encompass a village, town, or neighborhood. "In ancient imagery, the center of his territory is a man's 'house,' be it a home or a farm, a firm or a family, a dynasty or a church; and his 'city' marks the boundary of all the houses associated with his" (Erikson, 1969:176).

Society requests and requires families to be territorially based, to be oriented in space. Society's most common means of establishing social identifications are the answers to the questions: Name? Address? Or, less formally, Where are you from? which actually means, What was the place of your family of origin? Homeless persons are at a disadvantage to receive services when they cannot state a residential address, despite federal legislation intended to alleviate this problem. The societal concern with family territoriality is clearly expressed in this quotation: "Show me a man who cares no more for one place than another, and I will show you in that same person one who loves nothing but himself. Beware those who are homeless by choice" (Southey, 1959:508). Similarly, groups of people who are not identified with a particular or specified "home territory"; nomads, e.g., Gypsies (more accurately, "Rom"), Bedouins, migrant workers, or homeless persons, are often viewed with suspicion by others.

B.   Behavioral Aspects

Social control and *socialization* are characteristic functions of the family. The family is always a subsystem of its society and, as such, participates in the socialization processes of that society. It would be defensible to classify all socially defined dysfunctional families as failing to meet the requirements for socialization of its members. A central task of the family is to assure that its members are sufficiently acculturated to participate in the other societal subsystems that enable attainment of societal goals. For example, Project Headstart was instituted to supplement families that were not fulfilling (or might not fulfill) this expectation as society defined it—to socialize the children and, if necessary, the parents. Furthermore, the family is expected to control its members in order to prevent them from interfering with attainment of the society's goals; notice the recurring legal efforts to enforce parental responsibility for delinquent behavior of their children.

Billingsley's observation that responsibility for socialization is especially difficult for many African-American families continues to be true, three decades later (see also Taylor, Jackson, and Chatters, 1997). Despite the rise of a substantial African-American middle class and increasing integration economically, educationally, and socially, such families still "must teach [their] young members not only how to be human, but also how to be black in a white society" (Billingsley, 1968:28). While the family on television's "The Cosby Show" was portrayed as successful and middle-class, its star, producer, and writer, Bill Cosby, frequently points out the special demands and constraints placed on African-American families. Two indicators of these are the extraordinarily high number of young African-American men in penal institutions (about 25 percent spend some time in confinement), and the disproportionate number of African-Americans who receive the death penalty. In addition to the pressures that affect all families in America, an African-American family must cope with three additional facts of life:

1. a distinctive historical development;
2. the American stratification system which historically has relegated African-Americans to inferior, caste-like status; and
3. the social class and economic systems that keep most African-Americans in lower socioeconomic classes. (Billingsley, 1968:28)

Power in families is a topic that has received relatively little attention, except from feminist theorists. Kranichfeld stated that earlier research concentrated on men's power derived from outside the family, rather than women's power derived from relationships within the family. Also, research has concentrated on power relations between men and women, neglecting women's power relative to other family members.

In spite of all the mental, emotional, and physical hardships that women appear to have experienced simply by virtue of their membership in the female gender, they appear to be remarkably resilient and constructive in their approach to human relations. As a group, women continue to struggle for greater equality and justice, but as individuals *almost never do so by choosing to sever the bonds that connect them to other people,* from which they derive tremendous sustenance and reward. (Kranichfeld, 1988:232–233)

She maintains that since men and women experience "separate social realities," they wield different types of power. If power is the ability to achieve goals by affecting other systems' functioning, women have great power: "women do not just change the behavior of others, they shape whole generations of families" (ibid.:235). She holds that women's power derives, consistent with Chodorow's (1978) and Gilligan's (1982) views, from *caring* for others in the family, and maintaining deep emotional connections with them. "The message here seems to be that, when it comes to securing the kind of power that exists in the family realm, nothing—not superior physical strength, nor greater economic resources, nor culturally ascribed authority—can substitute for investment, attention, connection, and care" (Kranichfeld, 1988:239). Dowd cites evidence that single-parent families (nearly all headed by women) "are far less hierarchical, and far more cooperative and communal, than most two-parent marital families [and that children] in single-mother families are given more responsibility, and demonstrate higher self-esteem and aspirations than children from two-parent families" (1997:109–110). That is, power is distributed among family members.

Communication is increasingly emphasized as both the keystone of family interaction and the key to understanding family dynamics. Every family's behavior is influenced by the style and effectiveness of its communication. Communication is here used to denote the transfer of energy through meaningful symbols, both vocal and gestural—transfer of energy to accomplish system goals. The discussion of communication in Chapter 2 applies exactly to the family system: each family has a unique combination of communication patterns that strongly influence the behavior of its members. Communication practices are crucial to any understanding of family because of the importance and intensity of exchanges of feeling. These characteristic patterns of interaction operate with external systems as well as within the boundaries of the family. According to family theorist Don Jackson, the "redundancy principle" operates in family life: "The family will interact in repetitious sequences in all areas of its life, though some areas may highlight these repetitions (or patterns) more quickly and systematically than do other areas" (1970:121). Brodey described the *family dance*: "Each family has its own particular game, its rules and regulations. It has its rules of status, its rules of power, its techniques of movement" (1977:41–42). Maturana's concept of *autopoiesis* suggests that a family, as any other social system, strives to continue its existence; its characteristic processes serve to create and to maintain itself. *Change* must also contribute to survival of a system's identity (Maturana and Varela, 1980; see also Adams, 1988:61–64).

Communication in the family is extremely complex and subtle because of the number of functions served by the family. One energy exchange can convey a number of meanings, not all of them congruent. An example is a parent's directive to a child to do what the teacher says. Included in this could be several messages:

1. You ought to obey authority (to meet societal expectations).
2. But you should not be required to submit to unjust orders (to meet the child's developmental needs).
3. Nevertheless, do what the teacher tells you (to avoid conflict with the environment).
4. Keep out of trouble (and avoid conflict between parent and teacher, that is, between family system and environment).
5. Because if you don't you'll get it from me (meet parents' needs for societal approval of their parenting, and thus provides for the child's security, as well).

The child is expected to understand and comply with all these messages.

Adaptation is an essential family function. Because the family has consistently had the capacity to change its structure and function to adapt to marked changes in its environment, it has survived wars, industrial and technological revolutions, and traumatic societal disruptions that made traditional patterns of coping obsolete. The family calls upon the energies of its components and exchanges energies with the significant systems in its environment. The "utilitarianistic" family of Hong Kong is an example of creative adaptation to a turbulent environment (Lau, 1978). It expands to include nonrelatives, or distantly related relatives, as a means of securing external energy (including money). These members secure jobs or create businesses, perhaps a new hawker's stall in the streets, or a fish ball stand. If Hong Kong's economy falters, these "expanded" or "augmented" families share risk by contracting into less physical space and living on less income. The family may send a child to be educated (or to work) overseas to assure a means of emigration should Hong Kong experience economic or political difficulties.

Another necessary adaptive mode of the family is its assimilation of external stress as experienced by its members. Although other social institutions such as religious and fraternal organizations also fulfill the function, the family is expected to be the primary system wherein a person can relax ("unwind"), cast off externally adaptable role behaviors, and "be yourself." In some cultures the coffeehouse, bar, or the geisha perform this function for men; it is not clear how this function is performed for women in these societies. Perhaps sensitivity and support groups are substitutes for this family function.

A family is considered maladaptive when it cannot adapt to the changing demands placed upon it by its environment and its members. If it cannot or will not change, and devotes an undue proportion of its available energies to maintenance of existing structures (i.e., morphostasis), it will not be able to deal with external requirements and the individual development of its members. In essence, it maintains its previous behavior (assimilation; see Piaget in Chapter 8) and is thus dysfunctional. If, on the other hand, it is in a constantly unstable state of transition, it does not furnish the degree of stability its members require for repair of insults to their egos and for the chance to merely be oneself in an atmosphere of affirmative feeling. This leads to the final system aspects of the family.

C. *Evolutionary Aspects*

Steady state is an aspect of the family system, which must simultaneously change and remain the same. Throughout its life cycle the family meets ever-changing requirements from its members and from society. The marital dyad, for example, must modify its mode of functioning with the advent of the first child. A family may operate to its satisfaction and to that of society while the offspring are dependent, but run aground when the children need emancipation from the family. One possible reason for this is described as follows:

> The steady state of a family is maintained in various ways. . . . Family therapy observations have revealed . . . how the underlying system reciprocity is revealed by symptoms appearing in a previously asymptomatic member when the symptomatic one improves, and how a marriage may rupture when the symptoms which had keen built into the relationship are no longer present. (Sager and Kaplan, 1972:288–289)

All that was said about steady state in Chapter 2 applies to the family. Often the family in crisis is in a disruptive transition from one steady state to another. At such times, a family may be more open to importing energies, more amenable to interventive efforts (see Erikson's definition of *crisis* in Chapter 8). Some families tend to function only so as to reduce or eliminate pain (equilibrium) rather than to change affirmatively (steady state). It is not easy to achieve a sense of family as a system—as an entity in its own right, more than the sum of its members. Our Western cultural emphasis on the individual as the most significant system makes it difficult to conceive of the family as other than molder, background, or environment. Paradoxically, at the same time we categorize families as good or bad as measured by the social performance of their members. This leads to the pernicious doctrine that all problematic or antisocial behavior is rooted in the family in a cause and effect relationship. Of course, families may to some degree be responsible, but as society blames its families, it denies society's part in personal and social dysfunction. In the past, the "broken home" was especially maligned. This process is similar to family scapegoating, in which a family member is loaded with the responsibility for family pain and dysfunction. Thus the family both scapegoats and is scapegoated.

Human services professions are coming to understand the distinctive systemic qualities of family. Tolstoy's observation that all happy families resemble each other and each unhappy family is unhappy in its own way suggests that the resemblance may be more apparent than real. Perhaps each happy family, too, is happy in its own way. Each family is like others in having rules, games (sequences of events governed by rules), secrets, and ghosts. Each family is unique in that its rules, games, secrets, and ghosts are its own. Often, work with families is best conceived as aiding a family to discover what its own unique patterns are, how they disguise their unique patterns, and how the patterns operate.

SUMMARY

The family is a critical human system. It serves unique, yet constantly changing purposes for its subsystems (family members and combinations of family members) and suprasystems (society and parts of society).

The family is best defined from the viewpoint of the person within it. The definition should include those relationships that are "family" to that person: those with whom the person interacts and performs family functions within that society. In many ways, the family is the crucial intersection between culture and the persons within the culture, the point of most interaction and change. While particular aspects of the family may be better explained by one of the approaches we have discussed, a systems view best explains overall family system behavior, the changes the family undergoes, and the relationships that are cause and effect of those changes.

In recent years, family issues have largely been perceived as part of women's issues, and this rethinking and redefinition has broadened the marital and parental role expectations for both women and men. Family issues have moved to the center of the political arena, making it possible for politicians to insert themselves and their beliefs into family concerns (especially family planning and abortion). Legislating family matters diminishes tolerance for pluralism of family forms and functions. The fiasco of the 1979–1980 White House Conference on Families illustrates the hazards of politicizing the family. As one person observed, "diversity of family styles and traditionalism in family style peacefully coexist only as long as neither one gains actual or symbolic advantage over the other.

Planning for a White House Conference ruptured the peace between the two" (Steiner, 1981:45). Hunter discussed this event and this issues surrounding it, labeling it a "policy brawl" (1997:84).

What does the future hold for families in the United States? Popenoe waved danger flags:

> One of the key ingredients of a strong family is the presence of a rich subculture—a set of norms, symbols, humor and even language that is special to that particular group. . . . Over the course of life the subculture yields what has been called a "community of memory," a special cultural heritage that family members carry with them until death. . . . With the weakening of the family unit, the disinvestment in family life, this subcultural richness is disappearing. For those who have it, the tie to a rich family subculture is one of the most meaningful things in life. For those who do not, the commercially based cultures of mass societies serve as debased substitutes. (Popenoe, 1988,312–313)

Since families are interdependent parts of the fabric of society, they will continue to influence and be influenced by changes in other social institutions. Families will continue to have their unique position at the point where persons and culture meet; but the fate of the family is not assured.

SUGGESTED READINGS

Berger, Brigitte, and Peter L. Berger.
   1983   *The War Over the Family: Capturing the Middle Ground.* Garden City, NY: Doubleday.
      A provocative assessment of the range of family ideology. The authors' own position is that the bourgeois family is the necessary social context for the emergence of the autonomous individual required for political democracy.
Billingsley, Andrew.
   1968   *Black Families in White America.* Englewood Cliffs, NJ: New York: Simon and Shuster.
      A systems approach to the family that has been used as the small-map text for this chapter. Billingsley drew on experience of African-Americans to supplement and revise sociological analyses of the family.
Elliot, Faith Robertson.
   1986   *The Family: Change or Continuity.* London: Macmillan.
      Compact, straightforward study that suggests reality is more complex than Parsons's, Marxian, and feminist theories suggest; family is "outcome of the complex interplay of contradictory pressures."
Laird, Joan, and Robert-Jay Green, eds.
   1996   *Lesbians and Gays in Couples and Families: A Handbook for Therapists.* San Francisco: Jossey-Bass.
      Edited by a professor of social work and a professor of family and child psychology and with chapters by psychotherapists, psychologists, educators, and social workers, this is the best source on family treatment for this

population. It includes case examples, discussion from the various professional perspectives, and examines these families in cultural context.
Miller, Sally R., and Patricia Winstead-Fry.
   1982   *Family Systems Theory in Nursing Practice.* Reston, VA: Reston.
   An excellent text, recommended for other professions as well as nursing. Family systems theory is well integrated into nursing practice.
Pharand, Gisele R., Maria L. Sudermann, and Ray DeV. Peters.
   1988   "Comprehensive Assessment of Family Functioning." In Ray DeV. Peters and Robert J. McMahon, eds., *Social Learning and Systems Approaches to Marriage and the Family.* New York: Brunner/Mazel.
   A comprehensive overview of research methods and instruments.
Popenoe, David.
   1988   *Disturbing the Nest: Family Change and Decline in Modern Societies.* Hawthorne, NY: Aldine de Gruyter.
   An excellent comparison of families in the United States, Sweden, Switzerland, and New Zealand, which raises disturbing questions about the future of families in advanced industrial societies, as the efficacy of mediating systems such as family is reduced.
Skolnick, Arlene and Jerome H. Skolnick, eds.
   1997   *Families in Transition,* ninth edition. New York: Longman.
   As always, the Skolnicks have compiled a set of readings that are informative and provocative, covering a very wide range of information. The contributors are among the best and most authoritative writers on the modern family.
Slater, Suzanne.
   1995   *The Lesbian Family Life Cycle.* New York: Free Press.
   An admirable attempt to portray a modal scheme of development for families headed by lesbian couples. It illustrates features that these families have in common with heterosexual families, and features that are distinct. It depicts the early stages of a lesbian relationship very well, and presents the unique dynamics of the relationship.
Thorne, Barrie, and Marilyn Yalom, eds.
   1982   *Rethinking the Family.* New York: Longman.
   A feminist analysis of the family, highly useful.
Watzlawick, Paul, Janet Helmick Beavin, and Don D. Jackson.
   1967   *Pragmatics of Human Communication: A Study of Interactional Patterns, Pathologies and Paradoxes.* New York: Norton.
   An excellent text dealing with systemic communication in a family context. The analysis of communication patterning in the play *Who's Afraid of Virginia Woolf?* is especially interesting.

LITERARY SOURCES

Anderson, Robert Woodruff.
   1968   *I Never Sang for My Father.* New York: Random House.
   Portrays a relatively closed family system and the effects such closure has

on the children as they deal with becoming adults. The film version, starring Gene Hackman, is excellent.

Erdrich, Louise.

1985 *Love Medicine*. Toronto, New York: Bantam.

Sensitively written novel of a Sioux extended family by a Sioux author. The book beautifully illustrates systems aspects of families and tribe, which become apparent as layers of meaning and family history are laid one on top of another.

Guest, Judith.

1976 *Ordinary People*. New York: Viking.

A family coping with the aftermath of tragedy. Also available as a movie; Robert Redford received an Oscar as director.

Olsen, Tillie.

1976 *Tell Me a Riddle*. New York: Dell/Laurel Edition.

A small collection of short stories commenting with sensitivity and insight on common human experiences within a context of culture and family.

Pa Chin (or Ba Jin).

1972 *Family*. Garden City NY: Anchor.

The first novel in the trilogy *Turbulent Stream,* probably China's best known novel previous to the 1949 revolution. Based on the author's own experience, it describes a traditional Chinese family encountering modernization during and after the revolution of 1911.

Tan, Amy.

1989 *The Joy Luck Club*. New York: Putnam.

Chinese-American mothers and daughters deal with two cultures, two generations and their relationships to each other. Very highly regarded by critics.

FILMS AND VIDEOS

Dim Sum: A Little Bit of Heart (1985)

Tension between Chinese-American mother and daughter in San Francisco. Humor, warmth, and cultural change beautifully portrayed.

The Double Burden: Three Generations of Working Mothers (1985)

A documentary about three families—Mexican-American, Polish-American, and African-American, each with three generations of working women: "This film speaks eloquently to the diversity of working motherhood."

Dominick and Eugene (1988)

Two brothers, one "slow," are a family. Tom Hulce, of "Amadeus," works on a sanitation truck to support his brother in medical school. Fine acting, sensitively written.

Fanny and Alexander (1983)

Perhaps Ingmar Bergman's happiest film, of his extended family in Uppsala, Sweden, in 1907. In Swedish, with English subtitles.

The Great Santini (1979)

Robert Duvall is superb as an Air Force pilot whose family "hangs together" despite frequent moves and his dictatorial behavior. Told from the viewpoint of the adolescent son who frequently conflicts with the father, but learns family solidarity from him.

Home for the Holidays (1995)

This comedy/tragedy portrays the ambivalence and anger that emerges in a three-generation family during a holiday visit: "We don't have to like each other. We're family." Each member's feelings about their relationships, roles, and life-styles are heatedly revealed, but no resolution is reached. The parents maintain their way of adaptation, and the adult children each attempt to establish their own families as means of adaptation.

Homecomin' (1980)

This film is about a separated African-American family, and the effects on family members. The father grapples with his responsibilities to his son.

I Know Why the Caged Bird Sings (1979; made for television)

Based on Maya Angelou's autobiography, this is a story of survival, child abuse, and the strength of family ties among members of an African-American family.

I Never Sang for My Father (1970)

Gene Hackman as a forty-year-old still trying to play son to Melvyn Douglas, a tyrannical father. Profoundly moving.

The Schuster/Isaacson Family (1979)

A sixteen-minute documentary on a merged lesbian family. Includes interviews with the children. Short, but enough basis for discussion of values and nature of "family."

Sounder (1972)

An African-American sharecropper and his family. The father is sent to jail and the mother must rear the children. A moving film, with excellent acting by Cicely Tyson and Paul Winfield as the parents.

The Stone Boy (1984)

Robert Duvall is the unforgiving father of a boy who accidentally shot his brother and loses touch with reality. Emotionally powerful.

Too Little, Too Late (1987)

Families and friends of AIDS patients are profiled and interviewed. Their pain and isolation are conveyed by a mother whose son died of AIDS, and who is active in AIDS hospice programs.

The Vanishing Family—Crisis in Black America (1986)

This video documentary examines structures of African-American families, and difficulties in forming stable relationships among African-American teenagers.

The Person

> We live life forward, however perilously, al-
> though we retrace it backward, and after each
> travail we are lucky if we achieve a new equi-
> librium, never quite the one we left behind.
> —Max Lerner

> Our whole civilization is a masculine civiliza-
> tion. The State, the laws, morality, religion,
> and the sciences are the creation of men. . . .
> If we are clear about the extent to which all
> our being, thinking, and doing conform to
> these masculine standards, we can see how
> difficult it is for the individual man and also
> for the individual woman to shake off this
> mode of thought.
> —Karen Horney *

I. THEORETICAL APPROACHES

This chapter deals with the person as a human system and introduces
concepts of human growth and development that are congruent with
social systems theory. Some theorists have questioned whether persons
can be considered to be social systems; however, without the individual,
there would be no society and without the society there would be no
individual. Each determines the other. Social systems concepts explain
this interaction.

---

* Quoted in Westkott (1986:1).

Our approach to the person as a human system is developmental and cyclical; we draw from the works of a range of theorists, including Sigmund Freud, Carol Gilligan, Karen Horney, Lawrence Kohlberg, Daniel Levinson, and especially Erik H. Erikson and Jean Piaget. Their formulations are particularly congruent with social systems theory.

A. Psychosocial Approach to Human Behavior

The *psychosocial* approach (represented by Sigmund Freud and Erik H. Erikson) is introduced first, since this general view of human behavior provides the framework for this chapter's content on the human *life cycle*. The central theme of this approach is the interaction of the individual person (*psyche* = soul, spirit, or mind) with the *social* environment. From a systems viewpoint, the individual person is a human system who is both cause and effect of social systems. Therefore, when we examine persons' growth and development from psychosocial and systems approaches, it is important to make connections between developmental theories and societal provisions, i.e., social programs and institutions. Interaction among research findings, theories, and societal factors shapes the social provisions that will be made available; and in turn the availability of social provisions plays a role in shaping individual persons.

As the cycle of life unfolds, persons expand their interaction into systems of ever-larger magnitude. Figure 8.1 shows two of the many possible diagrams of this interaction. In either diagram, a person's growth and development is in a pattern of expansion, a movement outward. This chapter uses the life cycle theory of Erik Erikson as a framework to organize and describe the components and stages of that growth process. The psychosocial approach and Erikson's theory, in particular, are applicable in Western societies, and Erikson tested their applicability in India and in American Indian cultures, as well.

1. Sigmund Freud. Sigmund Freud was a physician, a physiologist, and a psychologist who treated persons with personality disturbances, and who originated psychoanalysis. From about the age of forty he wrote prolifically on many facets of personality; he pioneered the study of many of the subjects he chose. His theories were highly controversial, and continue to be. Whether one accepts his theories, knowledge of them is essential for researchers and students of human personality, not only of psychology and psychiatry but of literature and religion, because he drew upon and wrote about history, anthropology, and culture. His most influential works are *The Interpretation of Dreams* (1900), *The Psychopathology of Everyday Life* (1901), *Three Contributions to the Theory of Sex* (1905), and *The Introductory Lectures to Psychoanalysis* (1916, 1932–1936). *An Outline of Psychoanalysis,* published posthumously, is the most lucid and concise statement of his general theory. Despite revisions by later psychoanalytic

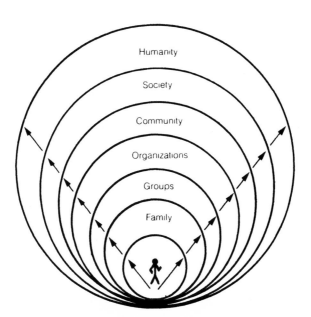

Figure 8.1.   Diagrams of a person's interaction with systems of increasing scale.

theorists, and devaluation of his ideas by critics, "He was an original thinker who radically altered prevailing views of human nature" (Brome, 1987:586).

We regard Freud's theory as one form of social systems theory. Freud's work must be considered in historical-cultural context. Science inherited the "clockwork," mechanistic view of the human organism from Sir Isaac Newton, but Freud broke with that tradition. Based on his therapeutic work with disturbed patients, he defined the human organism as a dynamic, complex system composed of physical energy and *psychic energy*. Freud's model was adapted from the physical sciences and the field of engineering (both hydraulic and electrical), hence his terminology of "forces" and "resistances."

Freud attempted to identify the structure, behavior, and evolution of the human psyche. The *id* is the source of energy for the human personality; it comprises the *libido*, essentially the sexual drive, and other unconscious drives and impulses that derive from human physiology. Its primary functions are the preservation and propagation of life (primarily via the sex drive); it operates on the "pleasure principle." The *ego* and *superego* evolve from the id. The ego's main function is to negotiate between the id and the external world (similar to the function of Piaget's schemas, described later); it operates according to the "reality principle," and controls intellect and perception; it is sometimes referred to as the "manager" of the personality. The superego is composed of social values that the person internalizes, sometimes in a rigid, judgmental way, sometimes in a flexible, tolerant way; it includes what is usually called "conscience." The ego also mediates conflicts between id and superego, employing a variety of *defense mechanisms*. These include (among many others) the sophisticated mechanism of *sublimation* (converting drives into intellectual desires; sex drive emerges as art or music or social power, e.g.), the more primitive *denial* of one's motivations and feelings, and *projection*, in which one's feelings are denied by claiming that it is others who have these feelings (a basic defense mechanism in paranoia). Personality disturbances result when the ego cannot resolve internal conflicts or threats from the external environment (either physical or social), and the person must rely too heavily on defense mechanisms.

Freud theorized that the personality evolves through several stages: *oral, anal, phallic,* and *genital.* Freud was true to his training as a physiologist, anchoring personality development in stages of organic development. Each stage is defined by the body tissues that are emerging and are most sensitive and that "demand attention" at that age. Psychological development might be arrested or fixated at any stage if unconscious conflicts were not sufficiently resolved during that stage.

a. Oral stage, the first year. If the child's personality development was arrested at this stage, it could be characterized by obsessive intake:

eating, smoking, talking, or alcoholism. One's development would be determined by the predominant oral mode: holding onto, biting, spitting out, or shutting out, each with its own specific character traits.

b. Anal stage, the second year. Fixation at this stage would largely be characterized by negative traits, including compulsivity, rigidity, desire to control, possessiveness, or passive resistance, although determination could be considered a positive trait. The reputed characteristics of this stage have entered into the popular culture with the current youth generation: "Don't be so anal!"

c. Phallic stage, ages 2–5. Freud concluded that this is the stage during which the Oedipal crisis (or its female counterpart, the Electra crisis) is resolved and the child identifies self by gender. He theorized that narcissism, arrogance, flamboyance, and prejudice resulted from fixation and that homosexuality resulted from arrested development at this stage. This may have ameliorated the view of homosexuality as a moral defect, but created another label, homosexuality as an illness, a failure to develop "normally."

d. Latency period, ages 6–12. Freud believed that while children demonstrated sexual behavior from birth, this stage is a quiescent time during which sexual curiosity and activity were repressed, after the resolution of the Oedipal crisis. Later psychoanalysts suggest that, instead, libidinal energies are redirected toward cognitive and social developments (compare Erikson's idea of "mastery" at this age, and Piaget's corresponding stage, later).

e. Genital stage (adolescence and adulthood). With the arrival of puberty, the person seeks others to love. Freud doubted that the stage of adult genital sexuality could be achieved without resolution of the earlier stages, and devoted his research and theorizing to problematic developments in the earlier stages, in particular internal psychological development, rather than social. That is, he focused on the person's internal structure, behavior, and evolution, and relationship to parents, almost to the exclusion of relationships with wider social systems. Erikson and other psychosocial theorists provide a fuller and more balanced view of adolescent and adult development.

2. *Erik Erikson.* The monumental task that Erikson undertook was to create and extend a conceptual framework for the complete life cycle, based upon Freudian theory, but substantially modified. Erikson's theory was first set forth in *Childhood and Society* ([1950, 1985, 1993] 1963). He published major revisions, refinements, and expansions in *Insight and Responsibility* (1964), *Identity, Youth and Crisis* (1968), *Life History and the Historical Moment* (1975), *Identity and the Life Cycle* ([1980] 1994), *The Life Cycle Completed* ([1982] 1997), *Vital Involvement in Old Age* (1986; coauthored), and *A Way of Looking at Things* (1987). He applied his theory

to the field of psychohistorical biography with two pioneering, monumental works, *Young Man Luther* (1958), and *Gandhi's Truth* (1969) for which he was awarded the Pulitzer prize; he also authored a study of Thomas Jefferson, *Dimensions of a New Identity* (1974).

Erikson's eight stages of the human life cycle are the organizing framework for this chapter for two reasons. First, it seems to be the only theory of human development that encompasses the complete life span. Second, his psychosocial approach to human development is particularly congruent with a systems approach, with its simultaneous attention to the individual and the environment; and with human services, with their emphasis on "person in environment." This chapter will introduce Erikson's thought by presenting a few key ideas from his formulation of the life cycle.

   a. *Erikson's view of the life cycle.*   This is based on the *epigenetic* principle. *Epigenesis* (from *epi*—"upon" and *genesis*—"emergence") means that each developmental stage builds upon, and in relation to, preceding stages. It is not merely that one stage succeeds another, but that each stage begins with the building blocks of the preceding stages and rearranges them, adding new elements and creating a structure that is new (at least to some significant degree). The building blocks include the physical, mental, psychological, and social aspects of the person that was created or reshaped in the previous stages.

The *potentials* for growth and development are all present in the human organism at birth; they emerge as the human organism matures. The parts arise out of the whole; each component (potential or capacity) has a special time for its emergence, until all the processes have run their course and the person develops into a functioning whole. Thus the human personality is an evolving system that contains its potentials in matrices that arise according to some general sequence. As these matrices emerge, they are interrelated, and in addition, the development of each matrix is dependent upon that which has gone before. Each alters the previously achieved balances. The stages are interrelated and, in systems terms, are synergistic.

Erikson's stages may be pictured simplistically as a set of teeterboards balanced upon each other (see Figure 8.2). To repeat: each level (or stage) depends upon the balance achieved in the previous stage, and an adjustment of any level involves a retroactive adjustment of all the preceding stages. The balance of each stage is the ratio of polar qualities that the person possesses at each stage. Bear in mind that it is not static, but a dynamic balance, a steady state subject to change.

   b. *Erikson's life cycle formulation.*   The life cycle and its stages are based in human genetic (physiological and psychological) energy but are, at the same time, totally dependent on social experiences. Erikson described the life cycle as the product of three processes: (1) *physical*, consti-

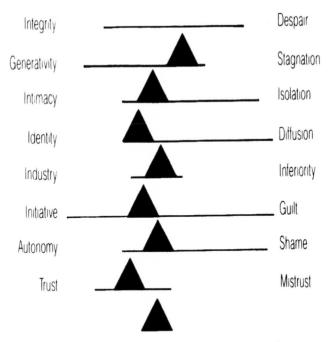

Figure 8.2.   Stages of life cycle according to Erikson.

tutional or somatic organization; (2) *ego*, the self as the organizing force, and (3) *social*, self-organization that is responsive to the rules and expectations of society and culture. In other words, the somatic process, the ego process, and the societal process equal the human life. The similarities and differences between this triad and the Freudian triad are important. The observation that Erikson's is an "ego psychology" and Freud's is an "id psychology" has some truth. In Erikson's theory, "A human being . . . is at all times an organism, an ego and a member of society and is involved in all three processes of organization" (Erikson, [1950, 1985, 1993] 1963:36). In our view, of course, these are three systems levels, and the person as system simultaneously participates in all three. Within Erikson's scheme, the unfolding of the human system is the intertwining of maturation (organism), education (ego), and socialization (society).

   The eight stages of Erikson's life cycle represent a synthesis of developmental (maturation) and social (learning) tasks. *Maturation* is the predictable course of growth for all members of a species, based upon shared physiological structure. *Learning* is unpredictable growth, new behavior based upon the individual experience of the organism and the accumulated learning of the culture. The distinction is similar to that between *genotype*, the inherited characteristics of an organism, and *phenotype*, the characteristics that emerge through the interaction of the organism's heredity with its environment. Growth, then, derives from the constant interaction of maturation and learning. The organism's potentials at any stage of development are determined by maturation, while its learning is a function of social experiences.

   c. *The idea of crisis.*   This is central to Erikson's theory. *Crisis intervention* is similar to Erikson's use of the term "crisis," which refers to a time of necessary change. The crises during growth and development, as Erikson uses the term, connote a heightened potential for development (or change) accompanied by greater vulnerability; an analogy is that the Chinese character for "crisis" contains elements of both "danger" and "opportunity." Crisis is not necessarily a negative state of affairs but rather an unavoidable occasion that requires some type of coping. This meaning of crisis has existed since antiquity. Hippocrates described crisis as an occasion of imbalance that required the "constitution" of the person to respond (i.e., cope) (Jones, 1923:ii–iv). In Erikson's view, the crises occur at their scheduled time, arising from the interaction of the organism's maturation and society's expectations. The outcome (not *resolution,* necessarily) is dependent upon the personality resources the individual has accrued up to that point and the opportunities and resources the person has available in the social environment.

   Erikson wrote most extensively and thoroughly on two of the eight crises of development—*basic trust vs. basic mistrust* and *identity vs. diffusion.* Attention to these particular periods of child development is not unique to Erikson, since infancy and adolescence have attracted the attention of much of child development research. In fact, infancy and adolescence *may indeed be* the two most critical phases of personality development. Erikson's theories about the first critical task of life, *trust vs. mistrust,* are compatible with the work of René Spitz (1965) in his studies of maternal deprivation and the establishment of an initial object relationship. Erikson's formulation is also consistent with the extensive literature on infant bonding and maternal deprivation. His ideas about adolescence are compatible with a host of theorists including Friedenberg (1962), Keniston (1970), and Goodman (1960).

   Erikson's critical developmental tasks are expressed as bipolarities. This formulation is consistent with general systems theory, that the dynamism of life derives from the fact of negative and positive charges with tension and movement between them. These bipolarities are not achievement scales to serve as measurable criteria of growth and development; one does not achieve *complete* trust and then move on to the next plateau, autonomy. The outcome of each of the developmental crises is a relative mix (a ratio) of the polar qualities and the developing person must cope with each subsequent task as it emerges at its proper time, as dictated by maturation and social expectations. In one sense, these critical task of

development are present at all times in each person's life and are directly
related to one another; Erikson attempted to illustrate this in his charts of
development.

Table 8.1 illustrates the interrelatedness of the various crises. This table
focuses on the crisis of adolescence, *identity vs. identity diffusion*, and illustrates how each of the earlier crises contributes to the readiness to cope
with this one and how it in turn influences the subsequent crises. It would
be possible to take any of the crises represented on the diagonal and fill in
the related boxes to show the relationship of that crisis to the preceding
and the following stages.

Erikson's worksheet (Table 8.2) illustrates his eight stages of the life
cycle on five dimensions. The second dimension (column B, radius of
significant relations) indicates the progression of interrelationships from
the dyad of the infant and nurturing person on through the broadening
hierarchy of social systems. The eighth stage includes all of humanity.
Columns C, D, and E concern social order, psychosocial modalities, and
psychosexual stages, and indicate the relatedness of these dimensions to
the other dimensions.

In our view, Erikson's life cycle scheme is a version of social systems
theory, based in the "natural" epigenetic principle. As the individual's life
cycle proceeds through successive steady states, it has the maturational
potential and the social necessity to be linked to, and be part of, ever-
wider social systems and ever-changing social environments. To fulfill
their functional destiny, persons must necessarily be engaged in transactions with these other social systems.

In summary then, Erikson's eight stages of the human life cycle represent necessary occasions for a person to unite biological, psychological,
and social forces. Erikson's theory stresses the adaptive and creative power of a person and respects each person's individual capacity to forge an
unique way of life. Erikson's faith in human social creativity is reflected in
his optimistic comment, "There is little that cannot be remedied later,
there is much that can be prevented from happening at all" (Erikson,
1950:164).

B. Cognitive Theory

1. Piaget. Jean Piaget was a systems theorist, and attended confer-
ences on general systems theory, exchanging ideas with other systems
theorists. Maier said:

> Piaget believes in universal order and suggests a single unity of all things
> biological, social, psychological, and ideational in living as well as nonliving
> systems. For him, as a biological scientist, "all living forms grow and devel-
> op in coherent, logical patterns." . . . All science is interrelated, and a theo-
> rem established in one branch of science is directly relevant to the laws and

Table 8.1 The Adolescent Crisis, "Identity vs. Identity Diffusion"

	1.	2.	3.	4.	5.	6.	7.	8.
I. Infancy	Trust vs. mistrust				Unipolarity vs. premature self-differentiation			
II. Early Childhood		Autonomy vs. shame, doubt			Bipolarity vs. autism			
III. Play age			Initive vs. guilt		Play identification vs. (oedipal) fantasy identities			
IV. School age				Industry vs. inferiority	Work identification vs. identity foreclosure			

	Time perspective vs. time diffusion	Self-certainty vs. identity consciousness	Role experimentation vs. negative identity	Anticipation of achievement vs. work paralysis	Identity vs. identity diffusion	Sexual identity vs. bisexual diffusion	Leadership polarization vs. authority diffusion	Ideological polarization vs. diffusion of ideals
V. Adolescence	Time perspective vs. time diffusion	Self-certainty vs. identity consciousness	Role experimentation vs. negative identity	Anticipation of achievement vs. work paralysis	Identity vs. identity diffusion	Sexual identity vs. bisexual diffusion	Leadership polarization vs. authority diffusion	Ideological polarization vs. diffusion of ideals
VI. Young adult					Solidarity vs. social isolation	Intimacy vs. isolation		
VII. Adulthood							Generativity vs. self-absorption	
VIII. Mature age								Integrity vs. disgust, despair

Source: Reprinted with permission from Erik H. Erikson, "Identity and the Life Cycle: Selected Papers," *Psychological Issues* (Monograph). New York: International Universities Press, 1959, Volume 1, p. 120.

Table 8.2 Erikson's Worksheet

	A Psychosocial crises	B Radius of significant relations	C Related elements of social order	D Psychosocial modalities	E Psychosexual stages
I.	Trust vs. mistrust	Maternal person	Cosmic order	To get To give in return	Oral-respiratory, sensory-kinesthetic (incorporative modes)
II.	Autonomy vs. shame, doubt	Parental persons	"Law and order"	To hold (on) To let (go)	Ana-urethral, muscular (retentive-eliminative)
III.	Initiative vs. guilt	Basic family	Ideal prototypes	To make (= going after) To "make line" (= playing)	Infantile-genital, locomotor (intrusive, inclusive)
IV.	Industry vs inferiority	"Neighborhood," school	Technological elements	To make things (= completing) To make things together	"Latency"
V.	Identity and repudiation vs. identity diffusion	Peer groups and outgroups; models of leadership	Ideological perspectives	To be oneself (or not to be) To share being oneself	Puberty
VI.	Intimacy and solidarity vs. isolation	Partners in friendship, sex, competition, cooperation	Patterns of cooperation and competition	To lose and find oneself in another	Genitality
VII.	Generativity vs self-absorption	Divided labor and shared household	Currents of education and tradition	To make be To take care of	
VIII.	Integrity vs. despair	"Mankind" "My kind"	Wisdom	To be, through having been To face not being	

Source: Reprinted with permission from Erik H. Erikson, "Identity and the Life Cycle: Selected Papers." *Psychological Issues* (Monograph). New York: International Universities Press, 1959, Volume 1, p. 164.

principles of other branches. Altogether, Piaget insists upon cosmic unity. (1988:19)

Phillips (1969:xii) described Piaget's conception of "the human brain as a vastly complicated system for the storage and retrieval of information; a system that becomes capable of increasingly complex operations; a system that changes in ways that are at least to some degree similar to the constructions that Piaget has given us."

Piaget was a biologist, but chose to study cognitive development, and cognitive theory, about the process of knowing and learning. Much of what has been done in this field can be traced to Piaget and his collaborators. With other researchers, he sought to combine biology, philosophy, and psychology in a "psychological and biological epistemology," or theory of knowledge. His greatest influence was on educational theory and practice. Piaget's emphasis on first-hand involvement, experience, and grappling with problems appropriate to the child's intellectual development was consistent with the educational philosophy of John Dewey, whose influence on American education has been profound. "What [Piaget] found significant is that in every case where acceleration [of learning] takes place, it results from a conflict arising in the child's own mind. It is the child's *own effort* to resolve a conflict that takes him or her on to another level" (Duckworth, 1996:39, emphasis ours). This is an example of self-development of the person as system.

Piaget's research methods were criticized because they were often unorthodox. He used psychoanalytic and qualitative research interviewing (which would be more acceptable today, because of the influence of Piaget, among others) exploring children's responses, especially their mistakes, to discern the rules by which they made them. Piaget questioned children while they were doing various tasks and between tasks, and also silently observed their behaviors; he invented over fifty new research techniques. Here is one example: The child was presented with a group of coins and a bunch of flowers. The child was then asked how many flowers could be purchased if each flower cost one coin.

Gui (four years, four months) put 5 flowers opposite 6 pennies, then made a one-for-one exchange of 6 flowers (taking the extra flower from the reserve supply). The pennies were in a row and the flowers bunched together: "What have we done?—*We've exchanged them.*—Is there the same number of flowers and pennies?—*No.*—Are there more on one side?—*Yes.*—Where?—*There* (pennies). (The exchange was again made, but this time the pennies were put in a pile and the flowers in a row.) Is there the same number of flowers and pennies?—*No.*—Where are there more?—*Here* (flowers).—And here (pennies)—*Less.*" (Phillips, 1969:5)

This exchange illustrates the flexible interview style and search for concepts in the child's thought that was typical of Piaget's methods. In this instance, it appeared to the child that if the objects were spread out there were more of them than if they were bunched up. indicating that the concept of transferability of numbers from one set of objects to another had not yet developed in this child. Piaget also took the "unscholarly" approach of studying his own children and performing small experiments to test their development.

The topics of Piaget's major works include "the construction of reality," "judgment and reason," "language and thought," "logic and psychology," "moral judgment," "the origin of intelligence," and "the psychology of intelligence." His major work is *Genetic Epistemology* (1970).

Piaget is regarded by some as being equal to Freud in his eventual impact on personality theory. "Both Freud and Piaget posited universal, biologically-driven stages of development that scale the individual's changing knowledge and interpretation of the environment" (Bornstein and Lerner, 1987:710). Piaget dealt in concrete detail with the major problems of logic, thought, and philosophy in the twentieth century that hindered our understanding of human behavior. Acceptance of his ideas, and their diffusion among teachers and researchers, have accelerated with the development and use of computers, which mimic the human mind. Piaget's work is important for the human services: he stressed invention, creativity, and the ability of the person to overcome past deficiencies or conflicts. He believed that "every time you teach a child something you keep him from reinventing it" (Phillips, 1969:120) and that

> The principal goal of education . . . is to create [persons] who are capable of doing new things . . . who are creative, inventive and discoverers. The second goal . . . is to form minds which can be critical, can verify, and not accept anything they are offered . . . we need pupils who are active, who learn early to find out by themselves, partly by their own spontaneous activity and partly through materials we set up for them; who learn early to tell what is verifiable and what is simply the first idea to come to them. (Elkind, 1968:80)

Duckworth, Piaget's colleague and translator, echoed both Socrates and Piaget: "You don't want to cover a subject; you want to uncover it" (Duckworth, 1996:7). This is a model of knowledge and learning that is most familiar in Western cultures, which emphasize individual initiative and innovation.

The basic ideas of Piaget are relatively easy to understand from a systems viewpoint:

a. Equilibrium. In Piaget's view, equilibrium is a steady state of the cognitive processes. He regarded equilibrium as a dynamic balance between the person and the environment, in which the person's knowledge and self-organization are adequate to understand what is experienced. It is a state of active compatibility between the person and the environment. There is positive feedback that confirms and continues to reinforce the person's developing capacity to understand and master the environment; this is similar to Erikson.

   b. Intelligence.   As a biologist, Piaget defined intelligence as a form of biological activity. It arises from the person's physiology and is always a part of the individual as a biological being. Its function is the same as that of other system processes: to preserve the organism. According to Piaget, intelligence is *both* the means and the end; *both* the activity of coping *and* the end state of compatibility between the organism and its environment. It is the maximum potential of the adaptive capacities; never fully realized, because no match of organism (or person) and environment is perfect.

> Piaget's view of the structure of intelligence is quite consistent with the systems view. Just as Freud's concepts of id, ego, and superego came from classical mechanical physics, so Piaget's concept of schema comes from Einstein's theory of relativity and is compatible with [Alfred North] Whitehead's and Dewey's philosophies. Piaget specifically refers to physics as being analogous to his own ideas, and many of his experiments deal with children's understanding of such physics concepts as velocity, time, and distance. Piaget has explicitly acknowledged a similarity between his own theories and those of Bertalanffy, the foremost general systems theorist. (Koestler and Smythies, 1971:65)

   c. Schemas.   The structural units that lie at the heart of Piaget's system are *schemas,* mediating processes that form frameworks onto which information can, indeed must, fit. These frameworks continually change shape, to accommodate to new information. A schema is "like a rule of grammar. Speakers create all sorts sentences they have never before heard, nor even produced themselves before. They have understood the rule of grammar. . . . Similarly, once the infant has made the connections, a [schema] is at his disposal, and [the child] uses it in all sorts of different . . . manifestations" (Duckworth, 1996:19). Intelligence has a structure and this structure is systematic and orderly. At any particular time it maintains an equilibrium that changes—that is, a steady state.

   Freud's and Piaget's conceptions of intellectual structure are compatible. Piaget was far less interested in the emotional content of schemas, although he recognized its presence. Piaget believed that thought begins as action; schemas are patterns of internalized actions, ranging from the most elementary reflex pattern to profound philosophical thought. Schemas are organized action sequences and behavior patterns that arise through association with each other. Reflexes become associated with other experiences, and such isolated schemas as sucking, grasping, looking, and hearing become larger and more comprehensive. For example, looking and sucking are coordinated into seeing-grasping-sucking the bottle simultaneously. Progressive refinements of schemes allow the child to see the bottle, hold it, turn it around, tilt it, lay it down, pick it up again, see that it is empty, cry, and so forth.

> Infants begin to act in intelligent ways from the day of their birth, that is, they make connections, seek consistencies and modify their actions. . . . [I]nfants proceed to carry out their reflexes in all possible situations, to modify them as necessary, and to figure out which actions in certain situations give rise to more possible things to do. They more they try to do . . . the better they are able to adapt . . . and the more they start to differentiate and to coordinate what they can do. They are making refinements and connections in their actions—"thinking" in their actions—long before there is any use of language (Duckworth, 1996:18–19).

As it matures the child will conduct these operations mentally—that is, to carry on the action internally, think it through, correct it, then try it, all without picking up the bottle. Piaget said that thought is precisely such actions and schemas, refined and modified endlessly. He carried this a step further by stressing that reality as we know it can only be this structure of associated and coordinated experiences. In other words, reality is structured by the schemas we have built up. "The totality of your [schemas] is the totality of what you know" (ibid.:19) "Schema[s] are intellectual structures that organize events as they are perceived and classified into groups according to common characteristics. They are repeatable psychological events" (Wadsworth, 1996:15).

The developing child self-organizes its schemas, and adapts them as new information and experiences are encountered. According to Piaget, adaptation takes two forms: *assimilation* and *accommodation*. The person attempts to fit new information into the old schemas, to interpret it as similar to previous experience; this is assimilation. Accommodation is modification of previous schemas to accept new information.

> Babies are born with eyes, hands, and mouths, but mouths cannot work unless there is light to look at; the grasping reflex cannot work unless there is something to grasp; sucking cannot work unless there is something to suck. Infants take in, incorporate, those parts of the world that enable them to do what they are organized do. In a quite literal sense, this . . . is assimilation.
>
> When infants modify their own organization in order to be able to incorporate yet more of the world, they are accommodating. The only food infants can take in at first is milk. Later they manage to *change their own structures,* in order to be able to take in more forms of nourishment. Similarly, they accommodate their mouth movements to a series of different objects, thus becoming able to enlarge the range of things they can suck. The

greater the flexibility of the structures for taking things in, the better. (Duckworth, 1996:99, emphasis ours).

Assimilation and accommodation are similar to *morphostasis* and *morphogenesis*, the maintenance or change of a system's structure in order to achieve a new steady state after the input of new energy / information. These two tendencies, like other polarities, are never mutually exclusive; there is always some balance (ratio) of the two.

   d.   *Stages of growth.*   Piaget identified four major stages of cognitive growth (ages given here are approximate). "Operations," as Piaget referred to them, mean formal logic, "the manipulation of abstract concepts and the mastery of reasoning" (Bornstein and Lerner, 1987:716), e.g., imagining a concept's opposite, or variations on it; or reversing the sequence in which something occurred, to identify the cause.

   (1) Sensorimotor stage, ages 0–2.   Piaget and Erikson similarly described the infant's profound egocentrism during the initial stage. At birth, the child has no awareness of a self. There is only sensation and reflexes. There is no distinction between self and environment, no consciousness yet to construct a boundary. Duckworth's description, above, is of this stage. The child begins to experience self as an active agent within an environment that is separate from itself, and to influence that environment. This is *coevolution*: the environment changes as the child changes; the parent encourages the child's expanding repertoire, and provides increasingly challenging opportunities for cognitive and motor development. It is Erikson's *trust vs. mistrust* stage, in which the child's trust in its own capacities, and in the reliability of the environment, develop.

   (2) Preoperational stage, ages 2 to 6 or 7.   In this stage, thought is intuitive rather than deductive or "logical." The child can abstract from experience, but is limited to concrete objects, and to only one aspect of an object at a time. "The beginnings of logic appear in the form of classifications of ideas and an understanding of time and number" (ibid.:716). The capability for reversibility, "running events backward" and to reason back to the beginnings of things, emerges now.

   (3) Concrete operations stage, ages 7 to 11 or 12.   Now that the child can "group" and classify things, the child can manage the logical tasks involved in mathematics, begin to understand scientific method and to understand concepts such as "conservation" (that a volume of water remains the same whether it is in a tall or short glass, e.g.; see the "Gui" illustration, earlier). With these intellectual tools, the child develops of objective certainty about the world, a sense of mastery of it, as Erikson described it in his stage of *industry vs. inferiority*. The child has achieved a temporary *equilibrium* or steady state in its relationship to the world.

   (4) Formal operations stage, age 12 through adulthood.   Now the person becomes capable of the full range of logical operations; the schemas are

fully developed, although they will continue to become more complex throughout life. The adolescent can imagine beyond his or her own experience. In Freudian terms, the ego can now fully idealize, testing reality against ideals. Everything is open to question, parents and authorities included; everything must be analyzed (and reanalyzed). This explains adolescence as the "idealistic" stage of life, and the usefulness of adolescents as the "advance guard" of cultural adaptation. It is no coincidence that the ideal of romantic love is the adolescent Romeo and Juliet. Adolescence, as we discuss later, is a time of crisis (in Erikson's terms) because the person system is physiologically, emotionally, and cognitively in upheaval.

2. The Development of Moral Judgment: Lawrence Kohlberg

Piaget hypothesized that all people pass through two phases of moral reasoning. In the first phase an objective and concrete morality is based on the constraints imposed by the powerful (e.g., adults) on the nonpowerful (e.g., children). In the second phase the person develops a subjective morality based on an abstract understanding of the contracts implicit in cooperative and autonomous relationships. Piaget's stress on the universal ordering of moral growth represents an approach that is quite distinct from relativistic, response-centred approaches. As such, it has stimulated considerable interest among developmental researchers. (ibid.:716)

Lawrence Kohlberg (1984, 1987), a psychologist, applied Piaget's theory to the development of moral judgment in children and adults. Piaget's studies of this aspect of human development date from the 1920s; Kohlberg's from the late 1950s. Kohlberg's methodology was to administer verbal and written descriptions of situations that asked children or adults to state what is "right" in each situation. For example, in the "Heinz" case, Heinz's wife is dying and the pharmacist has the rare medicine to cure her but will sell it only at a price that Heinz cannot afford. The respondent must decide what is "right," and why. Should Heinz steal the medicine? If not, why not? If so, why? Because he loves his wife or simply because she is a human being in jeopardy? What are the rights of the pharmacist? Should he be able to set any price he wishes? What of the pharmacist's right to private property that he created? Should Heinz or the pharmacist act according to the "golden rule" or some other universal rule? The answers given in this and other situations indicate the respondent's stage of moral development; these stages are adapted from Piaget.

Kohlberg identified six stages (and later a seventh that seems highly speculative), the first four of which emerge from his research. The fifth and sixth stages are logical extensions of the preceding stages, but they are criticized by other investigators for the lack of empirical evidence. The stages are grouped in pairs under three major headings.

a. Preconventional moral judgment. Kohlberg identified the majority of the population, which falls in stages 3 and 4, as being "conventional" in their moral judgments. Accordingly, stages 1 and 2 are "preconventional," centering upon self, and stages 5 and 6 are "postconventional," centering upon wider social systems, either societal or universal (all of humanity), in making moral judgments.

Stage 1.   In this earliest stage, judgments are based upon the direct consequences the child is likely to suffer. "Will I be punished for this or rewarded?" The child's calculation is simple and straightforward, and it is the first step beyond egocentrism; it represents the ability to take the perspective of another person.

Stage 2.   Now the child moves beyond stark reciprocity; it desires to please its nurturers. It anticipates the pleasure or displeasure of these "significant others." The child has differentiated self from other and views self *in relation to* other. The child begins to understand that the will or desires of the other person can change—that they can be changed by the child's actions, and that there is some standard of fairness or reciprocity to which the child can appeal.

b. Conventional moral judgment.   According to Kohlberg, stages 3 and 4 comprise the levels of development of most of the population; hence the label "conventional." One could assume that the distribution of the adult population falls within a classic bell-shaped curve, except that the shape of the "bell" would be quite high and quite narrow, since Kohlberg and his fellow researchers estimate that no more than 5 percent of the population have progressed beyond stage 5.

Stage 3.   The child now not only understands the other, but is capable of taking the role of the other, and can see the situation (and self) from the other's perspective. "Kohlberg refers to this sometimes as the 'Good-boy / Nice-girl' stage. One is motivated to observe rules in order to maintain relationships. The individual's conception of right at this stage is limited to people within his own circle and does not extend to a broad societal level" (Rosen, 1980:76).

Stage 4.   This stage can be called "social system and conscience" (ibid.:77). The child's reference is the entire society. There is a sense of obligation to conform and to obey its laws and fulfill its obligations. Laws are recognized as necessary and legitimate. There is now a conception of a moral code that extends beyond one's family and community systems. Judgments are based upon the rights of society. Vengeance, for example, is the right of society and is interpreted as "paying your debt to society." In a cogent sentence, Kohlberg suggests what underlies the attitude of the general public toward welfare and those who receive it: "Social inequality is allowed where it is reciprocal to effort, moral conformity, and talent, but unequal favoring of the 'idle' and 'immoral,' poor, students, etc., is strongly rejected" (ibid.:77). This, then, is the stage of conventional morality, and is manifested in such current programs as "workfare" and such slogans as "a hand up, not a handout," which are embodied in the 1996 federal welfare reforms and associated changes at the state level.

Kohlberg and his collaborators identified a substage (cleverly labeled stage 4B), which is a "moratorium" (Erikson's term; see later in this chapter) or period of limbo. During this substage, the person is in a transition state from stage 4 to stage 5 and, in confusion, alternates between relativism and absolutism in moral judgments. Roughly, this period falls between high school graduation (about age 18) and the midtwenties, approximately the "college (and perhaps graduate school) years." This poses a question that psychosocial theorists might ask: Is it that the institution of higher education causes such change, or does the developmental change during this period create the institution of higher education, to accommodate this cognitive/moral development? A systems answer might be that this is an example of mutual causation.

Kohlberg said that there are periods of "disequilibrium" between stages (similar to Piaget; we recognize them as phase transformations or transition states) and that the person in substage 4B is in such a disequilibrium. Kohlberg believed that stage 5, if it is achieved, occurs during the midtwenties, and that stage 6 does not occur until at least the late twenties. If these stages are substantiated by further research, they would tend to confirm Erikson's stages of adulthood as well as Kohlberg's.

c. *Postconventional stages of moral development.* Stages 5 and 6 are controversial, since there is less supporting evidence for them. Kohlberg has been accused of deriving these from philosophical premises, rather than empirical research. The person recognizes that societies' rules are relative, that they are sometimes arbitrary and subjective. Postconventional reasoning becomes possible with the arrival of formal logic, and begins at adolescence.

Stage 5.   Now the person entertains the possibility of changing unjust laws and challenging society's practices. The person looks beyond laws to the principles they embody, and questions whether the laws fulfill those principles. According to Kohlberg, the logical outcome of stage 5 is a democratic society. The person becomes aware that there may be two or more valid moral or legal alternatives and must choose between them. In this sense, the person in stage 5 seeks justice as a principle rather than simply obedience to the law. Equity (fairness based on specific criteria) is preferred over absolute equality. It is clear that Kohlberg has been influenced by a philosophy of justice such as that of John Rawls.

Stage 6.   Here are the idealized characteristics of the person who attains stage 6:

The rare person whose sociocognitive moral development has [progressed] to this stage of moral reasoning is fully autonomous. He is *completely decentered from society's expectations* and bases his resolutions to ethical conflicts upon universal principles of justice. . . . Universality, consistency and logical comprehensiveness are the central attributes. . . . Respect for the dignity of each individual, regardless of station in life, has reached a zenith. (Rosen, 1980:80–81, emphasis ours)

Kohlberg cited a philosopher's solution to the "Heinz" situation as an example of stage 6 moral judgments:

IF THE HUSBAND DOES NOT FEEL VERY CLOSE TO OR AFFECTIONATE WITH HIS WIFE, SHOULD HE STEAL THE DRUG? *Yes. The value of her life is independent of any personal ties.* The value of human life is based upon the fact that it offers the only possible source of a categorical moral "ought" to a rational being acting in the role of a moral agent. SUPPOSE IT WERE A FRIEND OR AN ACQUAINTANCE? *Yes, the value of a human life remains the same.* (Hersh, Paolitto, and Reimer [1979] 1983:80)

Stage 7. Kohlberg identified a seventh stage for which there is no supporting research data, as yet. His critics did not find convincing evidence for stages 5 or 6, either. Kohlberg acknowledged being influenced by Erikson and believed that this seventh stage occurs in elderly persons who find meaning in life, despite despair and doubt, by "identifying the self with cosmic perspective of the infinite" (Rosen, 1980:88). Kohlberg does not claim that this is a verifiable stage, but believes that among the elderly spiritual growth occurs that is qualitatively different from earlier moral stages. One wonders whether such spiritual growth might also occur among younger persons who face their own imminent death, with time to ponder its meaning.

Kohlberg's theories have received thorough and sometimes unfavorable reviews; but he has created the largest body of research on moral judgment and for that reason alone is significant. Some observations on his theory may be useful here. Persons do not inevitably progress through either Kohlberg's or Piaget's stages, as contrasted to Erikson's stages; Kohlberg stated that most of the population remains in stage 4.

One serious criticism of Kohlberg's theory is that his idealized persons in stages 5 and 6 (and certainly stage 7) are conceived to be "beyond culture" or "culture-free" (similar to Maslow's theory of the self-actualized person). This contradicts what we have said in Chapter 3 regarding the pervasiveness and power of culture. Socrates, Lincoln, Martin Luther King, Jr. (each of whom he cited), and—one could add—Gandhi were certainly not free of their respective cultures. One could maintain (as Erikson did of Luther, Jefferson, and Gandhi) that in fact they transformed their cultures through exemplifying certain principles that, in each case, underlay the laws and norms of their societies.

C. Theories Related to Gender and Sexual Orientation.

It is extremely important to note criticisms that have been leveled at the preceding theories regarding their focus on men, and Caucasian, heterosexual men in particular. In this and the following section, we will examine some theories of development that begin with other cultural, social, and biological premises. Gender (or more precisely, sexuality) is not solely female; that it is perceived so reveals the male norm in our society. "Masculinity and femininity are not like a set of clothes in a wardrobe which can be put on and off with ease. These identities feel more like a skin which can not be shed" (Wetherell, 1995:250).

1. Women's Development. Discussion of theories of women's development is placed here because at many points these theories contain critiques of, and advancements on, other theories including those previously presented. Some views of women's development, particularly within the last generation, may be described as feminist theory. Feminist theory "addresses the invisibility of women's experience and knowledge in domestic and public spheres, and redresses this injustice by reclaiming women's own history and language" (Butler and Wintram, 1991:6). This theoretical field begins with "An underlying feminist assumption" which permeates

> our thoughts, behaviour and attitudes . . . that patriarchy systematically oppresses women in every sphere of life. (ibid.:8)
> [Therefore,] it is crucial that any theory derived outside of feminism is considered critically for its value *for* women and, in addition, should not preclude the development of woman-based theory. (ibid.:20)

This present book may be evaluated by the same criteria, as well.

At this point, we should look at the reality of women's lives. In the United States, most women are in low-paid, unskilled jobs, although there have been increases of women in professional positions. Many have inadequate or no health insurance, and welfare "reform" will probably make this worse, at least in the short run. Most will receive a modest pension or none, and will fare better with "spouse" pensions than their own. Typically, employed women work the "second shift" unassisted, with little help in domestic chores or child care. About half will receive child support payments they are legally entitled to, and when they do, will receive about half the amount specified. Women are less often promoted and appear less often on the "fast track" at work, receive lower pay for similar work, and often hit the "glass ceiling." Women hold a relatively small fraction of executive jobs in work organizations, including higher education, although women are highly represented as creators and executives of small, entrepreneurial firms.

As Levinson says,

> The level and intensity of gender conflict have risen since 1980. We live in a state of gender warfare—often covert but with flare-ups of overt antagonism. . . . Harassment and discrimination take a greater variety of forms, gross as well as subtle. . . . There is growing public awareness that many women are abused, discriminated against, and hindered in their personal development.
>   . . . The conflict is not only between women and men. It exists also among women and among men. Our established customs, laws, and values are in question. (Levinson, 1996:417)

The cultural conflict is not new, of course. As Levinson points out, the writer Virginia Woolf addressed these issues eloquently in 1931 (Levinson, 1996:419–420).

   a. Karen Horney.   Born in Germany in 1885, Karen Danielson Horney was one of the first psychoanalytic patients (of one of Freud's colleagues), while she was a medical student, and became a psychoanalyst. Her early work elaborated Freud's basic themes, but she proposed a counterinterpretation using Freud's own ideas. As her theory evolved, she fundamentally diverged from Freud, proposing an alternative "cultural view of human development" rather than a Freudian intrapsychic (instinctual and sexual) view. After she moved to the United States in 1932, she found support among colleagues such as Harry Stack Sullivan and Erich Fromm. She anticipated ideas later advanced by Erikson, regarding the need for basic trust, and Maslow, regarding the need for "safety and satisfaction" (Westkott, 1986:68–71).

   Horney's theory of the psychology of women was based upon experience with her female patients, her own experience (as Freud's views were), and her experience as the mother of three daughters. In addition, her view of the impact of culture was influenced by the rise of Nazi ideology. "To understand female psychology, she proposed, one must account for this male-created social subordination of women. Thus, a psychology of women should be a social psychology, an explication of the interaction of psychic and social factors" (ibid.:12). For Horney, "inner conflict is the avoidable consequence of the contradictions and dehumanizing elements of civilization as transmitted by parents to their children" (ibid.).

   Horney described a "common present-day feminine type" in 1934; she traced its origin to the culture's conflicting definitions of femininity: "a patriarchal ideal of womanhood versus a more independent female identity" (ibid.:14). Women are devalued by the male-dominated culture; they are viewed as sexualized beings from childhood onward. Horney "believed that authentic care for others and mutual love in intimate relationships are possible" (ibid.:165), but recognized that the culture forced women to "overvalue love" as the primary source of self-esteem and validation. In consequence, women compete for the attentions of men (beginning with a rivalry between mother and daughter for the husband / father's affection) and suffer anxiety, self-doubt; other women are seen as "enemies." Thus women's inner conflicts originate in cultural devaluation and dehumanization and *then* are internalized, the converse of Freud's opinion.

Horney intended this analysis to apply to both genders, but feminist interpretations of her work emphasize its particular applicability to women. One author maintains that Horney's analysis explains the "relational traits that subsequent psychologists have more recently identified" (ibid.:5). Among these traits are "female altruism . . . the characterological need to care for others" (ibid.:134), the culturally prescribed imperative to nurture others and to make fewer demands on others for care. This trait has been addressed by Carol Gilligan.

b. Carol Gilligan. A former collaborator with Kohlberg at Harvard University, Carol Gilligan would presumably take issue with his conception of the morally autonomous person in stage 6, on the ground that separation from human attachment is more characteristic of males than of females. Gilligan applied Kohlberg's technique in her research with women; in particular, the "Heinz" problem. In her book, *In a Different Voice* (1982),* Gilligan provided an extension of Chodorow's theory of the importance of rearing by mothers, and maintained that the relationship to the mother is crucial to moral development and to the child's later mode of relationships with others. Because males ordinarily separate from their mothers in order to identify with their own sex, and females do not, males employ a mode of relating that is oppositional, separatist, and places more importance upon abstract (rational and impersonal) principles than upon relationships with others. Males' styles of relating are presumably more compatible with bureaucratic (including military) ways or organizing their lives and activities. Conversely, women are presumably more (but not exclusively) compatible with informal styles of organization and communication, even within bureaucracies; "networking" is more characteristic of women as a style of relationship and communication.

Gilligan's statement of the difference is that men and women see attachment and separation differently: men see connection as a threat, while women see separation as a threat. Women view the fundamental issue in relationships as *care* and responsibility, rather than rights and rules (Gill-

---

* We apologize for misstating the name of this book in the previous edition, and are grateful that a reader called this to our attention.

igan, 1982). Gilligan concluded that women's logic is based on equality and reciprocity rather than an abstract conception of justice. "Women . . . associate moral behavior with obligation, sacrifice, and inhibitions against hurting others. They are reluctant to make moral judgments about other people and perceive a conflict between power and care (Westkott, 1986:141).

There may be a negative aspect of this role, however:

> The female altruist is not only the selfless caretaker of others but also the great mediator of this vast web of competing needs. Thus the moral paralysis that keeps her from taking a stand which would favor one person over another. This is the underside of her affiliation.
>
>   Despite her tendency to idealize this female caretaking, Gilligan is aware of the quivering in the different voice and of the need to get beyond the condition in which morality is tied to [to quote Gilligan] "dependence on others and equated with responsibility to care for them." (ibid.:143)

This will occur when "the concept of relationship changes from a bond of continuing dependence to a dynamic of interdependence. Then the notion of care expands . . . to an injunction to act responsively toward self and others and thus to sustain connection" (Gilligan, 1982:149). Horney stated a similar, existentialist view in *New Ways in Psychoanalysis* in 1939:

> By making self-responsibility her fundamental therapeutic goal, Horney reclaimed judgment as a human capacity that is not reducible to sexuality (libido), guilt (superego), or accommodation to external reality (ego). Freedom and responsibility of choice that draw upon a whole real self, not a segmented and managed self, bring to bear perception, cognition, feeling, and judgment. (ibid.:207)

Horney's view is highly congruent with a systems view of the relationship of the person and larger systems. Conflict within the person mirrors conflicts in the culture and society, and alteration of the feedback cycle (through locating and validating the "real self") can heal: "From [Horney's] perspective growth is *self-directed* life itself, and at is core is the central inner force that is the real self" (ibid.:71; emphasis ours). While Gilligan focuses on *care* as a desirable characteristic for both genders, she acknowledges the same need as Horney for self-direction by women.

   c. *Daniel Levinson.*   Daniel Levinson, a psychologist, began to research women's development shortly after completing his study of men (discussed later in this chapter). The result was *The Seasons of a Woman's Life* (1996), an analysis of homemakers' and career women's experiences during their adult years.

   Levinson demonstrates a systems approach: "[T]he primary components of a life structure are the person's *relationships* with various others in the external world" (Levinson, 1996:22). He cautions that

It is important to distinguish between the development of the life structure and the development of the self. . . . The study of adult development inevitably goes beyond the focus on the self. It requires us to examine the life course, to study the engagement of self in the world. . . . As we learn more about the evolution of the life structure, we will have a sounder basis for studying the adult development of the self. (ibid.:29)

"Satisfactoriness of the life structure" is a highly significant factor in his analysis of women's lives:

[I]t refers to the structure's viability in the external world—how well it works, what it provides in the way of advantages and disadvantages, successes and failures, rewards and deprivations. Internally, it refers to the structure's suitability for the self, that is, what aspects of the self can be lived out within this structure? What aspects must be neglected or suppressed? What are the benefits and costs of this structure for the self? (ibid.:28–29)

Levinson reports that he was surprised by the "extent and power of the differences" between women's and men's lives, and attempts to capture this in the concept of "gender splitting":

a splitting asunder . . . women and men have lived in different worlds: culture, social institutions, everyday social life, the individual psyche. It creates antithetical divisions between women and men, between social worlds, between the masculine and the feminine within the self. It also creates inequalities that limit the adult development of women as well as men. (ibid.:38)

Levinson's research confirmed the effects on women, many of whom experienced what he calls "rock bottom time" during transition periods at about age thirty and age fifty: "a sense of being overwhelmed, of having no way to form a minimally good enough life. . . . For some the crisis involved considerable turmoil and conscious suffering; others were not clearly aware of the extent of their difficulties" (ibid.:94). The difficulties arose, in large part, because both societal expectations and women's expectations changed (both macro and microsystems).

[T]he traditional pattern is difficult to sustain. Most women who tried . . . formed structures that were relatively unsatisfactory—not viable in the world, not suitable for the self. The few who were more or less contented paid a considerable price in restriction of self-development. The career women tried to anticipate the future: to reduce the gender-splitting, to enter formerly "male" occupations, to work on equal terms with men, and to establish a family life in which homemaking and provisioning were more equally divided. Their lives attest to the pleasures and problems of innovation, of attempting to realize values not well supported by the current culture and institutions (ibid.: 415).

2. *Theories of Lesbian and Gay Development.*   Etiology of gay or lesbian sexual orientation is uncertain.

> There is no clear evidence from studies that family of origin relationships contribute to the development of homosexuality. . . . The causes of homosexuality remain a mystery, although research is becoming centered increasingly on genetic factors and the prenatal hormonal environment . . . as predisposing conditions for subsequent internal and developmental-social processes that lead to self-labeling as lesbian or gay. Most likely, there are multiple routes to adoption of a homosexual identity. (Laird and Green, 1996:7)

Freud believed that homosexuality was due to anal fixation or failure to resolve the Oedipal crisis. A behaviorist explanation is that the person finds same-sex experiences reinforcing or less aversive than heterosexual contact. The Kinsey studies in sexuality supported this interpretation: that first sexual experience determined subsequent choices (Kinsey et al., 1948). One study of brain structure indicated similarity between the brains of women and gay males, which might support an organic origin for homosexuality.

There is no clear evidence to suggest patterns of difference between the personality development of homosexuals, heterosexuals, and bisexual persons. However, it was not until 1973 that the American Psychiatric Association removed homosexuality from its list of pathologies; in 1991, it officially allowed gays and lesbians admission to its training institutes; and in 1992, allowed them to teach in these institutes and to become senior analysts (Clark, 1997:30–31). The American Psychological Association agreed in 1975 that homosexuality is not a mental disorder. There have been few studies of personality development among gays or lesbians, certainly not enough to propose a distinct scheme of development with any degree of confidence. However, "coming-out" models suggest four stages of identity development, leading from first awareness to full disclosure:

1.   First awareness

- An initial cognitive and emotional realization that one is "different: and a feeling of alienation from oneself and others
- No disclosure to others
- Some awareness that homosexuality may be the relevant issue

2.   Test and exploration

- Feelings of ambivalence that precede acceptance of homosexuality
- Initial but limited contact with gay and lesbian individuals or communities

- Alienation from heterosexuality

3. Identity acceptance

- Preference for social interactions with other gays and lesbians
- Evolution from negative identity to positive identity
- Initial disclosure to heterosexuals

4. Identity integration

- View of self as gay or lesbian with accompanying anger at society's prejudice
- Publicly coming out to many others
- Identity stability: unwillingness to change and pride in oneself and one's group (J. Sophie, in Clark, 1997:154–155)

This model indicates the resistance, or fear that may justifiably accompany a person's disclosure of gay or lesbian identity. It does not, however, sufficiently convey the isolation, self-doubt, and negative poles of Erikson's stages that are experienced by many gays and lesbians, in response to the fear and hostility they encounter in their social relationships. Most are reluctant to disclose to their families; most will disclose to friends and to siblings before the disclose to parents; many never disclose to parents, particularly if their family's culture (Hispanic and Asian cultures, e.g., are cited) is not receptive to homosexuality. Often, maintaining psychological defenses and keeping the secret require massive expenditure of energy, and closing off social exchanges. In a significant number of instances, the strain is too great; some studies report that 20–40 percent of gay and lesbian youths have attempted suicide; half of these have made multiple attempts, and they are two to three times more likely to commit suicide than other youths (Laird and Green, 1996:170). Families often find disclosure, or discovery, difficult to accept; outright rejection may result, or physical or emotional attacks. Relatively few families handle disclosure affirmatively and supportively, at least at first.

Homophobia is a word coined by George Weinberg in *Society and the Healthy Homosexual* in 1972:

> It suggests a phobic, irrational fear of people who are gay or primarily homosexual in orientation and, indeed, of anything having to do with homosexuality. . . . Homophobia may cover a person's fear of his or her own homoerotic feelings. . . . It is an irrational, illogical pathology driven by simple fear and the awesome power of buried anxiety. (Clark, 1997:9)

Whatever its origin, "No other issue taps into such a potential conflict more than the issue of homosexuality" (Wolfe, 1998:72). Wolfe reports that while 70 percent of Americans believe that same-sex behavior is "wrong," most people would live and let live. He believes that public opinion does not support gays and lesbians teaching in public (elementary and high) schools, but cites data showing that over 70 percent believe that it is acceptable for homosexuals to teach in higher education (ibid.:75). "That support can be explained on the grounds of respect for rights; in endorsing the right of homosexuals to teach, people are not necessarily endorsing homosexuality" (ibid.); apparently they fear for their children. Homophobia runs deep in American culture, despite respect for privacy and individual rights, and permeates all systems levels.

Wolfe draws a parallel between this prejudice and American attitudes toward bilingual education: "It is one thing to say that people's rights should not be denied and another to say that their identities should be respected" (ibid.:154). The cultural system, with its structure of privilege, its racial/ethnic and sexual attitudes, strongly resists change. Like all identities, cultural identity contains negative as well as positive elements. Identities change in response to crisis; social work and other professions have a deep responsibility to assist in the positive resolution of this cultural crisis.

D. Theories of Development: Some Observations

Freud's views were influenced by the *zeitgeist* of his culture: male dominance and the contention of powerful forces. Feminist views as represented by Horney and Gilligan, and more affirmative views of homosexuality invalidate Freud's chauvinistic opinions. In the long term, Freud's contributions are greatest in his recognition of the unconscious, his introduction of sexuality as a subject of academic and popular discussion, and his attempt to identify stages of human development that are grounded in physiology. History may rehabilitate his reputation as a groundbreaking theorist, but these are precisely the points on which contemporary theorists of women's development take issue, and on which advances in theory have occurred:

1. The unconscious is not an isolated subsystem; it is social as well as instinctual, and inner conflicts result from cultural conflicts.

2. Gender identification is a more complex (and social) process than Freud envisioned; while biology and sexuality are important components of identity, they are not the only, nor necessarily the *most* significant elements; the dynamics of the cultural system and family system are vitally important; and stages of growth (as demonstrated by Erikson and Piaget) are not solely determined by physiology but by feedback cycles between the culture, society, family, and person; description of the stages

must (as Erikson's does) include the characteristics and expectations of the cultural system, to be complete.

Summing up from a systems perspective, Freud posited the self, or personality, as a nearly closed system, with the exception of the intimate ties to parents during the initial stages; once the Oedipal crisis was resolved, the structure of the system underwent no further change. Each of the other theorists discussed here described the person as an open system, interacting with its environment throughout the life cycle. Erikson and Piaget viewed physiology as setting some parameters and general timetable within which growth occurred; there was a degree of inevitability about the stages of development. Kohlberg appeared to agree, but did allow for some exceptional persons to surpass the constraints of the social environment.

Horney, Gilligan, and Erikson seemed to agree about the openness of the person to other systems, although it appears that Erikson's description of male and female modalities of relationships is rejected by many feminists as too Freudian, too *essentialist* in the importance he gave to biological determinism. Among these theorists, Horney and Gilligan offer a "deep theory" of culture, maintaining that the cultural system penetrates the person system to the level of the unconscious self, creating an "idealized self" that obscures and displaces a "real self." An objective view of homosexuality recognizes the role that culture plays in shaping the experiences of gays and lesbians, and the defenses they must employ in order to withstand the systematic homophobia of our society; in this respect, they are forced to be *too open* to the dictates of the culture. It is only in recent decades that gay and lesbian cultures in the United States have been able to sustain sufficient autonomy and self-development to sustain permeable but protective boundaries.

II.   THE CRITICAL PHASES OF THE LIFE CYCLE

A.   *Establishment of Primary Attachment (Dependency and Trust) in the Parent-Child Dyad—The First Social System*

Initially, at least, we should not refer to the infant as an autonomous entity in itself. It is helpless, dependent, and must be cared for; it is "as one" with the other party to the dyad. It is now confined to being a component—something that is not true at any later time. It is a component of a system—a two-person system. In the prenatal environment, the developing organism is connected through the umbilical cord; in the first months of life, it is tethered by a "psychological cord" that must be stretched, and later severed (or transformed), to permit the developing personality to make other, wider, less exclusive social connections.

The newborn enters the world in a totally dependent state. Most of the first year is devoted to the effort to survive and to the formation and elaboration of adaptation devices that will achieve survival. During this early period, the infant is helpless and incapable of surviving by its own efforts. The nurturing person (or persons) compensates for, and supplies, what the newborn lacks. The newborn is initially in an *undifferentiated* state; that is, in the world of the newborn, there is no object or object relation (no conception of self, therefore no sense of anything that is not-self). The infant is profoundly egocentric; it is aware of nothing but its own internal conditions. Physiological organization is rudimentary, and there is no demonstrated psychic organization (in the sense of self, or ego or superego). Object relations will develop during the first year (Spitz, 1965).

1. *Trust vs. Mistrust.*   Erikson described the first crucial social task as a sense of *basic trust vs. basic mistrust*. By this, he meant the necessity to develop a *feeling* of trust in others and in one's self and for healthy (realistic) mistrust of one's environment (and of oneself, perhaps); that is, one learns to distrust snarling dogs, hot stoves, and strangers (and maybe one's jealous older sibling). Spitz referred to this first task as the initiation of an object relationship. In the Erikson formulation of the dimension of trust, the following elements are important:

(a)   The nurturing person becomes an inner certainty for the child, as well as an outer predictability. This state includes the qualities of consistency, continuity, and sameness of experience. These experiences and qualities become part of the child's identity.

(b)   (The infant develops a sense of being able to trust self and the capacity of its own organs to cope with urges; it learns to control its hands; it learns to control its bladder and bowel functions (the latter are very important social expectations).

(c)   This sense of trust in self and others forms the foundation for the later development of a sense of identity; this is an example of how Erikson's stages relate to one another.

(d)   Since the sense of trust / mistrust is essentially social, it is based in communication (particularly tactile, nutritive, and emotional) between the infant and the caring person(s). Bonding relies on the quality of these experiences.

Ever since Spitz's work in the 1930s on the effects of maternal deprivation, there has been controversy about whether the primary social attachment must be between infant and *mother*; it is fairly well accepted that is not necessarily only the biological mother. The necessary continuity, consistency, and predictability must be embodied in *some* particular person, but it can be a "caring or nurturing person" other than the biological mother, and not necessarily confined to only one person. This continues to be an important question regarding parents' usage of day-care centers for their infants.

The infant's primary needs are the oral, nutritive needs. The mouth is the initial receptor, the most sensitive and demanding tissue in the body at this time. Sensitive tissues develop in other erotogenic zones later; these are the basis of Freud's *oral*, *anal*, and *genital* stages. Erikson, too, employed the idea of physical *zones* and identified the zonal sensitivity of this stage as *oral-respiratory* and *sensory-kinesthetic* (the latter is compatible with Piaget's view). He stressed that these are incorporative modes: taking in. The child's first social activities focus on incorporation: *getting* and learning to *get*. During the later portion of this first, critical stage, the infant begins to give in return. To paraphrase Erikson, as the child evolves in the first months of life it could well say, "I am what I am given," next say, "I am what I can get," and finally say, "I am what I can give."

   2.   *Dysfunctional conditions.*   Within the initial dyad, the infant does not long remain a passive recipient. In her definitive theoretical review of object relations, dependency, and attachment, Ainsworth emphasized the important role of infants' behaviors both in eliciting parental responses and in active "proximityseeking" (Ainsworth, 1969:981). Transactions between a human system and its social environment are necessary to its definition of boundary of self; it is through the recognition of and interaction with "other" that the boundaries of self can be defined. If the boundaries of self do not become defined, *infantile autism* may result. If self is not differentiated from other, the resulting condition is referred to as *symbiosis*

   a.   *Maternal deprivation.*   A number of dysfunctional dyadic systems were identified and grouped under the rubric of maternal deprivation (Bowlby, 1962), which can be described both quantitatively and qualitatively. It usually refers to an *insufficiency of interaction* between the child and the nurturing person(s) and to the conditions in which the insufficiency seems to develop. The term "maternal deprivation" should be interpreted figuratively (it may be someone other than a mother, and may be insufficiency rather than total deprivation) rather than literally. It describes the effect upon the child more accurately than it describes the conditions which cause it. Some of these conditions are:

   1.   Absence of relationships: e.g., institutionalization or hospitalization of the infant with no provision for substitute nurturing. The danger of this was documented by Spitz in his writings and films (1965). This might happen in wartime conditions; in a state of widespread disease (such as the AIDS epidemic in some African countries, where 25 percent

are infected); or in extreme poverty or famine in which parents die or are severely ill, and social substitutions are unavailable.

2. Child's lack of response: Sufficient care is available, but the child is unable to interact because of previous deprivations, maturational deficiencies, or unknown causes. Not infrequently, parents of disturbed preschool children report that almost from birth, an infant was not responsive to cuddling and "gentling." Frequently a neurological deficit is suspected, but not always detectable.

3. Distorted relationships:

(a) Situations in which the child is *undifferentiated* from the parent, similar to the normal condition that the newborn experiences, but here the normal process of developing a somewhat autonomous self does not occur. The parent, also, does not distinguish between self and child; the boundary is not clear.

(b) Interlocking dependency, a symbiotic relationship wherein the parent "needs" to have a totally dependent infant and the child "needs" to have total mothering. Again, this is the normal circumstance of the newborn, but to prolong this condition distorts the child's development and prevents development of a healthy parent-child relationship. The Münchhausen syndrome, in which a parent induces illness in a child in order to maintain mutual dependency, is an example.

(c) The parent may assimilate the child as being certain aspects of himself (or herself) or identify the child completely with the qualities of another person. A measure of this is normal and desirable, e.g., seeing the child as having the parent's eyes or grandparent's chin, but when the total child is viewed as possessing the qualities of another, the child has little opportunity to differentiate self and establish self as a separate, autonomous and distinct person.

(d) The parent perceives the child as the embodiment of a single quality, such as stupid, evil, or totally demanding (when it is not so).

4. Insufficient relationships:

(a) A situation in which a mother (or other primary nurturer) provides insufficient opportunity for interaction. Examples are "crack mothers" or other addicts who may be incapable of providing sufficient interaction; acute mental illness of the primary nurturer might be another situation.

(b) The parenting person is unable to give emotionally because of her/his own isolation, coldness, cruelty, or learned inability to relate to others; this may have originated in the parent's own childhood family system.

(c) The parent may be narcissistic and involved with self so that no more than physical care is provided. The parent's system is so closed toward the child that little or no transaction of feeling is permitted.

(d) Circumstances exhaust the caring person's energies, and little love is available for nurturance of the child. These demands may come from within the family system (parental illness, e.g.) or from the environment (e.g., conditions of poverty, war, an epidemic, or systematic repression).

One or more of these distorted or insufficient relationships are often found in cases of child abuse.

b. Separation. Another form of defective dyad that complicates the child's efforts to establish a basic sense of trust is labeled *separation.* Deprivation refers to insufficiency of relationship; separation refers to interruption of an already established relationship, and to the need for continuity and predictability. Bowlby (1962:205–214) studied the effects of separation and concluded that a separation in the first three months of life is not disturbing to a child *if an adequate parent substitute* is provided. However, by the age of three months, the infant has formed an attachment (a dyadic system) with the nurturing person, and separation at this time is more likely to interfere with its efforts to establish basic trust. Prolonged separation between the ages of six and twelve months is most harmful and may not be reversible (ibid.:117–119). Bowlby described the possible results as an "affectionless character," an inability (or difficulty) to enter into intimate relationships with other persons, and an unfavorable ratio of mistrust to trust, in Erikson's terms. Bowlby also found that juvenile delinquency was highly correlated with separation experiences in the preschool years and suggested that early childhood separation is a causal factor for some delinquents, but this finding has been questioned.

B. Differentiation of Self within the Family System

The family system is the scene of the second and third of Erikson's crises of psychosocial growth. The mother-child dyad usually expands to become a three-or-more-person system for these tasks; while the third person may be husband / father, it may be grandmother or other nurturing person (see discussion of this in Chapter 7).

1. Autonomy vs. Shame and Doubt. This psychosocial crisis carries the special requirement for the establishment of a sense of self as an entity, distinguished from the environment. This parallels the child's development, which includes the capacity to manage certain physical functions (e.g., ambulation and elimination) as muscles and nerve systems mature. Assertion of self as an autonomous being, and uncertainty about its capacity to do so, compete within the child, who must risk relinquishing some of the comfortable dependency of the primary dyadic system.

The first assertion of self as an autonomous, self-developing system is through communicating, "No! No, I can *will* not to do what you want me to do." The well-known negativism of the two-year-old expresses this assertion of the will. In middle-class cultures, this negativism defies cultural dictates about toilet habits, neatness, and respect for others' property.

The corollary of negative assertion is self-control and independence. But if the family system places *too few* limits on assertive behavior, the child may be stranded out on a limb, not having internalized the capacity for self-management and direction. If the family system *overly* restricts opportunities to test the limits of its behavior, the child will not have the chance to experience itself as a autonomous and self-developing entity. At either extreme, the child will likely develop a sense of shame and doubt.

For the most part, these preschool years are centered in the family system, the primary social unit of the culture. It is within this microculture that the child becomes a person, a social being. This crisis of *autonomy vs. shame and doubt* occurs within the family system, in which it is critical to resolve the following issues:

a. Sense of self beyond the dyad. An awareness of autonomy, separate from the nurturing persons, must develop. The question, Where do they end and where do I begin? must be provisionally answered now, and is a question that arises again in adolescence, with full force.

b. Order in the social environment. Sensitivity to order is characteristic of this age. Children frequently insist on sameness in their environment and become distraught when important objects are relocated. The predictability, continuity, and consistency that were needed from the nurturing person in the first stage are now required from the physical environment. The environment must be trustworthy because the child now self-constructs from the environment. Learning to name objects provides the perception of stability in the environment (Piaget's concept of *conservation*), and allows the child a degree of control over it (Brown, 1965:267–276). Self-organization is possible only when the environment is sufficiently organized.

c. Assertion of will—self inserted into the environment. This occurs first in negation and then in affirmation. The child diligently attempts to be an autonomous, self-developing entity. First physiologically, then psychologically, and finally socially, children find (as Erikson described) they can will to *hold on* or to *let go*. Physiologically, maturation of sphincter muscles allows the child to hold on to, or let go; this is accompanied by psychological and social qualities of retention or release. If the society is extremely concerned about toilet habits, elimination may provide the child with a proving ground for a conflict of power and a test of weaponry. Toilet training is sometimes referred to as "breaking" the child as in breaking a wild mustang. To persuade the child to submit its will to that of the culture as represented by the family becomes crucially important. The child is encouraged to develop a willing capacity (and a capacity to will), congruent with the conformity and self-control that the culture so highly prizes.

Psychologically, a child can hold on to or let go of feelings ("put a cork in it" or "vent"), express frustration and anger directly through behavior or control it to please "others." If others communicate that these feelings are too dangerous to let out, the child may doubt its capacity to control emotions; it may also have a feeling of omnipotent power (a "blow-up" in more ways than one). If others cannot or will not provide ground rules, the child may feel internal anarchy and shame, not having experienced release and the power to control the release. In holding on to feelings, the child may not engage in enough transactions with others and may have insufficient feedback to establish self. In letting go, self-boundaries may not be established, and the environment continues to be indistinguishable from self. Clear but permeable boundaries, with a repertoire of flexible responses that are appropriate to environmental stimuli, would be a positive outcome, of course.

d. *Ambivalences—self-expression in the environment.* Dichotomies of feeling (ambivalences) are a characteristic of this crisis. A child may alternately express a sense of love and hate, a sense of independence and total dependence, or a sense of pleasure and displeasure. This rapid alternation of strong, opposite feelings must now be coped with for the first time, and how this is resolved will serve as the prototype for future life tasks. Erikson stated that the cultural solution for this dilemma is embodied in the culture's approach to law and order, in attitudes of social justice, punishment, and compassion.

e. *Communication.* Although language has developed, much communication continues to be nonverbal. Approval and disapproval are more important reinforcers of behavior and are conveyed by feeling, more than by word; the sensitive two- or three-year-old may be more responsive to parental feeling than to word meaning. The parent's prohibitive "no-no" may communicate prohibition or protection, approval or disapproval, challenge or censure, dependent upon the feeling behind the words. The child's thoughts tend to be concrete and fragmentary; the concepts grasped are specific and often literal. At any one time, the child may feel all "good" or all "bad." It is essential at these times that the parents not view the child as either all "bad" or all "good."

The child who does not develop a sufficient sense of autonomy may have little sense of self. Manifestations of this include cloying dependence, general anxiety, foolhardy behavior, expecting others always to be in control, and severe withdrawal. Severe and pervasive negativism may also indicate lack of sufficient autonomy. A sense of autonomy is manifest in a measure of self-regulation and a capacity to enter into social transactions as a discrete entity, that is, self-development.

In the latter preschool years, the primary social system continues to be the family, but the child is beginning to establish linkages to systems beyond the family: playmates, neighbors, extended family or family friends, and increasingly, adults and peers in organizational settings such as Headstart, day-care, and preschool. The qualities of self that the child has developed and brings to these new systems are crucially important.

2. *Initiative vs. Guilt.* The child's second psychosocial crisis occurs through its interaction with its social environment, the family system. With the sense of autonomy, and shame and doubt, accrued so far children must now explore who they are, and what their distinctive qualities are. The Oedipal conflict is central, as is the introjection of right and wrong. As Erikson views this task, the modalities are "to make" (to get) and "to make like" (to play). The bisexuality of the child, which has been apparent up to this time, is now directed toward a culturally defined gender. As Erikson viewed it, the masculine "making" is intrusive, the insertion of self into the social world to accomplish purposes, and the feminine form of "making" is inclusion of the social world to accomplish purposes (this implication that "biology is destiny" is viewed as sexist by feminist critics of Erikson). The genital tissue is hypersensitive at this stage, consistent with Freud's "phallic" stage (one may argue that Freud's view displayed gender bias).

In Erikson's view, the child's active insertion of self, or inclusive behavior, is accompanied by fear of rivalry and anticipated threat of punishment. Identification (or imitation) is a frequent method of coping with the child's compulsion to define self and with the culture's expectations that the child will be like the same-sex parent. Erikson stated that the child could say "I am what I can imagine I will be" (Erikson, 1968:122). The outcome of this crisis will be a mixture of a sense of initiative and a sense of guilt. The child with a favorable ratio of initiative will have purpose and direction as part of her/his adult character, will be self-motivating, and will be able to initiate social behavior and transactions.

This "initiative" crisis has certain common issues:

a. *Creating the self.* The essential psychosocial task now is to create a qualitative sense of self. This exploration begins in the family and then expands outward. Because of the arousal of awareness of genital sensations and the cultural expectations of sex differentiation, much of this is played out in the Oedipal context. The culturally desired outcome of the Oedipal complex ("complex" refers to sets of relationships) is the child's relinquishment of sexual interest in the parent of the opposite sex and identification with the parent of the same sex. Cultural ambiguity about sex-differentiated behaviors affects parents as well as the child. The child may identify with the "stronger" parent regardless of gender, and sometimes does not know with whom to identify. The child may continue to wallow in this task during later crises; energies may be preempted and later crises may be inadequately dealt with. Ideally, however, a favorable resolution is reached, and the child expands its fields of activity to other social systems.

b. *Creative use of play.* Play is an important mode of behavior during this crisis. As Piaget indicated, cognitive development has now progressed so that imagination can be controlled and used in various ways. Erikson considered play as "autotherapeutic," a rudimentary form of the adult capacity to create models and experiment with alternative behaviors without committing oneself. Erikson described three stages of forms of play:

> (1) autocosmic: the child's play begins with and centers on its own body;
> (2) microspheric: the small world of manageable toys; and
> (3) macrospheric: sharing of play with others, first in parallel fashion (playing together but apart) and then in concert. (Erikson, [1950, 1985, 1993] 1963:220–221)

In this crisis, two kinds of play are especially important. One is solitary daydreaming in which the child can fantasize, imagining what she or he would like to do and be. The second is peer play, wherein children together can work on solving their common concerns. Occasionally, play may carry fantasy beyond control or comfort and be frightening. Pretending is a reassuring way to establish the boundaries of reality, especially when adults occasionally share the "let's pretend" activities.

c. *Consolidation and integration.* This crisis is a time of transitional consolidation and integration. Exertion of self into the social environment with hope and expectation of influencing the environment involves a measure of trust in the predictability of environment and one's own predictability, as well as a measure of self-control or will. To be able to do this enables children to imagine how they might eventually influence the world. Because children are newly aware of, and concerned about, the intactness and integrity of bodies at this stage, they are likely to be sensitive to anything that threatens this (e.g., children being baked in an oven or eaten by wolves, as in fairy tales; but these tales allow children to face these fears and allay them). They may be frightened by their own fantasies of power and hold themselves responsible for any calamity that befalls others close to them. This is reinforced in many cultures by means of tales of what befalls disobedient or willful children, as means of inculcating rules of good behavior. Don't forget what happened to Pinocchio, Little Red Riding Hood, Hansel and Gretel, the Sorcerer's Apprentice, and Jack with his beanstalk. Beware!

Again, it is well to mention that the outcome of this crisis is a *ratio* of initiative and guilt. This is the critical time for the development of conscience, which can be a tolerant guide or a punitive slavemaster, but a conscience there will be. It is hoped that initiative will be directed toward "making" things work, in the sense of integrated behaviors, but it can be "making" things and people in the exploitative sense. A child who can emerge from these family-centered growth tasks with a robust sense of trust in others and self, a sense of autonomy as a person who is linked to others, and a sense of purpose is well on the way to a fulfilling life plan.

C. Definition of Self within Secondary Social Systems

1. *Industry vs. Inferiority.*   Erikson's next psychosocial crisis occurs in interaction with components of the community system: formal organizations (such as the school and the church) and informal organizations (such as the neighborhood and the peer group). As in all stages of development, physiological and cognitive maturation provide the capacities, and the culture furnishes the expectations. This is the period of development that Freud labeled *latency* (in which the sex drive is presumably dormant) and that Piaget called the phase of *concrete operations.* Erikson described this fourth crisis as *industry vs. inferiority.* "Industry" is used here in the sense of "being industrious," productive or competent. The dominant issues of this crisis are:

a. *Mastery.*   Now that the child is encountering wider social systems, it seeks to assert control over both its physical self and its environments: physical objects, social transactions, and ideas and concepts. It is the time to learn the technology and ways of one's culture; the institutionalized means to accomplish this are supplied by the culture, whose investment is in its own survival. The school is one such institution charged with transmission of the cultural technology. The Future Farmers of America and 4-H are organizations for communicating the culture of agricultural communities (and for 4-H, increasingly, urban culture as well). The "block gang" exists to transmit the ways of another specialized, local culture, often without "official" societal recognition. Games, contests, and athletics are also examples of institutionalized culture carriers (witness the English proverb, "Wars are won on the playing fields of Eton"). Churches, mosques, temples, and synagogues are other such institutions. The child participates in these organizations, developing a sense of self as competent and incompetent, in some ratio.

Entry into school is an important step to the child, to the parents, and to the culture. One of the very few clearly demarked way stations on the long trail to adulthood (other than religious rituals), it is the occasion when society ensures that each of its young members participates in an organized, institutionalized culture. In the Midwest, the phrase "kindergarten roundup" conveys the cultural investment in collecting the mavericks and commencing the long process of "breaking" them, of acculturation to technological society. An arbitrary age is set for such entry, two years younger than the legal requirement for compulsory school attendance in most states, and the social expectation exists that the child will be readied by the family. If children are indeed ready, they eagerly look forward to entry into this new world. If unready because energies are lacking, the child may have "problems." The child and parent(s) may not be ready for separation. The kindergartner may not be able to distinguish teacher from parent, or may not have self sufficiently organized to comply with the expectations for settled and cooperative behavior.

If the culture transmitted by the school is alien to, or opposed to, the culture of the child's family (as American Indians have often experienced, for example), the young child is in a difficult, indeed untenable, position. The technology and ways of doing things, and the sense of self and other, that the child has learned in that culture have, by this time, become a part of self. To accept a differing way or culture may be felt as an act of betrayal of self, family, and tribe. If so, the child may continue its efforts toward mastery outside the school, seeking mastery of its own culture, not that of others. The lack of participation in school by significant numbers of American Indian, African-American, and Hispanic youths may, in large part, be explained this way. Various writers have documented this as experienced by people of color in the United States. Acuña explained how the educational system serves to socialize the student into accepting and supporting the ways of the majority culture. He stated that this is accomplished by "erasing the [ethnic or racial group's] culture, language and values and replacing them with Anglo-American culture, language and values" (1972:146). Such socialization is clearly a means of social control.

The school has evolved as an overburdened carrier of culture as changes in technology and family functions have occurred; too much is expected of the schools, and some expectations are inappropriate. As society has been bureaucratized, so has the school. It is charged with preparing the young for participation in the existing cultural ways; hence the child experiences self as a functioning participant in a bureaucratic organization. "Preventive" intervention in schools, and early identification of difficulty, is based on the premise that a child's success in school predicts success in adult life, and that lack of success predicts adult failure; there is minimal evidence for this belief. Many who are unsuccessful in school are successful in other aspects of living, and vice versa.

Nonetheless, society expects the child to demonstrate mastery and competence primarily in the single institution of the school. This includes not only the technology of literacy but also physical mastery (Phys. Ed., intramurals, and athletic teams), arts and music, social mastery (social dancing, family life education), domestic skills (now often required of both genders), and such other technological competencies as driving an automobile and operating a computer. Public schools find it very difficult to complete all the assignments the culture gives them. The school has even been required to deal with this society's primary problems: racism, sexism, poverty, and the use of drugs.

   b.   Membership and participation in peer groups.   Peer group experience is a necessary element of the crucible in which mastery is tested. It provides a social system parallel to adult society (and intersecting with it on some occasions), with its own organization, rules, purposes, and activities. It is with the peer group that the child can test self and grow to mastery in social relationships with equals.

   The school is the primary system in which to construct a sense of competence; the other available secondary social system is the peer group. During middle childhood (latency), the child's primary connections continue to be within the family system; it is later in adolescence that the peer group may take precedence over family. The peer group of middle childhood is modeled after the culture within which it exists. At its best, it is not very visible to the adult world and has its own parallel culture passed from generation to generation (two or three years to a generation) with continuity, but with frequent innovations. Less positively, youth gangs can function in defiance of adult norms, although they may provide means of accomplishment (positive or negative) if youths cannot access constructive means of achievement.

   The peer group is likely to be strongest in direct relation to the stability of the population it draws from. The peer group of suburbia is likely to be weak and transitory, whereas the peer group in the small town or urban neighborhood may be stronger. Increasingly, adults have taken control of middle childhood's peer groups: activities are organized and conducted by adults. School functions are part of this control; Little League baseball exemplifies another part; the day camp and "away camp" are others. The attention to individual fulfillment through lessons in swimming, driving, tennis, golf, dancing, music, skiing, and so on, have diminished the availability of child-controlled peer groups. Other factors are the geographic separation of children from their parents who work elsewhere, perhaps in another community, and are not available to transport them, or to be nearby if needed. These adult-managed and supervised activities undoubtedly enable children to develop skills, but minimize opportunities to develop self through interacting freely in a peer culture. This may explain, in part, the phenomenon of "living together" (Popenoe, 1988:303) within a wider peer culture of young adults who are exploring their selves before committing to adulthood.

   c.   Outcome.   Again, the outcome is a ratio of polar feelings. A dominant sense of inferiority may result from a lack of ability, but most frequently it derives from (1) insufficient accrual of resources from previous crises, (2) unclear or unreasonable expectations by adults or peers, or (3) excessively high criteria by which to judge competence and mastery. The idea of a *sense* of industry or inferiority is important. It is the *feeling* the child has about his or her own competence that is crucial, not competence as measured by adult standards. The person who embarks into adolescence with a feeling that she or he can do at least one thing very well is in a favorable position indeed.

Mastery of the ground rules of life is important to children at this stage. Piaget (1932) found that they are quite occupied with "justice" and accept arbitrary or expiatory punishment as sometimes warranted. As they grow older, they favor the idea of retribution connected to the offending act and its natural consequences. Development of schemas for moral judgment forms the basis for organized social relations. Peer groups have fairness, social order, and "the rules of the game" at the core of their reason for existing.

The largest portion of children referred to child guidance clinics and school special services are aged eight to eleven; the problem most often described is "immaturity." Problems of middle childhood can be grouped under these general headings:

(1) Poor school performance.   The child's mastery of cultural technology does not measure up to the standards of the school and/or parents, or the child's school behavior disrupts learning its own learning, or others'.

(2) Symptoms not expected at this age, but not unusual in a younger child.   Some of these are incontinence, fearfulness, short attention span, hyperactivity, daydreaming, and not assuming expected responsibilities.

(3) Social inferiority (in Erikson's sense).   This may be the isolated child or the child who consistently associates only with younger children. A sense of social inferiority may be manifested by overcompensatory behavior (e.g., bullying or braggadocio). If societal expectations are excessive or opportunities for development of competence are too limited, a kind of cultural inferiority may result.

(4) Cultural incongruity.   As noted earlier, some children are placed in the difficult position of reconciling cultures or rejecting one of two cultures. If social systems in the child's environment (e.g., family, school, or peer group) recognize this and support the child by emotional support, counseling, providing opportunity to vent frustration, and playing out resentments against authority in a safe situation, the child may be able to reconcile conflicting demands. Unfortunately, however, children of color often experience a lack of understanding and support by persons in their environments.

2. *Summary.*   The middle years of childhood ("the wonder years") are the time for development of a sense of competence—to master self, social relationships, and the technology of the culture. The human system is relatively open to inputs from, and transactions with, the institutions of

the community beyond the family system while retaining a primary linkage to the family. The growing person emerges from this crisis with a sense of being somewhere on the continuum from industry to inferiority. Erikson's view was that the child's situation in this stage could be stated, "I am what I can learn to make work" (Erikson, 1968:127).

D. Transitional Self: Self-Development of Identity (Adolescenthood and Youth)

In Erikson's formulation, this is *the* transitional growth crisis. It is the time when biological and social imperatives demand that the evolving person organize and develop an identity that goes beyond an accumulation of roles. In our culture, this more or less coincides with that period referred to as adolescence. We prefer to use the term *adolescenthood* to convey that it is more than a transitory hiatus. The adolescent span of life has become a distinct life phase with its own culture, role expectations, and style, reinforced by cultural expectations (including consumerism).

The concept of *identity* has entered into the conventional wisdom, and references are replete to individual identity, group identity, organizational identity, and even national identity. Erikson used the term with precision, and applied it primarily to the individual person. He saw the social-psychological task at this age as one of integration, or more precisely *re*integration, of the various components of the person into a whole. It is a process of ego synthesis that culminates in *ego identity,* meaning an internal consistency and a continuity of meaning to others. This goes beyond the sum of childhood identifications and is not merely a synthesis of social roles. Again the concept is that of *sense* of identity, of which the person is aware. It is a state of being that cannot be viewed by others, or objectively evaluated by them.

> An optimal sense of identity . . . is experienced merely as a sense of psychosocial well being. Its most obvious concomitants are a feeling of being at home in one's body, a 'sense of knowing where one is going' and an inner assuredness of anticipated recognition from those who count. (ibid.:165)

Erikson first labeled the opposite pole *identity diffusion,* later *role confusion,* and in later writings *identity confusion* (Erikson, 1968). The term conveys the antithesis of integration, the dispersion of selves, and the alienation of the self. From a systems viewpoint, one could say that internal and external tensions compel the human system to integrate its components in order to undertake new purposes and responsibilities. If the components of personality are not brought together, the person is fragmented and has no solid sense of self. The person is not capable of putting energy to concerted use—the person is entropic. Schizophrenia, with its disorganization of personality components and particular disparity between thought and feeling, is the extreme form of such fragmentation. Interestingly, the earlier term for schizophrenia was *dementia praecox*, meaning "insanity of the young." Some theorists, Erikson among them, hold that true schizophrenia cannot appear until adolescence, since it is foremost a condition of pathology of identity and identification. A sensitive expression of this condition is:

> I am learning peacefulness, lying by myself quietly
> As the light lies on these white walls, this bed, these hands.
> I am nobody; I have nothing to do with explosions.
> I have given my name and my day-clothes up to the nurses
> And my history to the anesthetist and my body to the surgeons.
> (Plath, 1966:10)

Erikson focused much of his study and writing on the adolescent crisis, including *Identity, Youth and Crisis* (1968), *Childhood and Society* (1963), and "The Problem of Ego Identity" (1959). Two of the characteristics of adolescence he identified, the *moratorium* and *negative identity*, are particularly worthy of emphasis.

Moratorium refers to a socially approved period of delay wherein the person is allowed to, or forced to, postpone assumption of the full responsibilities of adult commitments. The culture relaxes its expectations and is more permissive; the person can try out a variety of identifications, modes of behavior, and roles without a commitment to see them through. The moratorium is both necessary and desirable to allow for integration, regrouping of forces, and the setting of life goals, in a culture that places a high value on individuality. The extension of adolescence into the "twenties" in the United States can be viewed as a socially imposed moratorium that may be unnecessarily long for some. Moratoria may occur at times other than adolescenthood for some persons. Often, they are times when important decisions must be made, or major changes in life goals are considered. If the individually determined moratorium is more prolonged than societal expectations allow, there is reason for concern, for example, Biff in *Death of a Salesman*.

> HAPPY: Well, you really enjoy it on a farm? Are you content out there?
> BIFF: *With rising agitation:* Hap, I've had twenty or thirty different kinds of jobs since I left home before the war, and it always turns out the same. . . . And whenever Spring comes to where I am, I suddenly get the feeling, my God, I'm not gettin' anywhere! . . . I'm thirty-four years old, I ought to be makin' my future. That's when I come running home. And now, I get here, and I don't know what to do with myself. *After a pause:* I've always made a point of not wasting my life, and everytime I come back here I know that all I've done is to waste my life.
> HAPPY: You're a poet, you know that, Biff? You're a—you're an idealist!

BIFF: No, I'm mixed up very bad. Maybe I ought to get married. Maybe I oughta get stuck into something. Maybe that's my trouble. I'm like a boy. I'm not married, I'm not in business, I just—I'm like a boy. (A. Miller, 1955:18–19)

Negative identity occurs because any identity is better than no identity at all. Negative identity is "an identity perversely based on all those identifications and roles which, at critical stages of development, had been presented . . . as most undesirable or dangerous and yet also as most real" (Erikson, 1968:174). Cloward and Ohlin's "opportunity theory" is consistent with this; when denied legitimate opportunity to achieve, youths will adopt illegitimate means. Confirmation of the person's identity comes from within ("this is what I feel like") and from without ("this is what you say I am"). This feedback cycle operates similarly for any identity. Although one's sense of identity may and often does change subsequent to adolescence, this is the crucial time for initial identity formulation, the greatest opportunity for such development, and the time of greatest vulnerability.

   1.   *Adolescenthood.*   There are more definitions of adolescence than there are definers. For a time, adolescence was synonymous with the teen years, but that is no longer an adequate definition. The idea of the "between years" is frequently encountered, but that has an implication of "floating." We will employ the following definition, recognizing that it, too, is open to dispute: "Adolescence is probably in all societies that period which comes after the biological and hormonal changes of puberty have set in but before the individual's incorporation into society as an independent adult" (Ktsanes, 1965:17). *Adolescence, then, begins with biology and ends by social definition: the beginning is organism, the process is organism interacting with culture, and the termination is culturally determined.* The seemingly unique element in adolescenthood in the United States is that adolescence has become a distinct cultural phase of life in the same sense as childhood and adulthood. The only qualification we would make is that adolescent *behavior* may begin before puberty, as adolescent culture is communicated to children in middle childhood (or even younger).

   Rather than reviewing all the elements of this Eriksonian crisis, we will approach it from a particular viewpoint. Freud is widely quoted as believing that the two elements of a successful life were the capacities to love and work. The task of identity formulation can be viewed as the prerequisite for loving and working. We will discuss briefly some of the characteristics of the adolescent and the culture that are important to development of these capacities.

   a.   The peer group.   The associations of the adolescent with peers are extremely necessary experiences. Typically, peer groups take over some of the parental roles of support and value-giving. Peers absorb much of the available social energy of the youth and become a primary reference group. The person can use peers to find self by projecting her/his ego fragments onto others. The person can experience and express feelings of tenderness toward others, beyond the family system, on new planes. Various roles are available to be tried and either accepted or discarded. An attitude of respect for competence develops in the peer group. In the peer society, the adolescent can begin to be a lover and a worker in close interaction with others. This experience occurred within the family system but only in the person's role as a child. Adulthood requires more of the person than continuing to be a loving, working child within its family.

For some youths, the peer group gains overriding importance, totally replacing the family. Such substitution of one kind of childlike dependency for another does not suffice for the creation of a unique identity. Some youths remain largely separated from peer groups and still manage to pull together an identity. Peers are, however, an essential part of adolescents' struggles to find out who they are, what they value, and what they want to become.

b.   Education.   The school continues to be the central social institution that it was during middle childhood. Increasingly, occupational choices are centered in the school experience. As students' choices of occupation have broadened and become minimally determined by their parents' occupations, it has become the school's responsibility to assist in this choice. Curricula are constructed to expose the youth to a range of potential occupations; performance is self-evaluated as well as judged by peers, parents, teachers, and guidance counselors, and the youth is guided in certain directions. A number of factors enter into determining the "real" possibilities for any given youth. Some of these are race, gender, socioeconomic status, and "intelligence" (which is usually defined by the narrow criteria of grades and intelligence tests). In a society where persons are signified by what they do rather than by who they are, one's choice of work role or, more precisely, occupational aspiration becomes central to one's sense of who one is and what one may become (see the discussion of bureaucracy and personality in Chapter 5). While many theorists comment on the absurdity of this institutionalization of identity development, it continues to be, for most youth, the sole societally approved means to acquire a sense of self as a worker and a potential worker.

2.   Adolescenthood and Culture.   The adolescent (a person between puberty and full status in matters of love and work) is an important person in our culture. There are certain clear manifestations of this importance. Economically, the adolescent has the status of a part-time worker and a full-time consumer. The jobs allotted to youth are usually service occupations rather than production and often are substitutes for parental role performance (e.g., babysitting, food preparation and serving, carrying grocery bags, and home maintenance, such as lawn care). This age group is a primary target of advertising and merchandising (and has at least one cable television channel devoted to its musical tastes). Whole industries in fashion and leisure time facilities cater to an adolescent market. Pop culture, fashion, food, and music styles originate in the youth culture and permeate the broader culture through the impetus of the advertising and distribution industries. Bloom's controversial book, *The Closing of the American Mind,* emphasized the pervasive influence of rock music in youth culture, stating, "Nothing is more singular about this generation than its addiction to music" (Bloom, 1987:68). A newspaper columnist provided this bemused parental view of adolescence, identity, and clothing:

> I doubt that my 13-year-old daughter wears anything that she owned last fall. Likewise, she won't wear anything next fall that she's wearing now. Clothes were always important to her, but in her seventh-grade year, they became her identity. (She would prefer her actual identity to remain a secret for the next five years, until she can relocate to a university in another state where all the kids are just like her, whatever that is.) (Shefchik, 1998)

There is a dual ambivalence that exists between adults and adolescents. This manifests itself in the family system, where parents and youths are both torn between wanting the youths to grow up and wanting them to remain children. The ambivalence appears in the community and broader culture as the adult envies the vitality of youth, whereas youth envies the power and control possessed by adults. Adults may covet youthfulness as a denial of death, while increasing evidences of age cause this denial to be more difficult to maintain. Similarly, youth may covet power and control because of the prolonged dependence the culture dictates. This dual ambivalence complicates the forming of a sense of identity because separation into opposing camps may contribute to premature closure of adolescent identity rather than moving on to adult identity. Such identity foreclosure is problematic in a society where choices are many and increasing in scope. The person who made an early commitment to a total, foreclosed identity may later find it necessary to engage in a moratorium in order to experiment with possibilities for change. This may be highly problematic if others (e.g., spouses) are expecting this person to continue with the foreclosed identity.

As Erikson viewed this, adolescenthood requires the culture to make adjustments because the generation coming up has absorbed the past, lives in the present, and must confront the future with new forms of living constructed of knowledge and experience not available to their elders. Mead (1970) pointed out that youth is, in fact, the arbiter of modern cultures. Youths find that construction of both their own life-styles and those of the culture is a bewildering task. Mead helped to explain why youth experiments widely in life-styles. As many writers conclude, each generation has a wide range of characteristics from which the culture can select those best suited to cultural survival. Each generation of youth can be considered a component of its culture system and, as such, a source of energy and tension: the primary means by which the culture accommodates to change. An example is the speed with which our culture (and most other world cultures) has adapted to electronic media. It is pre-adolescents and adolescents who have been the most avid "consumers" and masters of computers, video gaming, digital communication, and computer graphics. Many are now among the "under-30s" or young adults who create computer programs and adapt them to their worksites and occupations. Incidentally, it is no longer true that young males dominate this field; recent research indicates that women and men use the Internet in equal numbers.

As the culture system seeks a steady state, its youth component must interact with, and exchange energy/information with other components: age groups, organizations, institutions, communities, and families. In order for this to happen, the culture will change (accommodate) or seek to maintain the status quo (assimilate). Within this dynamic interaction, each person must seek an identity, and the culture its survival.

Ideology is a special concern of persons in the throes of the identity crisis. The adolescent has a special sensitivity toward, as well as a particular vulnerability about, ideology. As Erikson puts it so clearly, "It is through their ideology that social systems enter into the fiber of the next generation and attempt to absorb into their lifeblood the rejuvenative power of youth" (Erikson, 1968:134). Erikson's psychohistorical studies of Martin Luther and Gandhi demonstrate how persons' resolutions of the ideological aspects of their individual identity crises provided creative innovations that profoundly affected their cultures. Malcolm X, Martin Luther King, and Nelson Mandela are more recent examples of personal identity crises transmuted into the ideology of a culture (Malcolm X, 1966; Garrow, 1986; Branch, 1988; Mandela, 1994).

The special "virtue" that Erikson attached to identity is *fidelity*. The proclivity of youth to invest self in a belief, an idea, or a person with total commitment and faith is well-known: the search for the Holy Grail, the Crusades, the willingness to follow the knight in shining armor, be he Arthur Pendragon or Mao Tse Tung. To experience total and complete volitional commitment (in both work and love) seems a necessary element of an emerging identity.

The characteristic troubles of the adolescent identity crisis are legion. They may be grouped under the following headings:

1. *Psychosis* usually appears in the form of schizophrenia. This is a condition of extreme identity diffusion. The traits may be considered exaggerations of "normal" traits:

a. feelings of dislocation and estrangement;

b. total docility or exaggerated rebelliousness;

c. emotional lability; rapid mood swings;

d. feelings that "everyone is against me";

e. exaggerated idealism that seems to be a denial of reality; and

f. confused body image and sexual identification.

2.   *Neurosis* can also be described as identity confusion, in that there is a conflict between the ideal self and other selves. Neurosis is a conflict between antagonistic ideas, wishes, desires, or impulses that lead to entropy and disrupt psychological functioning. If they are extreme, the alternating excitability and lethargy of adolescents might be examples of this tendency.

3.   *Delinquency* is a socially defined response to inner demands and outer expectations. It may be the result of particular internal conflicts ("acting out" behavior), or it may be an individual or group rejection of cultural values of a larger system. The negative identity previously referred to may be manifested by delinquent behavior. While delinquency might be pathological it may, as said earlier, be better than no identity at all.

In summary, it can be said that the growth crisis of adolescence is the necessity of *self-*development. All subsystems of the adolescent personality—physical, cognitive, and emotional—are in rapid flux, an upheaval of the person's previous steady state. At the same time, the environment demands new linkages and energy exchanges with this new person; and the person seeks them, as well. "To be or not to be" states part of the issue confronting the adolescent. *What* to be or *what not* to be is the second part of the question. The later crises of adulthood are to a large degree dependent upon the outcome of this crisis. A person must be fairly certain and comfortable with self before successfully entering into a sustained, intimate, and constructive relationship with another

E.   *Perpetuation and Sharing of Identity (Adulthood)*

Adulthood has seldom been dealt with in theories of personality development, but perhaps because of the "baby boomer" generation, more attention is being paid (see, e.g., Sheehy, 1976, 1992, 1995; and Levinson, 1978, 1996). Erikson is notable for his attempt to conceptualize the adult period as an integral part of his life cycle formulation. Pertinent here are the sixth crisis, "intimacy vs. isolation," and the seventh, "generativity vs. self-absorption."

The critical task of *intimacy vs. isolation* is to enter in an involved, reciprocal way with others sexually, occupationally, and socially. One's sense of identity is merged with another to form a new primary social system. To put it another way, the person completes the transition from the *family of origin* to the family of procreation (or *family of orientation*). This psychosocial crisis addresses itself to the activities of love and work. If one is unable to merge an intact sense of self with others, the outcome is a sense of isolation and polarization of affect. The concept of alienation (discussed later in this section) is another expression of a sense of isolation. The theme of love, genital and reciprocal, is central to this crisis.

These first two adult crises that Erikson delineates are closely related; the second describes the task of *generativity vs. self-absorption*. This involves the task of active participation in establishing the next generation. Erikson explained why he chose to express the quality of feeling as "generativity" rather than creativity or productivity (Erikson, 1959:97). He saw the term *generativity* as being derived from "genitality" and "genes." This particularly emphasizes responsibility for perpetuation of the species and the culture. The theme of this crisis is *caring*: caring in the sense of nurturance and caring in the sense of concern for others. In his Jefferson Lecture, Erikson further elaborated his notion of the adult virtue of caring (Erikson, 1974). The polar sense of stagnation refers to caring primarily and essentially for one's self, along with pseudointimacy with others and indulgence of one's self. Stagnation can be viewed as the "closed" human system, defending its equilibrium and minimally engaging in transactions of feelings with others.

The adult period requires persons to maintain their own identities while sharing this sense of identity with others. The culture establishes social institutions, particularly procreative and child rearing, through which this task can be accomplished, e.g., schools and colleges, religious organizations, community organizations, and work organizations. At stake is a sense of well-being for the person, continuity for the culture, and survival for the species.

Other approaches to describing personality development in the mature years generally take one of two forms; either an idealized definition of maturity or a listing of the problems to be overcome. Sheehy's popular book *Passages* (1976), supports Erikson's contention that a person can, and does, "go home again," in the sense of redressing the balances of earlier stages. Levinson's view of adult development followed Erikson's ([1982] 1997; Erikson et al., 1986), and is highly compatible with a systems view, in that it stressed integration of "self-in-world." Levinson described a "life structure" in which the major components are the person's relationships with others.

There are both external and internal aspects in the total life structure and in every component within it. The external aspects deal with the persons, social systems, and other realities with which the individual is involved.

The internal aspects are values, desires, conflicts, and skills—those multiple parts of the self that are lived out in one's relationships. (Herbert, 1989:55)

Levinson identified distinct periods in the lives of men (his subsequent book on women is discussed later in this chapter):

A. The *novice phase of early adulthood*, ages 17–33: this phase has four tasks: (a) forming a dream, (b) forming mentor relationships, (c) forming an occupation, and (d) forming a marriage and family. Its subphases are:

(1) *Early adult transition*, ages 17–22, the boundary between adolescence and adulthood. Its primary tasks are to terminate preadulthood, to modify previous relationships, and to make steps into the adult world.

(2) *Entry life structure*, ages 22–28; the major task now is to establish a provisional life structure between self and society, involving occupation, love, peer relationships, values, and life style.

(3) *Age thirty transition*, ages 28–33; building a more satisfactory life structure.

B. *Culminating life structure*, ages 33–40; the two major tasks are to find a place in society and to strive to "make it."

Becoming One's Own Man—"BOOM" (ages 36–40) is a distinctive phase of the . . . period. The major developmental tasks of this phase are to accomplish . . . goals . . . to become a senior member in one's world, to speak more strongly with one's own voice, and to have a greater measure of authority.

C. *Mid-life transition*, ages 40–45, and Entering Middle Adulthood, ages 45–50, include the tasks of

(a) reappraisal of one's life, (b) individuation, and (c) modifying the life structure yet again. Levinson did not study men older than their 40's. (Herbert:57–63; emphasis ours)

Following Erikson and Levinson, it is possible to group the central social expectations for adults under four related headings:

1. Sexuality. Adult sexuality is an important part of intimacy and the sharing of identity. Genitality, in the sense of the capacity for full and mutual consummation of sexual potential, is characteristic only of adulthood. Sexual mutuality forms the foundation of the procreative family system. Sexuality is not confined to sexual activities, but includes generativity and child rearing.

2. Generativity and Child Rearing. The assumption of responsibility for transfer of the culture and nurturance of the young fulfills the destiny of the adult of the species. This requirement is particularly stressful for those without a firm sexual identity or the capacity to merge self-interest with the interest of others. Performance of this task, of course, is not confined to being a biological parent who rears a child. It includes participatory, generative roles that are gratifying to self and others, such as child care (including the health professions), teaching, child welfare and youth work, mentoring, training young employees, volunteering in social services or civic work, and other roles that benefit future generations. These are all generative forms of the adult task of participation in social processes.

3. Participation in Social Processes. To further the purposes of society and culture requires a measure of subordination of personal needs to the others. This is particularly stressful to those who are isolated and retain a primarily self-indulgent orientation. An additional complicating factor here is the perpetual cultural conflict between the values of individualism and social responsibility. One of the most important aspects of social participation is work.

4. Work. As Freud said, a work function is required for adulthood; work that is gratifying to self and to society. In our society (more than most, apparently) work is an organizing theme (the famous "work ethic"), and we construct our life-styles around it. In such societies, work provides an identification, represents social usefulness, and is a primary means of organizing a life. The usual response of the adult to a Who are you? question is more often than not an occupational response. When we meet someone who does not work, it is often difficult to relate to the person until it is determined why she or he does not work: something must be "wrong." Writings on the rehabilitation of schizophrenics have emphasized the necessity of employment if there is to be hope of continued remission. The most recent welfare reform legislation, the Personal Responsibility Act of 1996, espouses work as an answer to the problems of low-income families, and allows for benefits such as day care in order to facilitate employment.

Certain work identifications are still tied to the place of work ("I work in the mines" or "I work at WalMart") but other designations are also used. Now most people express work identification as either "I do" or "I am." Traditionally, the "I am" designation belonged to the classic professions of law, the clergy, and medicine, including nursing. The "I do" description is usually a shorthand job description ("I sell shoes" or "I wire circuit boards"). The press toward professionalization in a wide variety of occupations is an attempt to establish a work identification of the "I am" type, such as "I am a social worker," "I am a teacher," or computer programmer, or stock analyst. There are still symbolic workplace territories such as "She's in the navy," "He's in bonds and securities," "I'm in government," or "She's in politics." The escalation of occupational titles is another indication of the significance of work as a determinant of status and position. The farmer is now in agribusiness; the undertaker is a mortician or funeral counselor; the barber or beautician is now a stylist, and the salesperson is an account executive.

Erich Fromm (1962) presented a clear and concise exposition of the idea that the marketplace orientation of our society determines and maintains work identity. He suggested that one is valued not for what one is but for what one *seems* to be; this is then related to supply and demand. "Image" becomes crucial and the person must project the "right" image to be successful; the resumé becomes the person. Advertisers are concerned with product image, politicians with their public image, and professional associations with their profession's image. One's value as a person, said Fromm, is not self-defined but dependent upon value definitions by others using the criteria of the marketplace. Fromm described how this has led to the cult of adaptability, with emphasis on changeability.

Work identification has permeated our social systems to an extent we seldom recognize. Often, "problem" segments of our society are defined and labeled by work status:

a. The nonworkers. These include youth and the aged. These are not "unemployed persons"; they are clearly identified as *nonworkers*, not responsible to work. School is viewed as a kind of work and "student" serves as a work status (and is accepted on application forms as a proper answer to "Occupation?"). Organizations of, and in support of, the elderly (such as the American Association of Retired Persons) have been successful in redefining their status to allow them to continue to be active workers. For example, Social Security recipients may now continue to work, earning up to a certain amount before it affects their monthly benefit; this amount will steadily increase over the next few years, approaching the nation's average per capita income. This is acceptable not only because elders wish to continue in useful roles, but also because government policy aims to relieve the tax burden that younger workers may have to bear to support the rapidly increasing number of retired workers, particularly the looming population of "baby boomers."

b. Waste persons. As Carse said, "Waste persons are those no longer useful as resources to a society for whatever reason, and have become *apatrides,* or noncitizens. Waste persons must be placed out of view—in ghettos, slums, reservations, camps, retirement villages, mass graves, remote territories . . . all places of desolation, and uninhabitable" (1986:133). The same could be said, of course, regarding convicted criminals, and persons with certain disabling or disfiguring conditions, among others. American Indians were historically viewed as being in this category, as the "vanishing Americans"—a designation that fortunately is not, and never was, accurate. Opponents of abortion make the case that fetuses (or unborn children, dependent upon one's views) are at risk of being included in this category, as well.

c. The unemployed. These seem to be society's greatest concern. "Welfare reform" and "workfare" place primary emphasis upon putting the unemployed to work and rewarding persons who make the effort to seek and sustain work. The ablebodied, unemployed person violates social prescriptions. That person is without a work identification—in fact, the primary social identity may well be "unemployed." In the absence of demonstrated lack of jobs, or other obvious barriers beyond the person's control, such unemployment is often attributed to individual deficiency.

d. *The unemployable.* By changing the ground rules and expectations regarding work, as Goodwill Industries (note the use of "Industries") and sheltered workshops do, it becomes possible to remove some people from this classification. Youth Service programs (both public and private) serve the same function, converting untrained (and therefore unemployable) youth into apprentices preparing for careers. This provides opportunity structures in which "the right to work" can be realized.

The Americans with Disabilities Act (ADA) and similar legislation at the state level have made it possible for "differently abled" persons to find employment. Adaptation of work environments to accommodate workers with special needs and the use of facilitating technology (including computers) have "opened doors" to many who were formerly considered unemployable. A Supreme Court opinion in June 1998 included persons with HIV / AIDS among those covered by the ADA who must be given opportunities for employment.

e. *Alienation.* Lack of employment is a significant source of alienation. Alienation is a phenomenon of adulthood, since it is a condition of one's identity. It is, in some respects, the adult counterpart of maternal deprivation. Alienation means the absence or insufficiency of those vital, intimate connections with one's social environment that call forth and sustain one's identity. "Structural unemployment" itself fosters alienation as it breaks the connection between the person and the work environment, and between the person and the society. In most definitions, alienation also includes the feelings and perceptions that accompany these lacks, including the following:

(1) There may be lowered self-esteem, a gulf between societal expectations and perceived self. The person may also experience *self-estrangement* and *self-alienation,* a gulf between ideal and actual self, as though one were someone (or something) other than oneself.

(2) *Anomie* is a term coined by sociologist Emile Durkheim to convey what, in systems terminology, may be viewed as absent or faulty linkage with larger social systems. This is experienced as "rootlessness," "normlessness," or "meaninglessness." The person does not experience a culture of shared meanings, or a sense of shared norms of behavior. Recent observers have identified a new "underclass" of those excluded from opportunities for achievement, particularly victims of racism and discrimination (Wilson, 1987). A prime characteristic of this underclass is the

abandonment of any expectation of social mobility or approved achieve-ment within the "legitimate" social classes or structures. In such situa-tions, persons may create or join alternative subcultures, e.g., street gangs and criminal organizations, including drug traffickers.

(3) *Alienated* persons may perceive, correctly or not, that their values are not shared or supported by their social environments, and the con-verse, that they do not share society's (or family's) values.

One of the most frequently examined forms of alienation is *work aliena-tion*. Despite many studies that reveal some degree of dissatisfaction with work, research consistently indicates that most workers are largely satis-fied with their jobs. Women probably comprise the largest group of alien-ated workers (Levinson, 1996; see our discussion in Chapter 5). In addition to the reasons already mentioned, women face other alienating circumstances. They frequently are not taken seriously as career-minded workers. "Career women" who are mothers with young children have been described as being on the "mommy track" (Goodman, 1989a; Ehrlich, 1989:98–99), an "alternative" career line in which flexible schedules are a necessity, but in which advancement is slower. Whether this is fair, and whether it promotes or detracts from women's rights at the workplace, is a matter of much debate. Women often are not paid as much as men for performing the same jobs: women earn about 80 percent of men's wages per hour, about 76 percent per week, and 71 percent of annual salaries (U.S. Department of Labor, 1997). They report that they are overworked (particularly in the present climate of "downsizing" among corporations and institutions), their abilities are underutilized, they are less frequently advanced, and are less frequently chosen for specialized training.

(4) Demands on time: The average number of hours worked per week has gradually increased over the past few years, as companies have reduced the work force, in the name of "productivity." Women are espe-cially affected by the combination commuting time, hours worked, do-mestic chores and child care.

"Telecommuting," working by computer and telephone from their own homes, is increasingly common among so-called "knowledge" work-ers, although it is not available to most workers. This practice presumably has the advantages of reducing commuting time, more flexibility in work hours, more likelihood of being able to care for and supervise children at home (with reduced child care costs), and greater feeling of indepen-dence and being trusted (despite some concern about whether employers will be satisfied with the arrangement). Whether this practice truly frees more time (reports indicate that telecommuters may, in fact, put in *more* hours—for example in evenings and on weekends) is not clear. It is also not clear whether the total workload and stress of women telecommuters is reduced or, in fact, increased by not having structured "break times" and opportunities to "shmooze" with fellow workers.

In conclusion, the crises of adulthood are focused in the socially defined expectations for the person to intimately involve herself or himself with others in the creation and maintenance of the social systems that enable the culture and species to survive. An adult who does not do this will be isolated, self-serving, and stagnant. To paraphrase Erikson, the adult may say, "I am what I can love and care for and about."

F. Conservation of Identity (Elderhood)

This concluding stage of the life cycle can be characterized as the crisis of aging. *Conservation* refers to consolidation, protection, and holding on to the ego integrity one has accrued over a lifetime, in the midst of loss and divestment of usual roles and functions. The positive sense of "conservation" is that identity passes from one social context to another and yet remains the same. The self maintains its continuity and consistency from one social system to another.

Erikson's polarity during the waning years of life is *ego integrity vs. disgust and despair.* This is the culmination of the previous seven crises. Integrity refers to "the ego's accrued assurance of its proclivity for order and meaning—an emotional integration faithful to the imagebearers of the past and ready to take, and eventually to renounce, leadership in the present" (Erikson, 1968:139). It is the capacity of persons to accept their life histories, to see the effect they have had upon their world through their relationships, and to accept their mortality. The other pole, the sense of disgust and despair, is characterized by bitterness and refusal to accept death as the finite boundary of the personal life cycle. A positive resolution was expressed by Max Robinson, former ABC television "news anchor," the first African-American to hold such a position. Robinson died of AIDS in December 1988. In his last public appearance, Robinson said to students at Howard University: "Try to keep your integrity, because you're going to find out in life, at the end, that's all you've got."

A definition of "aging" or "age" is difficult to formulate to everyone's satisfaction. In one sense, the aging process begins at birth. Socially, age is defined by function, usually work-related. For example, most professional athletes are "old" by the time they are 35 (the minimum age qualification to become president), while a Supreme Court justice is thought to be still functional at 80. Some industries consider the 40-year-old worker as too old to be hired. Social security currently sets the age of retirement at 65 (soon to become 67). The "old elderly," age 80 and older, are the fastest growing segment of the American population. Birren suggested a utilitarian definition:

> A person is "old" or, better perhaps, "aging" when [the person] is so regarded and treated by contemporaries and by the younger generation and when [the person] has read the culturally recognized individual and social

signs symbolic of membership in the generation of elders. The only matter of individual choice open to the old person has to do with whether [the person] wishes to accept or postpone belief in [the] new identity and act accordingly. (1959:280)

Erikson commented, "it is perfectly obvious that if we live long enough, we all face a renewal of infantile tendencies—a certain childlike quality, if we're lucky, and senile childishness, if we're not. The main point is again a developmental one: only in old age can true wisdom develop in those who are thus 'gifted'" (cited in Evans, 1967:53–54). The tasks of aging in our culture were nicely summarized by Birren:

(1) To live as long as possible, at least until life-satisfaction no longer compensates for its privation, or until the advantages of death seem to outweigh the burden of life.

(2) To get more rest, relief from the necessity of wearisome exertion at humdrum tasks, and protection from too great exposure to physical hazards—opportunities, in other words, to safeguard and preserve the waning energies of a physical existence.

(3) To remain active participants in personal and group affairs in either operational or supervisory roles—any participation, in fact, being preferable to complete idleness and indifference.

(4) To safeguard or even strengthen any prerogatives acquired in long life, i.e., skills, possessions, rights, authorities, prestige, etc.

(5) Finally, to withdraw from life, when necessity requires it, as honorably as possible, without too much suffering, and with maximum prospects for an attractive hereafter. (1959:864–865)

The cultural definition has changed somewhat, however; notice the number of magazines, tours, and educational opportunities (e.g., Elderhostel) for active, financially comfortable elderly). "Disengagement," a once-predominant view of the aging process, seems to be only one option among many.

As earlier stated, aging is characterized by the theme of conservation. It involves relinquishing certain patterned investments of self (Levinson's "life structure") and adoption of other patterns. The nature of one's transactions with other human systems is necessarily modified. The elements of identity involved can be discussed under a few general headings:

1. *Work Role and Occupational Identification.* This probably has a more profound effect upon those with the "I do" work identification than upon those with an "I am" identification. The retired physician continues to be seen as "Doctor," but the retired shoe salesman is no longer a salesman. Willy Loman ("low man") in *Death of a Salesman* is an example of a person faced by a loss of work identity. Relinquishing the work role may be especially difficult because so much validation of one's worth is tied to this

role. Loss of work role often is accompanied by a marked reduction in income and the necessity of readjustment in standard of living. Women face losses (or at least changes) of role earlier when children leave home (the "empty nest") or their partners die; in addition, since about 60 percent of women are employed, they too face employment-related changes.

On the other hand, many of both sexes who retire from their work roles easily make the transition to a more leisurely pace of living. Most women whose husbands take "early retirement," at age sixty-two for example, retire at the same time, though they are typically younger than their husbands. Time is available to pursue other interests; the economic means may or may not be. In view of the large proportion of people who opt for early retirement, it is conceivable that the work identification of "retired" substitutes for an identification as active worker.

2. *Intimate Ties.* As a person's friends, acquaintances, and spouse die or become incapacitated, the elderly person is again faced with separation experiences faced as a child or young adult. Those who were part of one's personality system are gone. One must undergo the painful process of withdrawing (decathecting) attachments to them at a time when it is probably most difficult to establish new linkages to replace the former ones. One may not be able to modify one's own personality structure sufficiently to accommodate new attachments, and the social environment may not "reach out and touch" elders. One's environment tends to narrow, and perhaps the intensity of the remaining attachments is increased. Such attachments may become "overinvested"; for example, a pet or a formerly casual acquaintance may suddenly become all important. If no replacements or investments are accomplished, the person may turn inward, seeking energy internally, or may "bank the fires," attempting less and seeking equilibrium on a lower level of interaction with the environment.

Such withdrawal is not inevitable; some elders "blossom" as they are relieved of responsibilities for family and work. They revive latent interests or hobbies, e.g., travel, writing, volunteering, time with grandchildren, genealogy, or community and political involvement; the American Association of Retired Persons (for whom one is eligible at age fifty) has an extremely active and politically "savvy" membership. Ways are found to economize, or expectations are adjusted. This is truly a "golden age" for many elderly, whose involvement in larger systems increases rather than declines (Erikson et al., 1986).

As noted earlier, the average life span continues to increase modestly (in most of the world) and the health of elders continues to improve. Increased attention to diet and exercise are resulting in an extended period of active, productive retirement for many aged people, and the possibility of a "cure for cancer" (announced in 1998) may have profound effects on this age group. Their continued presence, whether as persons needing care or as additional resources for their adult children and grandchildren, will have significant effects on the social systems to which they are linked.

3. *Sexual Interests.* Although little research has been done on the sexual activity of the aged, findings indicate a gradual decline in sexual activity over the entire adult period; there is no sharp decline at any particular age. As overt sexual activity declines, aged persons may express or receive tenderness or affection in other ways; grandchildren frequently serve as recipients of affection from grandparents. Because our social stereotypes of the elderly indicate that such needs (for affection or specifically sexual) somehow disappear, we are often unrealistic about the behavior of the aged. Unfortunately, society's understanding of this is blocked by our tendency to deny sexuality in elderly persons. For example, some residences for the elderly prohibit physical manifestations of affection, do not allow the closing of doors when one has a visitor of the opposite sex, and in a few reported instances, prohibit holding hands. The available evidence indicates that sexual companionship (with or without sexual activity) is as important to most elderly persons as it is to those of earlier adult years. Recent newspaper articles report the discomfort that adult children often feel when confronted with their parents' sexual activity, in residences for elderly or nursing homes. Perhaps when "baby boomers" inhabit such facilities, stereotypes will change and more realistic perceptions of elders will result.

4. *Physical Abilities.* Physical abilities, particularly sensory and motor abilities, decline with age (although with attention to diet, exercise, and health care, decline may not be great, or rapid; the remarkable "once and future" astronaut John Glenn is a case in point. Physiologically, the number of taste buds declines with age, eyesight and hearing may suffer impairment, and walking may become more difficult. If these limitations occur, they necessarily handicap the aged person in maintaining contact with the accustomed social environment. In the extreme, the person's world may be narrowed to the walls of his or her own home, and to the television set.

The older person's self-concept may be threatened by these losses. An example is the sixty-year-old man who refuses to be beaten at tennis. The person's reaction may be to deny the losses and demand performance characteristic of an earlier age, or the reaction may be depression and unrealistic refusal to do what one is still capable of. It is common among the aged to make reasonable adjustments to less acute faculties—in other words, to make the best of one's abilities: to drive only in daylight, e.g., or to use a telephone in which the volume can be turned louder, or to wear a hearing aid. Such realistic adjustments are part of the person's integrity and maintenance of self.

5. *Intellectual Abilities.* Borrowing from Piaget, it could be concluded that as one's schemes multiply and more adequately account for one's experience, they become progressively less modifiable. Accommodation declines, while assimilation increases. The aged may exclude stimuli from awareness, to limit the energy exchange with those in their environment. The aged person may become less concerned with interpreting and storing new information and more concerned with preserving previous information, sometimes literally in the form of scrapbooks, possessions of a deceased spouse, or a house that was the family dwelling. Either of these intellectual patterns, becoming more closed or remaining open (or becoming *more* open), may be exercised to maintain integrity.

6. *Life Review.* A review of one's life might include the feeling that time is running out, that there are no alternatives possible "at this late date." In *Death of a Salesman,* Willy depends upon his son Biff to reassure him of his own integrity, but Biff has neglected to write to his father:

> BIFF: I was on the move. But you know I thought of you all the time. You know that, don't you pal?
> LINDA: I know, dear, I know. But he likes to have a letter. Just to know that there's still a possibility for better things. (A. Miller, 1955:55)

With our society's cultural emphases on youth, external appearance, and robust health, to the neglect of wisdom, experience, and the ability to cope with travail, the frail elderly may find themselves in a disadvantaged state and their integrity unnoticed and uncelebrated. As human systems, elders must find their steady state, their identity, among the social systems with which they are linked. Erikson said that a person "as a psychosocial creature will face, toward the end of . . . life, a new edition of an identity crisis which we may state in the words, 'I am what survives of me'" (1968:141). What survives are the human systems one has been related to and part of: persons, families, groups, organizations, communities, societies, and cultures. These human systems in turn affect other persons who are being born and who are developing. This is why Erikson calls it a life cycle—not the life of an individual, alone, but the cycle of life itself: the human system. He commented:

> Webster's Dictionary is kind enough to help us complete this outline in circular fashion. Trust (the first of our ego values) is here defined as "the assured reliance on another's integrity," the last of our values. . . . It seems possible to further paraphrase the relation of adult integrity to infantile trust

by saying that healthy children will not fear life if their elders have integrity enough not to fear death. ([1963] 1993:269)

CONCLUSION

In this book, we have examined and speculated upon social systems—human systems. We state in Chapter 7, "Families," that a family is to be construed as patterns of relatedness as they converge in a specific person. We can now say the same about all social systems: systems are patterns of relatedness as they converge in individual persons. Systems do not exist without persons; and persons can exist only because of social systems of which they are, or have been at some time in their life, a part. Understanding of the implications of this, and applying that understanding to one's life and practice, are the highest wisdom to which a systems approach can contribute.

SUGGESTED READINGS

Ainsworth, Mary D. Salter.
   1969   "Object Relations, Dependency and Attachments: A Theoretical Review of the Infant-Mother Relationship," *Child Development*, 40(4):969–1025.
      The definitive review of early attachment; grouped under headings of Psychoanalytic, Social Learning, and Ethological.
Butler, Robert N.
   1975   *Why Survive? Being Old in America*. New York: Harper and Row.
      A landmark work on the plight of the aged in U.S. society. Dr. Butler, a psychiatrist, was the first director of the National Institute on Aging. This book was awarded a Pulitzer prize in 1976.
Case, Robbie.
   1992   *The Mind's Staircase*. Hilldale, NJ: Erlbaum.
      Excellent review of Piaget's theory.
Clark, Don.
   1998   *Loving Someone Gay*. Berkeley, CA: Celestial Arts.
      "A pioneering gay therapist [clinical psychologist and professor] offers courageous and compassionate guidance for gay men and lesbians, their families, their loved ones and their counselors." It is also wise, tolerant, and occasionally indignant and angry. Particularly recommended are pages 295–308, on understanding and counseling gay and lesbian persons.
Duckworth, Eleanor
   1996   *"The Having of Wonderful Ideas" and Other Essays on Teaching and Learning*, second edition. New York: Teachers College Press.
      An excellent exposition of Piaget's ideas, by his collaborator and American translator. Highly recommended.

Erikson, Erik.
  1968 *Identity: Youth and Crisis.* New York: Norton.
  Erikson expanded on the critical task of identity formation; he also discussed the total life cycle. This book has been used as the small-map text for this chapter. For a thorough explanation of his life cycle formulation see *Childhood and Society,* second edition. (New York: Norton, 1963).
Fennell, Graham, Chris Phillipson, and Helen Evers.
  1988 *The Sociology of Old Age.* Milton Keynes: Open University Press.
  An excellent, comprehensive examination of old age as a social phenomenon. "Our priority has been to demonstrate both the 'normality' and diversity of older people and to encourage more wide-ranging perspectives," said the authors.
Freud, Sigmund.
  1949 *An Outline of Psychoanalysis.* New York: Norton.
  Freud's last book, published posthumously, it is a concise explanation of the principles derived from his life's work. It is strongly recommended that the reader be familiar with Freud's expression of his ideas rather than relying on interpretations by latter-day critics. A small book, it can be used in its entirety as a supplement to this systems text.
Group for the Advancement of Psychiatry.
  1989 *How Old is Old Enough?* Report No. 126. New York: Brunner/Mazel.
  This interesting little book attempts to provide psychiatrists with guidelines for assessment of psychological maturation, examining "historical, psychoanalytic, Piagetian, phenomenologic, and biological" evidence. Chapter 2 is a review of Piaget's theory.
Kuhmerker, Lisa.
  1991 *The Kohlberg Legacy for the Helping Professions.* Birmingham, AL: REP Books.
  An excellent, recent critique of Kohlberg's work; a major addition to the literature on moral development.
Laird, Joan, and Robert-Jay Green, eds.
  1996 *Lesbians and Gays in Couples and Families: A Handbook for Therapists.* San Francisco: Jossey-Bass.
  An extraordinary book. It should probably be required reading for every social work student (and for other professions, as well). It has long been needed, and it would be difficult to surpass in its scope, its scholarship, and the depth to which it addresses its subject. In addition, the authors draw upon their own experiences and those of colleagues and friends.
Levinson, Daniel J.
  1978 *The Seasons of a Man's Life.* New York: Knopf.
  1996 *The Seasons of a Woman's Life.* New York: Knopf.
  Levinson's scheme of adult development has been widely adopted. It is highly compatible with systems ideas and the "person-in-situation" view of the helping professions. His original contributions include the periods of "forming a dream," "forming mentor relationships," and "culminating life structure." His later book is the departure point for any discussion of women's adult lives; he examined "homemakers'" and "career women's" evolution from adolescence through midlife transition.

Maier, Henry W.
  1988   *Three Theories of Child Development*, fourth edition. New York: Harper and Row.
      The author, a social worker, compared and contrasted the theories of Erikson, Piaget, and Sears, and looked at them as bases for social work practice. An excellent resource.
Munhall, Patricia, L., ed.
  1994   *In Women's Experience*, volume I. New York: National League for Nursing Press.
  1995   *In Women's Experience*, volume II. New York: National League for Nursing Press.
      These are companion volumes authored by nurses, and published by the National League for Nursing Press. The readings are insightful and approach the experience of women from a unique perspective that adds depth to the study of human behavior. Highly recommended.
Phillips, John L., Jr.
  1969   *The Origins of Intellect: Piaget's Theory*. San Francisco: Freeman.
      Perhaps the best source for anyone wishing to read further about the contributions of Piaget. Especially useful are the Preface, Chapter 1, and Chapter 5.
Schuster, Clara Shaw, and Shirley Smith Ashburn.
  1992   *The Process of Human Development*, third edition. New York: Lippincott.
      Intended for students in nursing and other health professions, social work, and any other profession, this is a comprehensive and invaluable resource. It includes a short section on general systems theory.
Sheehy, Gail.
  1995   *New Passages*. New York: Random House.
      Like her earlier books, this is a popularly written but well-grounded study; in this instance, of "a historical revolution in the adult life cycle. . . . People are taking longer to grow up and much longer to die, thereby shifting all the stages of adulthood—by up to ten years." She identifies a "completely new frontier—Second Adulthood in middle life."
Westkott, Marcia.
  1986   *The Feminist Legacy of Karen Horney*. New Haven, CT: Yale University Press.
      A long-overdue and impressive assessment of the importance of Horney as a major personality theorist. Fundamental to the study of women's development.

LITERARY SOURCES

Ambrose, Stephen E.
  1996   *Undaunted Courage: Meriwether Lewis, Thomas Jefferson, and the Opening of the American West*. New York: Simon and Schuster.
      Superb psychological and intellectual biography of Meriwether Lewis, co-leader of the Lewis and Clark expedition. A tale of high personal and intellectual achievement and its tragic aftermath. An excellent illustration of a life lived in interaction with social systems.

Bergman, Ingmar.

> 1960   *Wild Strawberries*. In *Four Screenplays*. New York: Simon and Schuster.
> An elderly man reminisces about the past as a means of dealing with the present. Sensitively done.

McCullers, Carson.

> 1940   *The Heart Is a Lonely Hunter*. Boston: Houghton Mifflin.
> A man with a severe hearing loss cares for and about others. The movie version is beautifully done.

Miller, Arthur.

> 1949   *Death of a Salesman*. New York: Bantam.
> Miller's classic play of Everyman caught up in a world of change and attempting to live in the past; prophetic regarding the relationship of corporations and their employees.

Thompson, Ernest.

> 1979   *On Golden Pond*. New York: Dodd, Mead.
> Two elders struggling to maintain their integrity. The interaction between them and the youngster well illustrates Erikson's comment at the conclusion of this chapter, i.e., healthy children will not fear life if their elders have integrity enough not to fear death. The movie, with Henry Fonda and Katherine Hepburn, is marvelous.

FILMS AND VIDEOS

An Alzheimer's Story (1985)

> This documentary follows a family whose wife/mother is deteriorating, and their decision about a nursing home.

And the Band Played On (1993)

> This is an abbreviated version of Shilts's book of the same name. It is not a substitute for reading the book, but does capture the frustration of scientists by the politics of both medicine and government. It received Golden Globe awards for best motion picture made for television and for Matthew Modine as best actor.

Bill (1981; made for television)

> Based on the true story of our friend Bill Sackter, a retarded man who spent most of his life in an institution, but blossomed with the help of his friends Bev and Barry Morrow. Barry Marrow wrote the story, which won an Emmy, and the screenplay for the sequel, *Bill On His Own* (1983).

The Color Purple (1985)

> From Alice Walker's poignant novel, this illustrates Erikson's principle that much can be remedied later in life. Celie, an African-American girl, is viewed as unattractive and is mistreated by those about her. She finds support from her sister and from her husband's girl friend, and becomes a strong, self-determining woman who cares for others. Beautifully acted.

First Dance (1984)

> A young man wants to choose his date to the prom; he is gay. What are his rights as a person?

400 Blows (1952)
Francois Truffaut's early film illustrates the process by which a young boy is rejected by family and others, and survives by adopting deviant behavior. A fine film.

Freud (1962)
This is a credible attempt to present the main tenets of Freud's thought and his life, primarily through his work with one female patient. The television series "Freud" is even better.

Just Because of Who We Are (1986)
Physical and psychological harassment suffered by lesbians, and violence against them, is shown in this documentary. Personal stories of rejection, arrest, and attempts at "cures" are related.

Longtime Companion (1990)
"Perhaps the first film to put a face on the AIDS epidemic" (Internet Movie Database Ltd., 1998) It follows a group of friends from the beginning of the outbreak to its devastation of their lives. The title refers to the *New York Times'* refusal to acknowledge gay partnerships; instead survivors were called "longtime companions." Bruce Davison won an Academy Award for best supporting actor.

Philadelphia (1993)
Tom Hanks received an Oscar for this moving portrayal of a gay lawyer dying of AIDS who sues over dismissal from his firm. One of the first films in which a gay person is the main character, presented sympathetically. Bruce Springsteen's "Streets of Philadelphia" also won a best song award.

Serving in Silence: The Margarethe Cammermeyer Story (1995)
Colonel Cammermeyer, a twenty-year army veteran officer defied the "don't ask, don't tell" policy. She was supported by her children, father, her partner, and the Lambda organization. Glenn Close won an Emmy for Outstanding Lead Actress. Made for television.

The Sum of Us (1994)
An Australian film about a gay son and his straight father who love each other. Each is seeking the "right" partner, respectively. Not a "message" film; "very natural, entertaining story-telling" (Internet Movie Database Ltd., 1998).

The Three Faces of Eve (1957)
The real patient in this case has identified herself in recent years, and has told her own story. Joanne Woodward is credible as a tormented woman with multiple personalities who finds a self with the help of a psychiatrist.

To Live Until You Die: The Work of Elizabeth Kubler-Ross (1983)
This video shows Dr. Ross working with dying patients, and illustrates the five stages of reaction to dying which she identified.

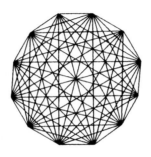

Epilogue

> What I propose . . . is very simple; it is noth-
> ing more than to think what we are doing.
> —Hannah Arendt, *The Human Condition*

This epilogue addresses the ideological, intellectual, and ethical foundations undergirding the social systems approach and its application to understanding human behavior. Does it make a difference what we perceive and believe? Emphatically, *yes!*

Within each of the domains in which "helping professions" operate, there exists divergence of opinion regarding the most effective means to accomplish change. For example, which will be more effective: basic research into the physiology of disease processes or greater concentration on environmental conditions that affect public health? Which will improve patient care more: intensified training of the nurse practitioner or restructuring the organizations that deliver health care services? In the field of human services, should there be more attention to clinical training of social workers or to training community organizers and policy analysts?

Practitioners, or students, often choose modes of intervention on the basis of beliefs and values that have not been articulated, examined, analyzed, and evaluated. The helping professions and professional disciplines that are oriented toward practical application of theory are often accused of intellectual shallowness and lack of philosophical clarity. Practitioners are criticized for failure to be explicit about their assumptions and suppositions, their definition of their competencies, the nature of their helping processes, and the goals of their activities. One critic charged: "I would argue that tacit (and therefore unquestioned) false assumptions have led to at least as many grievous mistakes as explicitly affirmed wrong conclusions" (Andreski, 1973:6). There is, beyond a doubt, some truth to these charges. We in the helping professions share idealism, impatience, and dissatisfaction with the world as it is. We seek pragmatic approaches to action. Frequently, our desire for change outdistances our willingness to examine thoughtfully the philosophical and intellectual structures that are the foundations of our practice. In this epilogue, we comment briefly on these intellectual and ethical foundations.

I. HOLONISTIC THOUGHT

A. Part-Whole Relatedness

In the first two chapters, particularly, and in subsequent chapters we introduced concepts of "partness" and "wholeness"; of oppositeness, duality, and polarities. Whether we are examining the idea of *holon* or seeking the locus of change in the various levels of social systems, we are dealing with the topic of part-whole relatedness; how one is related to the other. This is *systems thinking*, which provides a means to recognize and to understand the inevitable, simultaneous unity and separateness of part and whole. Ronald Jones stated the problem:

> From approximately 3,000 B.C. in the East when Emperor Fu His is believed to have discovered the idea of Yin and Yang as they are embodied in T'ai Chi, and since about 400 B.C. in the West when Heraclitus and Plato struggled with the problem of opposites, scholars have tried to resolve the mystery of how many parts come to be a unified whole. This adds up to a 5,000 year problem. Throughout the history of ideas the problem of One and the Many, of part-whole relations, of order and structure has appeared over and over again. Names we are all familiar with identify this as the *pons asinorum*. Nicholas of Cusa (fifteenth century), Giambattista Vico (seventeenth century), and more recently Cassirer, Whitehead, von Bertalanffy, Koestler, Sorokin, and Polanyi have made this problem *the* problem. The problem of the integration of differentiated parts, of harmony in diversity, is not merely a problem for idle, remote, and academic speculation.
>
> To make certain that this connection is clearly before us, let me elaborate a bit. It seems to me that the *sine qua non* of man's [*sic*] knowledge, happiness and existence is to be found in the idea of the reconciliation of differences. It matters little whether we talk about mental health and personality structure of whether we talk in the context of society. It matters little what size of the society is. It makes little difference whether the society is a marriage, a small group, a large industrial organization, a community, a nation or many nations, the basic issue is that of the reconciliation of the individual with the group, the organization, the integration of the parts into a unified whole. These issues are all matters of totality, wholeness, completeness, unity, order, structure. (Whyte, Wilson, and Wilson, 1960:284)

But this is not a "problem" in the sense of solving, curing, or otherwise having done with it. It is rather a perplexing mystery of human existence. Systemic thinking is a means toward perceiving the issue of the one and the many as a foundation for systems' survival and well-being. In fact, the One cannot exist without the Many, and the Many cannot exist without the One.

> Alfred North Whitehead described existence as part/whole activity. By that I mean that every actual thing is something by reason of its activity; whereby its nature consists in its relevance to other things, and its individuality consists in its synthesis of other things so far as they are relevant to it. (Curtis and Greenslet, 1962:61)

B.   Qualities and Polarities

The question of differences and opposites has always puzzled humankind. Aristotle dealt with it by holding that an entity, quality, or phenomenon must be *one thing or another*. A contemporary statement of that belief is "If you aren't part of the solution, then you are part of the problem." As the blues song puts it, "Is you is, or is you ain't, my baby?"

Earlier Greek philosophers Anaximander and Heraclitus postulated that differences must be merged or balanced into a state of wholeness. Hippocrates drew from the thought of Anaximander in developing the doctrine of "coction." According to the Hippocratic formulation, in the course of each disease there occurs a "crisis" in which either *coction* occurs or the patient dies. Coction is the action that integrates the opposing "humors" so that there results a perfect fusion of them all.

According to Hippocrates, "a disease was supposed to result when the equilibrium of the humours, from 'some exciting cause' or other was disturbed, and then nature, that is the constitution of the individual, made every effort through coction to restore the necessary balance" (Jones, 1923:lii). "Balance" is equivalent to steady state.

In Plato's *Phaedo*, Socrates insisted that the Hippocratic method is right, and then discourses on the nature of opposites:

> "Then don't consider it as regards men only," he said; "if you wish to understand more easily, think of all animals and vegetables, and, in a word, everything that has birth, let us see if everything comes into being like that, always opposite and from nowhere else; whenever there happens to be a pair of opposites, such as beautiful and ugly, just and unjust, and thousands of others like these. So let us enquire whether everything that has an opposite must come from its opposite and from nowhere else. For example, when anything becomes bigger, it must, I suppose, become bigger from being smaller before."
> "Yes."

"And if a thing becomes smaller, it was bigger before and became smaller after that?"

"True," he said.

"And again, weaker from stronger, and slower from quicker?"

"Certainly."

"Very well, if a thing becomes worse, is it from being better, and more just from more unjust?"

"Of course."

"Have we established that sufficiently, then, that everything comes into being in this way, opposite from opposite?"

"Certainly."

"Again, is there not the same sort of thing in them all, between the two opposites to becomings, from the first to the second, and back from the second to the first; between greater and lesser increase and diminution, and we call one increasing and the other diminishing?"

"Yes," he said.

"And being separated and mingled, growing cold and growing hot, and so with all; even if we have sometimes no names for them, yet in fact at least it must be the same everywhere, that they come into being from each other, and that there is becoming from one to the other?"

"Certainly," said he. (Warmington and Rouse, 1956:475–476)

Samuel Butler expressed a similar conception of polarities in *The Way of All Flesh*:

People divide off vice and virtue as though they were two things, neither of which had with it anything of the other. This is not so. There is no useful virtue which has not some alloy of vice, and hardly any vice, if any, which carries not with it a little dash of virtue; virtue and vice are like life and death, or mind and matter—things which cannot exist without being qualified by their opposite. (Butler, 1942:80)

The One and the Many is just such a set of unified opposites and partakes in the nature of opposites. Each system, as the observer recognizes it and separates it from its environment, is simultaneously part/whole or One/Many and contains a duality within itself; it can also be viewed as one pole of a larger duality. Again, it should be stressed that these are *ways of thinking*, not descriptions or discoveries of "reality."

It follows, then, that controversies over whether it is better to work toward changing individuals or to work toward changing society are of little practical consequence unless the inseparability is fully taken into account. It becomes apparent that both (One and Many) are inextricably responsible for change. Systems thinking provides a means to observe, understand, and intervene into these interactive processes.

II. IMPLIED VALUES AND ETHICAL POSITIONS

Most of the recurring questions about our social systems approach relate to values and ethics. Are there implicit values that should be explicated? Can a perspectivistic model be value free? Does a social systems approach remain simply descriptive, and thus mitigate against change? Does it favor maintenance of status quo?

In our judgment, there are certain value stances implicit in a social systems perspective. Holding no brief for the specific labels, we will discuss five aspects under the following rubrics: (A) interdependence, (B) interaction, (C) conservation and conflict, (D) change, (E) egalitarianism.

A. *Interdependence*

The systems view presented in this book begins with the postulate that each human or social entity exists and thrives as both whole and part. It cannot continue existence in isolation and therefore must participate in interdependent relatedness with other entities.

A dramatic example can be drawn from medieval times. The walled castle-keep, surrounded by a moat with a bridge that could be drawn closed and sealed, was designed to protect a community from attack. It often proved to be unassailable with the weapons available to the attackers. However, the adversary could simply make sure that the boundary was not crossed and that the castle remained isolated, to draw the occupants out, for in time the only alternative was death by starvation. The modern-day naval blockade follows the same strategy. A system, then, cannot be completely autonomous indefinitely. Neither can it exist without some measure of autonomy. Without some distinguishable quality of separateness it could not be defined or identified within its environment. To deny the quality of autonomy and separateness is to deny human and social existence. Interdependent relatedness is a melding of dependence and independence (autonomy) and is both desirable and necessary to the well-being of social systems.

B. *Interaction*

Similarly, interaction is essential and therefore desirable to systems' well-being. Energy exchange and feedback (as a regulatory mechanism) require and depend upon interaction. Furthermore, we assume that mutuality is a necessary aspect of interaction; systems interactions are reciprocal and cyclical. Mutuality of interaction is valued: systems affecting, and being affected by, other systems of the same magnitude (horizontal relations) and differing magnitudes (vertical relations). Interdependence and interaction are closely related, but not identical.

To illustrate: The Old Order Amish continue to employ the social sanction of "shunning" members who have seriously violated expectation of behavior. The practice of shunning allows the person to remain in the community system but prohibits others from mutual interaction with the person being shunned. Within this custom, the quality of interdependence remains largely unchanged, whereas the quality of mutual interaction is greatly diminished. One of the most severe punishments that can be inflicted on a human being is solitary confinement. This more extreme form of shunning prohibits energy exchange and feedback.

C. Conservation and Conflict

Conservation of system integrity is necessary and desirable to system vitality and well-being. Conservation is defined as "the act of preserving guarding or protecting; preservation from loss, decay, injury or violation" (*Webster's New Twentieth Century Dictionary of the English Language*, 1980:389).

Paradoxically, conservation and conflict stem from the same systemic source: a system seeks to protect its integrity in ways that might interfere with, or prevent the protection of, another system's integrity. The achievement of synergy, or constructive interchange, occurs only with effort and expenditure of energy. Entropy occurs without effort; conflict requires effort. In those situations where conflict can be avoided, it can be averted only with effort. Conflict, then, is not merely accidental and unfortunate: it is an inherent, legitimate, and frequently unavoidable event that is a direct result of system(s) striving for integrity (i.e., wholeness). As Stafford Beer (1981) put it, "Resistance is only people continuing to be who they are."

D. Change

Change, too, is necessary and desirable for systems' vitality. Without change, systems tend to "feed" on themselves or their environment, depleting the internal or external resources; to shrink, and eventually cease to exist, i.e., become entropic. Our view of systems presupposes an interactive balance between change and conservation, the mixture varying according to circumstances. In some instances, conservation requires change, especially for purposes of preservation from decay, injury, or violation. Change is the means for the genesis of "new life" for systems purposes, while conservation maintains or augments the "life stream" of the system.

E. Egalitarianism

Our social systems view is permeated by values of equality and equity. Interdependence and mutuality of interaction dictate that systems of varying magnitudes be perceived as being equally necessary to systemic functioning. Within a systems approach, the centrality of the concept of hierarchy strikes some as inimical to egalitarianism. However, hierarchy is a structural aspect of systems organization (and all life, human or otherwise) that, in itself, implies no value or power differential. It is the *abuse* of hierarchy in social systems that is objectionable: subjection of persons on the basis of artificial (or irrelevant) criteria that are designed to favor some dominant group, or extension of hierarchical power to areas of persons' lives where it is not appropriate or legitimate. Such hierarchies are based on power (used illegitimately), not on competence or priorities that are related to task performance. While some versions of social systems theory (Parsons, e.g.) may fairly be judged to maintain the status quo, we believe that ours does not; in our view, systems may undergo "phase transformations" to become much different social structures, if components and/or environments exert sufficient influence. Further, we believe that the social systems approach can be a tool for constructive change; in our view, it is grounds for optimism.

Egalitarianism does not imply maintenance of a status quo or an absence of conflict. Conflict is inherent within and between systems; and the fact that each system strives to maintain its integrity inevitably leads to conflict. Thus, egalitarianism does not denote absolute equality but rather a recognition that each system possesses its own "will to live," its place in the sun, and thus has as much right as any other system, subsystem, or suprasystem, to survive. It is the carrying out of this survival that requires a system to resolve values/ethics questions of interdependence, interaction, conservation, conflict, and change. It could be interpreted as tragedy, in the Greek sense of an unavoidable dilemma: in order to preserve itself, any system must engage others and risk "losing it*self*," that is, must risk its steady state. This conundrum applies to all systems. In order to thrive, each must change to some degree. This is the ultimate egalitarianism of the social systems approach.

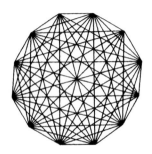

Bibliography

Acuña, Rodolpho. 1972. *Occupied America: The Chicano Struggle toward Liberation*. San Francisco: Canfield.

Adams, Margaret. 1971. "The Compassion Trap—Women Only." *Psychology Today*, November.

Adams, Richard. 1988. *The Eighth Day: Social Evolution as the Self-Organization of Energy*. Austin: University of Texas Press.

Adams, Scott. 1996. *The Dilbert Principle*. New York: HarperCollins.

Ahrons, Constance R. 1987. "The Binuclear Family: Two Households, One Family." Paper presented at the Sixth Annual Conference of the Stepfamily Association of America, Lincoln, NE.

Ahrons, Constance R., and Roy H. Rodgers. 1987. *Divorced Families*. New York: Norton.

———. 1997. "The Remarriage Transition." In Arlene S. Skolnick and Jerome H. Skolnick, eds. *Family in Transition*, ninth edition. New York: Longman.

Ainsworth, Mary D. Salter. 1969. "Object Relations, Dependency and Attachment: A Theoretical Review of the Infant-Mother Relationship." *Child Development* 40(4).

Anderson, Ralph E. 1981. Book reviews of Jeremy Rifkin, *Entropy*. In *Social Development Issues* 5:1.

Anderson, Walter Truett. 1995. "Moralizing Won't Bring Back Community." *Minneapolis Star-Tribune*, March 3.

Andreski, Stanislav. 1973. *The Prospect of a Revolution in the U.S.A.* New York: Harper Colophon.

Ardrey, Robert. [1966] 1971. *The Territorial Imperative*. New York: Atheneum.

Arendt, Hannah. 1962. *The Origins of Totalitarianism*. Cleveland: World Publishing Company.

Argyris, Chris. 1994. *On Organizational Learning*. Cambridge, MA: Blackwell.

Armour, Stephanie. 1998. "Many Turn to Start-Ups for Freedom." *USA Today*, June 8.

Auger, Jeanine Roose. 1976. *Behavioral Systems and Nursing.* Englewood Cliffs, NJ: Prentice-Hall.

Bailey, Kenneth. 1994. *Sociology and the New Systems Theory.* Albany: State University of New York Press.

Bales, Robert F. 1950. *Interaction Process Analysis.* Cambridge: Addison-Wesley.

Balk, David E. 1995. *Adolescent Development.* Pacific Grove, CA: Brooks / Cole.

Barnard, Chester I. 1938. *The Functions of the Executive.* Cambridge, MA: Harvard University Press.

Barnes, John. 1954. "Class and Committees in a Norwegian Island Parish." *Human Relations* 7(February).

Bawer, Bruce. 1996. "A Tale of Two Cities." *Advocate,* September 17.

Beer, Stafford. 1981. "Death Is Equifinal." Eighth Annual Ludwig Von Bertalanffy Memorial Lecture. *Behavioral Science* 26.

Bellah, Robert N., Richard Madsen, William M. Sullivan, Ann Swidler, and Steven M. Tipton. 1985. *Habits of the Heart.* Berkeley, CA: University of California Press.

Bengtson, Vern, Carolyn Rosenthal, and Linda Burton. 1995. "Families and Aging: Diversity and Heterogeneity." In Mark Robert Rank and Edward L. Kain, eds. *Diversity and Change in Families.* Englewood Cliffs, NJ: Prentice-Hall.

Benkov, Laura. 1997. "Reinventing the Family." In Arlene S. Skolnick and Jerome H. Skolnick, eds. *Family in Transition,* ninth edition. New York: Longman.

Berger, Brigitte, and Peter Berger. 1983. *The War over the Family: Capturing the Middle Ground.* Garden City, NY: Doubleday.

Bernard, Jessie. 1997. "The Good Provider Role: Its Rise and Fall." In Arlene S. Skolnick and Jerome H. Skolnick, eds. *Family in Transition,* ninth edition. New York: Longman.

Bertalanffy, Ludwig Von. 1967. *Robots: Men and Minds.* New York: Braziller.

Billingsley, Andrew. 1968. *Black Families in White America.* Englewood Cliffs, NJ: Spectrum.

———. 1988. *Black Families in White America.* New York: Simon and Schuster.

Birren, James E. 1959. *Handbook of Aging and the Individual.* Chicago: University of Chicago Press.

Blau, Peter. 1956. *Bureaucracy in Modern Society.* New York: Random House.

Bloom, Allan. 1987. *The Closing of the American Mind.* New York: Simon and Schuster.

Boehm, Werner. 1965. "Relationship of Social Work to Other Professions." In *Encyclopedia of Social Work.* New York. National Association of Social Workers.

Boguslaw, Robert. 1965. *The New Utopians.* Englewood Cliffs, NJ: Prentice-Hall.

Booth, Alan, and Ann C. Crouter, eds. 1998. *Men in Families.* Mahwah, NJ: Erlbaum.

Bornstein, Marc H., and Richard M. Lerner. 1987. "The Development of Human Behaviour." *Encyclopaedia Britannica,* fifteenth edition, volume 14:708–723.

Boss, Pauline. 1987. "Family Stress." In M. B. Sussman and S. K. Steinman, eds. *Handbook of Marriage and Family.* New York: Plenum.

Boulding, Elise. 1972. "The Family as an Agent of Change." *Futurist* 6(5).

Bowlby, John. 1962. *Deprivation of Maternal Care.* Geneva: World Health Organization.

Boyd, Robert, and Peter J. Richerson. 1985. *Culture and The Evolutionary Process.* Chicago: University of Chicago Press.

Branch, Taylor. 1988. *Parting The Waters: America In The King Years 1954–63.* New York: Simon and Schuster.

Brill, Charles. 1974. *Indian and Free.* Minneapolis: University of Minnesota Press.

Brodey, Warren M. 1977. *Family Dance: Building Positive Relationships through Family Therapy.* Garden City, NY: Anchor.

Brome, Vincent. 1987. "Freud." *Encyclopaedia Britannica,* fifteenth edition, volume 19:582–587.

Brown, Roger. 1965. "How Shall a Thing Be Called?" In Paul Musser, ed. *Readings in Child Development and Personality.* New York: Harper and Row.

Bruner, Jerome. 1968. *Toward a Theory of Instruction.* New York: Norton.

Buber, Martin. [1937] 1947. *I and Thou.* Edinburgh: Clark. [Originally in German, 1923.]

———. 1965. *The Knowledge of Man.* New York: HarperCollins.

Buchwald, Emilie, Pamela R. Fletcher, and Martha Roth, eds. 1993. *Transforming A Rape Culture.* Minneapolis: Milkweed.

Bull, Chris. 1994. "Suicidal Tendencies." *Advocate,* April 5.

Burr, Wesley R. 1995. "Using Theories in Family Science." In Randal D. Day, Kathleen R. Gilbert, Barbara H. Settles, and Wesley R. Burr, eds. *Research and Theory in Family Science.* Pacific Grove, CA: Brooks/Cole.

Burton, Linda M. 1996. "The Timing of Childbearing, Family Structure, and the Role Responsibilities of Aging Black Women." In E. Mavis Hetherington and Elaine Blechman, eds. *Stress, Coping and Resiliency in Children and Families.* Mahwah, NJ: Erlbaum.

Business Week. 1998. Quoted in Teresa McUsic, "Biography Shows GE's Welch Is Admired and Hated." *Minneapolis Star-Tribune,* June 12.

Butler, Robert N. 1975. *Why Survive? Being Old in America.* New York: Harper and Row.

Butler, Samuel. 1942. *The Way of All Flesh.* New York: Walter J. Black.

Butler, Sandra, and Claire Wintram. 1991. *Feminist Groupwork.* London: Sage.

Bütz, Michael R. 1997. *Chaos and Complexity: Implications for Psychological Theory and Practice.* Washington, DC: Taylor & Francis.

Cairns, Robert B., Glen H. Elder, Jr., and E. Jane Costello. 1996. *Developmental Science.* Cambridge: Cambridge University Press.

Campbell, D. T. 1958. "Common Fate, Similarity and Other Indices of the Status of Aggregates of Persons as Social Entities." *Behavioral Science* 3.

Caplow, Theodore, Howard M. Bahr, Bruce A. Chadwick, Reuben Hill, and Margaret Holmes Williamson. 1982. *Middletown Families: Fifty Years of Change and Continuity.* Minneapolis: University of Minnesota Press.

Capra, Fritjof. 1996. *The Web of Life.* New York: Anchor.

Carse, James P. 1986. *Finite and Infinite Games.* New York: Free Press.

Cartwright, Darwin and Alvin Zander. 1960. *Group Dynamics.* Evanston, IL.: Row, Peterson.

Case, Robbie. 1992. *The Mind's Staircase.* Hillsdale, NJ: Erlbaum.

Caudill, Harry M. 1963. *Night Comes to the Cumberlands.* Boston: Little, Brown.

Chodorow, Nancy. 1978. *The Reproduction of Mothering: Psychoanalysis and the Sociology of Gender.* Berkeley, CA: University of California Press.

Christaller, Walter. 1966. *Central Places in Southern Germany.* Englewood Cliffs, NJ: Prentice-Hall.

Clark, Don. 1997. *Loving Someone Gay.* Berkeley, CA: Celestial Arts.

Cohen, Bernice. 1988. *Global Perspectives: The Total Culture System in the Modern World.* London: Codek.

Coleman, Joseph. 1998. "Some Say Corporate Transfers Tear Apart Japanese Families." *St. Paul Pioneer Press,* June 9.

Coplon, Jeff. 1988. "Skinhead Nation." *Rolling Stone* 540.

Corey, Gerald, Marianne Schneider Corey, Patrick J. Callanan, and J. Michael Russell. 1982. *Group Techniques.* Monterey, CA: Brooks/Cole.

Corsini, Raymond J., and Danny Wedding. 1989. *Current Psychotherapies,* fourth edition. Itasca, IL: Peacock.

Coser, Lewis. 1964. *The Functions of Social Conflict.* New York: Free Press.

———. 1974. *Greedy Institutions: Patterns of Undivided Commitment.* New York: Free Press.

Cox, Fred M., et al. 1987. *Strategies of Community Organization: Macro Practice.* Itasca, IL: Peacock.

Coyle, Grace. 1948. *Group Work with American Youth.* New York: Harper and Row.

Curtis, Charles P., Jr., and Ferris Greenslet. 1962. The *Practical Cogitator.* Boston: Houghton Mifflin.

Dahl, Robert A. 1957. "The Concept of Power." *Behavioral Science* 2.

Davis, Phillip W. 1997. "The Changing Meanings of Spanking." In Arlene S. Skolnick and Jerome H. Skolnick, eds. *Family in Transition,* ninth edition. New York: Longman.

Day, Randal D. 1995. "Family Systems Theory." In Randal D. Day, Kathleen R. Gilbert, Barbara H. Settles, and Wesley R. Burr, eds. *Research and Theory in Family Science.* Pacific Grove, CA: Brooks/Cole.

Day, Randal D., Kathleen R. Gilbert, Barbara H. Settles, and Wesley R. Burr, eds. 1995. *Research and Theory in Family Science.* Pacific Grove, CA: Brooks/Cole.

De Kerckhove, Derrick. 1995. *The Skin of Culture: Investigating the New Electronic Reality.* Toronto: Somerville House.

Domhoff, G., and Thomas R. Dye. 1987. *Power Elites and Organizations.* Newbury Park, CA: Sage.

Donigian, Jeremiah, and Richard Malnati. 1997. *Systematic Group Therapy: A Triadic Model.* Pacific Grove, CA: Brooks/Cole.

Dowd, Nancy E. 1997. *In Defense of Single-Parent Families.* New York: New York University Press.

Drucker, Jane. 1998. *Families of Value: Gay and Lesbian Parents and Their Children Speak Out.* New York: Insight.

Drucker, Peter. 1982. *The Changing World of the Executive.* New York: Truman Talley.

Duckworth, Eleanor. 1996. *"The Having of Wonderful Ideas" and Other Essays on Teaching and Learning,* second edition. New York: Teachers College Press.

Dunn, Edgar. 1980. *The Development of the U.S. Urban System,* volume 1. Baltimore: Johns Hopkins University Press.

Durkheim, Emile. 1968. "Division of Labor and Interdependence." In Robert Dubin, ed. *Human Relations in Administration,* third edition. Englewood Cliffs, NJ: Prentice-Hall.

Durkin, James E. 1981. *Living Groups: Group Psychotherapy and General System Theory.* New York: Brunner/Mazel.

Ehrlich, Elizabeth. 1989. "Is the Mommy Track a Blessing—or a Betrayal?" *Business Week*, May 15.

Elkind, David. 1968. "Giant in the Nursery—Jean Piaget." *New York Times Magazine*, May 26.

Elliot, Faith Robertson. 1986. *The Family: Change or Continuity.* London: Macmillan.

El Nasser, Haya. 1998. "Ruling Puts Workplace Behavior under a Harsher Spotlight." *USA Today*, March 5.

Engels, Friedrich. [1884] 1902. *The Origin of The Family, Private Property and the State.* Chicago: C. H. Kerr.

Erikson, Erik H. 1950. In M. S. E. Senn, ed. *Symposium on the Healthy Personality.* New York: Josiah Macy, Jr. Foundation.

———. 1958. *Young Man Luther.* New York: Norton.

———. 1959. "The Problem of Ego Identity." In *Psychological Issues*, edited by George S. Klein. New York: International Universities Press.

———. 1963. *Childhood and Society.* First edition, 1950; 35th anniversary edition, 1985; latest edition, 1993. New York: Norton.

———. 1964. *Insight and Responsibility.* New York: Norton.

———. 1968. *Identity, Youth and Crisis.* New York: Norton.

———. 1969. *Gandhi's Truth.* New York: Norton.

———. 1974. *Dimensions of a New Identity.* New York: Norton.

———. 1975. *Life History and the Historical Moment.* New York: Norton.

———. [1951] 1985. *Childhood and Society*, 35th anniversary edition. New York: Norton.

———. 1987. *A Way of Looking at Things: Selected Papers from 1930 to 1980.* New York: Norton

———. [1980] 1994. *Identity and the Life Cycle.* New York: Norton.

———. [1982] 1997. *The Life Cycle Completed: A Review.* New York: Norton.

Erikson, Erik H., Joan Erikson, and Helen Q. Kivnick. 1986. *Vital Involvement in Old Age.* New York: Norton.

Etzioni, Amitai. 1964. *Modern Organizations.* Englewood Cliffs, NJ: Prentice-Hall.

Evans, Richard. 1967. *Dialogue with Erik Erikson.* New York: Harper and Row.

Farb, Peter. [1968] 1978. *Man's Rise to His Civilization as Shown by the Indians of North America from Primeval Times to the Coming of the Industrial State.* New York: Dutton.

Fellin, Philip. 1995. *The Community and the Social Worker.* Itasca, IL: Peacock.

Fennell, Graham, Chris Phillipson, and Helen Evers. 1988. *Sociology of Old Age.* Milton Keynes, England: Open University Press.

Ferguson, Kathy E. 1984. *The Feminist Case against Bureaucracy.* Philadelphia: Temple University Press.

Ford, Donald H., and Richard M. Lerner. 1992. *Developmental Systems Theory.* Newbury Park, CA: Sage.

Fowler, Robert Booth. 1991. *The Dance with Community.* Lawrence: University Press of Kansas.

Freire, Paolo. 1983. *Education for Critical Consciousness.* New York: Continuum.

French, Robert Mills. 1969. *The Community.* Itasca, IL: Peacock.

Freud, Sigmund. 1949. *An Outline of Psychoanalysis.* Translated by James Strachey. New York: Norton.

Friedenberg, Edgar Z. 1962. *The Vanishing Adolescent.* New York: Dell.

Fromm, Erich. 1942. *The Fear of Freedom.* London: Routledge and Kegan Paul.

———. 1955. *The Sane Society.* New York: Rinehart.

———. 1962. "Personality and the Market Place." In Sigmund Nosow and William H. Form, eds. *Man, Work, and Society,* New York: Basic Books.

Garrow, David J. 1986. *Martin Luther King, Jr., and the Southern Christian Leadership Conference.* New York: Morrow.

Gemmill, Gary, and George Kraus. 1988. "Dynamics of Covert Role Analysis: Small Groups." *Small Group Behavior* 19.

Geyer, Felix and Johannes Van Der Zouwen, eds. 1986. *Sociocybernetic Paradoxes.* Beverly Hills, CA.: Sage.

Gilligan, Carol. 1982. *In a Different Voice: Psychological Theory and Women's Development.* Cambridge, MA: Harvard University Press.

Giner, Salvador. 1976. *Mass Society.* London: Martin Robertson.

Glassman, Urania, and Len Kates. 1990. *Group Work: A Humanistic Approach.* Newbury Park, CA: Sage.

Gleick, James. 1987. *Chaos: Making a New Science.* New York: Viking Penguin.

Glennon, Lynda M. 1979. *Women and Dualism.* New York: Longman.

Godway, Eleanor M., and Geraldine Finn, eds. 1994. *Who Is This "We"? Absence of Community.* Montreal: Black Rose.

Goffman, Erving. [1961] 1973. *Asylums: Essays on the Social Situations of Mental Patients and Other Inmates.* New York: Doubleday.

Golembiewski, Robert T., and Arthur Blumberg. 1970. *Sensitivity Training and the Laboratory Approach.* Itasca, IL: Peacock.

Goodman, Ellen. 1989a. "The Mommy Track: Is It Fair?" *Minneapolis Star-Tribune,* March 17.

———. 1989b. "Abortion and Family Rights." *Chicago Tribune,* February 19.

Goodman, Paul. 1960. *Growing up Absurd.* New York: Random House.

Hall, Edward T. 1969. *The Hidden Dimension.* Garden City, NY: Doubleday

———. 1977. *Beyond Culture.* Garden City, NY: Doubleday Anchor Press.

Hall, Richard H. 1996. *Organizations: Structures, Processes, and Outcomes,* sixth edition. Englewood Cliffs, NJ: Prentice-Hall.

Handy, Charles. 1985. *Understanding Organizations.* Harmondsworth, England: Penguin.

———. 1993 *Understanding Organizations.* New York: Oxford University Press.

Hansen, Karen V., and Anita Ilta Garey, eds. 1998. *Families in the U.S.: Kinship and Domestic Politics.* Philadelphia: Temple University Press.

Hardcastle, David A., Stanley Wenocur, and Patricia R. Powers. 1997. *Community Practice.* New York: Oxford University Press.

Hasenfeld, Yeheskel. 1983. *Human Service Organizations.* Englewood Cliffs, NJ: Prentice-Hall.

Hearn, Gordon, ed. 1969. *The General Systems Approach: Contributions toward an Holistic Conception of Social Work.* New York: Council on Social Work Education.

Herbert, James I. 1989. *Black Male Entrepreneurs and Adult Development.* New York: Praeger.

Hersch, Patricia. 1998. *A Tribe Apart*. New York: Fawcett Columbine.
Hersh, Richard H., Diana Pritchard Paolitto, and Joseph Reimer. [1979] 1983. *Promoting Moral Growth: From Piaget to Kohlberg*. New York: Longman.
Hetherington, E. Mavis, and Elaine A. Blechman, eds. 1996. *Stress, Coping, and Resiliency in Children and Families*. Mahwah, NJ: Erlbaum.
Hetherington, E. Mavis, Tracy C. Law, and Thomas G. O'Connor. 1997. "Divorce: Challenges, Changes, and New Chances." In Arlene S. Skolnick and Jerome H. Skolnick, eds. *Family in Transition*, ninth edition. New York: Longman.
Hillery, George A., Jr. 1968. *Communal Organizations: A Study of Local Societies*. Chicago: University of Chicago Press.
Hine, Virginia. 1982. *Tarrytown Newsletter*.
Hirokawa, Randy Y., Dennis S. Gouran, and Amy E. Martz. 1988. "Understanding the Sources of Faulty Group Decision Making: A Lesson from the Challenger Disaster." *Small Group Behavior* 19(4).
Homans, George. 1950. *The Human Group*. New York: Harcourt, Brace and World.
House, R. J. 1975. "Etzioni's Theory of Organizational Compliance." In Henry L. Tosi, ed. *Theories of Organization*. Chicago: St. Clair.
Hunter, Floyd. 1953. *Community Power Structure*. Chapel Hill: University of North Carolina Press.
Hunter, James Davison. 1997. "The Family and the Culture War." In Arlene S. Skolnick and Jerome H. Skolnick, eds. *Family in Transition*, ninth edition. New York: Longman.
Huxley, Julian. 1964. *Man in the Modern World*. New York: Mentor.
Jackson, Don. 1970. "The Study of the Family." In Nathan W. Ackerman, ed. *Family Process*. New York: Basic Books.
Johnson, David W., and Frank P. Johnson. [1982] 1991. *Joining Together: Group Theory and Group Skills*. Englewood Cliffs, NJ: Prentice-Hall
Jones, W. H. S., translator. 1923. *Hippocrates: With an English Translation*. London: William Heinemann.
Juario, Rolf. 1989. "Secrets to Your Success." *Etc.* 6(7).
Kanter, Elizabeth Moss. 1970. "Communes." *Psychology Today* 3(2):70ff.
Katz, Alfred H., and Eugene I. Bender. 1976. *The Strength in Us*. New York: New Viewpoints.
Kauffman, Stuart. 1995. *At Home in the Universe: The Search for Laws of Self-Organization and Complexity*. New York: Oxford University Press.
Keniston, Kenneth. 1970. "Youth: A 'New' Stage of Life." *American Scholar* 39(4).
Kimball, Meredith M. 1995. *Feminist Visions of Gender Similarities and Differences*. New York: Harrington Park.
Kinsey, Alfred C., et al. 1948. *Sexual Behavior in the Human Male*. Philadelphia: Saunders.
Knowles, Louis L., and Kenneth Prewitt, eds. 1969. *Institutional Racism in America*. Englewood Cliffs, NJ: Prentice-Hall.
Koestler, Arthur. 1967. *The Act of Creation*. New York: Dell.
———. 1979. *Janus: A Summing Up*. New York: Random House.
Koestler, Arthur, and J. R. Smythies, eds., 1971. *Beyond Reductionism: New Perspectives in the Life Sciences*. Boston: Beacon.
Kohlberg, Lawrence. 1984. *The Psychology of Moral Development*. San Francisco: Harper & Row.

————. 1987. *Child Psychology and Childhood Education: A Cognitive-Developmental View*. New York: Longman.

Kosko, Bart. 1993. *Fuzzy Thinking: The New Science of Fuzzy Logic*. New York: Hyperion.

Kovel, Joel. 1976. *A Complete Guide to Therapy: From Psychoanalysis To Behavior Modification*. New York: Pantheon.

Kranichfeld, Marion L. 1988. "Rethinking Family Power." In Norval D. Glenn and Marion Tolbert Coleman, eds. *Family Relations*. Chicago: Dorsey.

Kroeber, Alfred Louis, and Clyde Kluckhohn. 1952. *Culture: A Critical Review of Concepts and Definitions*. Cambridge, MA: The Museum.

Ktsanes, Thomas. 1965. "Adolescent Educational Values and Their Implications for the Assumption of the Adult Role." In *Adolescence: Pivotal Period in the Life Cycle*. Tulane Studies in Social Welfare, Volume 8. New Orleans: Tulane University Press.

Kuhmerker, Lisa. 1991. *The Kohlberg Legacy for the Helping Professions*. Birmingham, AL: REP.

Kuhn, Thomas S. 1970. *The Structure of Scientific Revolutions*, second edition. Chicago: University of Chicago Press.

LaBarre, Weston. 1954. *The Human Animal*. Chicago: University of Chicago Press.

Laird, Joan, and Robert Jay Green. 1996. *Lesbians and Gays in Couples and Families*. San Francisco: Jossey-Bass.

Larwood, Laurie. 1984. *Organizational Behavior and Management*. Boston: Kent.

Lasch, Christopher. 1979. *Haven in a Heartless World: The Family Besieged*. New York: Basic Books.

Laslett, Peter. 1971. *The World We Have Lost*, second edition. New York: Charles Scribner's Sons.

————, ed. 1974. *Household and Family in Past Time*. Cambridge: Cambridge University Press.

Laszlo, Ervin. 1972. *The Systems View of the World*. New York: Braziller.

Lau, Siu-Kai. 1978. *Utilitarianistic Familism: The Basis of Political Stability in Hong Kong*. Hong Kong: Social Research Centre, The Chinese University of Hong Kong.

Lauffer, Armand. 1984. *Understanding Your Social Agency*. Beverly Hills, CA: Sage.

Lazarus, Edward. 1998. *Closed Chambers*. New York: Times Books.

Leslie, Gerald. 1967. *The Family in Social Context*. New York: Oxford University Press.

Levinson, Daniel J. 1978. *The Seasons of a Man's Life*. New York: Knopf.

————. 1996. *The Seasons of a Woman's Life*. New York: Knopf.

Lichterman, Paul. 1996. *The Search for Political Community*. Cambridge: Cambridge University Press.

Lidz, Theodore. 1963. *The Family and Human Adaptation*. New York: International Universities Press.

Lincoln, Yvonna S., and Egan G. Guba. 1985. *Naturalistic Inquiry*. Beverly Hills, CA: Sage.

Lind, Christopher. 1994. "When the System Farms the Farmers: What Can We Do About the Saskatchewan Farm Crisis?" In Eleanor M. Godway and Geraldine Finn, eds. *Who is This "We"? Absence of Community*. Montreal: Black Rose.

Lorenz, Konrad. 1963. *On Aggression*. New York: Harcourt, Brace and World.

Lyman, Stanford M., and Marvin B. Scott. 1967. "Territoriality: A Neglected Sociological Dimension." *Social Problems* 15.

Lynd, Robert S. and Helen Merrell Lynd. 1929. *Middletown*. New York: Harcourt, Brace and World.

———. 1937. *Middletown in Transition*. New York: Harcourt, Brace and World.

Maier, Henry W. 1988. *Three Theories of Child Development*, fourth edition. Lanham, MD: University Press of America.

Malcolm X (with Alex Haley). 1966. *The Autobiography of Malcolm X*. New York: Grove.

Mandela, Nelson. 1994. *Long Walk to Freedom: The Autobiography of Nelson Mandela*. Boston: Little, Brown.

Marriage Project Hawaii. 1997. "The Fluid Reciprocal Beneficiary Status." http://www.xq.com/hermp. August 13.

Marrow, Alfred J. 1969. *The Practical Theorist: The Life and Work of Kurt Lewin*. New York: Basic Books.

Marshall, T. H. 1964. *Class, Citizenship, and Social Development*. New York: Doubleday.

Maruyama, Magorah. 1966. "Monopolarization, Family and Individuality." *Psychiatric Quarterly* 40(1).

Maslow, Abraham. 1968. *Toward a Psychology of Being*. Princeton: Van Nostrand.

Mason, Mary Ann, Arlene S. Skolnick, and Stephen D. Sugarman, eds. 1998. *All Our Families: New Policies for a New Century*. New York: Oxford University Press.

Maturana, Humberto R., and Francisco J. Varela. 1980. *Autopoiesis and Cognition*. Dordrecht, Holland: D. Reidel.

Mayer, Milton. 1969. *On Liberty: Man vs. the State*. Santa Barbara, CA: Center for the Study of Democratic Institutions.

Mayo, Elton. 1945. *The Social Problems of an Industrial Civilization*. Boston: Harvard University Press.

McGrath, Joseph E. 1984. *Groups: Interaction and Performance*. Englewood Cliffs, NJ: Prentice-Hall.

McIntyre, Eilene L. G. 1986. "Social Networks: Potential for Practice." *Social Work* 31(6).

McKnight, John. 1995. *The Careless Society: Community and Its Counterfeits*. New York: Basic Books.

McLuhan, Marshall. 1965. *Understanding Media: The Extensions of Man*. New York: McGraw-Hill.

Mead, Margaret. 1970. *Culture and Commitment*. Garden City, NY: Natural History Press.

———. 1972. *Blackberry Winter*. New York: Simon and Schuster.

Meadows, Donella H., Dennis L. Meadows, Jorgen Randers, and William W. Behrens III. 1972. *Limits to Growth*. New York: Universe Books.

Mei, Yi Pao, Edwin G. Pulleyblank, and Wing-tsit Chan. 1987. "Confucianism." In *The New Encyclopaedia Britannica*, volume 16.

Menninger, Karl. 1963. *The Vital Balance*. New York: Viking.

Merton, Robert K. 1957. *Social Theory and Social Structure*. New York: Free Press.

Miller, Arthur. 1955. *Death of a Salesman*. New York: Bantam.

Miller, James G. 1972. "Living Systems: The Organization." *Behavioral Science* 17(1).

————. 1978. *Living Systems*. New York: McGraw-Hill.

Miller, Sally R., and Patricia Winstead-Fry. 1982. *Family Systems Theory in Nursing Practice*. Reston, VA: Reston.

Mills, Theodore. 1967. *The Sociology of Small Groups*. Englewood Cliffs, NJ: Prentice-Hall.

Minge, David. 1998. "Today's Farm Crisis Must Be Addressed." *Minneapolis Star-Tribune*, June 24.

Mingers, John. 1995. *Self-Producing Systems: Implications and Applications of Auto-poiesis*. New York: Plenum.

Monane, Joseph H. 1967. *A Sociology of Human Systems*. New York: Appleton-Century-Crofts.

Monge, Peter R. 1977. "The Systems Perspective as a Theoretical Basis for the Study of Human Communication." *Communication Quarterly* 25(1).

Mumford, Lewis. 1970. *The Myth of the Machine: II. The Pentagon of Power*. New York: Harcourt Brace Jovanovich.

Muncie, John, Margaret Wetherell, Rudi Dallos, and Allan Cochrane, eds. 1995. *Understanding the Family*. London: Sage.

Munhall, Patricia, L., ed. 1994. *In Women's Experience*, volume I. New York: National League for Nursing Press.

————. 1995. *In Women's Experience*, volume II. New York: National League for Nursing Press.

Murray, Charles. 1984. *Losing Ground*. New York: Basic Books.

Newman, Katherine S. 1997. "The Downwardly Mobile Family." In Arlene S. Skolnick and Jerome H. Skolnick, eds. *Family in Transition*, ninth edition. New York: Longman.

Northen, Helen. [1969] 1988. *Social Work with Groups*. New York: Columbia University Press.

O'Hare, William P., Kelvin M. Pollard, Taynia L. Mann, and Mary M. Kent. 1997. "African-Americans in the 1990s." In Arlene S. Skolnick and Jerome H. Skolnick, eds. *Family in Transition*, ninth edition. New York: Longman.

Olmsted, Michael. [1959] 1978. *The Small Group*. New York: Random House.

Olsen, Marvin. [1968] 1978. *The Process of Social Organization*. New York: Holt, Rinehart, and Winston.

Olson, David. 1983. *Families: What Makes Them Work*. Beverly Hills, CA: Sage.

————. 1993. "Circumplex Model of Marital and Family Systems: Assessing Family Functioning." In F. Walsh, ed. *Power to Change*. New York: Guilford.

Olson, David H., Yoav Lavee, and Hamilton I. McCubbin. 1988. "Types of Families and Family Responses to Stress Across the Family Life Cycle." In David Klein and Joan Aldous, eds. *Social Stress and Family Development*. New York: Guilford.

Oshry, Barry. 1995. *Seeing Systems: Unlocking the Mysteries of Organizational Life*. San Francisco: Berrett-Koehler.

Ouchi, William G. 1981. *Theory Z: How American Business Can Meet the Japanese Challenge*. Reading, MA: Addison-Wesley.

Papademetriou, Marguerite. 1971. "Use of a Group Technique with Unwed Mothers and Their Families." *Social Work* 16(4).

Parsons, Talcott. 1960. *Structure and Process in Modern Societies*. New York: Free Press.

————. 1964. "The Normal Family." In *Family Mental Health Papers*. Los Angeles, CA: County Bureau of Public Assistance.

Pasley, B. Kay, and Marilyn Ihinger-Tallman. 1989. "Boundary Ambiguity in Remarriage: Does Ambiguity Differentiate Degree of Marital Adjustment and Integration?" *Family Relations* 38(1).

Pei, Mario. [1966] 1984. *The Story of Language*. New York: Mentor.

Perrow, Charles. 1986. *Complex Organizations*, third edition. Glenview, IL: Scott, Foresman.

Pharand, Giséle R., Maria L. Sudermann, and Ray DeV. Peters. 1988. "Comprehensive Assessment of Family Functioning." In Ray DeV. Peters and Robert J. McMahon, eds. *Social Learning and Systems Approaches to Marriage and the Family*. New York: Brunner/Mazel.

Phillips, John L., Jr. 1969. *The Origins of Intellect: Piaget's Theory*. San Francisco: Freeman.

Piaget, Jean. 1932. *The Moral Judgment of the Child*. Translated by Marjorie Gabian. London: Kegan Paul.

————. 1987. *Possibility and Necessity*. Minneapolis: University of Minnesota Press.

Piaget, Jean (with E. Ackerman-Vailadao et al.). 1970. *Genetic Epistemology*. Translated by Eleanor Duckworth. New York: Columbia University Press.

Plath, Sylvia. 1966. "Tulip." In *Ariel*. New York: Harper and Row.

Popenoe, David. 1988. *Disturbing the Nest*. Hawthorne, NY: Aldine de Gruyter.

Presthus, Robert. 1962. *The Organization Society: An Analysis and a Theory*. New York: Vintage.

Price, Deb. 1998. "An Issue of Equality Still Is Waiting on Hawaii Court." *Minneapolis Star-Tribune*, June 24.

Prigogine, Ilya, and Isabelle Stengers. 1984. *Order out of Chaos*. New York: Bantam.

Putnam, Robert. 1995. "Bowling Alone, Revisited." *Responsive Community*, spring.

————. 1996. "The Strange Disappearance of Civic America." *American Prospect*, winter.

Ramsoy, Ødd. 1962. *Social Groups: As System and Subsystem*. Oslo: Norwegian Universities Press.

Reardon, Kathleen Kelley. 1995. *They Don't Get It, Do They? Communication in the Workplace—Closing the Gap between Men and Women*. Boston: Little, Brown.

Reid, Kenneth E. 1997. *Social Work Practice with Groups*. Pacific Grove, CA: Brooks/Cole.

Reik, Theodor. 1948. *Listening with the Third Ear*. New York: Farrar Strauss.

Richards, Stan, and Associates. 1974. *Hobo Signs*. Dallas, TX: Author.

Richardson, George P. 1991. *Feedback Thought in Social Science and Systems Theory*. Philadelphia: University of Pennsylvania Press.

Robbins, William G. 1988. *Hard Times in Paradise: Coos Bay, Oregon, 1850–1986*. Seattle: University of Washington Press.

Rodman, Hyman, ed. 1966. *Marriage, Family and Society*. New York: Random House.

Roethlisberger, F. J., and W. L. Dickson. 1947. *Management and the Worker*. Cambridge, MA: Harvard University Press.

Rogers, Carl. 1970. *Carl Rogers on Encounter Groups*. New York: Harper and Row.

Rose, Reginald. 1955. *Twelve Angry Men*. Chicago: Dramatics Publications.

Rosen, Hugh. 1980. *The Development of Sociomoral Knowledge.* New York: Columbia University Press.

Ross, Murray G. 1955. *Community Organization.* New York: Harper and Row.

Ross, Murray, and Charles Hendry. 1957. *New Understandings of Leadership.* New York: Association Press.

Rothman, Jack, John L. Erlich, and John E. Tropman, eds. 1995. *Strategies of Community Intervention,* fifth edition. Itasca, IL: Peacock.

Rowe, David C. 1994. *The Limits of Family Influence.* New York: Guilford.

Rubin, Lillian B. 1997. "Work and Family." In Arlene S. Skolnick and Jerome H. Skolnick, eds. *Family in Transition,* ninth edition. New York: Longman.

Sager, Clifford, and Helen Singer Kaplan, eds. 1972. *Progress in Group and Family Therapy.* New York: Brunner/Mazel.

Salzinger, Suzanne, John Antrobus, and Muriel Hammer. 1988. *Social Networks of Children, Adolescents, and College Students.* Hillsdale, NJ: Erlbaum.

Sandburg, Carl. 1955. "Chicago." In Oscar Williams, ed. *The New Pocket Anthology of American Verse.* New York: Pocket Library.

Schutz, Stephen J. 1993. *Family Systems Thinking.* Northvale, NJ: Aronson.

Schwartz, David B. 1997. *Who Cares? Rediscovering Community.* Boulder, CO: Westview.

Schwartz, Ed. 1996. *Net Activism: How Citizens Use the Internet.* Sebastopol, CA: Songline Studios.

Scott, W. Richard. 1998. *Organizations: Rational, Natural, and Open Systems,* fourth edition. Upper Saddle River, NJ: Prentice-Hall.

Scott, William G., and David K. Hart. 1980. *Organizational America.* Boston: Houghton Mifflin.

Segal, Lynne. 1995. "A Feminist Looks at the Family." In John Muncie, Margaret Wetherell, Rudi Dalos, and Allan Cochrane, eds. *Understanding the Family.* London: Sage.

Selznick, Phillip. 1996. "In Search of Community." In William Vitek and Wes Jackson, eds. *Rooted in the Land.* New Haven, CT: Yale University Press.

Senge, Peter M. 1990. *The Fifth Discipline.* New York: Doubleday.

Shaw, Marvin E. 1981. *Group Dynamics,* third edition. New York: McGraw-Hill.

Sheehy, Gail. 1976. *Passages.* New York: Dutton.

———. 1992. *The Silent Passage.* New York: Random House.

———. 1995. *New Passages.* New York: Random House.

Shefchik, Rick. 1998. "Closing Doors on School Year." *St. Paul (MN) Pioneer Press,* June 6.

Shilts, Randy. 1988. *And the Band Played On: Politics, People and the AIDS Epidemic.* New York: Penguin.

Simon, H. A. 1945. *Administrative Behavior.* New York: Macmillan.

Skolnick, Arlene S., and Jerome H. Skolnick. 1997. *Family in Transition,* ninth edition. New York: Longman.

Slater, Philip. 1974. *Earthwalk.* New York: Anchor.

Slater, Suzanne. 1995. *The Lesbian Family Life Cycle.* New York: Free Press.

Southey, Robert. 1959. "The Doctor." In *Oxford Dictionary of Quotations,* second edition. London: Oxford University Press.

Spenner, Kenneth I. 1988. "Social Stratification, Work, and Personality." *Annual Review of Sociology* 14.

Spitz, René. 1965. *The First Year of Life*. New York: International Universities Press.

Stack, Carol B. 1974. *All Our Kin: Strategies for Survival In Two Black Families*. New York: Harper and Row.

————. 1996. *Call to Home: African Americans Reclaim the Rural South*. New York: Basic Books.

Stegner, Wallace. 1992. *Where the Bluebird Sings to the Lemonade Springs*. New York: Random House.

Stein, Maurice R. 1960. *The Eclipse of Community*. Princeton, NJ: Princeton University Press.

Steinberg, Laurence. 1994. *Crossing Paths: How Your Child's Adolescence Triggers Your Own Crisis*. New York: Simon and Schuster.

Steiner, Gilbert. 1981. *The Futility of Family Policy*. Washington, DC: Brookings Institution.

Sullivan, William M. 1995. "Institutions as the Infrastructure of Democracy." In Amitai Etzioni, ed. *New Communitarian Thinking*. Charlottesville: University Press of Virginia.

Sweet, James A., and Larry L. Bumpass. 1987. *American Families and Households*. New York: Russell Sage Foundation.

Tönnies, Ferdinand. 1957. *Community And Society*, Translated by Charles P. Loomis. East Lansing: Michigan State University Press.

Taylor, Robert Joseph, James S. Jackson, and Linda M. Chatters, eds. 1997. *Family Life in Black America*. Thousand Oaks, CA: Sage.

Terkel, Studs. 1975. *Working*. New York: Avon.

Tuckman, Bruce W. 1965. "Developmental sequence in small groups." *Psychological Bulletin* 63.

U.S. Department of Labor, Women's Bureau. 1997. "The Earnings Gap between Men and Women." In *Information Please Almanac*. Boston: Houghton Mifflin.

Van Geert, Paul. 1994. *Dynamic Systems of Development*. New York: Harvester Wheatsheaf.

Van Maanen, John. 1988. *Tales of the Field*. Chicago: University of Chicago Press.

Vaux, Alan, 1988. *Social Support: Theory, Research, and Intervention*. New York: Praeger.

Veninga, Robert, and James P. Spradley. 1981. *The Work-Stress Connection*. Boston: Little, Brown.

Vigil, James Diego. 1988. *Barrio Gangs*. Austin: University of Texas Press.

Vogel, Ezra, and Norman Bell. 1960. *A Modern Introduction to the Family*. New York: Free Press.

Wadsworth, Barry J. 1996. *Piaget's Theory of Cognitive and Affective Development*. White Plains, NY: Longman.

Wallulis, Jerald. 1998. *The New Insecurity: The End of the Standard Job and Family*. Albany: State University of New York Press.

Warmington, Eric H., and Philip Rouse. 1956. *Great Dialogues of Plato*. Translated by W. H. D. Rouse. New York: American Library of World Literature.

Watzlawick, Paul, Janet Helmick Beavin, and Don Jackson. 1967. *Pragmatics of Human Communication: A Study of Interactional Patterns, Pathologies, and Paradoxes*. New York: Norton.

Webster's New Twentieth Century Dictionary of the English Language. 1980. Unabridged second edition. Cleveland: William Collins.

Weisman, Celia B. 1963. "Social Structures as a Determinant of the Group Worker's Role." *Social Work* 8(3):87–94.

Weiss, Penny A. 1995. "Feminism and Communitarianism." In Penny Weiss and Marilyn Friedman, eds. *Feminism and Community*. Philadelphia: Temple University Press.

Westkott, Marcia. 1986. *The Feminist Legacy of Karen Horney*. New Haven, CT: Yale University Press.

Weston, Kath. 1995. "Exiles from Kinship." In Mark Robert Rank and Edward L. Kain, eds. *Diversity and Change in Families*. Englewood Cliffs, NJ: Prentice-Hall.

Wetherell, Margaret. 1995. "Social Structure, Ideology and Family Dynamics: The Case of Parenting." In John Muncie, Margaret Wetherell, Rudi Dalos, and Allan Cochrane, eds. *Understanding the Family*. London: Sage.

Whorf, Benjamin Lee. 1956. *Language, Thought and Reality*. New York: Wiley/Technology Press.

Whyte, Lancelot Law, Albert G. Wilson, and Dona Wilson. 1969. *Hierarchical Structures*. New York: American Elsevier.

Whyte, William Foote. [1955] 1981. *Street Corner Society*, second edition. Chicago: University of Chicago Press.

Wilbers, Stephen. 1998. "Of Ego-Surfing Body Nazis and Other New Office Jargon." *Minneapolis Star-Tribune*, January 23.

Wilson, William Julius. 1987. *The Truly Disadvantaged: The Inner City, the Underclass, and Public Policy*. Chicago: University of Chicago Press.

Wolfe, Alan. 1995. "Human Nature and the Quest for Community." In Amitai Etzioni, ed. *New Communitarian Thinking*. Charlottesville: University Press of Virginia.

———. 1998. *One Nation, After All*. New York: Viking.

Wood, Julia T. 1994. *Who Cares? Women, Care, and Culture*. Carbondale: Southern Illinois University Press.

Woodruff, John. 1989. *China in Search of Its Future: Years of Great Reform; 1982–1987*. Seattle: University of Washington Press.

Woodward, Bob, and Scott Armstrong. 1981. *The Brethren*. New York: Avon.

Wuthnow, Robert, James Davison Hunter, Albert Bergesen, and Edith Kurzweil. 1984. *Cultural Analysis*. Boston/London: Routledge and Kegan Paul.

Zaleznik, Abraham, and Anne Jardim, 1967. "Management." In Paul R. Lazersfield, ed. *The Uses of Sociology*. New York: Basic Books.

Zimmerman, Carle. 1947. *Outline of the Future of the Family*. Cambridge: Phillips Book Store.

Zinn, Maxine Baca. 1997. "Family, Race, and Poverty." In Arlene S. Skolnick and Jerome H. Skolnick, eds. *Family in Transition*, ninth edition. New York: Longman.

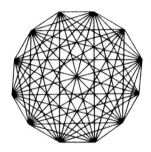

Literary Sources

Ambrose, Stephen E. 1996. *Undaunted Courage: Meriwether Lewis, Thomas Jefferson, and the Opening of the American West.* New York: Simon and Schuster.

Anderson, Robert Woodruff. 1968. *I Never Sang for My Father.* New York: Random House.

Bergman, Ingmar. 1960. *Wild Strawberries.* In *Four Screenplays.* New York: Simon and Schuster.

Branch, Taylor. 1988. *Parting the Waters: America in the King Years 1954–63.* New York: Simon and Schuster.

Dorris, Michael. 1987. *A Yellow Raft in Blue Water.* New York: Warner.

Erdrich, Louise. 1985. *Love Medicine.* Toronto, New York: Bantam.

Forster, E. M. [1921] 1954. *Howards End.* New York: Random House.

Golding, William. 1959. *Lord of the Flies.* New York: Capricorn Books/Putnam.

Guest, Judith, 1976. *Ordinary People.* New York: Viking.

Keillor, Garrison. 1985. *Lake Wobegon Days.* New York: Viking.

Kesey, Ken. 1962. *One Flew over the Cuckoo's Nest.* New York: New American Library.

Lee, Harper. 1960. To *Kill a Mockingbird.* Philadelphia: Lippincott.

Mailer, Norman. 1979. *The Executioner's Song.* New York: Warner.

Malcolm X (with Alex Haley). 1966. *The Autobiography of Malcolm X.* New York: Grove.

McCullers, Carson. 1940. *The Heart Is a Lonely Hunter.* Boston: Houghton Mifflin.

Miller, Arthur. 1949. *Death of a Salesman.* New York: Bantam.

Olsen, Tillie, 1976. *Tell Me a Riddle.* New York: Dell/Laurel Edition.

Pa Chin (or Ba Jin). 1972. *Family.* Garden City, NY: Anchor.

Rose, Reginald. 1955. *Twelve Angry Men.* Chicago: Dramatics Publications.

Solzhenitsyn, Alexander. 1963. *A Day in the Life of Ivan Denisovich.* New York: Praeger.

Solzhenitsyn, Alexander. [1968] 1969. *Cancer Ward.* New York: Farrar, Strauss, and Giroux.

Solzhenitsyn, Alexander. 1973. *Gulag Archipelago.* New York: Harper & Row.

Tan, Amy. 1989. *The Joy Luck Club*. New York: Putnam.
Thompson, Ernest. 1979. *On Golden Pond*. New York: Dodd, Mead.
Warren, Robert Penn. [1946] 1982. *All the King's Men*. New York: Harcourt, Brace, Jovanovich.

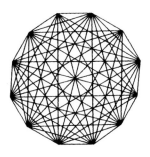

Glossary

Accommodation. Modification of the system to adapt to environmental conditions. See ACCOMMODATION, ASSIMILATION.

Adaptation. Action by the system to secure or conserve energy from the environment. Parsons's use of this term includes such action as well as the achievement of goals in the environment. See ACCOMMODATION, ASSIMILATION, FUNCTIONAL IMPERATIVES.

African-American. This is the preferred term for Americans of African descent, in that it refers to geographic origin rather than skin color, similar to "Caucasian," "European-American" (or "Euro-American") and "Asian-American." "Black" is used in this text in quotations from other sources, and in a historical context.

Alienation. This term has a wide variety of definitions. We consider that, fundamentally, it describes a state in which a person does not experience a synergistic linkage with a system (or component) that is significant to the person.

American Indian. This term refers to indigenous peoples of North America, specifically those within the United States. It is often used interchangeably with "Native American," although the latter also denotes other indigenous peoples such as Pacific Islanders. Other terms, such as "Natives," "First Nations" (in Canada), pueblos, Inuits (formerly referred to as "Eskimos") and Aleuts, and other specific tribes' names are also used. "Indians" is, of course, inaccurate, but some indigenous Americans hold that "American Indian" appears in treaties between the United States and the sovereign tribal governments and thus has historical value.

Assimilation. A form of adaptation in which incoming information is interpreted as being similar to previous information (i.e., fitted into old schemas). See ACCOMMODATION, ADAPTATION.

Autonomy. Independence from other components within a system. The components are related to a common suprasystem but are largely or entirely separate from each other. See AUTOPOIESIS.

Autopoiesis. Literally (from Greek), "self-made"; self-development and self-creation. There is theoretical disagreement about the degree of autonomy implied; Maturana and Varela seem to imply complete control of reproduction by the system; we caution that there is interdependence between part and whole, and perhaps between parts, along with significant autonomy and separateness.

Behavior. Short-term exchanges between components or systems that accomplish specific goals for the system. This includes socialization, communication, and social control. See EVOLUTION, STRUCTURE.

Body Language. Nonvocal communication expressed through touch, posture, facial expression, and movement.

Bond. The common interest, identification, or feeling of "we-ness" among members of a group (which can be as small as a dyad) that permits the group to exist as a system. See BOUNDARY, NETWORK, AND LINKAGE.

Boundary. The limits of the interaction of the components of a system with each other or with the environment. It is usually defined by intensity or frequency of interaction between systems and components. See DENSITY.

Bureaucracy. A distinct form of organization in which there is a relatively high degree of administrative centralization, hierarchical control, specificity of roles, and clearly identified role expectations. This form of organization is usually found in cultures that are highly elaborated, and it serves social control functions and goal achievement in the society.

Chaos and Order. In chaos theory (see below), "chaos" is defined as a completely entropic situation in which there is no exchange, relationship, or structure present. Any structure that arises is an example of "order." These definitions are counterintuitive, in that they seem to contradict usual meanings of these terms. It might be clearer to think of chaos as "unorganized" and order as "structured," but we may be stuck with these terms, for the near future at least. See CHAOS THEORY.

Chaos Theory. This conception of natural events holds that events occur in nonlinear fashion, due to extreme sensitivity to prevailing conditions, and that variations (or perturbations) are random, but occur within some identifiable parameters. The infinite variations of snowflakes, e.g., and of human events, have brought the natural and social sciences closer in recognizing and accounting for complexity and uncertainty. See LINEARITY AND NONLINEARITY, FEEDBACK CYCLE, and LOOP; see also ORDER and STEADY STATE.

Class. A scheme of classification of a particular society. Usually ordered by indices such as income, occupation, and education. See ROLE, STATUS.

Coevolution. This concept has gained importance recently. It is a modification of previous conceptions of the relationship between systems and their environments. The concept means that as systems evolve, so do their environments; in other words, that systems do not simply "adapt" or "adjust" to their environments, but influence the environments, as well, through feedback cycles. This has highly significant implications for the modification of the Darwinian view of evolution. In a broad sense, it redefines systems (particularly living systems) as active, and *autopoietic*; that is, *self*-developing. See FEEDBACK CYCLE.

Communication. In a narrow sense, the transportation of information between or within systems; in a broader sense, the transportation of energy, also. In this broader sense, information is considered a special form of energy. See INFORMATION.

Component. Synonymous with "part" (a part of a system). It may or may not be a system in itself, in contrast to a subsystem. See SUBSYSTEM.

Density. The degree to which energy / information can pass through a boundary; permeability of the boundary. (See Day, in Day, Gilbert, Settles, and Burr, 1995.)

Differentiation. Selectivity of function or activity among components of a system. "Division of labor" is one example. A function or activity is performed by one, or some, components and not others. This differs from specialization in that the component may perform other functions or activities in addition to the assigned, differentiated one. See SPECIALIZATION.

Disintegration. This means systemic death; components *desystematize.* "It is a movement away from organization into entropy and randomness" (Monane, 1967:159). See ENTROPY, ORGANIZATION.

Ecological Approach. This is an approach that is virtually synonymous with a systems approach. Specifically, it refers to "nested" systems, that is, from component to subsystem to suprasystem, and specifically to relationships between humans and their environments. Like systems theory, if calls for an analysis and specification of the context of the focal system.

Ecological Systems. A term used by some systems writers in the broad sense of systems that are hierarchically related. In biology and ecology, the term refers to the interactions of organisms and between organisms and their environments. See ECOLOGICAL APPROACH.

Elaboration. Used in reference to evolution of groups, this denotes increasing complexity and multiplication of parts of the system. We also use it to describe similar processes in other systems.

Energy. Capacity for action, action, or power to effect change. We use this term much as Parsons used "action." As increased interaction occurs, there is greater available energy. Richard Adams (1988) preferred the term "energy forms," which is a useful concept. Information is one form of energy. See ENTROPY, POWER, SYNERGY, SYNTROPY.

Energy Functions. Parsons specified four functions (or processes) that he saw as necessary in a system: adaptation, goal-directed activity, integration, and pattern maintenance. We identify other functions that we consider to be more descriptive—securing energy (S) and goal-direction (G)—and see these as occurring both externally (E) and internally (I); hence a set of four: SE, SI, GE, and GI. None necessarily takes precedence over the others. See GOAL-DIRECTED ACTIVITY.

Entropy. The tendency of systems to "run down," to distribute (or dissipate) energy randomly so that it becomes less accessible; the system thus becomes less capable of organized work. Prigogine, Maturana, Capra, and others argue that living systems violate this "second law of thermodynamics" by maintaining themselves in a high degree of disequilibrium "on the edge of chaos." See ENERGY, NEGENTROPY, ORGANIZATION, SYNTROPY, ORDER, CHAOS THEORY, EQUILIBRIUM.

Environment. Anything not included within the interactions of the components of a system (that is, within the interactional boundary) that affects the system. It may also be considered as anything that affects the system but over which it has little or no control. *Significant environment* refers to those systems or components that are capable of influencing the system in fundamental (as opposed to tangential) ways.

Equifinality. A systems principle that means that two different systems, if they receive similar inputs, will arrive at similar end states, even though they had different initial conditions. One illustration is that two children may grow differently, one "undershooting" and the other "overshooting" initially, but both will arrive at adulthood in good health and normal size if they are nurtured (both nutritionally and emotionally) similarly and adequately. Given newer ideas about nonlinearity and autopoiesis (see these terms), equifinality may be strictly a theoretical concept, considering the unpredictability of systems.

Equilibrium. Fixed balance of a relatively closed system, characterized by little interchange with the environment and avoidance of disturbance. Freud's concept of psychological structure fits this definition.

Ethology. The study of animal behavior, especially of innate patterns. Within the past generation, the theories of ethologists including Konrad Lorenz, Desmond Morris, Lionel Tiger, and Robin Fox became popular. Edward O. Wilson is the leading theorist of sociobiology, which suggests that human behavior is biologically determined in some significant ways.

Evolution. Longer-term change in a system's structure. The term describes which relationships have altered (and which have remained the same) and in what manner a system's functions are being performed differently at the end of some significant period of time. See BEHAVIOR, STRUCTURE.

Feedback Cycle. The process in which a system receives internal or environmental responses to its behavior and, in turn, reacts to these received responses by accommodating and assimilating the energy/information received, by altering the system's structure, and then engaging in altered exchanges of energy/information. See ADAPTATION, ACCOMMODATION, ASSIMILATION, COMMUNICATION, LOOP.

Focal System. This refers to the system that is the object of attention at a particular moment. It must be specified in order to be consistent with the demand that the perspective of the viewer should be stated. Systems analysts frequently label this the *target system* if the focal system is the system in which change is to be achieved. See HOLON, PERSPECTIVISM.

General Systems Theory (GST). A loosely knit set of theories derived from the natural and social sciences, which has generated useful hypotheses about similar (isomorphic) processes and structures across the range of living entities. GST comprises *social* systems theory, among many other varieties of living systems. This body of theory has evolved from the late nineteenth century to the present; Ludwig Von Bertalanffy in biology and Talcott Parsons in sociology are generally recognized as the progenitors of systems theory. One logical extension of GST is the "Gaia hypothesis" that the earth (and its environment of atmosphere and solar radiation) is a global ecological system that demonstrates the properties of a living system.

Goal. A desired steady state to be achieved by fulfilling a specific function of the system within some relatively short period of time. See PURPOSE.

Goal-Directed Activity (GE and GI functions). One of two kinds of energy functions, the other being *securing and conserving energy*. The process is the expenditure of energy (or distribution of information) to achieve system goals, either internally or externally.

Hierarchy. A form of organization that characterizes all viable systems. Hierarchy is a superordinate-subordinate relationship in systems in which any unit is dependent upon its suprasystem for performance of energy functions and must provide direction to its own subsystems. The hierarchy may be one of power, or simply of sequence (that is, one thing must precede another). This does not imply greater or lesser value to any partner in the hierarchical relationship. See HOLON.

Holon. Arthur Koestler's term, which denotes a system that is both part of a larger suprasystem and is itself a suprasystem to other systems. See FOCAL SYSTEM, SUBSYSTEM, SUPRASYSTEM.

Homeostasis. Fixed balance in a partially open system, characterized by very limited interchange with the environment and by maintenance of the system's present structure. The balance can change within very narrowly defined limits. See EQUILIBRIUM, STEADY STATE, CHAOS.

Id, Ego, and Superego. This is Freud's description of persons' psychological structure. The id includes the physiological processes and unconscious drives. The superego is the process that incorporates the socially derived "dos and don'ts." The ego is the process that mediates between the id and the external environment, and between the id and superego. We view this as a systems conception of the personality that attempted to identify and define the essential functions of the personality system. Freud's system was essentially closed, and the goal of the system was equilibrium.

Identity. Erikson defined this in several versions. The central idea is integration of the components of the personality, along with validation through interaction with the social environment. The result of these is *ego identity*, which is inner assurance of congruence between a person's feeling about self and others' feeling about the person. The concept has been loosely applied to other systems such as "national identity" and "racial identity." Identity is a steady state of the personality system but is richer in meaning than steady state. See STEADY STATE, SYNTALITY, SYNERGY.

Information. In the broadest sense, information is one form of energy. In a narrow sense, information includes signs and symbols that are exchanged. It is the content of feedback and communication. As opposed to "noise," it is *information*, organized so that it can be understood and utilized. See COMMUNICATION, FEEDBACK.

Institutionalization. One form of differentiation in which some component or subsystem is assigned (or assumes) responsibility to perform specific major functions for the system (usually a culture, society, or community but in a broader sense, in microsystems as well). The differentiated component or subsystem may specialize in this function. A new component or subsystem may carry out the function, or the assignment may be carried out by an existing component or subsystem. See DIFFERENTIATION, SPECIALIZATION.

Integration. One of Parsons's four functional imperatives. A system must ensure the harmonious interaction of its components in order to prevent entropy and in order to secure and conserve internal energy sources.

Isomorphic. Similarity of form between systems or components of systems. "Isomorph" is used in this book to point to similarities of structure, behavior, or evolution between different systems and levels of systems. For example, *feedback cycle* is applicable to all levels of systems from person to culture.

Linearity and Nonlinearity. In systems terminology, linearity means "straight-line" causation, in which "*A* causes *B*, which causes *C*." Nonlinearity means that causation is at least partially determined by *feedback loops*, in which later developments alter conditions that existed earlier, leading to new events and conditions. Examples include Erikson's stages, in which outcomes of later stages may alter the balances achieved in earlier stages.

Loop. This term is borrowed from cybernetics, computer programming, and engineering. It is a specific form of feedback, in which a system's output becomes input that modifies the system's functioning. That is, the system's own behavior supplies stimuli for system modification. See FEEDBACK.

Mission. See PURPOSE.

Morphogenesis. A system tending toward structural change. In actuality, all systems must simultaneously maintain a dynamic balance between morphogenesis (change) and morphostasis (maintenance) if they are to continue. See MORPHOSTASIS.

Morphostasis. A system tending toward maintenance of its current structure. See MORPHOGENESIS.

Negentropy. The word is a contraction of "negative entropy," meaning the reduction of random, unavailable energy via the importation of energy from outside the system. Recent theorists stress that a high degree of negentropy is the means by which systems maintain themselves "on the edge of chaos." See CHAOS, ENTROPY, SYNERGY, SYNTROPY.

Network. A set of persons linked together, although not necessarily each to every other. We refer you to the quotation from McIntyre (see Chapter 4, of this book); a network includes indirect links, different from a small group, which has only direct, face-to-face linkage between members. *Networking* is the usage or exploitation of such linkages to achieve specific, desired results. See BOND.

Open or Closed System. "Open" denotes energy exchange across a system's boundaries. "Closed" denotes lack of energy exchange across boundaries.

Order. See CHAOS.

Organization. The process of structuring a system's exchange of energy, both internally and externally. Persistent regularities of relationship between components make up the structure, or organization, of the system. See CHAOS, DIFFERENTIATION, ORDER, SPECIALIZATION.

Pattern Maintenance. One of Parsons's four functional imperatives. This refers to the necessity of the system to regulate and enforce legitimated behaviors in order to conserve energy and to achieve goals. We consider this to include our SI and GI functions. See ENERGY FUNCTIONS.

Perspectivism. In social systems theory, this means that any description or definition of a system must include an explicit statement of one's own position or intention with regard to that system and an explicit identification of the system that one is identifying as the focal system. Philosophically, the term denotes that any viewpoint is relative to one's own perceptions and relations to the system being described or defined, and to its environment. See our discussion of postmodernism in the Introduction to this edition.

Polarities. Opposite or contrasting qualities. Many of the systems ideas are conceived as polarities at opposite ends of a continuum. However, any system at any time is a mixture or ratio of two polar qualities, such as task *vs.* sentiment, adaptation *vs.* integration, and basic trust *vs.* basic mistrust.

Power. The capacity to achieve goals by the application or deprivation of energy to another system so as to affect its functioning.

Psychosexual. Generally, this refers to the Freudian stages of personality development (i.e., oral, anal, phallic, and genital). See PSYCHOSOCIAL.

Psychosocial. Generally, this refers to Erikson's life cycle formulation of personality development. This is a modification and extension of the Freudian psychosexual stages, with emphasis on social and cultural influences. See PSYCHOSEXUAL.

Purpose. A description or statement of a desired steady state to be achieved by assignment of goal achievement to a component or subsystem, and completion of the goal(s). Systems analysts frequently use "mission" to mean the same as purpose. See GOAL.

Role. A set of expectations about behavior that can be fulfilled by a person. It carries with it expectations of behavior that are defined and approved by systems in the persons' social environment. The role occupant generally has some leeway in interpretations of assigned behaviors. This is analogous to the theater, in which the playwright prescribes the role but the artist interprets through the performance. See STATUS.

Schema. Precisely used, this is Piaget's term for a single complex, or nexus, of associated responses that a person is capable of making. These responses, or behaviors, accumulate through experience, and are integrated into larger wholes as the person develops. We use the term to mean the integrated knowledge, experience, and interpretations that underlie any system's responses.

Securing and Conserving Energy. We designate this as one of two kinds of ENERGY FUNCTIONS in a system; the other is GOAL-DIRECTED ACTIVITY). The process is one of expending energy to secure further energy, or to reduce the expenditure of energy, as in minimizing intrasystem conflict. See ENERGY FUNCTIONS, GOAL-DIRECTED ACTIVITY.

Social Control. The use of energy by a system to assure that its components fulfill assigned functions (see PURPOSES and GOALS). Such activity includes socialization and enforcement of norms of behavior. The purpose of social control is to permit continued functioning of the system through reducing or preventing deviance (energy-diverting behavior) among the components. See SOCIALIZATION.

Socialization. One form of social control intended to assure the availability of components' energies to the system. The means to achieve this are primarily through assimilating the culture. Hence, education, indoctrination, and enculturation are forms of socialization. See SOCIAL CONTROL.

Specialization. Performance of a function or activity to the exclusion of other functions or activities, by a component of a system. A system may differentiate its components by allocating functions or activities among them; some components perform certain functions exclusively; that is, other components do not perform that function. If the component performs *only* the differentiated function, then it has specialized; if it performs other functions as well, it is differentiated but not specialized. The two are separate. See DIFFERENTIATION.

Status. A vertical dimension of ranking; it may be ascribed (assigned by society) or achieved (attained by dint of individual or group activity). See CLASS, ROLE.

Steady State. A total condition of the system in which it is in balance both internally and with its environment but is at the same time undergoing some degree of change (i.e, is not static). The word *steady* fails to connote the dynamic nature of systems, while the word *state* fails to connote a succession of conditions of the system. "Dynamic balance" or Bertalanffy's "flowing balance" connote these characteristics better. As noted earlier, steady state is maintained by a high degree of negentropy (importation of energy) in living systems "on the edge of chaos." Used fairly loosely and somewhat interchangeably with equilibrium and homeostasis, but distinct from them. See EQUILIBRIUM, HOMEOSTASIS.

Structure. The most stable relationships between systems and components (i.e., with the slowest rate of change). "Structure" describes which components or systems are related to each other during a given time period, but does not necessarily give details of the amount of energy exchange, or in what direction, or the functions being performed for each party to the relationship. It is thus a "snapshot," frozen in time, not a "movie." See BEHAVIOR, EVOLUTION.

Subsystem. A component of a system that is itself a system. It is one kind of component. See COMPONENT, SUPRASYSTEM, SYSTEM.

Suprasystem. A larger system that includes the focal system; a "whole" of which the focal system is a "part." See SUBSYSTEM, COMPONENT.

Symbolic Interaction. A theoretical perspective within social psychology that seeks to understand human behavior through study of the "social act." Such study attends to overt behavior and what the act symbolizes within the social context.

Synergy. Increasing the amount of energy available in a system through increased interaction of the components. Loosely, it may be described as the creation of new energy through compounding the actions of the parts, but this is a moot point in systems theory. See ENERGY, ENTROPY, NEGENTROPY, SYNTROPY.

Syntality. This is the unique character of a group; analogous to the "personality" of a person.

Syntropy. An innate drive in living matter to protect itself, to seek synthesis and wholeness; a hypothetical concept. See ENERGY, ENTROPY, NEGENTROPY, SYNERGY.

System. An organized whole made up of components that interact in a way distinct from their interaction with other entities, and that endures over some period of time. See COMPONENT, SUBSYSTEM, SUPRASYSTEM.

Territoriality. Refers to the proclivity of organisms, including humans, to seek, obtain, and defend an area or space of action. This serves to order and stabilize behavioral space. See ETHOLOGY.

Transition State. The condition of a system that is moving from one steady state to another. As discussed in the text of this book, transition states may be more frequent than steady states. However, every steady state is in transition, so it may be a "judgment call" as to whether at certain times a system is in steady state or transition. Like other polarities, it is a ratio: in this instance, of change or maintenance of current structure. See BEHAVIOR, EVOLUTION, MORPHOGENESIS, MORPHOSTASIS, STEADY STATE, STRUCTURE.

Name Index

Acuña, Rodolpho, 236
Adams, Margaret, 180
Adams, Richard, 9, 20, 189
Adams, Scott, 101, 133
Ainsworth, Mary D. Salter, 228, 257
Anaxmander, 265
Anderson, Walter, 96–97
Arendt, Hannah, 78, 263
Aristotle, 265
Armour, Stephanie, 125

Bacon, Sir Francis, 43
Bahrdt, Hans Paul, 80
Baily, Kenneth, 20, 161
Bales, Robert, 148, 161
Baridge, Betty, 74–76
Barnes, John, 74
Bawer, Bruce, 95
Bellah, Robert, 95, 176
Benedict, Ruth, 11, 138
Bengtson, Vern, 179
Berger, Brigitte, 193
Berger, Peter, 46, 63, 193
Bernard, Chester, 114–115
Berry, Wendell, 71
Billingsley, Andrew, 177–178, 188,
    193
Birren, James, 252–253
Blau, Peter, 109

Bloom, Allan, 243
Blumberg, Arthur, 138
Blummer, Herbert, 4
Boehm, Werner, 93
Boulding, Elise, 173
Boyd, Robert, 44
Brill, Charles, 73, 83–84, 91
Brodey, Warren, 189
Bruner, Jerome, 55
Buber, Martin, 64
Bull, Chris, 95
Burr, Wesley, 165–166
Bush, George, 31, 80, 109, 129
Butler, Samuel, 266
Butler, Sandra, 137, 141–143, 153–154,
    162, 257
Bütz, Michael, 1, 9, 20, 27–28, 30

Cairns, Robert, 28
Caplow, Theodore, 81, 88
Capra, Fritjof, 20, 27, 32
Carse, James, 39
Carter, Jimmy, 29, 129
Case, Robbie, 257
Cattell, R. B., 147
Caudill, Harry, 82–83
Chodorow, Nancy, 170, 189, 220
Clark, Don, 223–225, 257
Clinton, Hillary, 113, 167

Clinton, William, 14, 30, 80, 109, 113, 129
Cohen, Bernice, 67
Coleman, Joseph, 130, 131
Cooley, Charles Horton, 59, 60
Corey, Gerald, 153
Corsini, Raymond, 33–34
Coser, Lewis, 108, 123, 154–155, 160
Cox, Fred, 73
Coyle, Grace, 148

Dahl, Robert, 120
Darwin, Charles, 35, 39
Day, Randal, 185
De Kerckhove, Derrick, 67
de Tocqueville, Alexis, 78
Dewey, John, 92, 106
Domhoff, William, 89
Donne, John, 1
Dowd, Nancy, 167
Drucker, Peter, 132–133
Duckworth, Eleanor, 210–213, 257
Dunn, Edgar, 78
Durkheim, Emile, 119, 250
Dye, Thomas, 89–90

Einstein, Albert, 8
El Nasser, Haya, 125
Elliot, Faith, 193
Erdrich, Louise, 68, 167, 195
Erikson, Erik, 15, 24, 28, 32, 47, 77, 146, 154, 174, 181, 187, 201–261
Etzioni, Amitai, 105, 108–110, 121–122
Evans, Richard, 252

Farb, Peter, 15, 56, 67
Fennell, Graham, 258
Fellin, Phillip, 97
Ferguson, Kathy, 110
Flora, Cornelia Butler, 97
Ford, Gerald, 39, 129
Forster, E. M., 20
Fowler, Robert, 97
Freire, Paolo, 142, 143
Freud, Sigmund, 15, 23, 47, 61, 124, 159, 198–261
Friedan, Betty, 170
Fromm, Erich, 78, 109, 219, 249

Gandhi, Mohandas, 69, 201, 217, 244
Gemmill, Gary, 157–158
Geyer, Felix, 121
Gilligan, Carol, 170, 198, 220–221, 225, 226
Glassman, Uravia, 149
Gleick, James, 18
Glennon, Lynda, 110
Goffman, Erving, 122–123

Haley, Jay, 182
Hall, E. T., 52
Hall, Gus, 86
Hall, Richard, 67, 115–116
Handy, Charles, 108, 124–129, 133, 160, 162
Hardcastle, David, 97, 143, 152
Hasenfeld, Yeheskel, 118, 134
Hearn, Gordon, 2
Hersch, Richard, 180
Heraclitus, 1, 24, 265
Hillery, George, A. Jr., 74–75
Hiltner, Seward, 93
Hine, Virginia, 74
Hippocrates, 265
Hirokawa, Randy, 121–122
Hollingshead, August, 85, 86
Homans, George, 158
Horney, Karen, 77, 107, 197–198, 219–221, 225
Hunter, Floyd, 89, 193
Hunter, James, 45–46
Huxley, Julian, 48

Ihinger-Tallman, Marilyn, 185
Illich, Ivan, 64

Jefferson, Thomas, 47, 217
Jervis, Robert, 20
Jones, Ronald, 264
Juario, Rolf, 87
Jung, Carl, 157

Kauffman, Stuart, 40, 117
Kesey, Ken, xvii, 136
Kimball, Meredith, 64
King, Martin Luther, Jr., 217, 244

Kluckhohn, Clyde, 55
Knowles, Louis, 17, 88
Koestler, Arthur, 3, 5, 19, 20, 212
Kohlberg, Lawrence, 47, 198, 214–216,
    220, 226
Kosko, Bart, 40
Kovel, Joel, 140
Kranichfeld, Marion, 188, 189
Kroeber, Alfred Louis, 55
Kübler-Ross, Elizabeth, 155–156, 263
Kuhmerker, Lisa, 258
Kuhn, Thomas, 47

La Barre, Weston, 52–53, 67
Laird, Joan, 193, 223
Larwood, Laurie, 119
Lasch, Christopher, 179, 180
Laslett, Peter, 172–173
Laszlo, Ervin, 24
Lerner, Max, 197
Lerner, Richard, 39, 210, 215–216
Levinson, Daniel, 219, 221–222, 246–
    247, 258
Lewin, Kurt, 106, 138, 149, 152
Leopoldi, Aldo, 72
Lichterman, Paul, 95
Lidz, Theodore, 182
Lincoln, Abraham, 29, 129, 217
Lind, Christopher, 72, 82
Lorenz, Karl, 44, 55
Luhmann, Niklas, 40
Lussier, Roland, 73, 81
Lyman, Stanford, 53
Lynd, Helen Merrell, 81, 88
Lynd, Robert S., 81, 88

Maier, Henry, 259
Mailer, Norman, 21
Malcolm X, xviii, 38, 40, 77, 85, 183–
    184, 186, 244
Mandela, Nelson, 244
Marshall, T. H., 57
Marx, Karl, 107
Maslow, Abraham, 31, 47, 107, 117,
    138
Maturana, Humberto, 33, 189
Maudlin, Bill, 148, 157
Mayer, Milton, 137

Mayo, Elton, 106
McGrath, Joseph, 161
McKnight, John, 78, 85
McLuhan, Marshall, 82
Mead, G. H., 4, 59, 244
Mead, Margaret, 66, 165
Mel, Yi Pao, 63
Menninger, Karl, 61
Merton, Robert, 53
Miller, Arthur, 185
Miller, James, 114
Mills, C. Wright, 102, 168
Mills, Theodore M., 147, 159
Mingers, John, 40
Monane, Joseph, 9
Monge, Peter, 2
Moore, Michael, 132
Mumford, Lewis, 105
Munhall, Patricia, 259

Nixon, Richard, 109
Northen, Helen, 147, 155

O'Connor, Flannery, 71
O'Hare, William, 168, 177
Olmstead, Richard, 106
Oshry, Barry, 101
Ouchi, William, 131

Papademetrious, Marguerite, 162
Parsons, Talcott, 4, 102, 124, 167, 177,
    180
Pascale, Blaise, 23
Pasley, Kay, 185
Pei, Mario, 51
Pendragon, Arthur, 244
Phillips, John, 209, 259
Piaget, Jean, 13, 19, 24, 26, 32, 39, 46,
    191, 209–211, 213, 217, 231, 234,
    238, 256
Plato, 265
Popenoe, David, 168–169, 172, 179,
    185, 193
Presthus, Robert, 108
Price, Deb, 50
Prigogine, Ilya, 14, 18, 27, 33
Putnam, Robert, 94, 97

Quayle, Dan, 167

Ramsey, Ødd, 155
Reardon, Kathleen, 125
Reagan, Ronald, 80, 129
Reid, Kenneth, 139–140, 143, 155–156
Reik, Theodor, 61
Richardson, George, 18, 20, 41
Robbins, William, 83
Roethlisberger, F. J., 106, 148, 156
Rogers, Carl, 152–153
Rothman, Jack, 86

Salzinger, Suzanne, 86
Sandburg, Carl, 78
Schwartz, David, 65, 71, 101, 165
Schwartz, Ed, 96
Scott, W. Richard, 104–104, 110, 155–156
Segal, Lynne, 169–171
Sheeney, Gail, 259
Shelley, Mary, 49
Shilts, Randy, 85, 135, 261
Simon, Herbert, 105
Slater, Phillip, 171–172
Socrates, 217, 265
Spitz, René, 227–230
Stegner, William, 76
Stengers, Isabella, 18, 19, 27, 33
Sullivan, Harry, 77, 94–95

Taylor, Edward, 55, 188
Thompson, William, 23

Tolstoy, Leo, 165
Tönnies, Ferdinand, 72–73, 75
Tuckman, Bruce, 152–154, 156
Tzu, Chuang, 3

Van der Zouwen, Johannes, 121
Van Geert, Paul, 21
Van Maanen, John, 68
Vaux, Alan, 48, 86, 88
Veblen, Thornstein, 85
Veninga, Robert, 112

Walesa, Lech, 148
Warren, Robert, 40
Watzlawick, Paul, 37, 194
Weber, Max, 4, 56, 80, 107–109
Weinberg, George, 224
Weisman, Celia, 149
Weisman, Frederick, 145
Weiss, Penny, 95
Westkott, Maria, 259
Whitehead, Alfred North, 24
Whyte, William Foote, 156
Wolfe, Alan, 95
Wood, Julia, 64–65
Wuthnow, Robert, 45–47, 63–65, 68

Zaleznak, Abraham, 124
Zimmerman, Carole, 175–177

Subject Index

Adaptation, 34, 35, 37, 39, 44, 50, 78–79, 82, 85, 145, 149, 156–160, 172,173,190–191, 287
accommodation, 19, 24, 37, 39, 44, 79–80, 172–173, 212–213, 244, 254, 256, 287
assimilation, 24, 39, 79, 190, 212–213, 229, 244, 256
Adolescence, 204, 205, 207, 214, 216, 237, 239–245
defined, 241
Adulthood, 219–257, 259
African Americans, 50, 58, 64, 77, 86, 88, 167, 177, 188, 193, 236, 260, 287
Aging (elders), 83, 164, 252–257
AIDS (Acquired Immune Deficiency Syndrome), 62, 84, 85, 135, 141, 142, 196
Alcoholics Anonymous, 87, 141
Alienation, 3, 77–78, 111, 122, 181, 239, 246, 250–251, 287
depersonalization, 123
Ambivalence, 232,243
American Indians, 44, 50, 56, 68, 73, 75, 77, 79, 83, 86, 90–91, 195, 236, 287
Amish, 29, 75, 79, 98

Anomie, 250
Asian Americans, 68, 86
Atomic or molecular model, 3, 4, 9, 45, 46, 66
Atomistic view, 4–5, 74, 175
Authority, 31, 102, 124
Autism, 228
Autonomy, 32–34, 128, 156–157, 287
vs. shame and doubt, 230–233
Autopoiesis (See Self-development), 33–34, 189, 288

Behavioral aspects (See also Adaptation; Communication Feedback; Social Control; Socialization), 36–39, 124
communities, 88–92
defined, 24
families, 187–191
groups, 148–151
organizations, 103–113
Biocomputer, 49
Black Americans (See African Americans)
Body language, 51, 288
Boundary (See also Territoriality), 28–31, 53, 60

Boundary (*cont.*)
  communities, 77, 79, 80, 84, 86–87,
    90–91
  cultures, 60
  defined, 29
  families, 29, 185–187
  groups, 156–157
  open; closed, 15, 24–31
  person, 30–31, 228, 232
Bureaucracy, 53, 57, 58, 90
  bureaucratic personality, 110
  bureaucratic situation, 109–113, 126,
    129
  defined, 109, 288
  school as, 236, 242
Burnout, 112–113

Caring, 246
Caste (*See* Social stratification)
Causation, 4–6, 33, 72
  Linear and nonlinear, 16–19
Change (*See* Steady state)
Chaos theory, 16–19, 27, 288
  complexity, 17, 18
China, 195
  class, 58
  Tienamen Square, 58, 60
Childrearing, 62, 173
Chodorow's theory, 220
City
  central place theory, 78
  ecumenopolis, 81
  evolutionary stages, 81
  megalopolis, 81
Class, social (*See* Social Stratification),
    288
Coevolution, 166, 213, 288
Cognitive theory, 116, 209
Communes, 98, 128, 182
Communication, 2, 9, 31, 36–38, 50–
    53, 88, 92, 114–116, 194
  community, 91–92
  defined, 190
  families, 163, 189–190
  first social connection, 232
  groups, 151, 160–162
  nonverbal, 59–60, 232
  organizations, 102–103

Communitarianism, 95–96
Community
  as system, 71–99
  boundaries, 30, 79, 83–84
  compared
    to groups, 72, 145
    to organizations, 145
  defined, 76, 96–97
  gemeinschaft, 72–73, 126
  gesellschaft, 72–73
  institutions, 84–85, 90–91, 97, 122
  kinship, 75–76
  mind, 73, 82
  nonplace, 73, 75, 77, 79, 82, 83, 87,
    92–94
  place, 73, 74, 87
  power structure, 88–90
  sense of, 77, 93–94, 131
  social work as, 93
  utopian, 79, 98
Concrete operations, 235
Conflict, 12, 107–108, 240
  functions of, 160
  in groups, 154–155, 160
  in organizations, 107–108, 114
  in persons, 16
Control (*See* Power and control; Social
    control), 119–123
Crisis (*See also* Identity crisis), 191,204
Culture, 43–69, 123, 126–127, 131, 217,
    230–231, 235–236, 237, 238, 245
  adolescence and, 239,242,245
  analytic dimensions, 55–66
  and school, 62, 236–237
  defined, 34, 44–45, 55–56
  externalization and objectification,
    45, 48
  of communities, 72, 76
  of groups, 147
  of organizations, 124
  subcultures, 49, 181
Cybernetics, 14, 37, 108, 121

Day Care, 30, 62, 171, 228, 233
Decision-making studies, 88, 90,105
Delinquency, 230, 235, 244, 245
Differentiation, 34–35, 54, 62, 92–93,
    102, 118–119

communities, 73 ,84–85, 96
defined, 34, 289
families, 180, 186–187
groups, 147, 157–158
organizations, 34, 54, 103, 105
person, 230–235
Disorganization, 15–16
Dyad, child-nurturing person (parent-child), 226–232, 257
defective, 228–230

Ecological approach, 182, 289
Education, profession of, 88, 93, 180
Ego, 116, 124, 200, 203, 214, 227, 239, 291
defense mechanisms, 12, 15
integrity, 77
organizing process, 15, 32, 159
Egocentrism, 213, 215
Energy, 3, 9–14
defined, 9, 289
exchange (transfer), 9, 11–12, 13–14, 23, 29, 30, 33, 92, 97, 160–161, 256, 267–268
information as, 9–14, 92
power, 9–10, 36
psychic (libido, eros), 10
Energy functions (SE, SI, GE, GI), 8, 9, 11–14, 33–35, 76–80, 120, 161, 184, 186, 289
communities, 76–80
families, 184, 186
groups, 161
organizations, 76–80
person, 9
Entropy, 10–11, 15, 18, 90, 92, 111, 239
defined, 10–11, 268, 289
organizations, 112
second law of thermodynamics, 10
Epigenesis, 202, 203
Equality, 62, 216, 269
Equifinality, 57, 290
Equilibrium, 10–11, 25, 37, 210–211, 213, 216, 290
Equity, 216, 269
Ethology, 44, 51, 290
Evolutionary aspects (*See also* Morphogenesis and

Morphostatsis, and Steady state), 24–26, 39, 124, 129
communities, 80–83
cultures, 55–57, 62, 67
defined, 23–24
families, 162, 174–177, 191–192
groups, 146–156
organizations, 124–129
person (*See also* Life cycle), 198
society, 57
systems, 24–28
Externalization, 45

Families, 4, 6–7, 30, 165–196, 246
and economic system, 62, 168
and organizations, 183
approaches to family analysis
cause or effect, 172–174
evolving system, 174–177
functional approach, 179–182
social systems view of, 182–192
structural approach, 177–179
system of roles, 166–171
augmented, 178
binuclear, 179
biological universal, 49–50
defined, 183, 192, 257
extended, 167, 178, 185
functions, 16, 179–182
headed by lesbian or gay couples, 167, 171–172
lesbian family life cycle, 172
nuclear, 49, 167, 172, 174, 175, 177, 178
resilience, 175
scapegoat, 186–187
single parent, 168
utilitarianistic, 190
Family system, 6
and early childhood, 62, 159–160, 168–169, 180, 233
as system of roles, 166–171
boundary, 185–187
compared to community, 178
compared to group, 145, 146
compared to organizations, 110
disorganized, 16
highly organized, 183

Family system (*cont.*)
  power in (feminist analysis), 169
Feedback, 9, 32, 37–39, 115, 149, 153,
    211, 267
  confirming identity, 38
  defined, 37
  deviation-amplifying, -counteract-
    ing, -reducing, 38
  feedback cycle, 37–38, 39, 45–46, 60,
    113, 149, 241, 290
  negative, 37–38
  positive, 37–38
Feminism, 218
  feminist critiques, 95–96, 169
  feminist views of women's roles
    and families, 169–171
Feminist group work, 141
Fidelity, 244
Focal system (holon), 5, 6, 13, 290
Freudian theory, 124, 146, 159
  critiques of, 198
  psychic structure, 200
  stages of development, 200–201
  unconscious, 200
Functionalism, 4, 5
"Fuzzy thinking", 2, 17

Gangs, 156
Gays and Lesbians, 49–50, 87, 95, 167,
    171–172, 196, 223
Generalized other, 38, 45, 60
General Systems Theory (GST), xvii,
    1–3, 290
Generativity vs. stagnation, 146, 172,
    245–252
Gilligan's theory, 220–221
  moral development, 220–221
Goal, 104, 116–118, 144–145
  attainment (achievement), 13, 36,
    102, 110, 117,146
  defined, 116, 291
  displacement, 117
  multiplication, 118
  succession, 118
Goal-directed activity, 116, 148–149,
    291
  cultures and societies, 11–12, 15
  groups, 144, 145, 148–149, 159

organizations, 101, 106, 108–
    109
Group, 103, 137–164
  bond, 148, 149
  cohesiveness, 148, 149
  compared
    to community, 72, 145
    to family, 144–146
    to organizations, 145, 146
  consensus, 147–149, 160
  defined, 137–138
  evolution, 146–156
  norms, 147–148, 149
  quality circles, 119
  reference group, 60
  stages of group development, 149–
    156
  use of groups
    cliques and coalitions, 143–144
    consciousness-raising and social
      action, 142–143
    empowerment, 142–143
    social advocacy, 142
    growth groups, or human poten-
      tial, 139
    self-help, 140–142
    support, 87, 140–142, 190
    task groups, 143
    therapeutic, or remedial, 140
Group dimensions (*See also* Polarities),
    144–146
  adaptation/integration, 144–145
  expressive/instrumental, 144–145
  narcissistic/generative, 146
  primary/secondary, 46, 145–146

Hawthorne effect, 107
Head Start, 85, 90, 188, 233
Hierarchy, 31–34, 102, 109, 157, 269
  authority, 31–32
  communities, 83
  control, 31
  defined, 31–32, 291
  groups, 157–159
  of life cycle stages, 32, 201–204
  of needs (Maslow), 31
  organizations, 54
Hispanic Americans, 86, 99, 236

Holon (focal system), 2, 5–8, 138, 173, 183, 264
  defined, 5, 291
Holonistic thought, 8, 103, 264–266
Homeostasis, 25, 26
  defined, 25, 291
Homophobia, 224–225
Homosexual (gay and lesbian) development, 223
  stages of identity development, 223–225
Hong Kong, 73, 75, 190
Horney's theory, 219–220, 221
  psychology of women, 219–220
Human Services, 139, 202

Id, 124, 211, 200, 291
Identity, 15, 77, 147, 203, 239, 245–246, 258
  as steady state, 24, 26
  vs. confusion (diffusion), 16, 204, 239–245
  conservation of, 252–257
  crisis, 204–205, 245, 256
  defined, 291
  explained, 15–16, 239–240
  negative, 240–241, 245
  perpetuation and sharing of, 245–252
Ideology, 74, 244–245
  authoritarian, 77–78
  fascism, 78
Industry vs. inferiority, 235–239
Infant bonding, 227
Information, 9–10, 31, 32, 37, 91, 291
  as energy, 9–10
Initiative vs. guilt, 233–235
Institutionalization, 291
  in communities, 181–182
Institutions, 76, 84–85, 90
  greedy institutions, 123
  total institutions, 122
Integration, 145, 147, 159, 292
Integrity vs. disgust and despair, 252, 253
Intelligence, 211
Intimacy and solidarity vs. isolation, 181, 245–246

Iran, 109
Isomorph, 3, 159, 242

Kinship, 75–76, 178
Kohlberg's theory, 214–218
  moral judgment, 214
  stages of development, 215–218

Language (See Symbols and Symbolic Interaction), 50–53, 55, 59–62
  linguistic collusion, 51–52, 61
  structures reality, 52
Latency stage, 235, 237
Leadership, 123–124
  in groups, 158, 162
  in organizations, 124
Learning, 203
Levinson's theory, 221–222
  satisfactoriness of life structure, 222
  stages of development, 221
Life cycle, 202–204, 226–257
Linkage, 28–31, 35, 74
  defined, 29
  Loose coupling, 75
Locomotion, 149
Looking glass (self), 60
Loop, 17, 32, 154, 292

Mastery, 235, 236–239
Maternal deprivation, 204, 227, 228–230, 250
Matrimony, 129
Maturation, 203, 204
Men, 247
  househusbands, 62
  moral development, 247
  stages of development, 247
Mobilization for Youth, 85
Monopolarization, 182
Moral judgment, development of, 214–218, 220–221
Moratorium, 181, 216, 240–241
Morphogenesis, 12, 26–27, 85, 191, 213, 292
Morphostasis, 12, 26–27, 85, 191, 213, 292

Negentropy, 18, 19, 90, 131, 292
Neighborhood, 87, 235

Networks, Social, 73, 76, 86, 87, 92, , 29293
network therapy, 88
Neurosis, 244, 245
Nursing, xv, 2, 34, 88, 90, 93, 180

Object relationship, 204, 227, 257
Objectification, 45
Oedipal conflict, 166, 233
Organization, 3, 14–16, 37, 122
defined, 14, 16, 100–101, 292
disorganization, 15, 16
of communities, 78
of cultures, 54, 56–59
of families, 14, 62
of organizations, 105
of person, 15, 231–232, 240, 245
schemas as, 211–213
Organization as systems (See also bureaucracy), xvi, 101–136
compared
to groups, 146
communication in, 114–116
compliance, 102–103, 121, 122
conflict in, 107–108
control in, 104, 114, 119–123, 129–130
cultures, 124, 125–129
defined, 99–103
effectiveness of, 15, 117
efficiency of, 15, 111, 117
entropy in, 111, 131
goals (See Goal achievement), 13, 102–103, 114–118, 132
informal structure, 106–107
participation, 106–107, 130–131
power, 119–123, 108, 109
rationality in, 104–105, 106–107, 110, 114
Organization theories, 102, 103–108, 133–135
bureaucratic situation, 108–113
natural systems perspective, 103
conflict theory or structuralist theory, 107–108, 111
Human Relations theory, 106–107
rational system perspective, 103

classical (machine) model, 104–105, 108–109, 111
neo-classical, or decision theory, 105, 111
systems model, 113–114, 134–135
Theory Z, 130–131

Pattern maintenance, 180
defined, 13, 292
Peers, 241
adolescenthood, 241–242
childhood, 235, 237
play, 234–235
young adults, 178–179
Person, 257
as system, 4, 5, 15, 32
motor capacities, 55, 56
reasoning capacities, 55
sensory capacities, 54
Patrimony, 129–130
Perspectivism, 5, 6, 183, 192, 257
defined, 5, 292
Piaget's theory, 205, 209–214
intelligence and equilibrium, 210–211
schemas, 211–213
stages of development, 213–214
Play, 234
Pleasure principle, 146
Polarities, 4, 5, 24, 39, 293
assimilation/accommodation, 24, 39
Erikson's developmental tasks, 24, 202–205,226–257
explained, 204–205
groups characteristics as, 144–146
life as dynamic between, 204, 265, 266
necessary to differentiation, 231–232
Postmodernism, xi–xiii
Poverty, 230, 237
Power, 57, 88, 105, 119–123, 126, 188
and control, 31, 32, 36
defined, 120, 293
in organizations, 102, 104–105, 109–110, 119–123, 125–126
Professions, 2, 61, 88, 180, 248, 263–264

as differentiated functions, 35, 179–180
as nonplace communities, 73, 75
jargon, 60
territory, 93
Psychiatry, 61, 67
Psychoanalysis, 61, 166, 198–201,219
Psychosis, 244
Psychosocial approach, 198–205, 293

Rape culture, 66
Reality principle, 146
Reciprocal beneficiary law
Religion and spirituality, 63, 156
Retribalization
Roles, 57–59, 126, 166, 215, 248, 254–255
  community, 92
  defined, 124, 293
  groups, 157–158, 160
  in families, 16, 166–171, 186
  instrumental/expressive, 166
  male-father, female-mother, 31, 62, 167–172, 192
  organization, 102,125–126
  society, 57, 58
Roman Catholic Church, 29, 57

Scapegoating, 192
Schema, 211
  defined, 211–213, 293
Schizophrenia, 16, 52, 159, 239, 244–245, 248
School, 321, 235, 238, 242
  as culture carrier, 62, 235–236
  historical development, 67
  institutionalization of, 62
Scientific method, 63
Self, 60
  looking glass self, 38, 45–46, 60
  sense of, 230–231, 231–232, 235–239
Self-development (See Autopoiesis), 33, 209, 245
  self-organization, 33
Separation, 230, 254
Sexuality, 245, 247–248, 255
  adolescent, 245
  infantile, 233

family roles, 174, 180
  Oedipal crisis, 166, 233
Skinheads, 141, 181–182
Social behaviorism and social interactionsim, 4
Social control, 36, 88, 160, 187, 236
  communities, 84, 88–90, 95
  defined, 36, 293
  families, 187
  groups, 160
  organizations, 119–123, 127, 236
  professions, 122
Socialization, 36, 51, 88, 90, 203, 236
  communities, 90–92
  defined, 293
  families, 165–166, 187–189
  groups, 140, 159–160
  organizations, 122
  professions, 92–94
Social stratification (See also Roles), 85
  caste, 85–86, 188
  class, 57, 58, 59, 85–86, 188
Social systems theory (or model) (See Systems approach), xi, 1–21, 2
Social work, 2, 13, 34, 122, 163, 164, 180, 248
  as subculture, 60
Society, 43–69
  defined, 44–45
  organization of, 56–59
  subsystems, 62
  underclass, 57
South Africa, 12, 69
Specialization, 34–35, 58–59, 109, 110, 180, 186, 294
Status, 56, 57, 85, 123, 124, 294
Steady State, 26, 37, 116, 213
  change, 24–26
  community, 80, 84
  culture, 58, 243
  defined, 24–26, 265, 294
  families, 191–192
  groups, 147–149
  organizations, 107–108
  persons, 26, 211–212, 243–244, 256–257
Structural aspects (or characteristics), 28–35, 39, 124–129, 146

Structural aspects (*cont.*)
  communities, 83–88
  culture, 56–59
  defined, 23
  families, 183–187
  groups, 156–158
  organizations (*See* Organization theories), 121, 124–129
Structure, 104, 121
  defined, 294
  horizontal relationships, 145
  vertical relationships, 145
Super-ego, 15, 60, 124, 227, 200, 211, 227, 291
Symbiosis, 228
Symbols, 9, 53–54, 228, 229
  communication, 51–52, 59–60, 189–190
  symbolic interaction, 52, 59–60, 122
  symbolic rewards, 122
Synergy, 10–11, 118, 155
  Benedict's use, 138
  defined, 11
  in groups, 138, 145
  in organizations, 118, 131
Syntality, 117, 147, 157, 294
Syntropy, 11, 25, 294
Systemic thinking, 3
Systems
  defined, 2–8, 257, 294
  model, 2
  self-direction, 37
  variety of, 3, 4, 124
Systems theory (or model), xi, 1–23, 163, 263–269
  advantages of, xvii–xviii, 2, 3, 114, 266
  and social work practice, 2
  as "map", xv–xviii, 8
  as metaphor, xvi, 1

  as "skeleton", xvi
  as "umbrella", xvi
  as a way of thinking, 3
  nature of, xi, xv–xviii
  useful to human services, 101

Territoriality, 53–54, 295
  families, 187
  community, 74
  professional, 92–94
Third Ear, 61
Thought (capacity for), 48, 52, 55–56
Tools, 55–56
Transactional Analysis, 61
Transition state, 24, 27, 295
  bifurcation point, 27
  transformation, 27
Trust vs. mistrust, 204, 226–230, 256

Values, 111, 216–217, 267–269
  culture, 62
  groups, 147
  social classes, 57
Vietnam war, 29, 54, 59, 129

Wholistic view, 4
Women, 29, 87, 112–113, 162, 251
  abortion, 168–170, 172, 173, 179–181, 188, 192
  care (caring), 189
    moral development, 218–223
  Right to Life, 87
  role, 167
  stages of development, 218–222
Work, 77, 112–113, 242, 246, 248–252
  and class, 57
  and role, 58–59, 77, 253–254

Youth stage, 181, 239